MW01042902

FROM **CONFLICT RESOLUTION** TO **PEACEBUILDING**

CHARLES HAUSS
Alliance for Peacebuilding
George Mason University

ROWMAN & LITTLEFIELD
Lanham • Boulder • New York • London

Executive Editor: Elizabeth Swayze
Editorial Assistant: Megan Manzano
Senior Marketing Manager: Amy Whitaker
Interior Designer: Ilze Lemesis and Integra Software Services Pvt. Ltd.

Credits and acknowledgments for material borrowed from other sources, and reproduced with permission, appear on the appropriate pages within the text.

Published by Rowman & Littlefield
An imprint of The Rowman & Littlefield Publishing Group, Inc.
4501 Forbes Boulevard, Suite 200, Lanham, Maryland 20706
www.rowman.com

6 Tinworth Street, London SE11 5AL, United Kingdom

Copyright © 2020 by The Rowman & Littlefield Publishing Group, Inc.

All rights reserved. No part of this book may be reproduced in any form or by any electronic or mechanical means, including information storage and retrieval systems, without written permission from the publisher, except by a reviewer who may quote passages in a review.

British Library Cataloguing in Publication Information Available

Library of Congress Control Number: 2019949255

ISBN 9781538116296 (cloth : alk. paper) | ISBN 9781538116302 (pbk. : alk. paper) | ISBN 9781538116319 (ebook)

∞™ The paper used in this publication meets the minimum requirements of American National Standard for Information Sciences—Permanence of Paper for Printed Library Materials, ANSI/NISO Z39.48-1992.

To Doug Irvin-Erickson

BRIEF CONTENTS

CONTENTS

PREFACE FOR STUDENTS

IN THE FIRST SENTENCE of chapter 1, I set myself a challenge—to write a book that is unusual, interesting, challenging, and empowering. So, before you dig into the book itself, let me explain why I chose those four words.

Unusual Academic textbooks tend to be dry treatments of the conventional wisdom in a given field. A peace and conflict studies textbook has to be different. To start with, there is not much conventional wisdom when it comes to conflict resolution and peacebuilding, so what I chose to include and exclude matters. Also, I have been active participant in the evolution of peace and conflict studies, both as an activist and as a scholar, so this book includes more of my own experiences and perspectives than you are used to seeing in books of this sort. Add to that the fact that I've included two features that, make the book unusual. First, I encourage you to get in touch with me via www.charleshauss.info. Second, I also encourage you to disagree with me. Each chapter has at least one Out on a Limb box in which I discuss controversies surrounding a point I just made.

Interesting A textbook doesn't have to be boring, and I've tried to prove that here. You'll have to decide if I've succeeded or not. In any event, I have provided case studies featuring some of the more interesting initiatives and portraits of some of the most engaging people who do conflict resolution and peacebuilding work. I have had the privilege of working with some of them, I hope some of that excitement shines through here.

Challenging *From Conflict Resolution to Peacebuilding* is designed to be a challenging book, but not because the concepts underlying the field are hard to understand. As I say in the book, conflict resolution is not as hard as rocket science to understand, but it may be harder to accomplish. Therein lies the challenge. If I've done my job, you will have had to come to grips with one of the most difficult challenges humanity has ever faced.

Empowering I spend a lot of time discussing a statement George Lopez made in describing peace and conflict studies thirty years ago, when he called our field "Gloom and Doom 101." To be sure, there is plenty of depressing material in the pages to come. However, like Lopez wanted us to do then, I encourage you to get more involved, beyond simply taking more courses in the field. More important, I hope you can find a way to be part of the effort to resolve conflicts more constructively and to build a more peaceful world. Most important of all, I end the book by arguing that you have no choice. Whatever you do professionally or politically during for the rest of your life, you will encounter conflict, and plenty of it.

One last thing I love working with students, especially helping them figure out how to build a more peaceful world. That's why I created charleshauss.info and hold virtual office hours through it. And as my wife knows too well, I check my email all the time—chip@charleshauss.info.

PREFACE FOR INSTRUCTORS

THE PREFACE FOR THE students who are reading *From Conflict Resolution to Peacebuilding* revolves around four adjectives. This one, which I wrote for instructors, only uses one of them—*challenging*.

I know that teaching courses on conflict resolution and peacebuilding is challenging for many reasons. What to include? How practical do I want to get? How should my own views and experiences shape the course? How do I assess my students' work? How do I handle the conflict that will invariably break out in my classroom?

I'm sure you can add questions of your own!

I can't address all of those challenging questions here. I have taken some of them on in the instructor's guide for this book, which is available on my website, www.charleshauss.info.

More importantly, I know that teaching peace and conflict studies can be idiosyncratic, because we all answer the kinds of questions I just posed differently.

And because teaching about conflict resolution and peacebuilding as effectively as possible to as many students as possible sits at the top of my personal list of priorities, I'm available to help you improve the way you teach your own course. We can talk about teaching strategies. If you have access to a wired classroom, I can even "visit" your class.

The best way to start is by sending me an email at chip@charleshauss.info.

ACKNOWLEDGMENTS

I HAVE BEEN WRITING books for a long time. While I wrote every word in all of them, those words emerged from the communities I was a part of at the time. That's especially true for *From Conflict Resolution to Peacebuilding*, because it is the culmination of more than half a century of work and, therefore, brought me into contact with lots of people who shaped my thinking.

That starts with Doug Irvin-Erickson, whom I have only known for two years and to whom this book is dedicated. We met when I attended his book launch during the same week as President Trump's inauguration. During the Q&A, Doug started talking about building an architecture for conflict prevention in the US which was a far cry from the topic of the night—his biography of Raphael Lemkin. I was drawn to the idea. We started talking about it. Gretchen Sandles and I started sitting in on his courses. I realized that I had never seen a young faculty member work as well with students. We kept talking and organized a workshop on architectures for peace in the US. I asked Doug to be a coauthor of this book. His pretenure schedule didn't allow it, but our assumption is that he will join me in writing the second edition. To top it all off, he's a Yankees fan, too.

Gretchen Sandles and rest of the family come next. Gretchen and I have known each other since grad school at Michigan and have been married for nearly thirty years. Because she worked in the intelligence community, I never expected that we would share the peace studies part of my work. However, since her retirement, her Quaker roots have come to the fore, and she is an integral part of what we are doing about peacebuilding in the US at AfP. Her daughter and my step-daughter, Evonne Fei, provided the coffee mug I use to end the book—and a lot more. Our son-in-law, Igor Petrovski, keeps me politically honest—from my left flank. Their children, Kiril Petrovski and Mila Petrovska, keep me going, especially when Kiril introduces me to his friends as "my eccentric grandpa."

Authors usually put their publication team late in the list of acknowledgments. That won't work in this case. I've had a working relationship with Rowman and Littlefield for more than twenty years. Now, I'm working with them to expand American peacebuilding as you will see in chapter 13. Elizabeth Swayze put up with me through the publication of this book, including at times when I know I was driving her nuts. Megan Manzano filled in when Elizabeth just had to get away from me. Dhara Snowden has helped in a series of books we edit together, many of which found their way into this one, too. Susan McEachern and Jon Sisk did not participate much in writing this book but have been key members of my support team for those twenty years. Most of all, I have to thank Linda Ganster, with whom Gretchen and I are leading the project described in chapter 13.

I owe a lot, too to friends at AfP and its member organizations, including Liz Hume, Melanie Greenberg, Uzra Zeya, Jessica Bumgartner-Zuzek, Adam Wolf, Laura Strawmayer, Rick Barton, Bob Berg, Dick O'Neill, Lin Wells, Shamil Idriss, John Marks, John Paul Lederach, Peter Woodrow, Bernie Mayer, Sarah Federman, and more. Virtually the entire faculty at George Mason's School of Conflict Analysis and Resolution found its way into this book, as did plenty of its current and former students. In addition to Doug, huge thanks to Kevin Avruch, who was one of the first people I met when I moved to Washington and will have stepped down as dean by the time you read these words, and Nora Malatinszky, who helped me write part 5.

As anyone who knows me will attest, the Oberlin mafia is central to my life. I helped plan my fiftieth reunion while writing the final draft of this book. In that crowd were Peter Woodrow and Bernie Mayer again, but also Walt Galloway, Michael Jarvis, Bonnie Wishne, and Mike Lubas. When I was at Search for Common Ground, my classmate Roger Conner eased my way into the field of professional conflict resolution. Today's Oberlin brought me Bethany Gen, who also made part 5 possible. I've learned a lot from Steve Crowley, Steve Mayer, Cindy Frantz, and Amir Mahallati, who teach in its peace and conflict studies program. Most of all, I have to thank Helen Kramer, now of Resetting the Table, who started as my mentee when she was a sophomore. Five years later, the roles have been reversed. I now learn far more from her than she does from me.

Peacebuilders who know me also know about my debt to the Beyond War movement from the 1980s. Its leaders and the late Rush Kidder of the Institute for Global Ethics literally saved my intellectual life by helping me move away from the academic world of comparative politics to what I do now. Gene and Donna Richeson got that going. Len and Libby Traubman, Marty Hellman, and more keep it alive today.

Other people helped, too—none more than Dick O'Neill, who has been a friend for all but three of my seventy-one years. Also, Clark Baxter, Christen Kerr, Val Bunce, Ron Herring, and more.

But as much as I owe to all of those other people, I owe Kiril and Mila more. Never having had children of my own, I find being a grandparent especially rewarding—and baffling. But these two have kept me focused on the world we are leaving to them because we have done such a lousy job as its stewards.

Falls Church, Virginia
April 2019

ABOUT THE AUTHOR

CHARLES "CHIP" HAUSS has spent fifty years as an activist, scholar, and teacher. He currently serves as senior fellow for innovation and emeritus member of the board of directors at the Alliance for Peacebuilding and is a visiting scholar at George Mason University's School of Conflict Analysis and Resolution. In addition to four other books on peace and conflict studies, he the author of thirteen books on comparative politics. A regular blogger, he also maintains www.charleshauss.info.

INTRODUCTION

PART I

PART IV

PART V

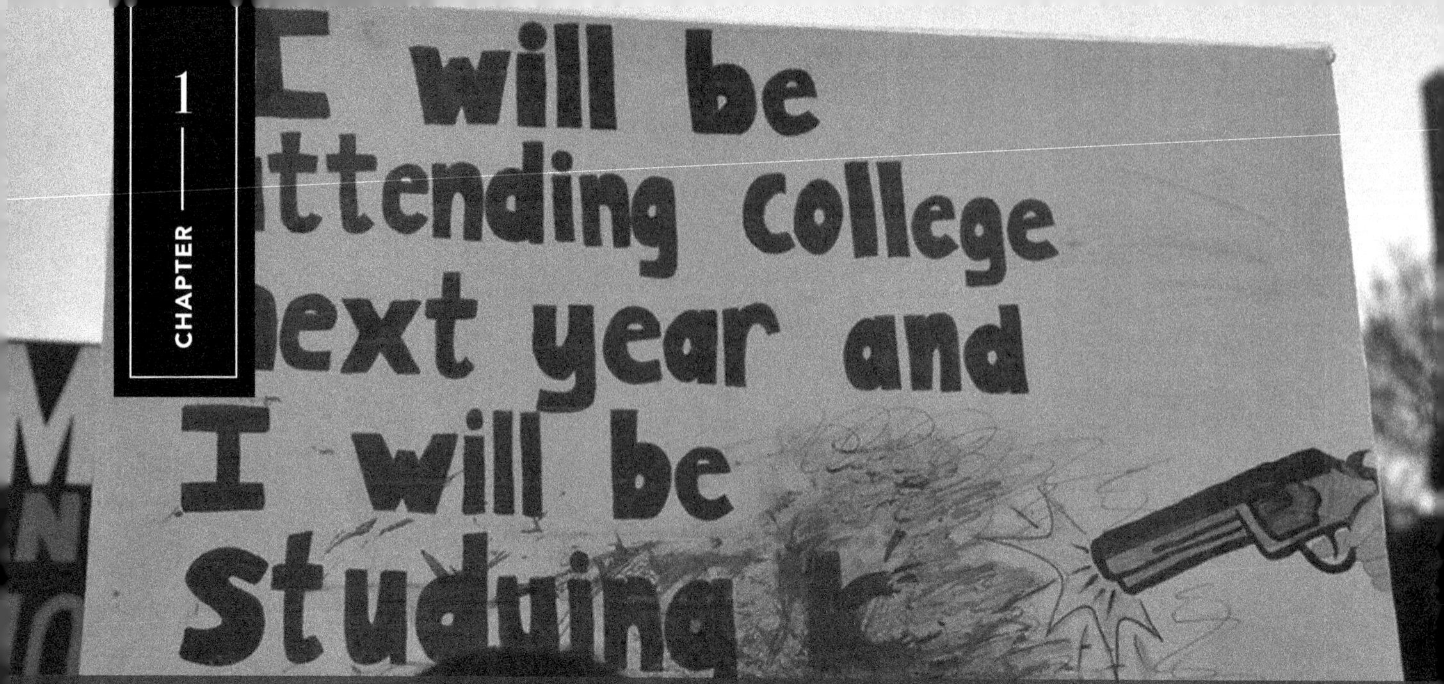

CHAPTER 1

Conflict Is a Fact of Life—Peacebuilding Is Not

THINK ABOUT IT

Most textbooks have a list of critical-thinking exercises at the end of each chapter. All too often readers ignore them, in part because they come at the end of the chapter and in part because they do not seem interesting or useful.

In this book, they appear at the beginning of the chapter so that you can think about them as you read. In this case, the single "think about it" exercise for this chapter is simple and does not come in the form of a question. Keep asking yourself how the points raised in the rest of this chapter help you better understand the conflicts you will begin mapping in the first Conflict Lab.

CORE CONCEPTS

A list of core concepts will also appear at the beginning of each chapter. It will draw your attention to key ideas that I will be introducing and/or giving particular attention to in the pages that follow.

conflict—a dispute, disagreement, or argument

do no harm—in peacebuilding, as in medicine, the commitment to avoid any action that could damage the patient or society

intractable conflict—complex problems that endure over extended periods of time and resist simple resolution

paradigm—a scientific theory or other all-encompassing mind-set that covers an entire field

peace—the absence of violent conflict

resolution—a settlement that ends or eases a conflict

wicked problem—problem whose causes and consequences are so inextricably intertwined that you cannot solve it quickly, easily, or separately, if you can solve it at all

The voyage of discovery consists not of seeking new lands but in seeing with new eyes.

—*Marcel Proust*

WELCOME TO WHAT I HOPE will be an unusual, interesting, challenging, and empowering book.

Unusual, interesting, challenging, and *empowering* are not words you usually associate with textbooks. If my experience is any indication, this book has to be unusual, interesting, challenging, and empowering because I assume that you enrolled in this class looking for new ways of understanding many of the world's most vexing problems and *then* doing something about them. Any book that is not unusual, interesting, challenging, and empowering would not help you reach such a goal.

CONFLICT LABS

I will start most chapters of *From Conflict Resolution to Peacebuilding* with a discussion either of its title or of the epigraph that begins it. I won't do that here. Instead, I want to throw you right into peace and conflict studies and do so in a way that should convince you that this is going to be an unusual book.

After you finish reading this section, do the first two Conflict Labs described in it. In doing them, you will identify and take a first stab at understanding two issues that you will be following in the chapters to come, where they will appear as Conflict Lab boxes. By doing the labs, you will learn how to build **conflict maps**,[1] which are at the heart and soul of peace and conflict studies because they help you both analyze how and why a problem exists and point you toward ways of solving it. This first pair of lab exercises should also help you to see that you already know quite a bit about peacebuilding and conflict resolution.

They can be done in a number of ways. You can do them on your own, but it's better if you do them in a group. You can do them with anyone, but since you will keep returning to them, it's a good idea to do them with a group of your classmates who can work as a team throughout the term.

I will describe the way I usually use them at the beginning of a workshop or the first day of a course when I have lots of sticky notes with me and am working in a room with a whiteboard. I also assume that if you do them in some other way, you can adapt my instructions. However you do the exercises, take good notes or better yet, take a picture of what you did, because we will keep coming back to your results in the next thirteen chapters.

The Global Version

In parts 2 through 4, I will show you how our field has grown. I will start with examples of grassroots conflict resolution initiatives and then build out to the national and international levels. That's the case because both the concepts and the progress we've made are easier to see if you start with issues that are close to home.

Here, however, it makes more sense to flip the order and start with the bigger issues that probably drew you to peace and conflict studies in the first place.

The first step is easy enough. Go to the *New York Times*, the BBC, CNN, Fox, or some other reputable news site. Each member of the group should pick an article or two that deals with a national or global conflict.

Had you done the exercise on the day I submitted the first few chapters of this book to the publisher, you would have found stories on Brexit, Donald Trump's disputes with a half dozen countries, and how European students are skipping classes to show their support for policies that would slow the rate of climate change. Even that day's sports page had its share of conflict since January 30, 2019, was the one hundredth anniversary of Jackie Robinson's birth, which led the *New York Times* to do an overview of the impact he had as the first African American major league baseball player.

Next, narrow your list until you agree on one issue that you think is particularly important and/or hard to resolve. Then, take no more than ten minutes and discuss the dilemmas faced by people who are dealing with that issue. Even in that brief period of time you should be able to see two things. First, with all due respect to rocket scientists, understanding conflict is not rocket science. Second, with all due respect to rocket scientists again, doing something about conflict and building peace can *actually be harder* than rocket science.

Once you've identified a few key themes, it is time for the sticky notes and whiteboard. Each of you should make three sets of sticky notes that briefly (after all, sticky notes are small for a reason) summarize:

- the controversy itself
- its causes
- its consequences

Don't worry about getting the details of the conflict right. You will have plenty of opportunities to revisit it in later Conflict Labs. My only goal here is to help you see that the field of conflict resolution and peacebuilding is both intellectually manageable and politically frustrating.

Put the sticky notes that summarize the conflict in the middle of the whiteboard. On the assumption that you have more than one note describing the conflict itself, arrange them in clusters that reflect the themes that emerged in your discussion.

If you had picked the war in Syria, you would probably have notes about the fighting that has killed tens of thousands and created more than a million refugees at the center of the board. Near it, you might have had other notes for the roles of ISIS, Russia, the US, and other global and regional powers.

Then, start putting up the notes listing the causes on the left side. As you did with the issue itself, rearrange the notes to form clusters of similar causes. Again, if you had chosen Syria, your clusters might have included divisions within the Muslim world, the origins of ISIS, Russian–American tensions, and Israel.

Once you have your notes clustered the way you want, draw arrows from the causes to the conflict itself and talk about how each of those then shaped the dispute, which is what the arrows represent. Last, but by no means least, look at the relationship among the causes themselves and add arrows between and among them, which will probably leave you with a set of important causes that are only indirectly related to your conflict.

Now, put the sticky notes listing the effects of the conflict on the right side of the board and draw a second set of arrows. In this case, however, point them outward from the conflict to those effects. Again, you will have a number of notes and arrows, including some for which the consequences are not a direct outgrowth of the conflict itself.

You should not have had much trouble getting to some obvious immediate effects, including instability in the rest of the Middle East or the 2015 refugee crisis in Europe. If you picked a particularly insightful set of stories, you might have drawn an indirect (and convoluted) connection between events in Syria and the so-called lone wolf terrorist attacks in Europe and North America.

After half an hour or so of rearranging sticky notes and arrows, you will probably end up with something that looks vaguely like figure 1.1. That is your first conflict map. I will defer discussing why these kinds of maps are important until the end of chapter 3, because you can't fully appreciate why they matter until I have put the entire field in historical and analytical context. So, don't worry about making sense of your map at this point.

FIGURE 1.1
Generic Conflict Map

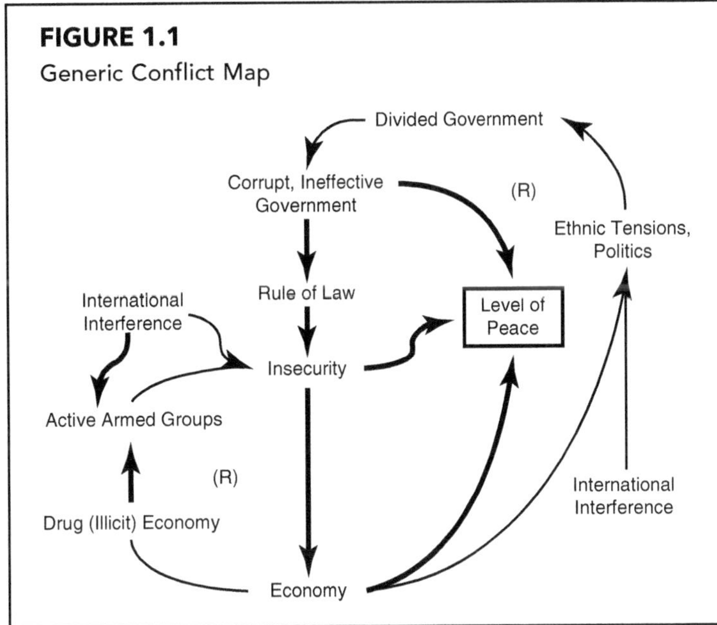

The Local Version

Once you've taken a picture of that map, do a second version of the lab that will help you see another point about conflict. We also have to deal with conflicts that take place much closer to home, some of which directly touch our own lives. That's important, because this book will help you see ways in which you can—but also sometimes cannot—use many of the same tools in dealing with all kinds of conflict, wherever and however they take place.

So, pick an issue that is dividing your country or your community. In this case, I can't really guide you, because I have no idea where you are (but see the box on the next page). Don't limit yourself to political issues. Be sure to look at the business news. You may even find an interesting story about a celebrity divorce in your local newspaper's style section. You can even pick an issue that has divided your campus or your community.

Do a second version of the exercise, and draw a second conflict map.

I did mine for Oberlin College, because I was helping plan my fiftieth reunion while I was finishing this book and was therefore spending a lot of time on campus. Oberlin has a long history of student activism which I helped lead in the late 1960s. Fifty years later, the college has had to deal with conflicts that pitted some students against the faculty, some professors against the administration, and the college against some local residents. The causes on my sticky notes included the fact that Oberlin was the first college to admit women and African American students, which means it has a long-standing commitment to diversity. On the other hand, many of the shorter-term causes grew out of the growing costs of higher education that limited what Oberlin could afford to do to meet current student demands. Their impact is easy to see in the difficulties the college has had in recruiting a diverse student body and faculty in recent years.

The Point of the Conflict Labs

I didn't ask you to do this exercise to test your ability to put sticky notes on whiteboards and move them around. Instead, I wanted to give you a first glimpse at what will be the interesting, challenging, and empowering features of this book:

- interesting, because the field itself is fascinating—even when you are not playing around with sticky notes and whiteboards
- challenging, because you have already discovered that most newsworthy conflicts are hard to resolve and that you and your fellow group members disagree on almost everything from the definition of your issues to the very meaning of terms like resolution
- empowering, because you probably also saw things that you can do to help solve these problems

In doing the exercises, you also probably stumbled across a number of the key points I will be making in the rest of this book. That starts with systems analysis, which is what maps like these point you toward. Although we will not get to systems approaches, per se, until the end of chapter 3, we will be relying heavily on maps like the ones you just did in almost everything that follows. You also saw that the kinds of conflicts we will be focusing on are complex, have deep roots, and have equally wide-ranging implications. Most importantly, you should not have had any trouble seeing that the world is filled with conflicts and that we are not dealing with most of them very well.

It will take the rest of this book to cover all the ground I've hinted at so far. In the process, I will help you see the field's core concepts, history, and accomplishments, as well as the challenges that we still face today. In particular, you will see how our field moved from the fringes of academic and political life towards the mainstream to the point that we can now think in terms of building a movement that just might be able to produce a global shift in the way we deal with conflict.

That means using the rest of this chapter to take a step back from those lofty goals and quirky exercises and put peace and conflict studies in perspective.

Right Where You Are

You may only be on page 6, but please put the book down *NOW!* Well, actually, after you finish reading this box.

You can get a lot from reading this book.

However, you might learn even more from the part of www.charleshauss.info devoted to this book.

Any book on peace and conflict studies is out of date even before it is published. Therefore, both the website and my weekly newsletter contain updates on the topics covered in this book.

The website will let you dig more deeply into the material by exploring the issues through a collection of videos, web links, and short articles that I either created or, more often, curated from elsewhere on the internet.

You can also use it to interact with me. You can send me an email, visit with me live when I hold weekly online "office hours," and connect with readers who are using this book elsewhere around the world. In fact, you can start doing so by sending me the results of your first exercise so that I can post versions of them for others to comment on and learn from.

FROM ANALYSIS TO RESOLUTION TO PEACEBUILDING

Peace and conflict studies is not an easy subject to master. That's not the case because the concepts we will be covering are hard to understand. Rather, the difficulties start with the fact that ours is a relatively new field that lacks a **paradigm** or a common core that everyone accepts around which a book like this could be written. The lack of a paradigm also means that we disagree a lot, whether "we" means practitioners who try to resolve conflict and build peace or scholars who focus on understanding conflict, its causes, and its consequences.

In the absence of a paradigm, the rest of this book will present peace and conflict studies in three stages while keeping the amount of disagreement and confusion to a minimum:

- The rest of part 1 will present the concepts at the heart of the analytical side of conflict and peace studies. In Marcel Proust's terms from this chapter's epigraph, I will be presenting the new set of eyes one needs to understand this complicated and growing field.
- Parts 2 through 4 will trace the way it has unfolded through three stages of practical work at both the grassroots and elite levels. I won't have time or space to cover everything, but will focus instead on the most important events and the ideas and approaches that were introduced at each one that are still in use today.
- Part 5 will explore the future, considering both where the analytical and practitioner communities are heading and how you might fit into it over the rest of your life. In Proust's terms again, we will begin to glimpse yet another set of new eyes we all may need in the future.

The first step in coming to grips with conflict is to start with three words—*analysis, resolution*, and *peacebuilding*. Coincidentally, they happen to be in the titles of the organizations I work for—the **Alliance for Peacebuilding** (AfP) and George Mason's **School for Conflict Analysis and Resolution** (S-CAR).

Superficially speaking, the two organizations are quite different. George Mason is, after all a university, so S-CAR's focus is on conflict analysis. As its name suggests, AfP is a network of **nongovernmental organizations (NGOs)** all of which employ practitioners whose job it is to build peace. Yet, many of S-CAR's students are more interested in resolving conflicts than in analyzing them. And AfP's staff members spend almost as much time working to improve the ways we understand conflict as they do actually resolving it.

Analysis. The first book I read in conflict studies as an undergraduate was Lewis Coser's *The Functions of Social Conflict.* Initially published in 1956, the book shook up the academic world by making the case that conflict can be useful as well as destructive. It is still assigned today, because it was also among the first books to systematically analyze the origins, current realities, and impacts that conflict has in people's daily lives.

In the sixty years since the book was published, conflict analysis has evolved into a field of its own, separate from Coser's sociology or my home discipline of political science. We went on and borrowed insights and analytical tools from other disciplines, including economics, history, anthropology, psychology, public health, medicine, environmental science, engineering, organizational behavior, and more.

In my day very few students who read books like Coser's were satisfied with its analytical insights alone. Most of us were activists who tried to apply what we learned in the classroom to the Vietnam War and the other conflicts that dominated the headlines at the time. Today the issues have changed, but it is still the case that many—maybe most—students who take peace and conflict studies courses want to use what they learn in the classroom to address the issues of the 2020s.

Resolution. In other words, this book has to go beyond analysis in two overlapping but somewhat different ways. The first of those involves conflict **resolution**.

As you will see in the next section, many of us were drawn to the field because of early research on the promise of **win-win** or **positive-sum** problem solving. Until Roger Fisher and William Ury wrote their pathbreaking book *Getting to YES* in 1981, many of us assumed that most conflicts had to end up like an athletic event that has a single winner and one or more losers. Whether we were talking about an election or a war or a baseball game, we took it for granted that the event had to have a **zero-sum** or winner-take-all ending.

By contrast, Fisher and Ury wrote about conflicts that were resolved in ways that benefited everyone as the term win-win suggests. And, as all baseball fans know, their idea has crept into our popular understanding of the way life works, because sportswriters now routinely talk about a trade being a win-win transaction that will benefit both teams.

Unfortunately, at the same time that win-win began making its way into the cultural mainstream, both academic analysts and practitioners in NGOs came to realize that a single win-win outcome rarely resolved what I will call an **intractable conflict**. Fisher and Ury wrote mostly about **transactional** conflicts, in which the parties argued about a salary or the size of a fence between two houses that could be settled once and for all on the basis of a single agreement. However, most of the issues—including the ones that I suspect you discussed in doing the Conflict Lab—require **transforming** the conflict by dealing with its underlying causes and consequences.

Today, most people who work in conflict resolution and peacebuilding base their work on building healthy **relationships**. In that sense, we share some goals with family therapists who try to improve the way parents, children, and other relatives get along. That can be hard to do as you might well know from your own personal experience. And as hard as it is for many families to work out their differences, it is harder to build healthy relationships when the conflict involves entire communities or countries.

Peacebuilding. That led many of us to think of peacebuilding as an ongoing process in which the underlying conflict may never actually disappear. Instead, the best we can do is to take steps to limit its impact and nudge the entire system in new directions that will at least begin addressing some of its causes.

Here, too, the picture is more complicated than the word peacebuilding might suggest. In particular, some of us with strong roots in transformational conflict resolution emphasize building bridges across ideological and other divides.

In My Voice

From Conflict Resolution to Peacebuilding is different from most other textbooks in one more way that I should make clear from the outset.

Most textbook authors keep their viewpoints to themselves. I could not do that here even if I wanted to, because you could discover where I stand on the issues covered in this book with a few mouse clicks.

More importantly, I was asked to write this book precisely because I have been a scholar, teacher, and activist for longer than I like to admit. Indeed, I was personally involved in a number of the case studies I will cover in parts 2 through 4. I also spend a good bit of time working with young people who want to find their own places in the field, which is rarely the case when I teach about comparative politics, a point to which I return in part 5.

Therefore, my editors and I decided that I should write it in my voice and include my own experiences.

At the same time, we also realized that I had to write the book in a way that would encourage you to challenge the conclusions I reached.

So, here is my email address:
chip@charleshauss.info

At the same time, colleagues with deeper activist roots are more likely to adopt tactics that challenge authorities in what I will call **contentious politics** later on.

CONFLICT IS A FACT OF LIFE—PEACEBUILDING IS NOT

The next step in understanding peace and conflict studies finally brings us to this chapter's title.

Conflict Is a Fact of Life

You don't have to read a book like this one to know that conflict is a fact of life.

Just think again about the Conflict Lab you just did. It didn't take you long to realize that the news is filled with social, political, and economic conflicts whose consequences can be global in scope.

Now, think about the last time you got into an argument with a friend, a coworker, or a relative, let alone the last time you hung up the phone on a telemarketer—something that I do at least once a week.

Identifying examples of conflict is easy. As you undoubtedly saw in doing the first Conflict Lab. However, many of us have a much harder time defining exactly what we mean when we use the term. In fact, conflict is the first of many ambiguous terms you will encounter in this book, which means that its definition is worth exploring in some detail before we go any further.

The *Oxford English Dictionary* starts by defining conflict in a way that almost certainly will not come as a surprise:

> a serious disagreement or argument, typically a protracted one

It goes on to supply a list of synonyms, which you will also probably find familiar:

> dispute, quarrel, squabble, disagreement, dissension, clash

Academics typically resonate most with the Oxford team's third definition, which sees conflict as:

> an incompatibility between two or more opinions, principles, or interests

Psychologists claim that people are in conflict when they:

> have, or show, confused and mutually inconsistent feelings

Oxford's lexicographers only included violence in their second definition of conflict as a noun, when they called it a:

> prolonged armed struggle

For our purposes, the two other words in the preceding definition are more interesting than the use of arms. We tend to be interested in conflicts that are prolonged or protracted. Precisely because they last (and last and last), the antagonisms that underlie them tend to fester, often getting worse over time. And make no mistake: the conflicts which we will focus on are struggles—armed or otherwise.

Intractable Conflicts and Wicked Problems

Not all forms of conflict are worth spending much time on here as you can see from a single, simple example. You and your friends may well end up disagreeing when you decide what to eat for dinner tonight. Pizza? Mexican? Burgers? Vegan? Sure, you may argue over what and where to eat, but those disagreements are not likely to lead to voices raised in anger, let alone fisticuffs.

Instead, most of us got to peace and conflict studies because we were fascinated by what Guy and Heidi Burgess refer to as intractable conflicts, which they define on their indispensable website, www.beyondintractabililty.org, as disputes:

> that last a long time, are damaging, and seem to resist all efforts to resolve them.

Many of us are drawn to peace and conflict studies because of our concerns about the international disputes that are roiling the world. As a recent report by the United Nations (UN) and the World Bank points out, there are almost no classical wars being fought today, if by that we mean ones in which the armed forces of one or more nation-state(s) fight against those of another government or alliance.[2] Instead, most wars pit states against other actors, usually rebel groups and/or terrorists. Some of these conflicts do spill across national borders, which we've seen in such different settings as the war in Syria or the migration crisis along the border between the United States and Mexico.

Today's conflicts tend to be particularly intractable when they revolve around **identity** issues, such as race, gender, ethnicity, and religion. As we will see in more detail in parts 3 and 4, they are hard to resolve because they do not readily lend themselves to compromise, let alone cooperative solutions, because they revolve around questions of who "I" am.

Intractable conflicts do not have to be international or global in scope. Many domestic issues, including some that play themselves out primarily at the local level, can be just as intractable.

To see that point, simply think about race relations in the US or any other country with a diverse population. Despite the progress made over the last fifty years, the history of racial inequality and the conflict it spawns are hard to avoid. In Northern Virginia where I live, many local schools and streets are being renamed because they currently honor leading Confederate officials from the Civil War. Our NFL team's nickname is a derogatory term once used to put down Native Americans. Most of my friends and neighbors think it is high time we changed the names of Jefferson Davis Highway and the Washington Redskins. At the same time, I know plenty of people who do not find those names offensive.

To complicate matters further, we are interested in more than just political conflict. My wife and I were divorced when we got together. We aren't alone—about two out of every five first marriages in the US ends in divorce. The divorce rates for second and third marriages are even higher. We've been lucky. We've blended our families well, but we know plenty of others that struggle with the emotional and—all too often—physical scars of family conflict. I assume that you do, too.

The recent popularity of mindfulness, yoga, and spirituality reminds us that conflict can be intrapersonal as well. One recent study estimates that one in five Americans has a mental health disorder that could, and should, be treated, but only half of them will ever seek that help. Although we won't get there until the end of part 4, I will eventually make the case that the more peacebuilders attain "inner peace," the more effective they will be in dealing with other people—especially those with whom they disagree.

Some of us have begun to think of intractable conflicts as **wicked problems**. The term was first coined in the 1970s by two urban planners who were frustrated by the slow progress they and their colleagues were making in addressing the problems plaguing America's inner cities. They referred to them as wicked problems, not because they were evil, but because their causes and consequences are so inextricably intertwined that you cannot solve them separately, easily, or quickly—if you can solve them at all.

Beyond Gloom and Doom 101?

If we were to limit ourselves simply to analyzing protracted conflicts and wicked problems, peace and conflict studies would be a depressing field indeed. However, because we also are interested in resolving conflict and building peace, we try to move beyond what George Lopez called "Gloom and Doom 101" in characterizing our field in his 1988 presidential address to what is today's **Peace and Justice Studies Association**.

As he saw it, there were plenty of reasons why we had trouble presenting plausible alternatives to the Cold War tensions of the day. Among them was our assumption that dealing with intractable conflicts required the use—or at least the threatened use—of **power**. Few of the people in the room that day questioned the political scientists' classic definition of that term, which Robert Dahl had laid out in a still-famous 1957 article:

> A has power over B to the extent that he can get B to do something that *B would not otherwise do*.

Power is something A (or I) exert over B (or you). Sometimes A can utterly defeat B (or I can utterly defeat you). However, few conflicts lend themselves to clear winners and losers these days. Instead, the loser (B or you) resents having lost and all too often spends his or her time figuring out how to get back at A (or me).

Whether we like it or not, it is hard to get people with whom we disagree to comply with our wishes, especially if we don't **trust** them or if they come from some other group we tend to think of in stereotypical terms. They, of course, are the problem, so we wait for them to take that first step. They, of course, think exactly the same way about us and wait for us to take the first step. All too often we end up at an impasse—or worse.

The bottom line is simple and depressing. We assume that we will have to threaten to use force in order to get what we want, at least when the stakes of a conflict are high. That need not involve physical violence in at least one way that you have undoubtedly experienced—when your instructor threatens to take one-third of a letter grade off for each day you turn an assignment in late. Some conflict analysts go so far as to argue that such practices are tantamount to psychological—if not physical—violence.

In other words, many of us blend our understandings of conflict, power, force, and all forms of violence together. You can even see that in the word conflict itself which has two Latin roots. When used as a prefix, *con-* almost always means "with"; *-flict* has as its root the Latin word for "fire." Put simply, when we are in conflict, we are playing with fire.

Increasingly, conflict resolution and peacebuilding are based on another—and more hopeful—definition of power, which we will get to beginning in chapter 3. For now, however, assume that Dahl's definition is still on target. In that case, it is easy to see why most of us dread having to deal with conflict and why Lopez felt we were spending the bulk of our time (unnecessarily) depressing our students!

Conflict Resolution Is Never Easy

This book is based on the challenging assumption that we can escape Gloom and Doom 101. Lopez believed that, too. In fact, he used his speech to goad the first generation of peace and conflict studies professors into exploring alternatives to the conventional definitions of conflict and power in what we taught, wrote, and did as activists.

Many of us who were in the room that day were already fascinated by the ideas underlying the then new field of conflict resolution and peacebuilding. But Lopez wanted us to understand that turning those ideas into reality was not going to be easy. Thirty years later, his words still ring true.

The 1980s had been a fertile decade for creating new ideas about peace and conflict. As I noted earlier, the most widely cited book on conflict resolution then and now, Roger Fisher and William Ury's *Getting to YES*, was published in 1981. The next year, Search for Common Ground became the first American NGO to dedicate itself exclusively to the peaceful resolution of conflicts. In 1983 George Mason University in Fairfax, Virginia, created the first degree-granting academic program in conflict resolution.

As you will see, we have added a lot to our store of knowledge since then. However, we still know a lot more about how we get into conflict than we do about how we can get out of it. To make matters worse, many respected thinkers, including most political scientists, assume that definitions of power like Dahl's are the only viable ones. From that perspective, conflict resolution involves the use of "power over" one's adversaries and leads to zero-sum outcomes that have a single winner and one or more losers.

That mind-set holds for all forms conflict, including war. Countries have taken up arms against each other since the dawn of recorded history. Our bloody history suggests that those conflicts continue until one side wins a decisive victory or both sides agree that they have reached a stalemate and reluctantly decide to stop killing each other. But it also applies to elections, baseball games, disputes with your college administration, and just about everything else.

All too often marriages that could be saved end up in divorce. All too often disagreements at work turn into shouting matches. All too often political disputes in Washington, London, Delhi, or Johannesburg end up in gridlock or worse. All too often, international disagreements slide into war, whether between states or—as is more often the case today—between a government and its opponents.

And Peacebuilding Is Even Harder

Things do not always have to turn out that way, which is where peacebuilding comes into play. As with understanding the problems that conflicts pose, the dictionary is, once again, a good place to start.

As they did with the word conflict, the Oxford etymologists provide several different meanings of peace. The first definition starts with:

> freedom from disturbance, serenity, and calm

In this sense, peacefulness emphasizes mental rather than political states and includes synonyms such as:

> tranquility, equanimity, calmness, composure, ease, and contentment

On the other side of the coin Oxford lists agitation and distress as antonyms, which it could also have used as synonyms for conflict.

Only the second definition refers to the issues that were probably on most of your sticky notes:

> freedom from or the cessation of war, civil disturbance

In this definition, too, achieving peace at least implicitly involves overcoming conflicts that give rise to war or civil disobedience.

Academics often warn their students to be wary of dictionary definitions because they do not always go deeply enough into the meaning of a term. That certainly is true here, because both of those definitions understate what peace involves.

You can see that in a distinction has been at the heart of academic peace studies for thirty years—the distinction between **negative** and **positive peace**, which was first made by the Norwegian scholar **Johan Galtung** (1930–). The Oxford and most other dictionary definitions are negative in the sense that they define peace as the absence of war, whereas positive peace refers to conditions that address the root or underlying causes of the conflict.

Obviously, it is hard to begin building positive peace as long as people are fighting. However, Galtung was among the first scholars to point out that you can only build lasting peace if you also address the structural, institutional, economic, identity-based, and other issues that give rise to what I called wicked problems a few paragraphs ago. As you will see dozens of times in the pages to come, we can never make their historical origins disappear. However, we can work toward **reconciliation** in which the parties to a dispute find long-term solutions to the problems that put them (and often their ancestors) in conflict with each other in the first place.

All of this is another way of saying that long-term peacebuilding is even harder than conflict resolution. Every day's news reminds us that even reaching a basic agreement about a conflict in the Middle East or health care in the halls of Congress is never easy. The minute you focus on long-term, lasting solutions, the difficulties grow exponentially. When you get to broader goals like what I will later call peace writ large, peacebuilding might well seem like nothing more than pie-in-the-sky idealism.

SEEING WITH NEW EYES

As will be the case with many chapters in this book, this one begins with a statement from outside of peace and conflict studies that might seem to have little or nothing to do with the field—at least on the surface. However, because our field is new and draws on so many other academic disciplines, it is important to see how their insights can help us come to grips with conflict resolution and peacebuilding.

That is particularly true of this first chapter. You should be wondering why you should pay attention to anything written by the French novelist Marcel Proust who wrote this famous sentence more than a half-century before the world's first peace and conflict studies programs were created. Still, his notion that true discovery comes from "seeing with new eyes" will be central in the rest of this book and, I suspect, in the ways you deal with conflict in the years to come.

Seeing with new eyes will come into play in two main ways here. First, most approaches to conflict resolution involve reframing the issues in a dispute in ways that open the door to solutions that no one had thought of before. Second, and more importantly, we will spend a lot of time considering the role of **mind-sets** and paradigms in shaping the ways people "see" and think about conflict resolution and peace.

Some of us—myself included—are convinced that we need to dramatically change the way we deal with conflict through what is known as a paradigm shift. Others doubt that a paradigm shift is necessary and, even if it is, doubt our capacity to pull one off (see the Out on a Limb box on the next page).

Whatever conclusion you end up reaching, you cannot understand the issues underlying peace and conflict studies without paying attention to paradigm shifts. We will do so beginning at the end of chapter 2.

OUT ON A LIMB

This call for a paradigm shift marks the first time that I have gone out on an "intellectual limb" by presenting material that not everyone reading this book will agree with. Whenever I do so again, I will include this image and a short explanatory box.

I decided to include these boxes because it is all but impossible to write a dispassionate textbook about peace and conflict studies. Moreover, as you are about to see, those of us who have been in the field for decades do not agree on what should be included in a book like this one.

That said, you should be aware of it when I do go out on a limb because those are precisely the times when you should be the most willing to question my conclusions.

And send me an email at chip@charleshauss.info to let me know how and why you disagree.

THREE ERAS

We will spend the rest of part 1 exploring the analytical core of peace and conflict studies. Then, parts 2 through 4 will focus on how the field has grown in the thirty-five years since the first academic programs were created in two ways. S-CAR's Sara Cobb also developed a model for understanding how the conflict resolution field has evolved in three periods, which you can explore in more detail in the textbook she coauthored with Sarah Federman and Alison Castel.[3]

We will start by considering the progress we have made during three overlapping periods which AfP has been calling Peacebuilding 1.0 through 3.0. Not everyone uses those terms or divides the history of our field in this way. Nonetheless, the end of the Cold War and the terrorist attacks on 9/11 produced dramatic enough interruptions and disruptions in our work to think of its trajectory in terms of the birth of the field in the 1980s, its consolidation in the 1990s, and its coming of age during the first two decades of this century.

At first, we asked fairly simplistic questions and came up with reasonably simplistic solutions. A mere thirty years later, we find ourselves taking on challenging problems like the ones you talked about in the first Conflict Lab. We have not abandoned many of the analytical insights or practical tools we developed along the way. Instead, we have added ideas and practices that have gotten us to the point that terms like win-win are part of our everyday conversation.

One last caveat. Peacebuilding 3.0 is not the end of the story. Some of us are already thinking about the next phase of our work. So, the book will need a fifth part in which we consider how the field should grow and how you could play a role in its evolution. But as you will see when we get there, Peacebuilding 4.0 comes with a question mark because no one fully knows what the next phase of our work will entail.

Peacebuilding 1.0: Getting to Yes and a Bit Beyond

It is no coincidence that modern conflict resolution and peacebuilding studies date from the 1980s. In showing how and why that was the case here, I will limit myself to the US, but a similar case could be made for the rest of the world during those years, as you will see in part 2.

Memories of the Vietnam War were fresh in most people's minds when President Ronald Reagan's election intensified tensions with the Soviet Union and paved the way for a new arms race. Many feared that the world was closer to an all-out nuclear war than it had been at any time since the Cuban missile crisis of 1962.

Critics of the new administration responded in a number of ways. Many activists were drawn to efforts, such as the Nuclear Weapons Freeze Campaign, that were designed to stop production of those bombs and missiles so that we could eventually cut back on or even eliminate them altogether. Others began exploring a different pathway toward a more peaceful world whose roots lay in other wings of earlier peace movements, including the Fellowship for Reconciliation and the World Federalists.

The modern conflict resolution and peacebuilding field emerged when people began to add insights from books like *Getting to YES* to the traditional peace movement's agenda. While Fisher, Ury, and their colleagues focused on industrial disputes and organizational management, some of us began to see how win-win conflict resolution could also help to lead us out of the arms race and the other geopolitical tensions of the day.

Until then, these new forms of conflict resolution had primarily been used elsewhere. Many American states, for example, no longer let divorcing couples go to court unless they had tried to work things out with a mediator first. Large law firms began including mediation as a service they offered clients, ranging far beyond divorcing couples to major corporations and star athletes in what became known as **alternative dispute resolution (ADR)**. It was during these years that the philosopher and pollster Daniel Yankelovich began writing about the power of **dialogue**, or discussions that were so powerful that they left no one who participated in them unchanged.

It took people who were not part of the traditional peace movement(s) to make that broader connection to global conflicts. In academia, the retired Australian diplomat **John Burton** (1915–2010) was hired by George Mason University to create the first graduate program in conflict resolution in the US. Burton himself never thought of himself as a peacebuilder. Rather, his own work revolved around the idea that conflict exists because people resent the fact that their basic **human needs** are going unmet.

Clockwise from top left: Roger Fisher, William Ury, John Burton, and John Marks

Meanwhile, **John Marks** (1943–) created **Search for Common Ground**, which was the first NGO to focus exclusively on what we would now call peacebuilding. Marks had joined the US Foreign Service after graduating from college. After serving an initial tour of duty in Vietnam, he quit the State Department in protest against the war. He spent the next few years working in conventional political life. Soon, however, Marks began looking for an alternative to **win-lose** politics and the broader cultural norms that undergirded that way of dealing with global and national problems. Search for Common Ground engaged in new forms of **Track II diplomacy** with the Soviet Union. Search (as it refers to itself)

was even better known for making television programs featuring Soviet and American luminaries talking about disarmament and peace using the then novel technology of video tapes.

Other groups began experimenting with even more disruptive technologies, including the then mind-blowing spacebridge telecasts that simultaneously brought Soviets and Americans onto the same screen. Meanwhile, hundreds of American tour groups went to learn about the Soviet Union, including a group of students I took there in January 1986.

Two key themes held these initiatives together:

- We thought in terms of two parties who disagreed about a single or, at most, an overlapping set of issues. A mediator or facilitator (or **third party neutral)** helped the parties in a dispute to at least move closer to a win-win outcome, as illustrated in figure 1.2.
- We assumed (although we rarely articulated it) that rational actors could solve their problems by reframing the question or thinking about issues rather than positions. We did explore the irrational sides of human behavior when, for instance, we talked about the **image of the enemy** and other **stereotypes** in workshops. However, we agreed with Fisher, Ury, and others when they talked about the importance of getting the parties to a dispute to focus on their general interests rather than on their specific demands, because the emotional nature of their initial demands often got in the way of finding common ground.

As important as these breakthroughs were, they were not endorsed by everyone. Many activists and early peace studies scholars did not agree with the notion that we could or should be neutral. As they saw it, the problem lay with out-of-touch leaders in Washington, Moscow, and beyond, which meant that there was every reason to still think in we versus they terms.

Many of them preferred what Charles Tilly and Sidney Tarrow called **contentious politics**. As they saw things, individuals and organizations that were on the political fringes could only begin to make a difference and shift public policy if they themselves threatened to use force and coercion to get the attention of the people in power.

The end of the Cold War, however, pushed those ideas onto the intellectual back burner at least as far as the academic conflict and peace studies communities were concerned. They have returned to prominence in recent years, but they were not important enough at the time to deserve much space in this brief historical overview of Peacebuilding 1.0.

FIGURE 1.2
Mediation, Deliberation, and Dialogue

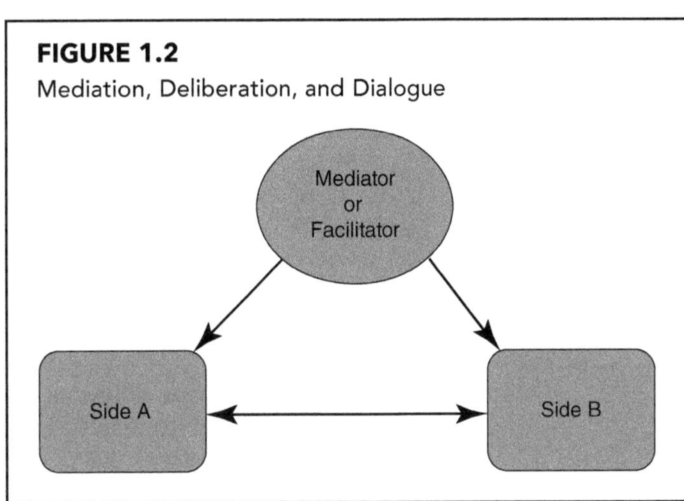

Peacebuilding 2.0: Human Security and the Problem of Identity

The period came to an abrupt halt when the Cold War ended. If you could invent a time machine and return to the early 1980s, you would find that just about everyone assumed that the Cold War would drag on indefinitely—if we didn't end human civilization, that is.

Then, in the blink of an historical eye, the superpower conflict ended when the Berlin Wall came down in 1989 and the Soviet Union collapsed two years later. In less than five years, President **Mikhail Gorbachev** (1930–) opened the clichéd Pandora's box, unprecedented reforms were introduced in the Soviet Union, and the impossible happened. At the time many of us (myself included) felt that we were entering what Presidents **George H. W. Bush** and Gorbachev referred to as a new world order in which the world's powers would settle their disputes more peacefully and constructively.

They were wrong.

I was wrong.

We all should have known better.

All of a sudden, we had to deal with a host of conflicts that had been papered over by the superpower rivalry. This started with fighting between two Soviet republics—Armenia and Azerbaijan—that began during the Cold War's dying days. It soon spread elsewhere in what was then the communist bloc, especially in the bloody civil wars that broke out as the former Yugoslavia disintegrated. Meanwhile, existing conflicts in other places like South Africa, Northern Ireland, East Timor, Somalia, and Rwanda now made the headlines because people were dying in the tens or even hundreds of thousands.

Some peacebuilding groups failed to make the transition. Many of the organizations whose *raison d'être* was ending the nuclear arms race stayed alive but lost much of their impact as their issues receded from center stage. Others failed to find new issues that grabbed their members' attention and disappeared altogether.

A few groups, including Search for Common Ground, realized that ending the Cold War was not the same thing as ending conflict. Even before the Cold War ended, Search began turning its attention to the Middle East and beyond. It also explored new ways of addressing disputes, including the use of the mass media when it made its first television soap operas around peacebuilding themes that we will explore in part 3.

The most important analytical breakthroughs came in a series of reports issued by the Carnegie Commission on Preventing Deadly Violence. More than Fisher and Ury or the people they had inspired, the Commission focused on **preventing** conflict in the first place.

We also had to work in places where efforts to prevent conflict had failed, and peacebuilders were called in to help reconstruct war-torn societies. The most important realization in that respect was that getting to yes on a single peace agreement or other "deal" was never enough. Postwar reconstruction involved a lot more than rebuilding a country's infrastructure, rewriting its constitution, and the like. Among other things, we had to deal with the human, trauma laden costs of conflict through what peacebuilders call **reconciliation**, in which the parties to a dispute truly work through their differences and find ways of living with each other.

One brief example should help you see why reconciliation is important and how different it is from anything that was on our agenda in the 1980s—the events in South Africa following the 1990 release of **Nelson Mandela** after twenty-seven years in prison. To this day, the country's peace process is best known for its **Truth and Reconciliation Commission (TRC)**, which was co-chaired by the Nobel Prize laureate and Anglican priest **Desmond Tutu**. The country's new leaders realized that they could not prosecute the perpetrators of apartheid and hope to heal the country's divisions. Therefore they drew on the new idea of

restorative justice and literally tried restoring broken relationships rather than sending guilty parties to prison. Tutu, in particular, drew on a concept used in much of southern Africa, ***ubuntu***, which can be translated as "a person is a person through another person" and therefore stressed the importance of positive relationships.

The TRC could grant amnesty to perpetrators on both sides if they openly confessed to what they had done and, more importantly, showed remorse for their actions. After three years of hearings and the publication of its final report, South Africans learned about almost all of the crimes committed by both sides during the apartheid years and took some important steps to improve relationships between whites and blacks that are still being felt a generation later.

Change was also afoot in what we now call the international community, especially at the UN. Not only did it do more to forge peace in global hotspots but it also launched two related initiatives that propelled the field forward in ways that have continued ever since.

The first came when it introduced the idea of **human security** in its Development Programme's annual report in 1994. Its lead author, Mahbub ul Haq, made the case that what we mean by security had to be expanded in the post–Cold War world:

> The world can never be at peace unless people have security in their daily lives. Future conflicts may often be within nations rather than between them—with their origins buried deep within socio-economic deprivations and disparities. The search for security in such a milieu lies in development. not in arms.[4]

These ideas first came to the broader public's attention when the UN published its eight Millennial Development Goals (MDGs), which included ending extreme poverty, promoting gender equality, combatting HIV/AIDS and other diseases, reducing child mortality, and more. The MDGs were designed to structure the UN's work for the first fifteen years of this century.

The words peace and conflict were largely missing from the MDGs and supporting documents. However, it was hard to imagine how the world could make much progress on (m)any of these fronts without tackling conflict resolution and peacebuilding along the way.

Last, but by no means least, the proliferation of programs led some people to begin thinking about how practitioners could and should work together. More academic programs were created. By the end of the century, at least ten American universities were granting graduate degrees in some aspect of conflict resolution and peace studies. Most law schools introduced courses in mediation, negotiation, and conflict resolution.

They were accompanied by the birth of professional organizations. Inspired in part by the Hewlett Foundation, the Association for Conflict Resolution was created in 2000 as a professional association for mediators, educators, and others, most of whom worked in the US. At about the same time, Hewlett worked with a group of American based NGOs and academic institutions that did most of their work abroad to form what is today's AfP. Similar initiatives took place elsewhere in the world, culminating in the creation of the **Global Partnership for the Prevention of Armed Conflict** (**GPPAC**).

Even national governments realized that they had a role to play. As hard as it may be for some people to believe, the US took the lead. The Clinton administration

FIGURE 1.3
Peacebuilding 2.0

created ADR offices in all federal departments and agencies to resolve internal disputes, some of which have proven to be extremely successful. More importantly for the purposes of this book, Congress passed a law creating the **United States Institute of Peace** (**USIP**) in 1983. It was only in the 1990s, however, that it became one of the few places in Washington where people from the left and right could easily come together to talk about questions of war and peace.

When AfP looked back on this period in the early 2000s and began calling this work Peacebuilding 2.0, we used the diagram that appears here as figure 1.3. Don't worry if you can't read all the words on the "petals" of that "daisy." They include the range of issues I have talked about so far in this section and then some. The key thing to note at this point, is that it placed peacebuilding and peacemaking at the center of the "daisy" on the assumption that if we were to create a more peaceful world, we would simultaneously tackle all of those other issues.

Peacebuilding 3.0: Wicked Problems and Complexity

Peace and conflict studies changed dramatically again after a second sudden and unexpected event—the terrorist attacks on New York and Washington on 9/11. As you will see in part 4, it took both the academics and the practitioners a long time to figure out how to respond.

When all was said and done, we realized that conflict was such a common feature in the human experience that there was very little we could leave out of peace and conflict studies. As a result, most peacebuilders—if not conflict resolution professionals—adopted a systems approach that views peace and conflict in holistic terms. I already pointed you in that direction with the first Conflict Lab, and we will have to spend a lot more time on these issues later. At this point, it is enough to see the main ways in which our practical work has evolved over the last twenty years—and remember that these issues will not appear in the book until we get to part 4 as important as they may seem to you today.

Terrorism and violent extremism. We have, of course, always worked on **terrorism** and, as it is now usually referred to, **violent extremism**. To be honest, the results have been mixed, but we are in good company in that respect. No one has developed strategies that have had much success in ending terrorism. What we can say is that military leaders and others have taken important steps toward accepting the peacebuilders' notion that we cannot defeat terrorism through the use of force alone. Instead, we will have to gradually undermine support for it by addressing the social, economic, and political problems that gave rise to this kind of violence in the first place.

Do no harm. By the end of the 1990s, we had already realized that some things peace and conflict resolution practitioners tried did not work. We also discovered that some things we did actually made natters worse as a result of their indirect or third order effects, which you may have stumbled on in doing the exercises at the beginning of this chapter. Therefore, many of us adopted a peace and conflict studies version of the Hippocratic Oath which all doctors swear to uphold—**do no harm**.

Sustainable development. We also realized that peace could not be built or conflict transformed unless we put the immediate issues in a larger context. Some scholars had already understood that by the end of the 1990s. Johan Galtung did so when he wrote about structural violence. John Burton did the same when he stressed how unmet human needs gave rise to conflict.

The UN, in particular, spearheaded the global efforts to think more holistically, beginning with its introduction of the idea of human security. In 2000, it adopted a set of Millennium Development Goals that guided its work for the next fifteen years. In 2015, the MDGs were replaced by the far more sophisticated and interconnected **Sustainable Development Goals (SDGs)**. The SDGs were also more important for our purposes, because they marked the first time the UN had explicitly included peacebuilding in one of its core documents.

Mind-sets. The 9/11 attacks and the changed global situation they led to also had important indirect effects on the way conflict resolution and peacebuilding specialists do their work, most notably in our growing interest in paradigm shifts. In the rest of this book, we will spend a lot of time focusing on paradigms and the way they affect the issues you talked about while doing the first Conflict Lab. Here it is enough to see how our personal paradigms or mind-sets have come to shape peace and conflict studies.

For example, the Stanford psychologist Carol Dweck talks about fixed and growth mind-sets. People with the former tend to resist change, while those with the latter perspective on the world are more open to it. More generally, feminists, the Black Lives Matter movement, and others have forced peacebuilders and others to think more deeply about the ways entrenched mind-sets, such as our **implicit biases**, shape the way we deal with the world. The same holds for the growing interest in self-awareness, resilience, and the like by the millions of people who practice yoga, have meditative practices, and generally bring spirituality into their lives.

Progress—Take 1: The SDGs

To whet your appetite for the rest of this book, this chapter has three boxes that suggest how much progress we have made—and how far we still have to go. This first one starts us off with a global issue. The Sustainable Development Goals obviously have not brought world peace, and no one dreamed that they would do so by the time they expire in 2030.

However, they are important steps forward in three main ways. They mark the first time that the UN or any other major international organization included peacebuilding and cooperation among its key goals. They also reflect the growing understanding that achieving sustainable development will require addressing all of the world's wicked problems. Finally, their authors included concrete "deliverables" against which progress will be measured for each of the seventeen goals.

All that has led conflict resolution and peacebuilding practitioners to put a renewed emphasis on personal growth and truly "walking the talk." As a result, problem-solving workshops and other small-group encounters we have always conducted now dig much more deeply into the participants' personal paradigms as well as their overt attitudes toward the other side. That has led us to stress values people have known about for centuries such as **empathy** or the capacity to see an issue from someone else's perspective, including your adversary's. At the same time, some of us began drawing on the work of neuroscientists who talk about the "plasticity" of our minds and are exploring ways that we can "rewire" our brains so that we are more likely to turn to nonviolent ways of dealing with conflict.

Fostering a culture of peace. Closely related is the now widespread belief that we have to build support for peacebuilding and conflict resolution everywhere. Traditional diplomacy has always been the province of trained foreign policy experts, most of whom were older, well-educated men. Even the Track II initiatives you will see in parts 2 and 3 rarely involved more than a few hundred individuals. Now, there is a growing realization that average citizens also have to change the values and assumptions they use in confronting the conflict in their daily lives, whether at home, at work, or in their dealings with government.

Changing them by fostering cultures of peace might seem like a daunting task given the state of the world today. At the same time, there are signs that people are interested in exploring alternatives to the status quo. Evidence for that proposition can be found both in the limited public opinion polling on support for peace in the US and Western Europe and in the growing popularity of yoga, meditation, and spirituality I mentioned a few paragraphs ago. To speed up the process of cultural change, a number of my colleagues have been working with advertising agencies and screenwriters as well as conventional mainstream journalists as we try to find ways to shift the narrative when it comes to dealing with divisive conflict.

Bright spots. Even those of us (including me) who argue most vociferously for a paradigm shift understand that we can't achieve peace in one fell swoop. Therefore, we see the need for a gradual approach in which we build on a series of **incremental changes** and take support for peacebuilding and constructive forms of conflict resolution to scale.

Critical here are what business professors Chip and Dan Heath call bright spots. If they and more scholarly experts who prefer terms like outlier or positive deviant are right, there will always be examples of "things that work" no matter how dire a situation might seem at the moment. In this respect, the Boston-based

Progress—Take 2: Cure Violence

Although mediators and other conflict resolution professionals have always done so, the peacebuilding community is just beginning to focus attention to problems closer to home. Many of these efforts build directly on the kinds of initiatives first used in the Global South, which we will see in part 3.

Some of the more promising ones are based on different ideas altogether and therefore hold out a lot of promise, especially for those of us who think we need to think "outside the box" of conventional conflict resolution and peacebuilding.

Particularly promising here is **Cure Violence**. Originally founded in Chicago by a public health doctor, Cure Violence uses an epidemiological approach to violence prevention, viewing it as a "disease" whose "spread" has to be prevented. It uses trained "interrupters," many of whom are themselves former gang members and ex-offenders, to defuse situations that could turn violent. After the tensions subside, others work with the community to address the underlying issues that led to the violence. Cure Violence has been so successful in Chicago that its model has been adapted for use in other American cities (New York, Baltimore, Kansas City, and New Orleans) and in a few other countries (Canada, Jamaica, Iraq, Syria, and El Salvador).

CDA published a book about communities that intentionally "opted out of war."[5] More generally, we began to look for these bright spots and to figure out if anything about those experiences could be replicated elsewhere.

The home front. Most of the conflict resolution and peacebuilding organizations I will be discussing in part 3 were based in the Global North but did most of their work in the Global South. The 9/11 attacks were the first of many events that convinced those organizations that they had to work on the issues facing their own countries as well.

The last two decades have been difficult ones in the Global North as we had to come to grips with our own wicked problems, including immigration and the identity issues it spawns and exacerbates, climate change, gender and economic inequality, and the rise of populism on the left and right. Then came the Brexit referendum in the UK and Donald Trump's election. We all began to think about the unthinkable, as Nik Gowing and Chris Langdon describe the crises we face in countries like my US or their UK.[6] As a result, more and more peacebuilders are working on problems at home, some of which are unfolding literally around the corner from their homes or offices.

New coalitions. Many practitioners (though not as many academics) have realized that we therefore have to build broader political coalitions. Given the origins of the field, it is hardly surprising that most of us started out on the political left. However, as you will see countless times in the course of this book, there is no reason why peace and conflict studies should only appeal to political progressives.

Indeed, as ideas developed by the likes of Fisher and Ury found homes in legal and corporate circles, they gained support among people who would rarely define themselves as leftists. Similarly, many military officers grew frustrated by their inability to defeat terrorist groups and began to focus on the roles they could and should play both in conflict prevention and post conflict reconstruction. Meanwhile, religious leaders from all faiths began exploring ways in which their different spiritual traditions could lead believers to reject violence and pursue peace. Finally, many businesses in the technology sector and beyond have made cooperative problem solving the norm in the way they manage themselves,

Progress—Take 3: Campus Climate

There is a lot of talk these days about ideological divisions and political correctness on college campuses—and not just in the US. There is undoubtedly a fair amount of truth to the criticisms that often get made about the antagonisms on campuses, some of which even gets directed at peace and conflict studies programs.

The popular media too often miss the conflict resolution work that is already being done on campuses around the world. We will return to that in part 5. Before we get there, you should find out about what is happening at your college or university. Is there a campus mediation service? A dialogue and deliberation center? An organization of peace activists? What are your campus's offices of religious life or its athletic department doing to deal with campus problems?

starting in the human relations department and often extending all the way to the C Suites and the corporate boardroom.

The return of contentious politics. Because many of those issues are so divisive, we now have to do our work in a world in which contentious politics mattered for the first in a generation (see the box on Disagreement Comes with the Territory on page 27). That started with the debate over the best way to respond to terrorism. The initial shock and unity after the 9/11 attacks soon gave way to heated debate during the months leading up to the US-led invasion of Iraq in 2003. Divisive issue after divisive issue filled the news. Activists and academics alike realized that the problems facing the world were no longer "out there" in the Global South but affected their lives at home, wherever home might happen to be. As Americans, that happened on dozens of fronts with such issues as our own ideological divisions, the Black Lives Matter and #MeToo campaigns, terrorism and other perceived threats to our national security, and, of course, now, the Trump presidency.

TWO ENTRY POINTS

I asked you to do two separate versions of the Conflict Lab at the beginning of this chapter because peace and conflict studies has its roots in disputes at all levels from your immediate household literally to the planet as a whole. Ideally, any introduction to peace and conflict studies should explore all of them. However, we cannot hope to cover all forms of conflict and its resolution in an introductory course. You can, however, begin to explore some basic similarities and differences at the micro and macro levels as I will do in the three chapters of parts 2 through 4 and as summarized in table 1.1:

- The first will put the period in its historical context and return to the key concepts introduced in part 1 that were critical for understanding the events of those years.
- The second will explore conflicts that take place at the grassroots and interpersonal levels and stress the ways individuals think and act.
- The third one will continue the analysis with conflicts that take place at the national or even the global level and therefore involve disputes over public policy.

TABLE 1.1 Levels and Eras in Conflict and Peace Studies

	Micro	Macro
Peacebuilding 1.0 The Beginning	*Getting to YES* Mediation	Cold War Track II
Peacebuilding 2.0 After the Cold War	Identity Reconciliation	The Global South Human security and positive peace
Peacebuilding 3.0 The Current Period	Holistic approaches Personal paradigms	Complexity Global paradigms

Micro

The lasting impact of the first phase can best be seen in the continued popularity of *Getting to YES*, which put alternative dispute resolution on the intellectual map. By the time, the book was published, Fisher and Ury had already created Harvard's **Project on Negotiations (PON)** at its law school, and some of the book's profits allowed it to become an intellectual hub that draws on faculty from many different disciplines who teach at all of the major universities in the Boston area. While PON has plenty of experts who work on national and international disputes, it is best known now for the work it does in legal and corporate circles.

Mediation and negotiation are also included in almost all law, business, and public administration curricula. Most corporate human resources officers and most university student support professionals now incorporate ideas developed by Fisher, Ury, and similar authorities in their work.

No one would claim that cooperative problem solving is the norm in the private sector. All you have to do is to look at the number of lawsuits in the news or the ruthless "gotcha" competition in today's business world to realize that win-win is by no means the decision-making tool people turn to first. What's more, much of what is done in the name of negotiation and deal making has next to nothing to do with the values one finds in *Getting to YES*, starting with President Donald Trump's first book.[7]

Macro

Because they drew most of us into the field, I will spend more time on the broader social and political issues that require some kind of public policy-based solutions. You will have no trouble seeing that we have made far less progress on higher level conflicts.

Still, we have made some progress.

As we will see in more detail in the next chapter, fewer conventional wars are being fought today than at most times in recorded history. And we have created institutions and adopted norms that have helped us discover ways of settling disputes without recourse to war. Still, there would be no need for you to take this course if cooperative problem solving were the norm at the national or global level. Instead, I assume that you share my frustration with the lack of progress we have made over the years.

In documenting the lack of progress, I will keep referring to a concern raised by Julia Roig, CEO of Partners Global, while we were drafting the document that introduced the idea of Peacebuilding 3.0. She wondered why we didn't have a seat at the "grown-ups' table" when it came to making public policy about everything from war and peace to climate change to race relations.

In one sense, Roig was right. Few people with a background in peace and conflict studies sit on any of the world's equivalents of the US National Security Council. In another sense, she overstated her case. When I first became an activist in the late 1960s, and then again during the first period we will be covering in part 2, we were all but totally excluded from policy-making circles.

That is not the case today. As you will see in part 4 we sometimes sit at the grown-ups' table at the local, national, and global levels. We are not there when all key decisions are made. We do not get what we want most of the time. We are far from achieving the paradigm shift I have dedicated my professional life to.

But we can at least see some glimmers of hope.

TOWARD PEACEBUILDING 4.0?

That takes us to part 5 and one final way in that this is an unusual book.

Most people who take courses in peace and conflict studies because they already have a long-standing interest in the subject. Many also hope that their first course will lead to an undergraduate major, graduate study, and even a career. Even the students who never take another course in peace and conflict studies understand that they will be dealing with the issues raised in the course for the rest of their lives.

In other words, I assume that you are like the students I have worked with over the years. You will want me to go further in two main ways, which are covered in the final two chapters.

Chapter 13 lays out the future of our field and the way a Peacebuilding 4.0 might affect students, scholars, and practitioners alike. Because the students I work with have asked for it, chapter 14 discusses ways you can empower yourselves as students, professionals, and citizens.

I also wrote these two chapters in a doubly unusual way.

First, I sat in on Professor Douglas Irvin-Erickson's introductory course in fall 2018 while I was finishing this book. In order to help me, he agreed to give the students an unusual final exam. Instead of the traditional test taken during finals week, he asked them to hand in two short papers, one exploring the issues that they thought the conflict resolution and peace studies community had to tackle next and the other explaining how they saw themselves fitting into the field during the rest of their lives. We both told them that I would incorporate their ideas into part 5 of the book. Doug also reassured them that he would not penalize them if they concluded that the field had no future or that they did not anticipate personally being a part of it. Rather, their grade would be determined by how well they made their case, whatever that happened to be.

Second, I invited two students to join me in writing the final two chapters, because it was not intuitively obvious to me that a seventy-year-old author should be giving advice to twenty-year-old students. Nora Malatinszky was then

Disagreement Comes with the Territory

Even though there is only one Out on a Limb box in this chapter, don't assume that we are a single unified field. In fact, at least one prominent scholar or activist whom I know and respect would have disagreed with every major point I have made this far including:

- Balancing analysis and activism?
- The issues we should focus on?
- The places where we should work?
- The role of violence in human nature?
- The need for a paradigm shift?

a junior at George Mason. She had taken Doug's course in her first year, worked in S-CAR's library (where we met), and is already well on her way to a career that explores the links between corruption and peacebuilding in her native Hungary. Bethany Gen was then a sophomore at Oberlin College, where she had already been paired with me in an experimental program that connects underclass students with older graduates on the assumption that the student and graduate could both learn from each other. In this case, I helped Bethany clarify her career goals, while she has helped me see the importance of gender in peacebuilding and turned me into a long-distance fan of Oberlin's women's soccer team.

SOME FINAL THOUGHTS

In ending this chapter, I want to make three last points before you dig into conflict resolution and peacebuilding.

What Isn't Included

There are dozens of topics I could easily have included but chose to leave out. For example, the threat of nuclear war will pretty much disappear after the end of part 2. Although traditional forms of negotiation and diplomacy are important, they won't feature prominently in rest of this book either.

In order to keep this book (reasonably) short and to avoid adding themes that would make its core lines of argument harder to follow, I have concentrated on:

- issues from earlier generations that are still on the agenda today
- ideas and social forces that gave rise to modern peace and conflict studies
- initiatives that have the greatest potential for bringing about large-scale, nonviolent social change

It Doesn't Always Work

While writing this book, I had two conversations that reminded me that conflict resolution and peacebuilding are not always the answer.

The first grew out of a dilemma that Doug raised toward the end of his class. He asked the students what they had learned that might help a German Jew who was about to be shoved into a cattle car and sent to a concentration camp and all but certain death during the Holocaust. For one of the few times all semester, not a single hand went up.

The second is something I heard a lot from my activist classmates as we were planning our fiftieth college reunion. We had all "majored" in ending the war in Vietnam, and many of us built careers that touched on conflict resolution and peacebuilding. Nonetheless, some of them made the case that not even the contentious politics versions of peace and conflict studies offered solutions to the problems we face today, ranging from war and terrorism to the rise of populism in countries like the United States.

In one key respect, both Doug and my Oberlin classmates are right. As convinced as I am that conflict resolution and peacebuilding offer useful ways of dealing with all of today's problems, I know that plenty of difficult problems we face do not lend themselves to the kinds of solutions you will be reading about in the next thirteen chapters.

There Are No Magic Wands

Finally, I also want to make certain that you see one last, related point.

Despite what many self-proclaimed conflict resolution or peacebuilding gurus might want you to think, there is no single pathway to peace. There is no one-size-fits-all solution, let alone a magic wand you can wave to end disputes. You can't think in terms of conflict as some sort of Rubik's Cube that you can twist and turn until you find *the* solution in which you end up with the equivalent of having all the squares of a single color on each side.

Dozens of books, websites, and videos at least hint that their creators have the answer. Don't believe them. Almost all of them have partial answers. But that's all they have.

There is no single way to either understand or to solve any of the problems you will be considering in the rest of this book. Physicists may think they are close to developing a unified theory of everything. We aren't even in the ballpark.

In other words, treat everything you learn about conflict and peace skeptically.

Starting with my prose.

KEY TERMS

Concepts

alternative dispute resolution (ADR), 16
conflict map, 3
contentious politics, 9
dialogue, 16
do no harm, 21
empathy, 22
human needs, 16
human security, 19
identity, 10
image of the enemy, 17
implicit biases, 21
incremental changes, 22
intractable conflict, 2
mind-set, 14
negative peace, 13
nongovernmental organization (NGO), 7
paradigm, 7
positive peace, 13
positive-sum, 8
power, 11
prevent, 18
reconciliation, 18
relationships, 8
resolution, 8
restorative justice, 19
stereotypes, 17
Sustainable Development Goals (SDGs), 21
terrorism, 21

third-party neutral, 17
Track II diplomacy, 16
transactional, 8
transformational, 8
trust, 12
ubuntu, 19
violent extremism, 21
wicked problem, 11
win-lose, 16
win-win, 8
zero-sum, 8

People

Burton, John, 16
Bush, George H. W., 18
Galtung, Johan, 13
Gorbachev, Mikhail, 18
Mandela, Nelson, 18
Marks, John, 16
Tutu, Desmond, 18

Organizations, Places, and Events

Alliance for Peacebuilding, 7
Cure Violence, 23
Global Partnership for the Prevention of Armed Conflict (GPPAC), 19
Peace and Justice Studies Association, 11
Project on Negotiations (PON), 25
School for Conflict Analysis and Resolution, 7
Search for Common Ground, 16
Truth and Reconciliation Commission (TRC), 18
United States Institute of Peace (USIP), 20

DIG DEEPER

Fisher, Roger, and William Ury. *Getting to YES* New York: Houghton and Mifflin, 1982. Still the single most influential book in the field.

Hunter, John. *World Peace and Other Fourth Grade Accomplishments*. New York: Houghton, Mifflin, Harcourt, 2014. A delightful account of how John Hunter's fourth-grade students achieved world peace and forty-nine other goals. It also teaches the reader a lot about the principles underlying this book.

Lederach, John Paul. *The Little Book of Conflict Transformation*. New York: Good Books, 2015. A slim but stunning volume by arguably the closest peacebuilding gets to having a rock star.

Mayer, Bernard. *The Dynamics of Conflict Resolution: A Practitioner's Guide*. San Francisco: Jossey-Bass, 2000. The first book by one of the leading theorists about mediation, who also happened to be my undergraduate housemate.

Richmond, Oliver. *Peace: A Very Short Introduction*. New York: Oxford University Press, 2014. Part of a wonderful series of very short introductions to academic disciplines by one of the best young scholars in the field.

United Nations/World Bank. *Pathways to Peace: Inclusive Approaches to Preventing Violent Conflict*. https://openknowledge.worldbank.org/handle/10986/28337. A book-length overview of the world's problems, with some ideas for what could be done about them.

NOTES

[1] Terms in bold can be found in the list of key terms at the end of each chapter and in the glossary at the end of this book.

[2] United Nations/World Bank, *Pathways to Peace: Inclusive Approaches to Preventing Violent Conflict*, www.openknowledge.worldbank.org/handle/10986/28337.

[3] You can find more details on thinking in terms of three eras in Sara Cobb, Sarah Federman, and Alison Castel, eds, *Introduction to Conflict Resolution: Discourses and Dynamics* (London: Rowman & Littlefield International, 2020).

[4] UNDP, Human Development Report: 1994 (New York: United Nations Development Programme), http://hdr.undp.org/sites/default/files/reports/255/hdr_1994_en_complete_nostats.pdf.

[5] Mary Anderson and Marshall Wallace, *Opting Out of War* (Boulder, CO: Lynne Reinner, 2015).

[6] Nik Gowing and Chris Langdon, *Thinking the Unthinkable* (London: John Catt, 2018).

[7] Donald J. Trump. *Trump: The Art of the Deal* (New York: Random House, 1987), chapter 1.

Forks in the Road

THINK ABOUT IT

This chapter is filled with questions that are important here and are worth returning to frequently in the rest of this book.

- How do the issues raised by Secretary General Gutteres affect your life and those of the people around you? Are there other issues you would add to his list? Does his rather dismal depiction of the world seem accurate to you? Why (not)?
- Steven Pinker and scholars like him paint an optimistic picture of humanity's long-term evolution. Do you agree?
  - If you agree, how would you explain the fact that there is so much fighting in the world today?
  - If not, how would you explain the trends he and other scholars have written about?
  - If you are having trouble coming down on one side or the other on the two statements, ask yourself how both of these interpretations could be true.
- Are we at the kind of fork in the road that Thomas Friedman talks about? Is power changing in the way Dacher Keltner envisions?
- Depending on how you answer the previous question, do you think we need a paradigm shift? If so, how would you go about creating one?

CORE CONCEPTS

evolution—the science of how species and individuals change in profound ways over time

exponential change—rapid, accelerating growth

globalization—the interconnection of worldwide systems of interaction

network—collection of interdependent components of an integrated system

paradigm—basic values and assumptions underlying an academic field or human behavior

power—the ability to get others to do what you want

VUCA—volatile, uncertain, complicated, and ambiguous

As a species, we have never before stood at this moral fork in the road—where one could kill all of us and all of us could fix everything if we really decided to do so.

—Thomas Friedman

We live in perhaps the most dynamic moment in human history when it comes to power.

—Dacher Keltner

MANY STUDENTS TAKE COURSES IN peace and conflict studies in part because they are worried about the world's problems and because they are looking for credible and even creative alternatives to the current state of affairs. There are literally dozens of intellectual paths that peace and conflict studies activists can take when they try to blend the sense of urgency that stems from those worries with the optimism offered by those credible or creative alternatives.

Like many of my colleagues, I often use the term **crisis** as a jumping-off point in describing them. Most people in the Western world do not think that crises are a good thing. To see why, think about these two examples.

Some of my political scientist colleagues are convinced that the events like election of Donald Trump or Britain's decision to leave the European Union (Brexit) have put democracy in crisis. Can the governments of the US or the UK cope with the new pressures? Could they go the way of Nazi Germany? Or worse?

Two parents are yelling at each other again and talking about getting a divorce. Their children overhear them, sit in the corner, and whisper to each other. What's going to happen to us? Where will we live? Where will we go to school? Do they still love us?

Crises can lead to catastrophe as the Germans discovered after 1933. Even when they don't have catastrophic results, they can leave permanent scars, as my sister and I learned after our parents got divorced—and we had already graduated from college by then.

There is, however, another way of thinking about a crisis that the conflict resolution and peacebuilding community learned from two unlikely sources—Chinese calligraphy and modern medicine. The Chinese use two characters as their equivalent of the English word crisis—"danger" and "opportunity." As in the case of my two examples, a crisis is dangerous because it can lead to a political mess or a messy divorce. But it also contains opportunities. So, to continue with the linguistic analogy to Chinese, seizing those opportunities requires learning from and overcoming the dangers.

For physicians, a medical crisis occurs when a patient hovers between life and death. Either outcome is possible. A person in a medical crisis is simply at a turning point, albeit one with (literally) life-or-death consequences.

These unconventional ways of thinking about a crisis bring us to the statements by Thomas Friedman and Dacher Keltner which will be at the heart not only of this chapter but of the rest of this entire book. People rarely talk about the two of them in the same breath. Keltner is a cutting-edge experimental psychologist who built on more than twenty years of data from his lab in reconsidering the use of power in his latest book. Friedman is an award-winning columnist for the *New York Times* who is best known for his insightful analyses of global trends and his use of catchy phrases he coins to describe them, like "the world is flat."

If they are right, we are at a turning point in human evolution. As Friedman sees it, we are at a fork in the road that, in Keltner's terms, could change the way we deal with conflict because we could—and perhaps should—redefine power. In short, studying peace and conflict today means that just about everything that matters to social scientists and average human beings is up for grabs.

Those kinds of sweeping statements rarely make their way into textbooks. However, if I'm right, peace and conflict studies has to be based on them.

To see how and why that might be the case, we will start at the present, take a big step backward in time, and then return to the present. In the process, I hope you see how we ended up at Friedman's fork in the road and why seeing with Proust's new eyes is vital for getting to Keltner's way forward.

THE STATE OF THE WORLD: 2018

If you had heard **UN** secretary general **António Gutteres**'s somber New Year's message on December 31, 2017, you might not have gone out to party that night.

> Dear friends around the world, Happy New Year.
>
> When I took office one year ago, I appealed for 2017 to be a year for peace. Unfortunately—in fundamental ways, the world has gone in reverse.
>
> On New Year's Day 2018, I am not issuing an appeal. I am issuing an alert—a red alert for our world.
>
> Conflicts have deepened and new dangers have emerged.
>
> Global anxieties about nuclear weapons are the highest since the Cold War.
>
> Climate change is moving faster than we are. Inequalities are growing.
>
> We see horrific violations of human rights.
>
> Nationalism and xenophobia are on the rise.
>
> As we begin 2018, I call for unity. I truly believe we can make our world more safe and secure. We can settle conflicts, overcome hatred and defend shared values.
>
> But we can only do that together.
>
> I urge leaders everywhere to make this New Year's resolution: Narrow the gaps. Bridge the divides. Rebuild trust by bringing people together around common goals. Unity is the path. Our future depends on it.
>
> I wish you peace and health in 2018.
>
> Thank you.[1]

In barely a minute and a half, he put his finger on five of the world's most pressing problems, which we will address in beginning this chapter, because they go a long way toward defining why Friedman thinks that we are at a fork in the road.

Deepened conflicts and new dangers. By one count, there were fifty-four armed conflicts taking place around the world in January 2018 (see table 2.1). One could quibble over whether some of the smaller ones should have been included, but there is little or no ambiguity when it comes to the bloodiest ones, each of which killed more than one thousand people in 2017.

The data in that table lead to a few conclusions that echo Gutteres's point:

- Next to none of these are traditional wars that pit two or more countries against each other.
- Most are civil wars, although many of them spill across national lines, including the uprising in the Maghreb listed in the second row of the table, which killed people in six North African countries.
- Many of them have deep historical roots that date back to the end of World War II, if not before.
- A few of the smaller ones showed signs of ending (e.g., Colombia), but far more of them remain powder kegs that could go off again and once more take thousands of lives as they have in the past (e.g., Israel/Palestine or the various Kurdish separatist uprisings).
- Many involve terrorism, in which the lines between political conflict and criminality are blurred.

Nuclear weapons. The threat of nuclear war loomed over every international crisis during the Cold War. Afterward, the chance of an all-out, civilization-destroying "nuclear exchange" all but disappeared. Therefore, many of us started worrying less about the nuclear threat as you will see in the transition from part 2 to part 3.

As Secretary General Gutteres warned, however, nuclear weapons are back on the agenda in at least three ways. First and most ominously, the

TABLE 2.1 | Conflict in the World: 2018

Number of People Killed	Number of Conflicts	Examples
10,000 or more	4	Afghanistan, Iraq, Syria, Mexican drug war
1,000–9,999	14	Myanmar, Somalia, Maghreb uprising (North Africa), Boko Haram (Nigeria), South Sudan, Yemen
100–999	18	Kashmir, Democratic Republic of Congo, Naxalite rebellion (India), eastern Ukraine
Under 100	22	Colombia, Kurdish separatism, Israel/Palestine

UN General Secretary António Gutteres

US and the Democratic People's Republic of Korea (North Korea) began threatening each other with nuclear weapons almost as soon as **Donald Trump** (1946–) was elected President of the US in 2016. Second, the Trump administration pulled out of the 2015 agreement that limited Iran's research program that could easily have led to their creation of a nuclear arsenal. Finally, both Russia and the US announced plans to modernize their existing arsenals.

It is true that the kind of war between the superpowers that could kill up to half of the world's population and end civilization as we know it is "off the table" for the moment. Nonetheless, Gutteres is correct in warning that any use of nuclear weapons is unthinkable in ways that remind me of a wryly understated bumper sticker I had on the back of my car in the 1980s: "One nuclear bomb can spoil your whole day."

Climate change. Of the five issues the secretary general raised, climate change will receive the least attention in this book until part 5 even though it is the most serious danger facing humanity today. In fact, the world's major political and business leaders—other than the current administration in the US—acknowledge that climate change is a clear and present danger to human civilization and the planet as a whole.

Tons of carbon dioxide, methane, and other gases are accumulating in the atmosphere. Once there, they trap the sun's energy close to the surface of the earth, heat the planet, and produce what are euphemistically known as "extreme climate events." If overall levels of those so-called greenhouse gases reach their predicted level by 2030, we may pass a point of no return. We are already seeing warmer temperatures in most parts of the world, rising sea levels, shrinking polar ice caps, and unusual weather patterns which could become so devastating that our very way of life becomes endangered.

We are also beginning to see the indirect impact of climate change on a number of regional disputes. Most analysts are convinced that the Syrian conflict is worse than it otherwise might have been because of the climate change–related drought that has affected the region for the past decade. Similarly, recent devastating hurricanes in the Caribbean and the southeastern US have sparked conflicts over recovery aid that did not turn did violent but future ones could well become so, as Omar al-Akkad so devastatingly depicts in his novel, *American War*.

Most peacebuilding and conflict resolution specialists understand the dangers posed by climate change. However, because we are just beginning to see how it will exacerbate conflicts around the world, we have not yet found ways to fully incorporate the climate into our work, which is why it will be little more than an afterthought until we get to part 5.

Violations of Human Rights. In 1948, the UN adopted the Universal Declaration of Human Rights, which many people believe is the international body's greatest achievement. Yet, seventy years later, Gutteres claimed that basic human rights were being threatened in unprecedented ways. Even with the defeat and/or collapse of the world's most notorious totalitarian regimes, human rights abuses are anything but rare. The **UN Office of the High Commissioner for Refugees (UNHCR)** estimated it supported forty-seven thousand victims of torture and twenty-five thousand enslaved people in 2017 alone.

The persecution of the Rohingya in Myanmar that began in the second half of 2017 provides a glaring example of what he was warning us about. Their only "crime" was the fact that they were Muslims who lived in a country that is overwhelmingly Buddhist. More than a million Rohingya were forced to flee to neighboring Bangladesh because they feared being massacred in what the UN called "a textbook example of ethnic cleansing."

The Rohingya, of course, were not alone. Two years earlier, about one million refugees streamed into Europe from Syria, Iraq, Afghanistan, and much of Africa. No one knows how many women and children are held against their will around the world. And, of course, we in the US are debating the fate of up to eleven million immigrants who are living in our country without the proper legal authorization.

You might question whether or not all of these cases involve human rights violations. However you come down on that front, one statistic should put the severity of these problems in perspective. The UNHCR had a total budget of just under $130 million in 2018, which was less than two-thirds of what my beloved New York Yankees paid their twenty-five-man roster that year.

Identity. By using terms such as nationalism and xenophobia, Gutteres reminds us that twenty-first-century conflicts largely revolve around **identity**. These are not new issues. After all, humans have always had a tendency to divide the world into **ingroups** and **outgroups**. But, they are taking on new life today, which you will see when I introduce the idea of imagined communities in part 3.

American readers should have no trouble seeing the impact of identity-related issues. Immigration. Black Lives Matter. Taking a knee when the national anthem is played. LGBTQ rights. Civil War monuments. If you aren't an American, you have undoubtedly encountered dozens of examples of identity-based conflicts wherever you live or study.

On the day I wrote the first draft of this section, the president of Poland signed a bill that would ban most accusations that its citizens were guilty of genocide during the Holocaust. Throughout Europe, nationalistic and xenophobic movements burst into the political mainstream. It wasn't just the industrialized countries of Europe and North America. As you are about to see, religious and ethnic antagonisms have been at the heart of most recent protest movements around the world.

TOWARD THE FORK IN THE ROAD

In short, it is easy to be pessimistic and to decide that peace and conflict studies still needs a healthy dose of the Gloom and Doom 101 I emphasized in chapter 1. But peace and conflict studies emerged as a distinct field of study precisely because it does offer constructive alternatives, which is why I find phrases like a fork in the road so appealing.

This is also where Proust's idea of seeing with new eyes and adopting a new paradigm come into play. In particular, some recent social science research has cast the broad sweep of human history in a new light that lends itself to more optimistic conclusions. These scholars realize that we face urgent problems. But

OUT ON A LIMB

The rest of this section is controversial, because these research findings seem to fly in the face both of what drew most of us to the field in the first place and what is taught in most history courses. Therefore, you will probably find it helpful to contrast this interpretation of global history with the one(s) you were exposed to in other courses and try to figure out how scholars can analyze the same evidence in such dramatically different ways.

they make two claims that we have to take seriously because they help us see why we might be able to take the more hopeful fork in Friedman's road:

- The world has never been less violent, no matter which indicators of violence you choose to focus on.
- That is the case because our ancestors created ways of avoiding violence that also enabled them to overcome some of the most vexing problems that their societies faced.

Our Better Angels

The most influential (and controversial) of these works is **Steven Pinker's** *The Better Angels of Our Nature.*[2] The book presents a wealth of data which we won't go into in any detail here, because some of the analysis requires more mathematical training than most readers of this book (or its author) have. That said, you don't need to have an advanced degree in statistical analysis to see his main point, which he summed up in the second sentence of its preface:

> Believe it or not—and I know that most people do not—violence has declined over long stretches of time, and we may be living in the most peaceful era in our species' existence.

Like most modern historians and anthropologists, Pinker doubts that humans ever lived in any kind of bucolic state of nature when people got along so well that there was little need for violence of any kind. While there is a lot we don't know about those earlier societies, the available evidence suggests that twenty percent or more of all deaths in hunter-gatherer societies occurred on the battlefield. In the bloody twentieth century, the corresponding number was well under one percent.

The first real governments arose about five thousand years ago, at about the same time that people began to farm and live in settled communities. Pinker suggests that those early states were based on a trade-off. The states protected their citizens from the dangers of an amazingly violent world; their citizens, in turn, were expected to give those new rulers their unquestioned loyalty.

That set off the dynamic that Pinker and other scholars have documented. Since then, most indicators of violence have declined at such rapid rates that they are hard to present in a conventional graph because they follow the trajectory of what mathematicians call a **power law**, versions of which will feature prominently in the rest of this book, starting with figure 2.1.

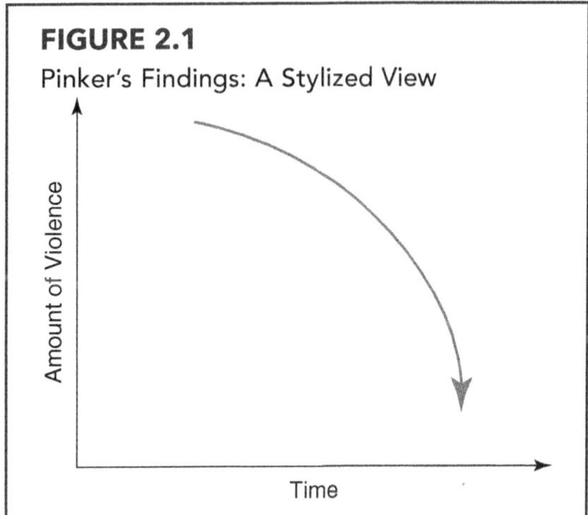

FIGURE 2.1
Pinker's Findings: A Stylized View

The most important of those shifts began in the sixteenth century, when the **Renaissance** and **Reformation** ushered in new ways of thinking in much of the Western world. Support for these new ideas continued to grow over the next century as the **Enlightenment** and other movements put new ideas like freedom, democracy, capitalism, and socialism on the public agenda.

At first, these trends seem to run counter to an argument like Pinker's. After all, these were the years that brought us newer and more lethal weapons, the wars of religion, European revolutions, and imperialism. That experience also led a series of thinkers to develop theories that stress our reliance on at least the threat of violence, none of whom was more important than **Thomas Hobbes** (1588–1679), who stressed the need for a strong state that could keep society from tearing itself apart.

In his day, Europe was a violent place. Hobbes himself lived through the wars of religion that swept Europe and were the bloodiest conflicts in human history up to that point. Prisoners were routinely tortured, most notably by the Inquisition, which jailed people simply because they were not Catholics. Traveling the highways and the high seas was far from safe. People paid to watch executions of criminals whose infractions might not even warrant prison time today. Most notoriously of all, Europeans enslaved Africans and decimated the population of the Americas. Of course, they weren't alone. Slavery was a common practice in most parts of the world.

Then, something remarkable happened. The death rate due to violence started plummeting in ways that mirror the general or "stylized" picture in figure 2.1. Interstate wars that political scientists have focused on have all but disappeared—at least for now. Even the insurgencies, terrorist attacks, and other instances of armed conflict today kill a much smaller share of the population in whatever countries are involved.

The sharp reduction in other forms of violence is even easier to see. Murder rates are way down. Piracy and highway banditry are now limited to a few isolated and particularly lawless parts of the world. Despite the recent concerns about sex slaves and others who are held in captivity, the world abolished legalized slavery more than a century ago. In my lifetime, we have also seen a dramatic expansion in the list of people at least legally covered by those basic provisions and guarantees of human rights, including most racial and ethnic minorities, women, and the LGBTQ community.

At first, peace studies scholars pushed back against findings like Pinker's. After all, they flew in the face of the carnage of the two world wars, instances of **genocide**, and other bloodshed that had led the political scientist Rudolph Rummell to coin the term politicide in describing the twentieth century. Now, however, most of us have come to terms with those findings and see how they can be blended into an understanding of the world that also includes the perils of twentieth- and twenty-first century warfare.

Why These Changes Occurred

These is much less agreement on why these changes took place. Most of those disagreements, per se, need not concern us here. However, three different lines of reasoning in the scholarly literature are worth mentioning, because they help show how these historical trends inform our understanding of conflict resolution and peacebuilding today.

The Hobbesian legacy. Central to any interpretation of the decline in organized violence is the creation of larger and more effective states. Hobbes and theorists like him started with pessimistic assumptions about human nature that were embedded in his most famous one-liner—that life is "cruel, nasty, brutish, and short."

That led them to support a strong state that Hobbes called a **Leviathan**. Only such a state could keep society from ripping itself apart. Hobbes, of course, was writing at one of those revolutionary moments when it was his side—the English monarchy—that was in danger of being destroyed.

Here, it is critical to see that Pinker and scholars of his ilk turned conventional interpretations of Hobbesian dynamics on their heads. Most students of political theory emphasize the elitist and even authoritarian implications of Hobbesian assumptions. Pinker, however, added an intriguing twist to the argument. Yes, that kind of state could control its citizens in ways that feudal monarchs could not even dream of. At the same time, however, the state provided mechanisms for settling disputes that did not involve the use of (as much) force. In more recent times, this line of thinking can be found in the writings of **Max Weber** (1864–1920), who defined the state as the institution that holds a "monopoly on the legitimate use of force" in a given territory.

For our purposes, that viewpoint can perhaps best be seen in international relations where the so-called realists argue that **anarchy** is the defining characteristic of the global system. Because there is no international state, there is no ultimate arbiter that keeps power-hungry governments that pursue their national interests from going to war with each other.

Modernity. In that sense, the Hobbesian legacy revolved around using power as defined in chapter 1 to bring the better angels of our nature to the fore. There is another school of thought that puts the decline in violence in a different and potentially more upbeat light. Key here was the thinking of the much less well known **Norbert Elias** (1897–1990). Elias was a German Jewish intellectual who spent most of his adult life in the UK after he fled Nazi rule.

Elias and analysts like him argued that we have found more effective and nonviolent mechanisms for solving our disputes not only because we have figured out how to use power better but also because modernity allowed us to see better alternatives and then put them into practice. In fact, Pinker showed the importance of Hobbesian and these other explanations that are based on new **norms** and other shared values when he tried to combine the two toward the end of *The Better Angels of Our Nature:*

> Dominance is an adaptation to anarchy, and it serves no purpose in a society that has undergone a civilizing process or in an international system regulated by agreements and norms.[3]

When Pinker (citing Elias) speaks of a civilizing process, he is referring to what most social scientists think of as the widespread adoption of deeply held values and widely shared norms that help determine how people act in difficult situations. Using that same logic, the large-scale adoption of new norms can be thought of as a shift in what we political scientists more often refer to as a country's or a community's **culture**.

Whichever term you use, global norms have changed dramatically in the last few centuries. While there have been many twists and turns, we have become more tolerant and inclusive. We have developed democratic and other institutions that nudge us toward cooperative rather than violent problem-solving techniques. Even in international relations, we have found ways of overcoming anarchy by creating norms about the use of chemical weapons or international trade, some of which have been codified in international law, if not in formal treaties.

Put in terms that Hobbesians would recognize, we have made progress that leave us less reliant on Leviathan-like institutions because we have found other ways to provide for our security and reach our collective goals. Then, because we are more secure than our ancestors, we have been able to develop trust in each other as well as the other norms that the likes of Elias champion. No one in this intellectual camp denies the importance of what Hobbes and his intellectual descendants wrote about. However, they are convinced that we have overcome some of the obstacles that once seemed baked into our human nature. To see that, consider these words from Pinker's most recent book:

> Human beings are fitted by evolution with a number of destructive motives such as greed, lust, dominance, vengeance, and self-deception. But I believe that people are also fitted with a sense of sympathy, an ability to reflect on their predicament, and faculties to think up and share new ideas—the better angels of our nature, in the words of Abraham Lincoln.[4]

Elias and his intellectual descendants are important here because of the role they played in helping us understand the rise of modernity. That said, I could have written this chapter without mentioning them. However, I included them because I will return to these themes in part 4 and especially in part 5, where we will consider the need for what some call a culture of peace, while others begin creating a broader social movement in support of conflict resolution and peacebuilding.

The liberal peace. These two strands come together in what British scholars in particular called the **liberal peace** (American readers should be sure to read the L-Word box on the next page). Peacebuilders and conflict resolution specialists who are also interested in large-scale disputes invariably—and sometimes unconsciously—endorse programs that take a strong state (Hobbesian) and capitalist market (liberal in the European sense of the term) for granted.

Concerns about the liberal peace will not feature prominently again in this book until parts 3 and 4 either. Nonetheless, you should remember that the most widely used peacebuilding tools have their origins in the social changes that helped create the economic and political conditions that led to capitalism, democracy, and the like.

With the end of the Cold War, it has become much harder to build support for socialism or any other alternatives to the liberal peace. However, you should be aware that many peacebuilding and some conflict resolution specialists question how much we can accomplish if we continue relying on the current paradigm, which is yet another reason to think in terms of forks in the road.

The L-Word

American students are often confused by the word *liberal*. In the US, it is used to describe people who support an interventionist government. Everywhere else, however, it means almost exactly the opposite—antagonism to government intervention in the economy and other policy areas in which individuals can make decisions on their own. The term will be used in this more widely understood sense in the rest of this book when describing the liberal peace. When talking about American liberals, I will use another term like progressive or leftist.

Is War Obsolete?

In the end, we may never be able to say whether the Hobbesian realists or their critics like Elias better explain the decline in violence. However, neither of them helps us come to grips with one of today's most important and controversial issues.

The costs of warfare and violence have risen at the same time that the number of violent and warlike events has gone down. In other words, we should never underestimate the fact that modern warfare kills more people more quickly and more indiscriminately than anything that came before.

To cite but the most obvious example, World War II killed about fifty million people in the span of six years. A single bomb killed about seventy thousand each in Hiroshima and Nagasaki. That many people or more died in the following months and years because it takes that long for the effects of radiation to take their toll.

One key reason is that the kind of progress that made Elias's civilizing process possible also allowed humans to invent weapons that can do more harm than anything our ancestors could have dreamed of in Hobbes's day. The machine gun. The airplane. Chemical and biological weapons. The atomic bomb. Add to that the fact that we can make them in unprecedented quantities and can deliver them using militaries that have grown to a size that was only made possible after the Industrial Revolution paved the way for the emergence of strong states.

There is no reason to believe that we have reached the end of the line as far as the development of new weapons and delivery systems is concerned. It could hardly be otherwise when the US spends around $700 billion a year on "defense," while the rest of the world spends even more.

All of this has led some activists toward the startling conclusion that war is obsolete. They don't use that term in the way most of think of obsolescence. Instead, they rely on a dictionary definition of the term, which suggest that something becomes obsolete when it has outlived its usefulness or no longer serves the purpose for which it was created.

It is in that sense that many of us now argue that war is obsolete. Any conventional international relations course includes Karl von Clausewitz's definition of war as "an extension of normal politics by other means." Even when he wrote two centuries ago, his ideas were not new. He was simply the most recent in a long series of experts stretching back to Thucydides, who is known to this day for claiming that "the strong do what they can and the weak suffer what they must."

Thucydides, Clausewitz, and today's realists all saw war as an inevitable (albeit often regrettable) by-product of international relations because governments pursued their national interests in a Hobbesian world in which there is no equivalent of the national Leviathan that could maintain law and order in the international system and thereby prevent states from going to war. However, undesirable they may have been, wars occurred because competing states could not solve their differences otherwise.

That line of reasoning becomes controversial once we add one of their often unspoken assumptions. In the simplest terms, Clausewitzean wars end when they result in a **zero-sum** or **win-lose** outcome in which one side wins. History is filled with examples of that kind of war, including the two world wars, both of which Germany and its allies lost. As the archaeologist Ian Morris has argued, the fact that a country ended up losing a war often turned out to be an important turning point in its evolution—a point we will return to in the next section.[5]

If war is obsolete today, it is because armed conflict rarely results in the kinds of outcomes Morris wrote about. To see that, think about the wars that the US has been involved in since 1945. There have been a few key clear-cut victories, including the invasions of Grenada and Panama in the 1980s. There has been one defeat that almost everyone acknowledges—Vietnam. Its other major conflicts turned into tense stalemates (Korea, Serbia/Kosovo) or have continued with no definitive end in sight (Afghanistan, Iraq, and the related antiterrorist efforts).

It's not just peace activists who are beginning to reach this conclusion. As you will see in chapter 12, many serving and retired military leaders are convinced that we cannot solve (m)any of today's international disputes using armed force alone. To be sure, American military might is unsurpassed by orders of magnitude. Still, even its well-equipped military seems less and less capable of winning what are known as **asymmetrical wars** in which one side is much more powerful than its adversary—at least on paper.

Even when it looks as if one side wins, victory can disappear in the blink of a historical eye. The US and its allies easily overthrew the Taliban's government in Afghanistan and Saddam Hussein's regime in Iraq, but those victories simply led to more intense and deadlier fighting. Similarly, Russian troops easily occupied Crimea in 2014, but doing so did little to end the **low-intensity conflict** along its broader border with Ukraine.

Don't get me wrong. We can—and do—still go to war. The problem from a peace and conflict studies perspective is that governments can no longer rely on war and other forms of organized violence to settle disputes once and for all.

The same is true in many respects at the domestic level. In the US, we have fought wars on crime, drugs, and poverty in recent years. Like the wars fought abroad, none of them has seemed to work.

TAKING THE RIGHT FORK IN HUMAN EVOLUTION

With this historical material in mind, we can now return to Friedman's comment at the beginning of this chapter and use it to point us toward what might be the **evolutionary** challenge facing our generation—which we will also return to in part 5. To see why, consider four of its key phrases. In doing so, keep in mind the fact that Friedman often gets criticized for overstating things with his use of catchy phrases:

- **As a species.** Friedman is convinced that the choices we face concern us all. Not just citizens of some parts of the world. Not just the elites. Not just the intellectuals. But all of us.
- **Never before.** Whether it is the all but sudden destruction of a nuclear war or the more gradual impact of climate change, the stakes are higher than they have ever been because of the progress we, as a species, have made.
- **Kill us all or fix everything.** Forks in the road imply choices between alternatives. This may be one of those places where Friedman overstates things, but he is on to something when he says our choice is between massive destruction (if not exactly killing us all) or making unprecedented progress (if not quite fixing everything).
- **Fork in the road.** Robert Frost made the image of the fork in the road famous in his poem "The Road Less Taken." If the likes of Friedman are right—and that is a big if—we may be facing one of those forks right now in a way that may force us to act, again, as a species.

With the exception of a few creationists, almost everyone accepts the key principles developed by Charles Darwin and his intellectual descendants. Evolutionary scientists never accepted the popular, stereotypical conclusions of nineteenth-century social Darwinists who believed in the survival of the fittest in which only the roughest and toughest survive. In fact, most environmental scientists today reject anything resembling those ideas and argue, instead, that evolution "favors" the species that can best adapt to a changing environment.

In the case of peace and conflict studies, that means at least considering the possibility that we are in the beginning stages of the next great phase in human evolution or, literally, a huge fork in the road. Our challenge is not to forge the kind of physical evolution that Darwin focused on, which is beyond our control. Instead, it is to take the next step in something we do control—our social or mental evolution.

Analysts who think in terms of choosing a fork in the road today tend to break history down into a series of phases in social evolution in which our ancestors made quantum leaps by developing new institutions, norms, and practices they used to solve their problems. No one has put this historical pattern of meeting new challenges more succinctly than David Ronfeldt. He spent most of his career as a national security analyst at the RAND Corporation, where he became interested in what is referred to as net-centered warfare (including terrorism) late in his career. As his health began to fade and it became clear that he would never find the energy to turn his ideas into a book, he made a twenty-three minute video that is all but required watching for a book like this one:

www.youtube.com/watch?v=UBulH9_04vc

Ronfeldt argued that human history has progressed through three main periods, each of which had its own dominant form of governance and may now be entering a fourth. He may not have gotten the details right—the video is only twenty-three minutes long, after all. Still, his periods mesh with those used by many professional historians:

- The first one began with the creation of tribal societies in which small groups of people began banding together at more or less the time that humans invented agriculture and started living in settlements that required some form of government in order to keep their inhabitants safe and secure.

- We then created larger and more hierarchical institutions that were able to govern larger territories, including the classical empires and institutions like the Roman Catholic Church.
- With the Renaissance, the Enlightenment, and the Industrial Revolution, we created larger institutions that governed more people and gave more of them a say in making the decisions that shaped their lives. That led to a world that included markets, democracy, the nation-state, the liberal peace, and the other indicators of modernity discussed in the previous section.
- He went on to suggest that we are in the initial stages of yet another great transformation in which the **network** will become the defining social institution. As is always the case in the early phases of such a great transformation, we are having a hard time understanding the exact dynamics of the changes that are taking place all around us.

Still, if Ronfeldt and dozens of other better-known (but longer-winded) social theorists are right, our world has four defining characteristics that grow out of the networked nature of our world that will require the kinds of conflict resolution and peacebuilding that this book addresses if we are to meet our evolutionary challenge.

Moore's Law and Rapid Change

The first characteristic can be traced back to a statement supposedly made by Heraclitus twenty-five hundred years ago—change is the only constant. We have no way of knowing if he was right then. There is little doubt that his statement holds true today.

In technology circles, the accelerating rates of change Heraclitus referred to is often illustrating by using something known as **Moore's law**. In 1965, Gordon Moore, the cofounder of Intel, noted that the number of chips that could be placed on a single integrated circuit doubled every eighteen months, while the price of the resulting computer was cut in half.

That "law" has held for more than fifty years and has helped lead to some amazing innovations. Your smartphone has more computing power than the Apollo astronauts had when they landed on the moon in 1969. Similarly, the Macs and iPads I used to write this book were roughly one hundred thousand times faster than the first Mac 128 I bought in 1984. Together, they cost a lot less than that technological dinosaur, whose best current use is as a doorstop.

It's not just technology. Accelerating change can be found just about everywhere you look. In the late 1960s, Alvin and Heidi Toffler began writing about what they called **future shock**. They showed that half of all human inventions were produced during the previous twenty years. When they updated their research a decade later, they found that the number of years needed to double the number of inventions had been cut in half. They called it future shock, because they felt people were ill-equipped to deal with rapid rates of technological and other change in much the same way that we suffer from culture shock when we move from one country to another.

In mathematical terms, Moore, the Tofflers, and the like are writing about accelerating or **exponential** rates of change as described by the generic equation

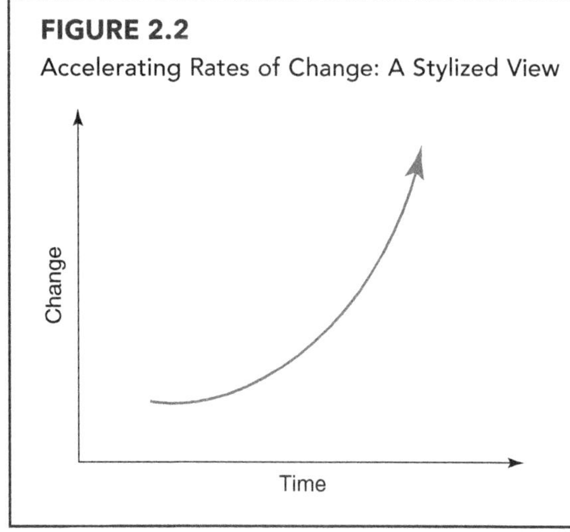

FIGURE 2.2
Accelerating Rates of Change: A Stylized View

$y = x^n$, which is depicted in figure 2.2. Because x (the number of inventions or innovations) grows at an accelerating rate over time, the growth in its value shoots up and to the right for much the same reason that the value of a savings account keeps growing because the balance accumulates compound interest.

If you look back at figure 2.1, which depicts the decline in violence, you will note that it looks much the same, except that the curve suddenly slopes sharply downward. It, too reflects an exponential rate of accelerated change. If you are mathematically inclined, the relevant equation takes the form of $y = x^{-n}$.

Metcalfe's Law and Globalization

Globalization is one of the most widely used—and misunderstood—concepts in the news today. It is normally thought of as a series of economic changes that are "shrinking" the world as laid out by the Levin Center at SUNY-Albany on its www.globalization101.org website:

> Globalization is a process of interaction and integration among the people, companies, and governments of different nations, a process driven by international trade and investment and aided by information technology. This process has effects on the environment, on culture, on political systems, on economic development and prosperity, and on human physical well-being in societies around the world.

Just as with Moore's law, technological change provides us with a useful metaphor for seeing that globalization is more than just an economic phenomenon. It touches all areas of life in ways that have profound implications for peace and conflict studies.

This law is attributed to another high-tech pioneer, Robert Metcalfe, who is best known for inventing Ethernet, which was the dominant technology that allowed computers to talk to each other before WiFi. Because he was trained as an electrical engineer who specialized in telecommunications, **Metcalfe's law** is usually presented as it is in figure 2.3, using images of now obsolete rotary dial telephones.

If there are two telephones in a network, you can only talk with one person at the end of the line. Under these circumstances, telephones are not very useful.

If, however, there are five telephones and users, the network becomes a lot denser and more useful. Now, instead of one, there can be as many as nine two-way conversations. Add seven more phones, and the network grows to twelve nodes, while the number of possible conversations reaches sixty-six.

There is, in fact, a simple equation in which n is equal to the number of phones in the network:

$$Y = (n)(n - 1)/2$$

If you are even the slightest bit mathematical, you will have realized that Metcalfe's law also behaves in an exponential manner. As you add more nodes to any network, the number of possible interconnections shoots up in ways that echo figure 2.2.

Our networked world does not resemble Metcalfe's telephones. Real-world networks are messier because they are less complete. Obviously, we do

FIGURE 2.3
Metcalfe's Law

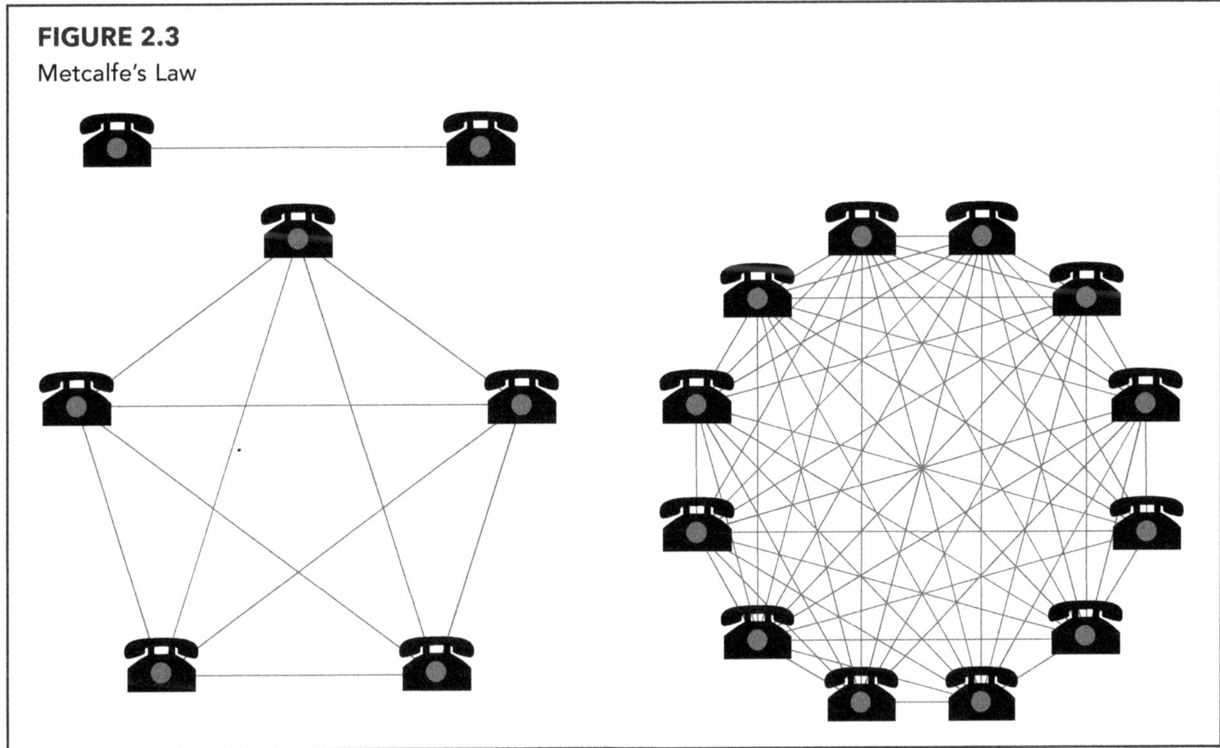

not make phone calls to everyone with whom we are directly connected, and the connections we do make often follow indirect and circuitous paths involving the now clichéd term six degrees of separation. From that perspective, global networks often look more like figure 2.4—every node is connected to every other one, but many of those connections follow indirect and circuitous paths.

For our purposes, focus on the fact that Metcalfe's law shows why networks get denser the larger and more interconnected they become. As the word globalization suggests, you and I are connected to more people who live and work in more places around the world.

FIGURE 2.4
A Generic Network

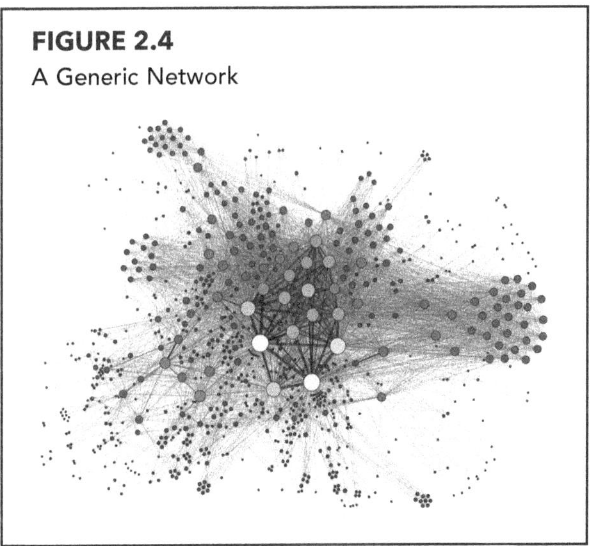

Wicked Problems, VUCA, and Complexity

This journey through history with its side trip into technology may seem to have taken us away from peace and conflict studies. In fact, it brings us back to at least the global half of the first Conflict Lab.

When you did that exercise, I asked you to analyze two conflicts and presented figure 1.1 as a simplified, generic model of what a systems map looks like. At this point, simply think about the similarities between your map or figure 1.1, on the one hand, and figure 2.4, on the other. In both of the figures, all the component parts or nodes are interconnected in a web. Figure 1.1 only has a dozen or so components. Figure 2.4 has thousands and more accurately reflects the interdependence of a globalizing world. As such, it reflects a key reality of life in the twenty-first century.

We are all interconnected.

On one level, that has always been true. Authorities as different as cutting-edge environmental scientists and traditional spiritual leaders tell us that the world has always been a single interconnected whole. However, as the debate over climate change shows, those interconnections matter a lot more today than they did even in the 1960s.

Recent research has uncovered some of the human dimensions of that interconnection. Early network scientists, for example, demonstrated that there is a hint of truth to the cliché that no more than six degrees of separation exist between you and everyone else on the planet. That statement itself is almost certainly an exaggeration. Are you really only six indirect steps removed from a Rohingya refugee? Or Pope Francis? Or Lionel Messi? Or Beyoncé? Or my grandchildren?

Even if we are more than six degrees of separation apart from most people in the world, we are all more interconnected now than our ancestors ever were. More of us travel to more places. New telecommunications tools allow us to learn about and even "friend" people from around the world, many of whom we have never met and never will meet face-to-face. On the day I finished this chapter, I had a board of directors meeting for Build Up^, whom you will meet in chapters 11 and 13. The seven board members were born in five different countries; all of us have worked internationally; and no one thought it surprising that we met via Zoom, which gave us crystal-clear video and audio even though we were working in four different time zones on four different continents.

That's not just true because more of us study abroad, use social media, and attend meetings using international video teleconferencing services. We see these trends play themselves out in most of the issues that are at the heart of conflict resolution and peace studies—from the use of internet-based mediation tools to the disruptions caused by the upsurge in the number of migrants fleeing the world's hot spots.

In other words, it may always have made sense to think of the world in terms of an interconnected system. As recently as fifty or one hundred years ago, however, we could get away with not doing so. If I am right, we ignore our interconnections at our peril today. That's why I briefly introduced the idea of **wicked problems** in chapter 1 and will return to them frequently in the rest of this book. Others prefer using the term VUCA (for volatile, uncertain, complex, and ambiguous) to describe a world of wicked problems. That, too, is a term I will return to frequently in the pages to come.

The Long Haul

Thinking in terms of networks also leads us to focus on the longer-term implications of our actions. Most social, political, and economic analytic schemes revolve around immediate outcomes, such as a decrease in the crime rate after a new policy is adopted, the policy changes that followed an election, or the daily ups and downs of the stock market.

Sometimes we can get away with focusing on the short run. Increasingly, however, the impact of our actions does not end on election day or a victory on the battlefield. It can take a long time before some of their impact can be seen, which is where the volatility, uncertainty, **complexity**, and ambiguity of modern life come into play.

CONFLICT LAB 2

Ask yourself how the broad historical trends shaped the two conflicts you considered in chapter 1. Not all of them may be relevant in each case. However, to the degree that they are, ask yourself the following:

- How do they reflect the long-term historical trends discussed here, including accelerating rates of change, globalization, networks, and wicked problems?
- Can you imagine resolving them without taking their long-term evolution into account? Why (not)?
- Do they seem to require something like a paradigm shift?

Even more important are what scientists call second-, third-, and even "*n*th"-order or indirect causal relationships in complex networks like those depicted in figure 2.4, which draw our attention to the often convoluted **feedback** loops among an institution's component parts that can lead to unexpected and often dramatic results.

PARADIGMS AND PARADIGM SHIFTS

I have been (over)using the metaphor of a fork in the road for a reason. One or more of the "forks" could lead to fundamental shifts in the way that we deal with conflict, which you have to understand if you truly want to master the material covered in a basic peace and conflict studies course. You don't have to agree that such a shift is necessary, let alone possible. You should, however, take seriously the proposition that everything you have seen so far in this book suggests that we need something akin to a paradigm shift.

Paradigms and paradigm shifts entered academia with the publication of Thomas Kuhn's *The Structure of Scientific Revolutions* in 1962.[6] As he saw it, real steps forward in human understanding do not happen through what he called "normal science" in which researchers work in their laboratories and publish their findings in obscure journals. Instead, fundamental progress is only made when a scientific community adopts a wholly new worldview. He called these scientific revolutions, but as his idea moved out of the physical sciences, we began referring to them as paradigm shifts instead.

From Kuhn's perspective, scientific revolutions or paradigm shifts follow a common pattern, which he illustrated with a number of examples, including the development of modern astronomy:

- **Anomalies.** Discrepancies or anomalies appear in the old paradigm that placed the earth at the center of the universe. Thus, when Galileo invented the telescope he and his fellow scientists learned that their predictions based on a geocentric or earth-centered depiction of the movement of heavenly bodies were wrong.
- **Making the data fit.** Because they all "knew" that the existing paradigm was "correct," they adjusted the formulas they used for measuring the movement of heavenly bodies to fit their preconceptions. In essence, they added epicycles (like curlicues) to their orbits so that the moon, the planets, the sun, and the other stars still revolved around the earth.

- **The new paradigm**. Then, Nicolaus Copernicus had the scientific equivalent of an epiphany. He realized that the conventional wisdom itself was wrong and devised a new paradigm that placed the sun rather than the earth at the center of the solar system.
- **Revolution**. In the process, Copernicus touched off a struggle between supporters of the heliocentric (sun-centered) and geocentric (earth-centered) paradigms, which is one of the reasons why Kuhn used the term scientific *revolution*. It took two centuries, but Copernicus's disciples finally won. By that time, of course, Copernicus himself was long dead.

From Conflict Resolution to Peacebuilding is obviously not a book about scientific revolutions. However, it is based on the assumption that we address conflict today using a few usually unspoken assumptions that amount to a paradigm and that we should be open to changing it.

Einstein's One-Liners

Most of us think of Albert Einstein as the twentieth century's most famous scientist. Few of us, however, think of him as a social commentator. Far fewer yet turn to him as a source of one-liners. Yet, he was both. And as strange as it may seem, three of his one-liners will help you see why we have to at least take the idea of paradigm shifts seriously in peace and conflict studies.

Einstein may not have been the author of the first one, although it is usually attributed to him. Whoever is responsible for it, the statement makes sense here:

> Insanity is doing the same thing over and over again and expecting different results.

To see why this first statement is important, simply think about the number of times political leaders proposed what they claim would be bold new policies to end the fighting in Afghanistan or Syria that are nothing more than a variation on the ones that have not worked well in the past and show little promise of doing so in the future.

The second one-liner begins to point us in the direction of a paradigm shift. We know for certain that this one was his idea. However, he never used it in a formal publication and it, therefore, appears in multiple forms when people refer to it today. In my experience, this version best conveys what we think he meant:

> You can never solve a problem by using the same level of thinking you used in creating it.

OUT ON A LIMB

Not all of my colleagues agree that we need a paradigm shift in the way we deal with conflict. If, in fact, a paradigm shift could or should be in order, it will have to extend to all of the ways we make all of the decisions that shape our lives. Therefore, I decided to make it one of the key organizing principles underlying this book. If you disagree, I am eager to hear why you reached that conclusion so that we can discuss it further.

Our list of pending problems is long and shows every sign of getting even longer. At the same time, our existing tool kit for solving them does not seem to be getting us very far. If Einstein is correct, that is the case because we are trying to address today's rapidly changing world using dated ideas and ideals that had a lot to do with creating the problems in the first place.

In one of his more famous (and, in this case, accurately transcribed) statements, Einstein also suggested that a paradigm shift begins when people consciously adopt new ways of understanding and responding to their problems that are the equivalents of seeing with Proust's new eyes. With that in mind, he included the following sentence in a telegram he sent to two hundred prominent Americans shortly after the end of World War II in which he urged them to stop the nuclear arms race in its tracks:

> The unleashed power of the atom
> has changed everything
> save our modes of thinking
> and we thus drift
> toward unparalleled catastrophe.

There is no question that this one is relevant for the subject matter of this book. That's the case because the statement has four interesting components, which are reflected in the way I have diagrammed it here. We can dispense with the first three fairly quickly and then spend the rest of the section on the implications of the final one.

The first appears at the beginning and the end of the sentence and is the part we tend to gloss over today because the "unparalleled catastrophe" of an all-out nuclear war is not likely to occur in the foreseeable future. Second, Einstein said *everything* had changed, not just warfare. Even within a few weeks of Hiroshima and Nagasaki, he realized we were entering a new era in all areas of life and not just in politics. Einstein died before the word globalization was invented, but he knew that something like it was in the offing. Third, he used a powerful verb—*drift*—to describe our condition that is powerful because of the very weakness it conveys. In old western movies, a drifter was a cowboy who rode aimlessly from town to town. A sailboat is adrift if there is not enough wind to allow the person at the helm to steer it. Finally, he went on to say that everything had changed except for our modes of thinking or the values and assumptions that shape our lives. Therein lies a good way of thinking about the need for a paradigm shift.

I first started working with this statement during the nuclear arms buildup in the 1980s when the Beyond War movement diagrammed the sentence along the lines of figure 2.5. Many of my colleagues were engineers and liked to describe Einstein's notion that the unleashed power of the atom has changed everything as what scientists call a phase transition, as when water freezes or boils. Quickly—even suddenly—a substance changes form. From this perspective, the invention of the atomic bomb changed everything, which we tried to convey with what my engineering friends called the step function in figure 2.5.

FIGURE 2.5
Einstein—Take 1

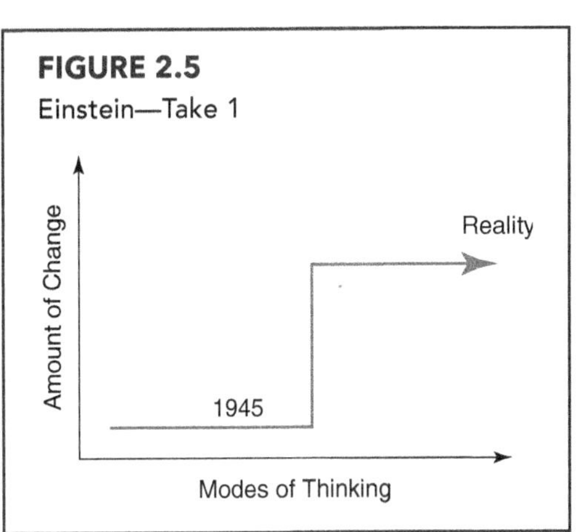

Except for our modes of thinking. Einstein also pointed out that the values and assumptions we used in dealing with international relations were more or less the same as the ones we had used before the bombs were dropped on Hiroshima and

FIGURE 2.6
Einstein—Take 2

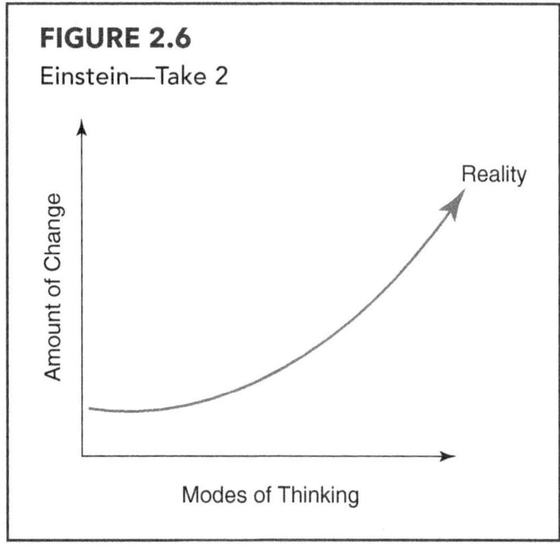

Nagasaki. In essence, Einstein was vainly trying to warn his contemporaries that they faced a huge gap between the changed realities of the nuclear age and our unchanged modes of thinking which that left us drifting toward nuclear catastrophe.

After the Cold War ended and the threat of nuclear war receded, I adapted the chart for the new environment we suddenly found ourselves in after 1989, which I have presented here as figure 2.6.

In the years since the end of the Cold War, there has not been the social or political equivalent of a phase transition in which everything changed with the possible exception of the terrorist attacks on 9/11.

Instead, I want to make the case that the realities of political, social, economic, and environmental life have been changing at an accelerating rate, as depicted in the curved arrow in figure 2.6. The curve, in fact, has the same basic shape as all of the ones I have used to depict exponential growth or decay that suggest the centrality of rapid change in our lives today.

This second depiction of Einstein's statement is also useful here because it can point us in two possible directions we could take at our fork in the road, whereas figure 2.5 suggests that a paradigm shift is our only viable alternative. You would reach that conclusion, too, using figure 2.6 *if* you read the evidence in this book and decided that the world we live in today is best understood as lying out somewhere near the right end of that chart where the gap between the reality we face and our political paradigm is immense.

If, on the other hand, you think that our situation is more like one represented by the left side of the chart and that the gap is not very wide, then you would be more inclined to conclude that we don't need a paradigm shift and decide that incremental changes that tinker with the status quo will be good enough.

The rest of this book works on the assumption that you ended up close enough to the right end of figure 2.6 that you are at least open to the idea of a paradigm shift. Even if you ended up closer to the left-hand side, learning about paradigm shifts in peace and conflict studies is worth your time.

Did Dacher Keltner Get It Right?

During the course of this chapter, I have taken you a long way out on an intellectual limb by looking at the broad sweep of human history and some current changes in the human landscape, both of which might seem far removed from peace and conflict studies. In ending it, I want to begin showing you why this material is relevant by returning to Dacher Keltner's words that I used to begin this chapter.

Whether you end up deciding we need a paradigm shift or not, studying peace and conflict will lead you to (re)consider what we mean by **power** and its role in human relationships at all levels. Robert Dahl's definition, which I introduced in chapter 1, is still the one you find most frequently both in academia and the real world of political life. However, in the rest of this book, you will see that power does not have to be something I exert over you, and that that realization can be game-changing.

One of the reasons that we still have the pressing global problems that Pinker refers to is that the holders of power wield it less effectively than they did even half a century ago. As Moisés Naím puts it, power today is both more concentrated and more fleeting than it used to be.[7] Wealth, and the power that come with it, is held by fewer people. In that sense, populist movements on the left and right lash out against the perception as well as the reality that "they" have too much power, in ways that have echoed throughout much of the world.

The concentration of power is occurring even more rapidly outside of politics. Massive corporations dominate economic life with what are increasingly global brands.

A generation ago, we might have focused on General Motors, Volkswagen, or Toyota as examples of giant, global corporations. Today, our attention and our critical eye are more likely to be drawn to Google, Apple, or Microsoft. But the point is the same. The economic as well as the political decisions that matter seem to be made by fewer and fewer people representing fewer and fewer interests.

Paradoxically, one can also make the case that people on the top of all those hierarchies are *less* powerful than they used to be. Power within them may be concentrated in fewer and fewer hands. However, those "hands" are less and less able to determine what happens, whether at the national (ending the recession), local (stopping urban violence), or nonpolitical (preventing people from sharing copyrighted music on the Internet) level.

When Naím argues that power is more fleeting, he is also echoing what economists mean when they say that it isn't fungible because it cannot easily be transferred from one policy area to another or from one time to another or from one place to another. To cite but the most obvious example, the US may be the wealthiest country and have the most powerful military in the world, but neither its riches nor its weapons have done much to help it defeat terrorism or slow climate change. Even corporate giants like Dell and General Motors have seen their market shares plummet in the face of competition from Lenovo and Toyota and found it hard to transfer their clout from one economic sphere to another or to protect themselves from upstart companies that challenge their prominent positions.

From that perspective, the use of power as traditionally defined has its costs. When I exert power over you, it tends to breed resentment, and unless I utterly defeated you or convinced you that I'm right, you will seek ways to retaliate against me.

That has always been the case, but the consequences of using power in these traditional ways were limited because the problems we faced were rarely global in scope. Now, that is the norm.

The question then becomes, how are we going to redefine what me mean by power so that the system "grows" over time and allows us to take the more hopeful looking fork(s) in Friedman's road?

To see why that might be the case, briefly consider four of Keltner's most important conclusions:

- Power is inherent in all relationships and exists whenever we set out to alter the "states of others."
- Power can come from empowering others in social networks, which occurs when we are empathetic, express gratitude, and share empowering stories with others that mobilize and empower them.

- We give power to those who advance our goals and what we think is the greater good.
- However, when we get power in the traditional sense, it tends to "go to our heads" and lead us to act impulsively, to be disrespectful and lack civility, to create stress in our environments, and the like. In other words, once we get power, we have created the seeds of its own destruction.

To be honest, it took my colleagues as least a generation to see that the stakes of conflict resolution and peacebuilding include just about every relationship in which power is involved. It will take me the rest of this book to show how and why that *might* be the case. In order to get there, we have to take one more introductory step and see how we have come to understand conflict itself.

KEY TERMS

Concepts

People

Organizations, Places, and Events

DIG DEEPER

Goldstein, Joshua. *Winning the War on War: The Decline of Armed Conflict Worldwide*. New York: Plume, 2011. This book has not gotten as much attention as Pinker's, but it might be more useful here, because it is less methodologically challenging.

Johnson, Steven. *Where Good Ideas Come From: The Natural History of Innovation*. New York: Riverhead, 2010. By perhaps the best author on the creation of new ideas. Johnson is less sanguine than I am about paradigm shifts, but I read everything he writes. He's that good.

Keltner, Dacher. *The Power Paradox: How We Gain and Lose Influence*. New York: Penguin, 2016. Based primarily on experiments Keltner has done in his social psychology lab. However, it is filled with implications for our VUCA world, which we will discuss shortly.

Kuhn, Thomas. *The Structure of Scientific Revolution*. Chicago: University of Chicago Press, 1962. The bible on paradigm shifts. It can be hard reading for someone who is not that familiar with the history of science.

Morris, Ian. *War! What Is It Good For? Conflict and the Progress of Civilization from Primates to Robots.* New York: Farrar, Straus, and Giroux, 2014. Very few peacebuilders agree with his conclusions that wars have led to major, constructive change, but it is an argument we need to consider.

Naím, Moisés. *The End of Power: From Boardrooms to Battlefields and Churches to States, Why Being in Charge Isn't What It Used to Be.* New York: Basic Books, 2013. By far the most thought-provoking book on globalization and its implications for the use of power.

Pinker, Steven. *The Better Angels of Our Nature: Why Violence Has Declined.* New York: Penguin, 2011. The best of a series of books on the shifting nature of conflict. It has received a lot of criticism, but the findings themselves are hard to contradict.

NOTES

[1] www.un.org/apps/news/story.asp?NewsID=58370#.WnmUBpM-dUN. This site also has a YouTube version of the message that you can watch.

[2] Steven Pinker, *The Better Angels of Our Nature: Why Violence Has Declined* (New York: Penguin, 2011).

[3] Pinker, *Better Angels*, 528.

[4] Steven Pinker, *Enlightenment Now: The Case for Reason, Science, Humanism, and Progress* (New York: Viking, 2018), 45.

[5] Ian Morris, *War! What Is It Good For? Conflict and the Progress of Civilization from Primates to Robots* (New York: Farrar, Straus, and Giroux, 2014).

[6] Thomas Kuhn, *The Stricture of Scientific Revolutions* (Chicago: University of Chicago Press, 1962).

[7] Moisés Naím, *The End of Power: From Boardrooms to Battlefields and Churches to States, Why Being in Charge Isn't What It Used to Be* (New York: Basic Books, 2013).

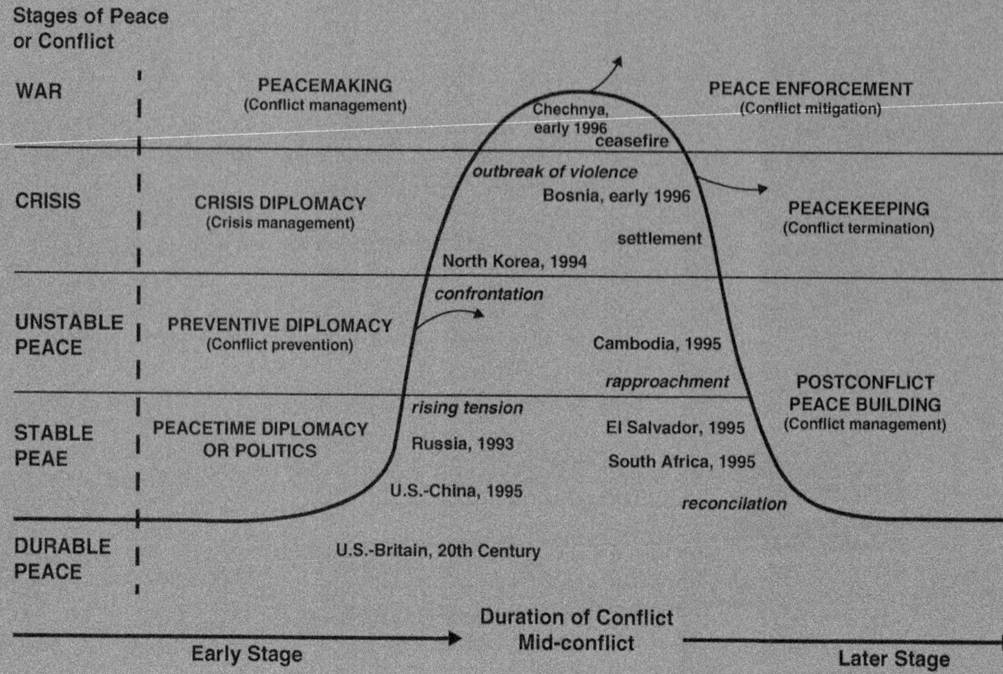

Seeing Conflict with New Eyes

THINK ABOUT IT

This chapter introduces the nuts and bolts of conflict resolution and peacebuilding. It traces models and theories of change that were developed in each of the periods covered in parts 2 through 4. However, each helps us to understand conflicts in general and not just during the years when it was developed.

To start with, make certain you understand why models and theories of change matter. Then, make certain you see how each new set of models deepened our understanding of the ways conflict can be understood and what could be done about it.

Finally, because this chapter covers so much important ground, it has three separate Conflict Labs, one for each pair of basic models. I will wait to ask specific questions until we get to those exercises. For now, it is enough to ask a single question that applies to this entire chapter.

Why are models and theories of change needed both to study and to help resolve conflicts as different as the two you mapped in chapter 1?

CORE CONCEPTS

conflict map—in systems approaches, a way of visually presenting the contours of a dispute

conflict prevention—stopping conflict from breaking out

crisis—a turning point

Lund curve—visual way of understanding conflict developed by Michael Lund

peacebuilding—processes that lead to stable or positive peace

peacekeeping—processes that prevent former adversaries from returning to war

structural violence—causes of conflict that reflect inequalities of power

systems—an approach to studying conflict (or anything else) that views it as a wholly interdependent phenomenon

As societies have become healthier, wealthier, freer, happier, and better educated, they have set their sights on the most pressing global challenges.

—*Steven Pinker*

We're not only in a zero-sum game. We're in a vicious circle. Is there any way out?

—*Amy Chua*

WHEN I USED THE STATEMENT BY Marcel Proust to begin chapter 1 I had a pair of bifocals in mind. People whose eyesight deteriorates to the point that they need bifocals end up with two sets of lenses. One of them lets them see better when they look into the distance. These were the lenses we explored in chapter 2. Here we turn to the new set of eyes that let us take a closer look at conflict and its resolution. This second pair of lenses will let you see how and why conflict resolution and peacebuilding specialists have chosen to take their own forks in the road.

To see why, consider the two statements that begin this chapter.

The first is by the same Steven Pinker whose optimistic reading of history helped bring us to a fork in the road. His most recent book, *Enlightenment Now*, from which these words were drawn, even more optimistically calls on our generation to return to the values that made so much of that progress possible over the course of the last few centuries.

Amy Chua is a law professor who stressed the dangerous nature of modern political life in her book. *Political Tribes*. She is far more pessimistic than Pinker in part because she regrets our retreat into identity-based "silos" and the resulting hostility so many of us feel toward those we disagree with.

Taken together, they point to a dilemma that is at the heart of peace and conflict studies. On the one hand, as I have at least hinted at in the first two chapters, most of us are convinced that viewing life in **zero-sum** terms is a major contributor to the problems we face. On the other hand, despite being, as Pinker says, "wealthier, freer, happier, and better educated," we haven't made much progress in dealing with "the most pressing global challenges."

Just about every expert in peace and conflict studies is convinced that the choices that might take us out of that dilemma all start with seeing with "new eyes" that let us "view" our differences in a more constructive and creative light. That does not mean that we all support the idea of a paradigm shift or any of the specific pathways that you will encounter in the rest of this book.

To understand any of them, however, you do need the second set of lenses that let you see individual conflicts more clearly. After doing so, we will be able to move on and consider how peace and conflict studies evolved to the point that it now deals with the world's most vexing problems and has made some progress in dealing with at least some of them.

NEW EYES

Chapter 1 made the case that there is no single roadmap we all use in analyzing and resolving conflict. Given the problems facing the world and the differences within the peace and conflict studies community, it could hardly be otherwise.

That said, we do not analyze or resolve conflict whimsically or randomly. In the years since the first peacebuilding NGOs were created and the first academic conflict resolution programs were formed, we have learned a lot.

An introductory textbook is never the place to dig deeply into the methodologies that scholars and/or practitioners use. However, you can't make sense of the way our field evolved unless you also see how we have come to expand our understanding of two key concepts that have shaped the ways we have approached that fork in the road:

- In the absence of a commonly accepted paradigm or overarching theory, we rely on **models** to structure our understanding of conflict.
- Practitioners, in particular, also use theories of change to help them design and assess their conflict resolution and peacebuilding efforts although we won't get to them until the second half of this chapter.

Mature sciences have explicit paradigms that structure entire disciplines. Unfortunately, peace and conflict studies does not have its equivalent of the periodic table of elements or neoclassical economics. As a result, both our academic research and our peacebuilding projects lack the conceptual rigor we find in those fields.

That does not mean that our work lacks analytical grounding. Instead, our best work is guided by models or simplified depictions of the phenomenon we are interested in.

Models come in a variety of forms. Scott Page, for example, is best known for computer-based formal models that combine a series of "if/then" statements with dozens of feedback loops. Others are mathematical models that transform social relations into a set of equations whose values can be calculated. These kinds of models can be sophisticated and productive, starting with the ones on altruism and cooperation in complex systems that won Elinor Ostrom the 2009 Nobel Prize in Economic Sciences. However, very few readers of this book have enough mathematical or computer science training to critically assess them.

For our purposes, the most useful models are simple, visual representations of more complicated phenomena. While you can find these kinds of models in all of the sciences, the best way to understand their role is to think about children's toys rather than conflict or chemistry for one simple reason. Thinking in these terms lets us avoid a lot of the jargon that gets used whenever academics talk about any kind of research methodologies.

To be precise, think about the Lego Chinook rescue helicopter. On February 5, 2019, you could buy a kit to make one for just under fifty dollars. I know, because I thought about buying one for my grandson. With its 303 pieces, you can build the helicopter itself, a crook's hideout, and an escape vehicle. The kit also has two police officers, two crooks, and one bear (I do not know why it includes a bear).

My grandson (who was eight when I wrote these words) knew full well that the model helicopter isn't real and will not fly. In fact, the helicopter, the crooks, and the escape vehicle can't do anything, but that's not the point. The rotors, wheels, and people are realistic enough for him to learn a bit about how a helicopter flies, a criminal robs, or a getaway car speeds along the highway.

No model ever shows you exactly how or why something works because it is a simplified representation of some complicated phenomenon you are interested in—in our case, conflict rather than helicopters. Therefore, a good model is simple enough and realistic enough for you to see how the conflict (or helicopter) operates by focusing your attention on features like the cockpit or the rotor.

We will consider six models. Although all can be used for every conflict, I will use pairs of them to illustrate the key insights from the three phases of our work that you will be exploring in parts 2 through 4. Each will allow you to interpret data about conflict far better than you could have without using a model. Each pair will also help you to understand how and why peace and conflict studies has become a more fascinating—and at times confusing—field.

TWO BASIC METAPHORS

Recall that chapter 1 narrowed this book's scope by focusing on intractable conflicts that lend themselves more to **transformational** rather than **transactional** resolution. The six models you are about to see will narrow it even more, because each improves our ability to "see" key aspects of intractability in ways that have guided both our academic research and our practical work.

Structural Violence and Underlying Causes

During the 1960s, **Johan Galtung** introduced the idea of **structural violence**, which took us beyond the specifics of a dispute as it might be presented on television or in a newspaper. That said, the term can be confusing, because Galtung rarely had physical violence in mind. As he saw it, violence went far beyond physical coercion, because he was among the first to see how **power** can be used to perpetuate inequalities along race, gender, class, and other lines and keep people from meeting what John Burton called their basic human needs. In that sense, structural violence can occur without a fist or weapon being raised in anger.

Physical violence is relatively easy to measure using indicators like the number of deaths, injuries, and arrests. Harder to measure, but no less important, is the degree of structural violence. As an example, progressive American readers can point to laws that make it more difficult for African Americans to vote. On the other end of the political spectrum, conservatives typically talk about the way affirmative action laws make it harder for white men to get admitted to universities or get hired.

Were he to coin the term today, Galtung might not have called it structural violence, because he was really referring to the **norms** and values that sustain those inequalities through racism, sexism, homophobia, and the like. By that logic we could also refer to structural violence as a conflict's underlying causes.

Galtung often used the image of an iceberg when discussing structural violence or the underlying causes of conflict in general. As figure 3.1 shows, ninety percent of a physical iceberg lies below the surface of the water, and we all learned in elementary school that you cannot "melt" an iceberg if you only change the portion of it that you can see.

FIGURE 3.1
Galtung's Iceberg

CONFLICT LAB 3.1

Because this chapter focuses on how the methods that peace and conflict analysts use have evolved, it has three Conflict Labs, each of which will ask you to dig more deeply into the conflicts you decided to map in chapter 1.

Take both of them and ask:

- Are their underlying causes clear in the ways the conflict manifests itself? Can you imagine ending them once and for all without addressing those underlying causes of what Galtung called structural violence? Why (not)?
- How do the conflicts play out at each of the three levels Lederach includes? If any one of them is missing from either of the conflicts, ask yourself why that is the case and what it would take to get people at that level involved.

So, too with structural violence. Even half a century ago, Galtung made the case that you have to dig below the surface and address a conflict's underlying causes if you want to have a lasting impact that does more than address its "surface" symptoms. Although not everyone will go as far as he did, it is important to see how economic inequalities, cultural norms, and the other root causes of a conflict perpetuate it and even lead to the threat and/or reality of physical violence (see Conflict Lab 3.1).

Lederach's Conflict Triangle

You will encounter **John Paul Lederach** (1955–) many times in the rest of this book because he is one of the field's true superstars who has been able to combine uncanny intellectual insights with a lifelong commitment to grassroots fieldwork. Even in his earliest works, he wrote about three levels at which conflict resolution and peacebuilding initiatives take place and how they unfold differently at each one of them (see figure 3.2). While I will treat each level separately here, note that most conflicts can take place at some or all of them, as you will see as you dig deeper into the conflicts you have been working on since the first Conflict Lab exercise.

Lederach has done most of his own work at the grassroots level, where he thinks of himself as **accompanying** local peacebuilders. As we will see in chapter 11, he does so because he is convinced that local residents have the best

Johan Galtung, John Paul Lederach, Elise Boulding, and Kenneth Boulding

ideas about conflict in their own communities and that no two peacebuilding efforts are the same.

He also knew from his earliest work in remote areas of Nicaragua that grassroots activism alone would never be enough. To make a lasting difference, activists had to convince local, regional, and eventually, national leaders to change, too.

In part 2 you will see that the conflict resolution and peacebuilding community has not always been comfortable working with national elites and vice versa. Still, farsighted thought leaders like Lederach have understood that conflict resolution work had to be integrated into broader movements for social change that addressed Galtung's structural violence and the underlying causes of a dispute.

FIGURE 3.2
The Lederach Triangle

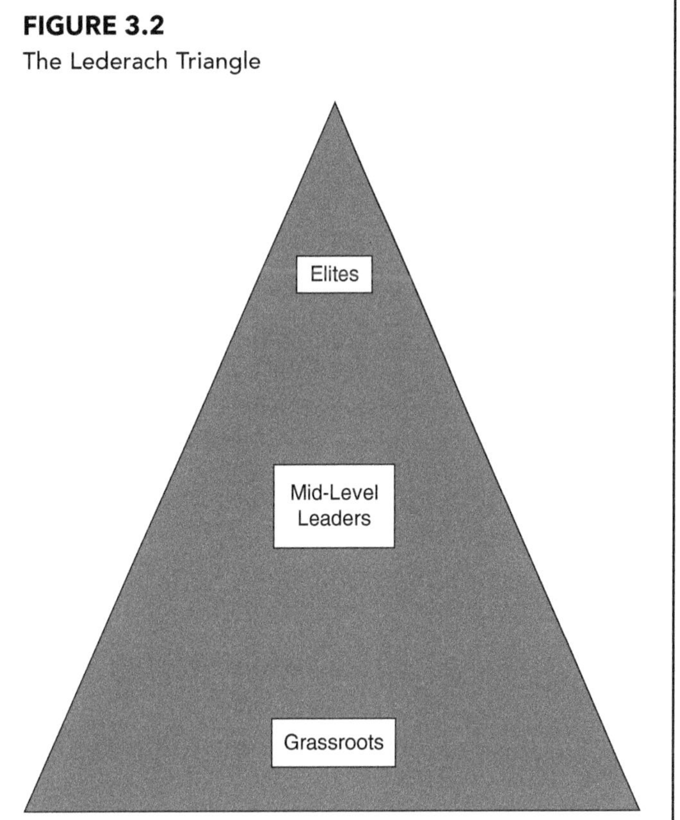

HOW CONFLICTS EVOLVE

Not surprisingly, models like Galtung's tended to reinforce beliefs that peace and conflict studies revolved around Gloom and Doom 101. Exploring the submerged portion of the "iceberg" did little more than convince earlier generations of students and activists that the underlying causes of intractable conflicts were deeply entrenched in public institutions and popular cultures. And, as we will see in part 2, few activists or academics saw any real hope of influencing national and international level elites no matter how much success they had at the grassroots level.

Then, **Elise** (1920–2010) and **Kenneth** (1910–1993) **Boulding** began exploring questions that should have been on our radar screens years earlier, which also helped us see more of the complexities involved in peace and conflict studies. That, in turn, led to the development of two similar and very useful models that structured much of what became Peacebuilding 2.0 by getting us to see that we could escape the bleak picture painted by the likes of Galtung if we understood what can best be called the life cycle of a typical conflict.

Imagining a Peaceful Future

The Bouldings deserve a prominent place in this chapter, because they were among the first to draw our attention to the ways conflicts changed and how they could end. That, in turn, makes it easier to see why the second pair of models will deepen your understanding of peace and conflict.

Kenneth was best known for his work on defining what stable peace would look like. As odd as it might seem, this is something early peacebuilders only thought about in the vaguest and most idealistic terms. Not Kenneth Boulding. He defined the term **stable peace** as "a situation in which the probability of war is so small that it does not really enter into the calculations of any of the people involved."[1] When that happens, conflict resolution takes the form of **diplomacy** and other normal decision-making techniques rather than the kind of outside-the-box interventions we will see in parts 2 through 4. I once heard Boulding tell a group of students that you could determine just how stable the peace between two governments was by measuring the amount of dust on the war plans each defense ministry had prepared for invading the other country.

To see what stable peace looks like in real life, think about the relationship between the US and the UK since the beginning of the twentieth century. At the interpersonal level, simply think about your neighborhood when it gathers for a picnic and nothing seems to divide one family from another.

Elise was more interested in how a society moves toward stable peace, starting with our ability to articulate what the world would be like when and if a given conflict had been resolved. She agreed with other analysts of her generation, like Benedict Anderson, who wrote that what we think of as racial, religious, or ethnic identities are the result of what he termed imagined communities. In other words, identities and other core values were created by people and were, therefore, subject to change. She, in particular, sought to build a global culture of peace in which all people—and especially women, poor people, and members of minority groups—would be involved in defining the future society they wanted to create.

Michael Lund's Curve and the Defense Department's Phases

Rarely does a single image shape a field as much as the one developed by Michael Lund did for peace and conflict studies after it appeared in a number of USIP publications in the second half of the 1990s (see the figure on page 54). As an aside and in anticipation of what you will see in chapter 12, the United States Department of Defense (DoD) developed a similar model at about the same time. The two were so similar that I only need to include one of them here and chose Lund's because it is more familiar to peace and conflict studies scholars. The two were created independently. In fact, Lund and the DoD architects of their five-phase model have never met each other to this day.

Even before we consider the chart in depth, be aware that people who use models like these often fall into two traps that are at least implicit in the smooth shape of Lund's curve:

- There is nothing inevitable about the steps or phases it outlines. Durable peace does not always degenerate into a tense standoff, let alone into actual fighting. And, as we have seen in Iraq and Afghanistan in recent years, "simply" ending or reducing the fighting by no means inevitably leads to anything like stable peace.
- It presents conflicts as what the British would call one-off events that have a beginning and end. However, as even your brief examination of conflicts while doing the first Conflict Labs undoubtedly suggested, ending one phase of a conflict in Lund's terms often paves the way for another outburst. In other words, a full analysis would probably consist of a number of these curves laid side by side.

Both Lund and the American military analysts focused on international disputes. But, you can map conflicts closer to home along the same trajectory. In your home neighborhood, the calm may be broken when new neighbors on your block start selling drugs to strangers who suddenly start visiting your street.

Tensions mount. You may all be reluctant to call the police, but you are also worried about the safety of your family.

Stable peace. The two models start where Kenneth Boulding left off with what Lund calls durable peace and the American military labels Phase 0. At this point, existing disagreements are minor and easy to resolve for the reasons Boulding suggested.

From unstable peace to crisis. Then, something disturbs the relationship. Tensions mount. In what military planners call Phases 1 and 2, foreign policy goals shift to what Lund termed preventive and then crisis diplomacy in which leaders start looking for alternatives to war. Sometimes they succeed. The US and Great Britain had their share of differences during the twentieth century, but their relationship never could have been described as tense. That was not true of the relationship among what were then the Yugoslavian republics in the 1980s. In less than a decade, reasonably stable peace gave way to a standoff in which that ethnically diverse country slid rapidly toward civil war.

Conflict. Sometimes the diplomatic efforts don't work. Fighting breaks out as it did in the former Yugoslavia in 1991. Military descriptions of the curve pay more attention to what it calls Phase 3, when the fighting continues until something happens that somehow ends it. This is the period in which peace is rarely on the agenda. If it is, it is in the form of **peacemaking**, in which one side physically tries to impose its will on the other. That can take the form of a series of military campaigns. Or, in the case of that hypothetical neighborhood, you and your neighbors can finally summon up the courage to call in the police who conduct a raid during which shots are fired.

Keeping the peace. All conflicts eventually end. In the original version of the chart, Lund focused on cease-fires and negotiating sessions like the one in Dayton, Ohio, that ended the bulk of the fighting in Bosnia. At this point in the life cycle of a conflict, something has to be done to make certain that a fragile truce holds. Often, the international community decides to send in a **peacekeeping** mission composed of lightly armed troops who try to keep the two sides from fighting again. More often than not, the UN sends in these troops. In the Bosnian case, however, the troops were deployed by an ad hoc coalition led by the US, NATO, and the European Union. No matter how it is done, what the military calls Phase 4 usually involves some kind of military presence in which at least one side threatens to use force, as was the case in Bosnia well into this century. In the case of the hypothetical neighborhood, the police will pay close attention to what happens at the drug dealers' house *and* how their neighbors deal with them.

Return to stable peace. The final stage is the one in which professional peacebuilders have the most experience, because it can lead to the return to the durable peace depicted on the left side of the chart—if and only if the root causes of the conflict have been addressed. In what Lund calls postconflict **peacebuilding** and others refer to as **reconciliation**, the parties to a dispute find ways of coming to grips with the issues that led them into the dispute in the first place. As you will see in more detail toward the end of part 3, our best example comes from South Africa in the years after the apartheid government was replaced by a multiracial democracy led by **Nelson Mandela** and the **African National Congress**. For example, its Truth and Reconciliation Commission allowed perpetrators of racial injustice during the apartheid years to escape prison time if they both acknowledged what

CONFLICT LAB 3.2

This chapter's second lab explores the ideas raised by the Bouldings, Michael Lund, and the anonymous military planners.

Like this chapter's first Conflict Lab, you might not need a lot of time to do this one, but it will almost certainly be a challenge. Consider each of your conflicts and ask three questions about them:

- Did stable peace ever exist between the parties to the dispute in the past?
- What would stable peace between them look like at some point in the future?
- What would it take for them to get there?

Then, trace the trajectory of the two conflicts along Lund's curve, knowing full well that they have not reached stable peace yet. If they had, you probably wouldn't have chosen them. This time, ask yourself why no one was able to keep the conflict from deepening at each of the major turning points along his curve.

they had done and sincerely apologized for their actions. As powerful as its hearings were, they by no means resolved all of the country's problems. Nonetheless, they did allow one-time enemies to rebuild their relationships on a more constructive footing in much the same way a reconciling couple tries to do after a painful separation. Or, in the case of those hypothetical neighbors, they talk through their feelings about the history of drug sales and find ways of integrating the one-time dealers into the ongoing life of the community.

Despite the similar trajectories they traced in their respective models, peacebuilders and the military *initially* drew very different conclusions from these models as far as theories of change were concerned.

Peacebuilders found themselves tailoring their efforts around the kind of conflict they faced on the ground. Rarely did we have a significant presence during the military's Phases 2 or 3 because the situation was too dangerous for us to do the kinds of work you will see in part 3. Instead, we focused on preventing the outbreak of fighting and helping the parties reconcile after it stopped.

I emphasized the word *initially* two paragraphs ago because by the time we got to Peacebuilding 3.0 and the less than successful military interventions in Iraq and Afghanistan, some military leaders had adopted theories of change that are remarkably like ours. As you will see in far more detail in chapter 12, they adopted Presidential Directive 3000.05 in 2004 which gave the same priority to conflict prevention and postconflict reconstruction as it did to war fighting. You will also see that those priorities still exist only on paper. Nonetheless, a growing number of current and retired officers have come to the conclusion that there are no purely military solutions to the geopolitical dangers facing countries like the US. Although they might not put it quite this way, even some military leaders are beginning to be convinced that war is obsolete.

CONFLICT MAPPING

The final pair of models are the newest and most sophisticated. They are also best suited for analyzing the wicked problems of a **VUCA** world for which they were designed. However, they are also more complicated and harder for beginning students and experienced professionals to use for reasons that will be clear once you dig into Conflict Lab 3.3.

Theories of Change

Before you do so, I need to take a short detour and have you consider an important addition to the field that did not take the form of a model which I briefly mentioned on page 55. You rarely encounter **theories of change** in mainstream social sciences. There, the researcher's main goal is to understand why events and trends occur.

Because we also want to influence everything from public policy to popular culture, we have had to go farther which is why theories of change matter so much to us. In the simplest terms, a theory of change is a series of if/then statements. For example, *if* we make it harder to people with mental illness to get access to guns, *then* there will be fewer school shootings in the US.

The Center for Theory of Change defines their subject as:

> essentially a comprehensive description and illustration of how and why a desired change is expected to happen in a particular context. It is focused in particular on mapping out or "filling in" what has been described as the "missing middle" between what a program or change initiative does (its activities or interventions) and how these lead to desired goals being achieved. It does this by first identifying the desired long-term goals and then works back from these to identify all the conditions (outcomes) that must be in place (and how these related to one another causally) for the goals to occur. These are all mapped out in an Outcomes Framework.

Adding them has allowed our work to reflect the more complex realities of the post-9/11 world.

USAID's Conflict Assessment Framework

In the decades after the end of World War II, leaders of the world's wealthiest countries created national development agencies to help spur economic growth and end poverty in the Global South. At first, their staffs only worked on economic development. However, since many of the world's poorest countries were also the site of most of the world's wars, these agencies' leaders quickly realized that they had to deal with conflict resolution and peacebuilding as well.

After decades of limited success on either the development or the conflict resolution front, they decided that they should do their homework before embarking on projects that can cost hundreds of millions of dollars, take years to complete, and affect the lives of everyone in a given region or country. Most of their models start with a **conflict map** that serves as a starting point for their own staff members and for the subcontractors who typically implement these programs.

Typical here is the US Agency for International Development (USAID), which issued the second edition of its **Conflict Analysis Framework** or **CAF** in 2012 (see figure 3.3). It is by no means the only one worth considering here.

FIGURE 3.3
The USAID Conflict Assessment Framework

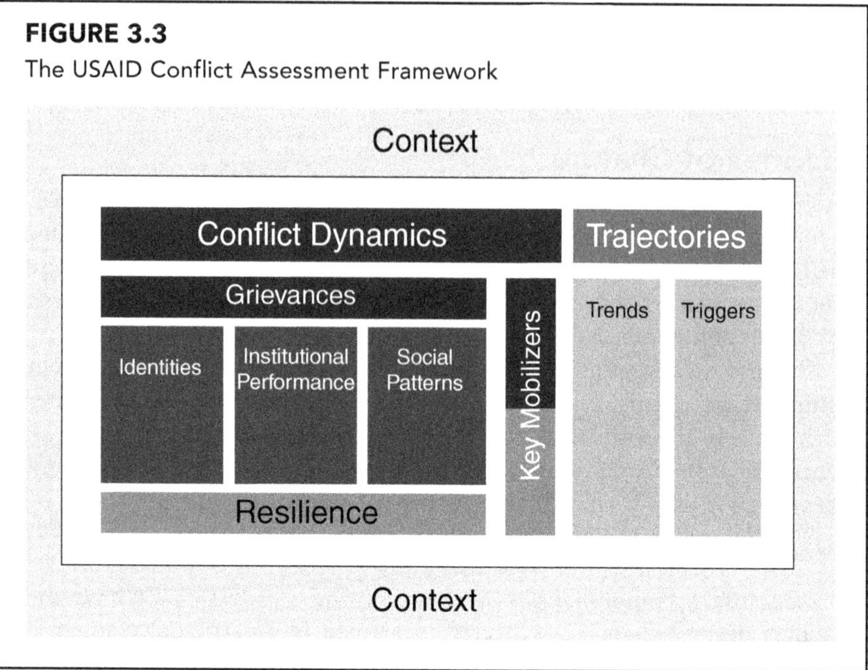

However, I chose it because it guides users through five analytical "baskets" that are used in planning most peacebuilding projects today.

The first task is to identify what the USAID team calls the conflict dynamics and map their trajectories. I could go into what they mean in more detail here, but you have already seen most of what they had in mind in dealing with the Lund curve. It is far more useful for our purposes to concentrate on the four clusters of causes.

Grievances. The framework starts by having users focus on the specific **grievances** that are on the agenda before a dispute breaks out. The fact that USAID puts this much emphasis on grievances is important because it draws our attention to the issues at stake and makes it hard to claim that a conflict has more to do with lawlessness and is the work of "mere" criminals as policy makers often insist.

The term grievances covers a lot of ground that can be broken down into these two subcategories:

- the issues people are upset about and how intensely they feel about them
- the extent to which grievances build on each other and become turned into wicked problems because the individual issues blend inexorably into each other

Precipitating causes. Like all the frameworks, the CAF encourages us to consider the immediate or precipitating causes or conflict mobilizers, which consist of the individuals and organizations that turn often vague grievances into concrete actions. We all know from our own lives that being angry alone is not enough to spark us into action. It takes something or someone to get people to act, whether that is to vote or take to the streets.

Deeper causes. This third set of causes sets the CAF apart from most other governments' assessment protocols by highlighting the kinds of issues that lie below the surface of Galtung's iceberg. In other words, grievances have to be understood as an outgrowth of broader social and political trends that can lead to wicked problems:

- **Social patterns**. These start with national and regional data about the distribution of wealth and other patterns one would cover in an introductory sociology course. Many of us, of course, are interested in conflicts in other kinds of settings. On a typical American college campus, we would be looking at things like its size, residence patterns (e.g., if there are fraternities and sororities), its endowment, or even its physical location.
- **Institutional performance**. USAID focuses heavily on **state** performance. As political scientists define the term, a state includes not only the formal government but also any other institutions that can shape average people's lives, often including the private sector. Politics exists and power is used everywhere, including on college campuses. There, for example, we would explore policies adopted by the school's administration and faculty, but at least at the college I attended, students have also protested against the independent contractor who runs the dining halls, local businesses, and even what some alumni have done and said about divisive issues.
- **Identities**. This third cluster will actually prove to be the most important in parts 3 and 4. As noted earlier, a person's **identity** refers to the answers he or she gives to such basic questions as "who am I?" and which are at the heart of the most vexing issues facing the world today. At the macro level, anger toward "the West" fuels ISIS and other terrorist groups. Similarly, you don't have to dig too far below the surface to see misinformation about the Muslim world, if not outright Islamophobia, in much of the West's reactions to such movements. Closer to home, identity issues around race, gender, and, less often, religion are dividing American campuses as well as society as a whole.

Resilience. I also chose to use the CAF because it stresses one reason why conflict might not turn ugly. USAID also wants its staff to consider the sources of **resilience** in the society it is working in. Typically, resilient societies have procedures in place that allow citizens to resolve their grievances without using violence, which are often buttressed by a national culture that leads them to choose conventional rather than contentious ways of solving their problems.

Toward a Systems Practice

The CAF has worked well enough for USAID whose projects are expected to show results in reasonably short periods of time. As a result, they haven't had to deal with the model's most glaring shortcoming. At best, it gives a snapshot of a country's problems when we often need the equivalent of an extended-play video instead.

If, on the other hand, you want to address the root causes of a dispute, you normally have to dig deeper and take a longer time doing so. Here **systems** analysis is more appealing, because it provides us with the equivalent of that video.

In writing this section (and indeed this entire book), I drew heavily on analytical tools developed by the **Omidyar Group**. Because the various parts of the Omidyar network deal with more than just conflict resolution, they tend to present their work in terms of systems thinking in general, which I will apply more directly to any kind of conflict here.

They argue that we need these kinds of **holistic** approaches when we deal with the **complexities** of conflict and most other issues today, especially when there is no obvious, single path to take in dealing with them. The resulting maps are based on **complex adaptive systems** theory, which can take us beyond the static pictures that emerge from the CAF.

In addition to identifying all of the actors in a map like the CAF, it prioritizes the relationships among them. As I have already suggested on several occasions, systems theorists take for granted the fact that everything we do directly or indirectly affects everything and everyone else. The very act of taking indirect effects and the long term into account is filled with implications for the way we understand conflict and design peacebuilding projects today. All that is a convoluted way of saying that systems maps help us see the way systems evolve over time.

Complexity scientists add the word adaptive to their self-definition because everything anyone does also reshapes the system itself. More importantly, they rarely think in terms of the chaotic or formless systems that are often discussed in the popular press. Rather, almost all systems we would be interested in have some kind of order, but it both emerges from its inner workings and, more importantly for our purposes, changes or "adapts" whenever it is disturbed.

A good-sized team of designers and researchers will take weeks or even months constructing a full systems map. Its members start with the kind of sticky note exercise and crude systems map that I had you do in the first Conflict Lab. They then spend a lot more time refining the map again and again until it ends up looking like figure 3.4 which the Omidyar team built with AfP's learning and evaluation team.

I know that you do not have either the time or the expertise to create anything like this map at this point in your career. However, there are a few key characteristics of a fully mapped system that are useful for understanding and dealing with conflict for people who are just starting either their academic or professional careers.

When looking at figure 3.4 don't worry about the terms or any of its other details. In fact, if you are reading this book on a screen, you might not be able to read the print. Instead, focus on the chart's overall structure. Note that it consists of a bunch of boxes and unboxed sets of words that are linked with arrows that denote cause and effect.

The formal mapping process begins with something that is implicit but does not appear in figure 3.4 or most systems maps you will encounter. One of the first things a systems mapping consultant does is to help you clarify how you want that system to change. In Omidyar's case, they ask you to define a **guide star**, which represents the long-term or ultimate goal you want to reach. Then, they ask you to define a number of near stars or shorter-term goals that you can realistically get to over the next five or ten years. Thus, in one recent report, it illustrated what it meant by the two kinds of stars using the example of a map it developed for the way multinational corporations obtain products manufactured in the Global South.

FIGURE 3.4
A Peacebuilding Systems Map

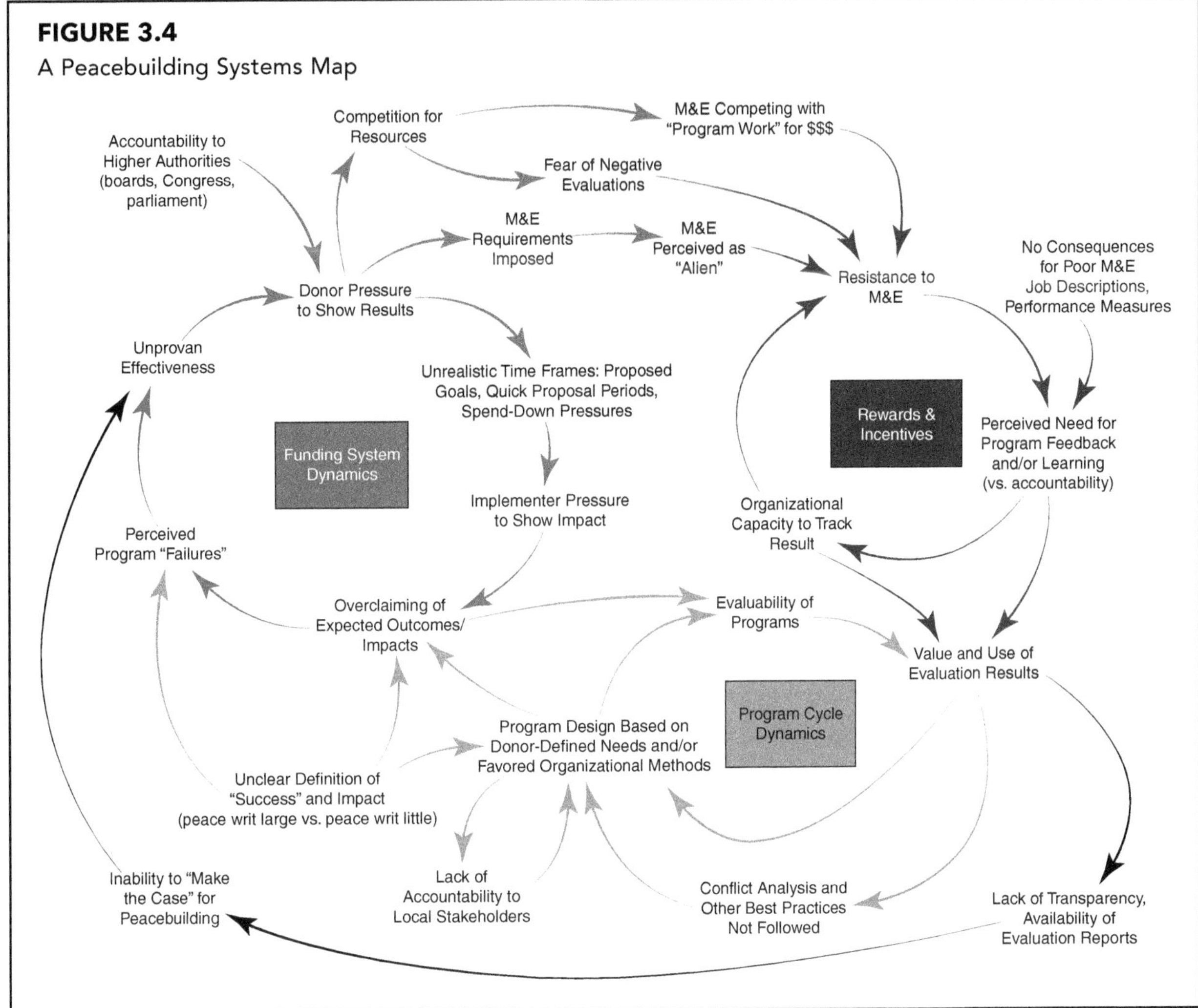

guide star—a system that eradicates the worst forms of human exploitation in corporate supply chains

near star—a new standard of corporate supply chain practice that will increase responsibility and decrease the use of labor abuse

They next chart the **environment** that is formally outside the system itself and may also not appear in the map, as is the case in figure 3.4. Those external social, political, and environmental factors are important in determining the context in which we work, and deciding what is "in the system" itself or "part of its environment" is always a judgment call. However, systems analysis focuses your attention on the things that can be changed as part of reaching either a guide or a near star. In other words, as you move from analyzing a problem to doing something about it, systems approaches lead you to the elements that can be and/or need to be changed in order to reach your goals.

The next step they would take in advising a team actually doing a project is to put the oldest set of causes (known as the upstream ones) to the left of the more recent ones. Then, they do the same thing with the desired consequences, which are not surprisingly known as the **downstream** effects to the right, so that all of them point toward the guide star.

Systems analysts eventually get to the main points included in a map based on the CAF. In this case, however, one doesn't try to fit (sometimes awkwardly) the evidence into categories represented by the boxes in figure 3.3. You get there by working inductively and letting the patterns in the data emerge as you proceed.

At this point, the participants invariably begin to see that some of the clusters hang together in the kind of circular structures that are known as **feedback** loops. They help you focus in on the key dynamics by naming each of the loops as you did in the boxed terms in the middle of each loop. The mere act of coming up with names itself helps direct you to the most important loops and allows you to see the core structures that hold the entire system together.

The loops show how causes and effects literally feed off each other. In other words, they show how what happened "today" impacts what happens "tomorrow." I put today and tomorrow in quotes here because feedback loops can be found in just about kind of any time frame. As figure 3.4 suggests, a full systems map contains dozens of feedback loops, while the system as a whole can be seen as a single interconnected loop that can be described in much the same way that a filmmaker constructs and describes a storyboard long before shooting begins.

Political scientists first studied feedback in the calmer days before the protests against the Vietnam War began and people largely trusted their political leaders. In those days, effective government action led to increased faith in and support for government in most of the American population. That led many citizens to become politically active, but in ways that reflected that support. There was relatively little protest. And, as what we now know to be an overly rosy interpretation put it at the time, decision makers got constructive input from the general public, which led to even more effective public policy that would keep the loop moving in ever more constructive directions.

Whether or not that analysis was accurate fifty years ago, it certainly is not today now that less than effective government action in a host of public policy arenas has left more and more people around the world dissatisfied with their governments. More of us today are disengaged. If we are involved, we tend to be making tougher and tougher demands on our policy makers, who have a harder and harder time making public policy.

These two types of loops are often called **vicious cycles** and **virtuous circles**. The former are used to depict deteriorating or **dysfunctional** systems, whether they are national governments or families teetering on the brink of divorce. Far less attention has been paid to the inelegantly labeled **eufunctional** systems that grow over time because their whole is literally greater than the sum of their parts. Yet, as you will see, creating that kind of virtuous circle is what conflict resolution and peacebuilding are all about.

Most loops contain several kinds of links. Some will strongly reinforce existing patterns. Others will be disruptive enough to produce fundamental change. There is no a prior way of determining the kind of link you are dealing with. That's why developing a map requires a lot more time and effort than I can expect you to devote to any mapping effort.

Next, focus on the feedback loops that tie the entire system together, which reveal what the Omidyar Group calls its **deep structure** and is built around the most important of the loops. One rarely discovers a system's deep structure by doing yet more research either in the lab or in the field. Instead, it requires taking a step back from the data—in this case the first version of your map—and figuring out which loops are most important and tying them together.

That usually involves moving your loops around your whiteboard and brainstorming. Eventually, you will find a central loop that you can turn into a narrative that amounts to the linchpin to the entire system.

Unlike the first five models we considered, this kind of systems approach actually has its theory of change built into it. You will see that in the next step which is based partially on intuition and partially on the empirical research that the mapping team conducts in between its sessions with the sticky notes and whiteboard. Peter Senge, who did more than any other single person to introduce systems approaches to corporate life, advised his clients to identify the places where they had the most potential for **leverage** over the entire system, which he defines as:

> seeing where actions and changes in structures can lead to significant, enduring improvements. Often leverage follows the principle of economy of means: where the best results come not from large-scale efforts but from small well-focused actions.[2]

Some loops are easier to change than others. Unfortunately, many of us tend to focus on what the Omidyar team calls frozen spots or those system components that are most resistant to change.

Instead, systems theorists would have us focus on:

- the idea of **bright spots** as popularized by business school professors Chip and Dan Heath, which consist of the subsystems that are actually working fairly well, no matter how dire the overall conflict may seem. Mainstream social scientists are more likely to use the term **positive deviants** or **outliers** to describe people, events, or trends that seem to point us in more positive directions[3]
- places where there seems to be the most energy for change, which may or may not be at an existing bright spot
- the potentially positive ripple effects of our actions are easiest to anticipate

Many who use systems in the corporate world call this kind of work **design thinking** as popularized by companies like IDEO and Pixar which use lots of verbs that begin with the letter "I," such as ideate, iterate, improvise, and innovate. They start out making crude systems maps or, in Pixar's case, storyboards. Gradually, they flesh out the map in the ways I suggested here until they are ready to build a cheap, quick prototype, often made out of Styrofoam and plastic. They keep experimenting until they create something that works and can be taken to

CONFLICT LAB 3.3

You should now be able to see why I had you use sticky notes for the exercises in chapter 1.

Since I have no idea how you recorded them, I have written this lab exercise on the assumption that you can re-create the pictures you drew and updated since then. For each of the conflicts you picked in chapter 1 do the following:

- Determine how each of the causes you identified fits into the CAF framework. If you now realize you left something out, make a sticky note for each theme you have uncovered since you first did the exercise.
- Then rearrange your old and/or new sticky notes so that they resemble figure 3.4 as fully as possible. Again, upstream causes go on the far left, while downstream causes go on the far right, with the conflict dynamics themselves in the middle:
- Be sure to identify what you think are the key feedback loops that make up the deep structure and reinforce the conflict dynamics, making it hard to resolve.
- Then identify what you think are the most important leverage points or loops that can either be changed most readily or show the greatest likelihood of changing the entire system for the better.

As you did in chapter 1 keep a record of what you did, and if possible, hold on to the sticky notes themselves. You will return to these exercises again in parts 2 through 4.

market which they often refer to as a minimum viable product. All along the way, they assume that they will make mistakes. The key is to learn from them and improve your product, whatever it happens to be.

A single example should illustrate that point. Systems thinkers in the corporate world talk fondly of the fact that James Dyson made 5,172 prototypes of the vacuum cleaners that bear his name before he came up with one that actually worked.

Those of us who deal with intractable conflicts cannot afford the time it takes to make that many mistakes. What's more, making a vacuum cleaner that doesn't work rarely has negative unintended consequences for society as a whole. Poorly defined peacebuilding processes do, as we will see with the use of what we will call do no harm principles in part 4.

CHUA AND PINKER/CONFLICT AND CRISIS

Unlike the first two chapters, I did not spend much time in the body of this one building an argument around the epigraphs that began it. I should do so in ending it, because the tools I have just discussed help you see both how we can both avoid Chua's pessimistic future and have a chance of turning Pinker's optimistic goals in to reality.

This time, a return to chapter 2's discussion of the word **crisis** should help you see why thinking in terms of models and theories of change can take us beyond their dilemma. As we saw at the beginning of that chapter, the Chinese bring together the characters for *danger* and *opportunity* to convey what English speakers do when they use the word *crisis*. In that sense, the Chinese term can be thought of in the same way medical doctors use the term. To them, patients who are in a medical crisis hover between life and death, their survival dependent on the way their health turns at that critical moment.

Put simply, we are at a crisis or turning point when it comes to conflict and violence. On the one hand, we can continue with business as usual in dealing with conflict and violence, in which case we might end up with the gloomy-looking future Chua fears. Or we could use tools like the ones discussed in this chapter to create the kind of hopeful paradigm shift that Pinker seems to have in mind.

In other words, it's time to shift gears and dig into concrete examples that show how and why the field has grown.

KEY TERMS

Concepts

accompaniment, 58
bright spot, 69
CAF, 63
complex adaptive systems, 66
complexity, 66
Conflict Analysis Framework (CAF), 63
conflict map, 63
crisis, 70
deep structure, 69
design thinking, 69
diplomacy, 59
disruption, 68
downstream, 68
dysfunctional, 68
environment, 67
eufunctional, 68
feedback, 68
grievances, 64
guide star, 66
holistic, 66
identity, 65
leverage, 69
models, 56
norms, 57
outliers, 69
paradigm, 56
peacebuilding, 61
peacekeeping, 61
peacemaking, 61
positive deviance, 69
power, 57
reconciliation, 61
resilience, 65
stable peace, 59
state, 65
structural violence, 57
systems, 65
theory of change, 63
theory, 56
transformational, 57
vicious cycles, 68
virtuous circles, 68
VUCA, 62

People

Boulding, Kenneth and Elise, 59
Galtung, Johan, 57
Lederach, John Paul, 58
Mandela, Nelson, 61

Organizations, Places, and Events

African National Congress (ANC), 61
Omidyar Group, 65

DIG DEEPER

Chenoweth, Erica, and Maria Stephan. *Why Civil Resistance Works: The Strategic Logic of Non-violent Conflict*. New York: Columbia University Press, 2011. A well-researched book on how contentious politics can lead to peace.

Lederach, John Paul. *Building Peace: Sustainable Reconciliation in Divided* Societies. Washington, DC: US Institute of Peace, 1997. A wonderful book that discusses not only the triangle considered here but also the concept of reconciliation, which will feature prominently from part 3 onward.

Lund, Michael. *Preventing Violent Conflict*. Washington, DC: US Institute of Peace, 1996. The source of figure 3.3 that helps one think about conflict dynamics as well as prevention.

Page, Scott. *The Model Thinker: What You Need to Know to Make Data Work for You*. New York: Basic Books, 2018. A basic book on why models are important by a professor of computer science and political science at the University of Michigan.

Ricigliano, Robert. *Making Peace Last: A Toolbox for Sustainable Peace*. London: Routledge, 2015. A thoughtful book by the leading expert on the use of systems analysis in peacebuilding.

Schirch, Lisa. *Conflict Assessment and Peacebuilding Planning: Toward a Participatory Approach to Human Security*. West Bloomfield, CT: Kumarian, 2013. Slightly older and more applied than Ricigliano's book, but still a good overview of the use of systems in conflict resolution.

[1] Kenneth E. Boulding, *Stable Peace* (Austin: University of Texas Press, 1978), 13.

[2] Peter Senge, *The Fifth Discipline: The Art and Practice of the Learning Organization* (New York: Doubleday Business, 1990), 1140.

[3] Chip Heath and Dan Heath, *Switch: How to Change When Change Is Hard* (New York: Crown Business, 2010), chapter 2.

PEACEBUILDING 1.0

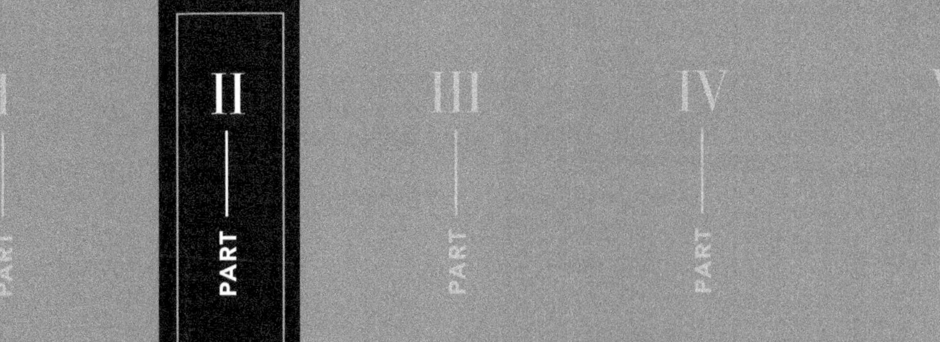

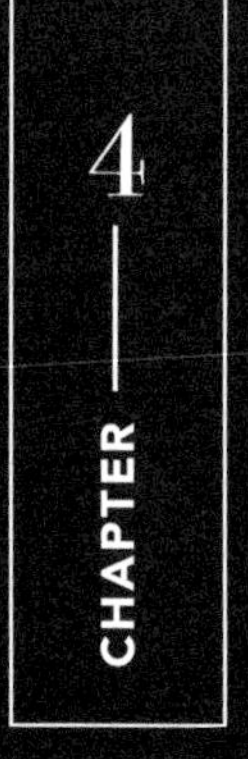

Beyond Gloom and Doom 101

THINK ABOUT IT

In parts 2 through 4, the Think About It boxes will help you connect the chronological material covered in that chapter to the concepts and tools introduced in part 1.

In this chapter, I make the case that a commitment to nonviolence is a common denominator to the entire field during all three time periods. Does it have to be? Can you imagine conflict resolution and peace studies initiatives that do not share that kind of commitment? Why (not)? If you can envisage the use of violence, how might it have played itself out during the 1980s?

By that same token, how would you balance the conflicting desires for broad coalition building and cooperative problem solving with the demands of contentious politics today?

CORE CONCEPTS

contentious politics—the use of disruptive tactics to change state policy

image of the enemy—a psychological term for the ways we tend to stereotype or demonize our adversaries

mode of thinking—another term for a personal paradigm or mind-set

The unleashed power of the atom has changed everything save our modes of thinking and thus we drift toward unparalleled catastrophe.
—*Albert Einstein*

WE ARE ABOUT TO SHIFT intellectual gears.

Part 1 defined this book's agenda along with a set of analytical "eyes" you can use in understanding peacebuilding and conflict resolution. Now, parts 2 through 4 will explore how the field has evolved by focusing on what it has—and has not—accomplished.

This chapter begins that journey by briefly returning to the conceptual material I introduced in part 1, something I will also do in the first chapters of parts 3 and 4 as well. Rather than repeating what you have already seen, these chapters will use those ideas to set the historical context and suggest why those earlier practitioners and scholars focused on a particular set of issues and adopted a particular set of tactics at that particular time. In this case, that starts with the creation of peace and conflict studies as a stand-alone academic discipline and the formation of the first organizations that were committed to putting what are often abstract ideas into practice.

As you dig into the material covered in the next nine chapters, remember that the division of the field into three stages and two levels is arbitrary. Many of the analytical tools and concrete examples you will be considering straddle both levels and that you will find traces of many of them in all three periods. Note, too, that I have not tried to present a comprehensive overview of any of the periods. Instead, I have focused on themes that defined peace and conflict studies at the time and/or continue to shape the field today.

THEN AND NOW

The Conflict Labs in part 1 may well have left you frustrated. On the one hand, you should not have trouble seeing how conflict resolution and peacebuilding activists could change the world. On the other hand, it is hard to make the case that we've made a lot of progress toward building what the John D. and Catherine T. MacArthur Foundation calls "a more just, verdant, and peaceful world."

There is good reason to feel frustrated. However, the first lesson to learn from part 2 is that we have actually made an amazing amount of progress in less than forty years.

If you could put yourself back at the start of the 1980s, you would have found yourself at a time when MacArthur's goals would have seemed like an impossible dream. Only a few colleges and universities had any kind of peace studies program. In the US, most of them were at schools that had been founded by religious denominations that had a strong commitment to peace to begin with. Only a handful of scholars, such as Johan Galtung and the Bouldings, were writing about peace, and their work was not taken seriously by mainstream academics.

Meanwhile, there were plenty of issues to worry about (see table 4.1). Revolution in Iran. The Soviet invasion of Afghanistan. Uprisings growing out of the dying gasps of formal colonialism. The renewed arms race. To be sure, there were organizations protesting against official policies on each of those issues, while a generation of young activists were being drawn to new causes, including gender and the environment. On balance, however, the social and political winds were shifting rightward.

Now, think about where we were in 2019 when I finished this book. While there is good reason to be frustrated by or even depressed about the events swirling around us, we have come a long way.

Most colleges and universities now offer some peace and/or conflict studies courses, and you can get a degree in the field at hundreds of institutions around

TABLE 4.1 | Key Events: The 1980s

Year	Event
1970s	OPEC oil embargo Iranian Revolution Soviet invasion of Iran
1980	Election of Ronald Reagan
1982	First major freeze demonstrations
1983	Gorbachev becomes secretary general of CPSU
1986	Reykjavik summit
1989	Fall of the Berlin Wall
1991	Collapse of the Soviet Union

the world. Most lawyers and diplomats have some training in mediation and conflict resolution. Terms like win-win and at least some of the values that underlie them have become a part of mainstream culture.

To be honest, when I first read *Getting to YES*, encountered George Mason University's (GMU) new program in conflict analysis and resolution, and met the leaders of the Beyond War movement (see the next chapter), I never dreamed that we would make this much progress. And I'm an optimist.

The key to that surprising growth lies in Einstein's sentence that starts this chapter, which, of course, you also encountered in chapter 2. Here, I will examine if from a slightly different angle because the peace movement was rekindled by the beginning and end of the sentence rather than by its middle. As Cold War tensions increased and progress on arms control stalled, millions of people in the Western democracies and the Soviet bloc began to take the threat of an "unparalleled catastrophe" seriously again after years of superpower détente.

Not all of the protest movements you will encounter in part 3 survived the decade. The ones that did *and* then contributed to the creation of the modern peace and conflict studies community all took the middle of the sentence, with its discussion of modes of thinking or paradigms seriously, too. Some of us also began to see that "everything" had changed and was going to continue changing faster and faster. Some of us, too began to see the potential in what came to be called **alternative dispute resolution**. Still others began to realize that we need profound social and political change at precisely the time that the then main alternative to the status quo—Marxism—was losing its appeal.

But, exploring those issues now would mean putting the clichéd cart before the clichéd horse. First, you have to see how peace activists began by returning to our roots in the **contentious politics** which we inherited from the new left of the 1960s. Only then does it make sense to see how some of us blended new ideas about conflict resolution with a desire for peace to create the networks we see today, many of which were in place by the middle of the 1990s.

Before digging into that material, keep one more thing in mind. We did not have everything figured out by the end of this first period, and we will don't today. As the Out on a Limb boxes in the rest of this book will attest, we still disagree among ourselves on some very basic issues. Do we need a paradigm shift? How much emphasis should we give to systems and complexity theory? How much of our time should be given to protesting against what's wrong rather than building bridges to what I'll be calling strange political bedfellows? And more.

Still, by the end of the 1980s, most of us understood that we had to go beyond what George Lopez called Gloom and Doom 101. When the 1980s began, it was clear what members of the peace and conflict studies community were against. By the end of the decade, we began a subtle shift that today leaves us emphasizing, instead, what we are for.

NONVIOLENCE

The one constant in all three periods is our commitment to **nonviolence**. That said, we are not of one mind about what nonviolence entails or if we have to adhere to all of its tenets all of the time.

Still, that commitment goes a long way toward defining who we are. It starts with the ubiquitous peace symbol that begins this chapter. It was first used by British activists who opposed the Cold War and nuclear arms in the 1950s. Its origins lie in the now obsolete symbols of semaphore, in which soldiers and others designated letters by raising their arms (often holding flags) in patterns people could recognize and make sense of. The peace symbol brought together its symbols for *N* (nuclear) and *D* (disarmament). Few remember those origins today, but, as you will see in the next two chapters, they go a long way toward helping you understand the way peace and conflict studies began.

For the most part, our commitment to nonviolence and the imagery of the peace symbol have been an asset. However, the popular equation of nonviolence with **pacifism** has often left many of us reluctant to work with some potential partners, including the military, which, as we will see in part 4, has become an integral part of what I do.

Principles

The origins of modern nonviolence can be found in all of the world's major spiritual traditions, some of which are thousands of years old. Modern nonviolence, however, is an outgrowth of a number of nineteenth- and twentieth-century movements, most notably those led by **Mohandas Gandhi** (1869–1948) in India and **Martin Luther King Jr.** (1929–1968) in the US. Considering the two men together here is no coincidence. As a young man, King visited India to learn what he could about the recently assassinated hero of the movement that had just freed India from British rule. That visit went a long way toward shaping King's strategy for confronting segregation and inequality in the US. The lessons he drew from India's struggle for independence and his own campaign for racial equality in the US remain one of the most comprehensive statements about what nonviolence is—and is not

Many of the conclusions he reached and the actions he led fly in the face of the image of Dr. King that gets bandied about each year when Americans celebrate his birthday. We tend to remember King, Gandhi, and others like them as superheroes who touched the hearts of everyone. Peacebuilders, however, should also recall that they were radicals who consciously used nonviolence to force the powers that be to change and were willing to do everything necessary—short of using violence—to make that happen.

King laid out his own version of radical nonviolence in his book *Stride toward Freedom*, which he wrote shortly after the end of the 1957 Montgomery bus boycott.[1] Not everyone agrees with everything King proposed in the twenty pages he dedicated to nonviolent struggle. Nonetheless, versions of his five main principles are at least implicitly at the heart of just about all of the analyses and initiatives you will encounter in the rest of this book.

Agape comes first, even though it is often left out of most treatments of King's beliefs and tactics. Originally a Greek term, it refers to a form of love found in Christianity and other spiritual traditions that defines how we should deal with everyone, including people we deeply disagree with. King, of course, saw agape in Christian terms and drew on biblical stories like the last supper, at which Jesus said:

> You have heard that it was said, You shall love your neighbor and hate your enemy. But I say to you, Love your enemies and pray for those who persecute you, so that you may be sons of your Father who is in heaven; for he makes his sun rise on the evil and on the good, and sends rain on the just and on the unjust. For if you love those who love you, what reward have you?
>
> — Matthew 5:43–46, RSV

More generally, proponents of radical nonviolence firmly believe in the principles of the Golden Rule, a version of which can be found in all major spiritual traditions. Do unto others as you would have them do unto you. In so doing, they anticipated one of the key implications of systems theory. What I do today will be fed back to me later. In this case, the violence I exert toward my enemies will invariably come back to haunt me.

Confront forces of evil, not evil individuals. As you can see any time you follow an election campaign, it is easy to demonize one's opponents. However, Gandhi and King insisted on the fact that evil rarely resides in individuals, even individuals who oppress the poor and the weak. Rather, the problem lies in the social and other forces that give rise to the evil behavior. Those underlying conditions should be the target of the protest.

Treat opponents with dignity. You might be surprised at how formally dressed the leaders of the 1962 March on Washington were as seen in the photograph on the next page. In part, that was a sign of the times. More importantly, it reflected Dr. King's belief that protesters had to treat their opponents with respect. Like all practitioners of nonviolence, King discouraged the use of stereotypes or what psychologists call the **image of the enemy** which lead us to turn the people we disagree with into caricatures of real human beings.

Do not react to violence with violence. Demonstrators who took part in protests that King and Gandhi led went through extensive nonviolence training. They were taught how to react to violence in nonviolent ways that often included accepting arrest and even spending time in jail, which both of those men used to expand their support.

Nonviolence is a sign of strength. Gandhi, in particular, chafed whenever anyone spoke of his actions as passive resistance or claimed that nonviolence is a weapon used by the weak. Rather, he and King argued that they had chosen nonviolence because it showed how strong they were. First, it allowed protesters to occupy the moral high ground. Second, as you can see in film clips those days, images of club-wielding police officers and others who resort to violence actually build support for the protesters, who react to them with dignity.

The March on Washington for Jobs and Freedom, August 28, 1963

Tugged in Four Directions

As powerful as the commitment to nonviolence has been, it has never unified the peacebuilding and conflict resolution world around a single goal or strategy. As you will see in the rest of this chapter and, in fact, the rest of the book, that commitment has tugged us in four often incompatible directions. They are important enough that I will, first, lay them out in general terms to end this section, do so again in an Out on a Limb box that reflects how they have affected my own career, and then use the rest of this chapter to show how they shaped the first period in the history of peace and conflict studies.

Broadening support. Gandhi, King, and the successful activists you will encounter in parts 2 through 5 had one other thing in common. They dramatically broadened support for their cause. While they rarely wavered when it came to their core beliefs, they learned how to present causes like Indian independence and American civil rights in ways that appealed to people who did not define themselves as radicals. Again, a glance at photographs taken at the March on Washington in 1962 or the Women's March the day after President Donald Trump's inauguration shows crowds in which committed radicals were outnumbered by average citizens.

The role of protest. I have spent the bulk of my career trying to build those broad coalitions, often by appealing to people who are more conservative than I am. I started out, however, as part of movements in which we stridently made demands on the American and other governments.

Most practitioners of contentious politics one encounters in peace and conflict studies are committed to nonviolent protests. Still, there are some individuals and organizations that claim to be building a more peaceful world but are willing to use violent tactics, including the AnfiFa activists in the US and Europe. However, they are rarely included in peacebuilding coalitions. Indeed, relations between these kinds of organizations and our community are often tense at best.

There are gray areas in which organizations that at least started out with a commitment to nonviolence ended up engaging in armed resistance, most notably the ANC in the thirty years before Nelson Mandela's release from prison and the end of the apartheid regime (see part 3). In these cases, nonviolent activists only became willing to take up arms when they (reluctantly) concluded that they had no other option.

Personal growth. Many of us have learned that fully practicing nonviolence requires personal growth that goes far beyond the refusal to take up arms.

OUT ON A LIMB

You will not be able to escape these sometimes contradictory "tugs" if you decide to continue studying peace and conflict resolution and, especially, if you pursue a career in the field. You can see that in the ways that they have shaped my career. It's up to you to see how dealing with them might shape yours.

I came of age at the end of the civil rights movement and describe myself as having majored in ending the war in Vietnam as an undergraduate. I wrote my PhD thesis and first book on the far left in France. In short, I started out in contentious politics and wanted to work for radical change. In fact, Charles Tilly, who coined that term, was one of my mentors and a lifelong friend. My radicalism has tempered some over the last half-century. However, no one would ever mistake me for a conservative.

At the same time, even in my most radical days, I saw the need for building broad coalitions. I have also always understood that there will inevitably be some tension between building those coalitions and staying true to your core beliefs. That manifests itself today whenever I work with never-Trump republicans or military officers.

Finally, I have spent a lot of time on my own personal growth since I started working with the Beyond War movement, which I will discuss toward the end of chapter 5. There are real questions, however, about how much I need to have a spiritual practice or how deeply I have to explore my personal paradigms. In the 2010s, that tension has played itself out in a personal conflict over the trade-off between spending time doing active peacebuilding and spending time meditating and "working on my self" in other ways.

The successful organizations that I will be profiling in the next nine chapters all devote significant resources to the intellectual and personal growth of their staff. Among other things, they stress the importance of truly listening to and representing the voices of the people who live in conflict zones. Similarly, many emphasize the importance of fully living one's personal values, such as being able to leave one's ego at the door.

A tilt toward the left? It should already be obvious that peacebuilding and conflict resolution have traditionally been associated with the political left. That need not be the case. There is no reason why cooperative problem solving and a more peaceful world should not appeal to people from all points on the political spectrum. However, because of the way the field has evolved, I often joke that our biggest diversity challenge at AfP is to attract more conservatives.

CONTENTIOUS POLITICS

As you will see in the next two chapters, our first instinct was to return to our 1960s-era roots in contentious politics. Indeed, it was our preoccupation with what was wrong with the status quo that prompted George Lopez to refer to our field as Gloom and Doom 101.

In other words, the first glimmers of what became today's peace and conflict studies definitely did not start with anything resembling getting to yes. Instead, we started by saying an emphatic no to militarism and injustice and set out to build movements that would force political and other leaders to change.

Many of us have deemphasized these kinds of approaches as we and our field have aged. Nonetheless, we did begin with contentious politics, and the analyses, strategies, and tactics to which it leads are still at the heart of many peace movements today.

What Contentious Politics Is

Then and now, most peace activists who engaged in contentious politics drew on the work of **Gene Sharp** (1928–2018), who was a Quaker activist and scholar whose ideas on nonviolent protest shaped many of the so-called color movements and revolutions that swept countries like Egypt, Ukraine, Iran, and Myanmar over the course of the last two decades. Analytically speaking, I find that the broader social movement analysis developed most notably by Charles Tilly and Sidney Tarrow takes us further, and I will rely on them here.

In their most recent work, Tilly and Tarrow defined contentions politics somewhat inelegantly as:

> interactions in which actors make claims on other actors' interests.[2]

While Tilly and Tarrow's prose may never win them a literary prize, their words tell us a lot about both the protest movements of the 1980s and more recent efforts to take peacebuilding efforts to scale, as you will see repeatedly in the rest of this book.

All of the activists you will encounter in the next two chapters tried to force themselves onto the national agenda. They had no choice. They were on the outside looking in at—and therefore clamoring to get into—the places where key decisions were made.

Tilly and Tarrow's work is also a useful jumping-off point because they realized that building a successful social movement always takes time and unfolds in a complicated process that has two main components, as summarized in figure 4.1.

Building a movement. The first challenge is to build a movement that is big and loud enough that the authorities have to take notice. For our purposes, we can break that effort down into three broad categories, all of which take place once a group of movement entrepreneurs have developed the ideas that crystallized what I called the grievances in discussing the USAID CAF in chapter 3. Typically, that includes both creating contending groups and blending their efforts together through some sort of coalition, as represented in the bottom half of figure 4.1, by:

- Building support for the movement's cause. The ways movement entrepreneurs do this, of course, have changed since the nineteenth century, which was the focus of much of Tilly's own research. Still, even with the growth of the internet and other forms of mass communication that have accompanied globalization, this is by no means an easy task, as you will see repeatedly in the rest of this book.
- Coordinating the efforts of a number of those groups once they have been created. As we will see in the case of the American nuclear freeze movement, doing so was no mean feat. The challenges only get more difficult when

FIGURE 4.1
Contentious Politics

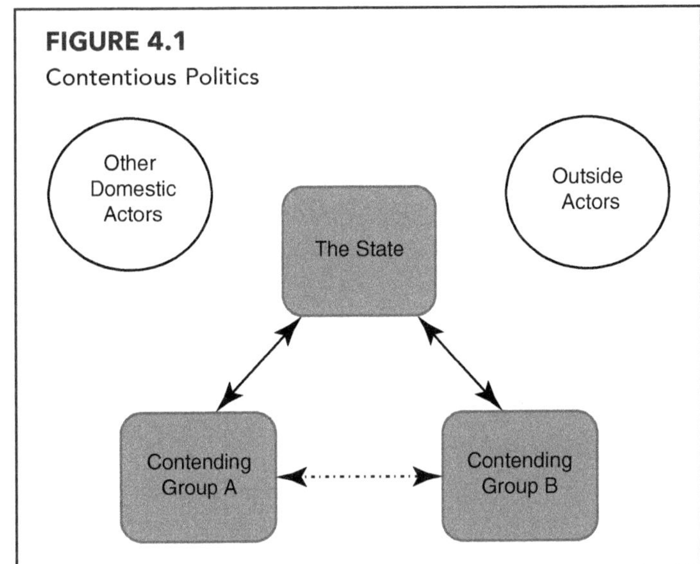

movements become transnational, as they increasingly have been in the forty years or so since the modern peace and conflict resolution communities were created.
- Acting as a **broker** or entrepreneur who can take the movements to **scale** at the national (or, today, supranational) level after an initial growth spurt ends, which protesters of the day failed to do.

The specific tactics contending groups choose vary from place to place and time to time. They all can be located on a spectrum that ranges from letter writing and attending demonstrations on one end to civil disobedience and organizing nonviolent revolutions on the other.

Challenging the state. Tilly and Tarrow also helped us see that we should study social movements in context. The people and institutions they want to influence also shape what they do and the impact they might—or might not—have when they make "claims on other people's interests."

That's the case because many contending groups will find that the relevant decision makers are unwilling to meet their requests and demands. How that plays itself out varies in the following ways, all of which also reflect the degree to which a given country is democratic as well as the upward arrows and the two circles in figure 4.1:

- The institutional arrangements and officeholder behavior largely determine what Tilly and Tarrow call a country's **opportunity structures**. Constitutional and other provisions may not go so far as to dictate the kinds of organizations that are allowed to operate—although some authoritarian regimes have tried to do just that. Not all of those influences have their origins in the country in which the movement operates, as you will see in Eastern Europe in chapter 6.
- States also have different **capacities**, which is a political science term that reflects their ability to carry out or implement a given policy or program. Other things being equal, governments that cannot make good on their policy promises leave themselves vulnerable to protest from contesting groups, something Americans have seen repeatedly since the 1970s in poorly conceived policies and the declining trust in leaders that followed in their wake.
- All regimes impose some restrictions on the ways people can legally express their grievances. All democracies, for example, ban certain kinds of demonstrations. Those restrictions are, of course, far more significant—and far more worrisome—under less democratic regimes. Authoritarian states, by contrast, can repress or otherwise limit most forms of dissent.

Why It Matters

As scholars like Sharp, Tilly, and Tarrow saw things, social movements had to force leaders to comply with their demands. Political and other authorities were not likely to give up power as defined in chapter 1 without a struggle. By their logic, if we wanted to win, we had to use confrontational tactics.

Note in passing that Tilly and Tarrow did not rule out the use of violence. In fact, Tilly always argued that contending groups should assume that they would have to use at least some violence before they could have a hand in making the kinds of policy changes the likes of Galtung or the Bouldings had in mind.

Protest movements that followed these kinds of strategies accomplished a lot, including returning nonviolent regime change to the world's political agenda.

CONFLICT LAB 4.1

Get together a new small group or reconvene the one that met in chapter 1 and pick a conflict that you all know about. Ask yourselves how applying the principles of contentious politics could be used in analyzing it:

- Can you identify ways in which the principles of contentious politics help you understand the conflict?
- What are the contending groups? What other ones might exist?
- Do they work together? Why (not)? What could they do differently to increase their influence?
- Does the state resist their efforts? How? What could be done to force the state to change?
- What other actors do you need to consider both at home and abroad?

Contentious protests produced independence in India and inspired the American civil rights and antiwar demonstrations in the 1960s. However, the end of the Cold War built new support, in particular, for Sharp's ideas, which would go on to inspire dozens of nonviolent insurgencies in once authoritarian regimes, some of which we will encounter later on.[3]

In presenting this material in person, I often play "It Isn't Nice." Written by Malvina Reynolds, it became an anthem of the American civil rights movement in the 1960s after it was sung by the likes of Pete Seeger. In fact, I usually play a version of it sung by a chorus of middle school students with Seeger playing backup banjo that was recorded just a few years before his death (www.youtube.com/watch?v=vnK0FpLIsNk). I have reprinted its first stanza below, but the lyrics alone don't do the power of her words justice. Nonetheless, you can easily see how they touch on what Sharp, Tilly, and Tarrow were getting at in ways we will return to frequently in the pages to come.

> It isn't nice to block the doorway,
> It isn't nice to go to jail,
> There are nicer ways to do it
> But the nice ways always fail.
> It isn't nice,
> It isn't nice,
> But if I've told you once, I've told you twice,
> If that is Freedom's price,
> We don't mind.

COOPERATIVE PROBLEM SOLVING

In the end, contentious politics could only take us so far, for reasons that will become clear in the rest of part 2 and are reflected in the title I chose for this book—*From Conflict Resolution to Peacebuilding.* Combining conflict resolution with peacebuilding might seem obvious now. In the early 1980s, the two seemed to inhabit separate universes.

While the details of what happened during the last two decades of the twentieth century are not all that important today, I do want you to see that by the end of the 1980s, the field's pioneers had created the broad outlines of an academic discipline and a professional community of practice that would take on its current form in the 1990s after the Cold War ended.

Mediation and Negotiation

Everyone interested in any aspect of peace and conflict studies is expected to read *Getting to YES* early in his or her career because it is one of the few books we all agree is central to the field. It had the impact it did because it was readable and filled a number of gaps in law, diplomacy, organizational dynamics, and a few other fields in which professionals had long hoped to find an alternative to **win-lose** or **zero-sum** decision making.

Similarly, the book did not appear out of thin air. It reflected the ongoing work of Harvard's **Project on Negotiations (PON)**, which was created by Fisher, Ury, and Bruce Patton in the late 1970s and took on its current name and form in 1983.

In its early days, PON was a consortium of scholars based at Harvard, MIT, and Tufts and now has participants from Boston's vast academic community. It has always been housed at the law school, but it has drawn on scholars from a host of disciplines. Its current director, Guhan Subramanian, for example, is the first person ever to have been granted academic tenure in both Harvard's Law and Business Schools.

Curiously, with the exception of Fisher, few of PON's founders had much experience dealing with international conflict, and his background was in international law and diplomacy rather than in the peace movement. Fisher, Ury, and Patton (who formally became a coauthor of *Getting to YES* with the publication of the second edition) essentially used the proceeds from the unexpectedly massive sales of the book to fund the day-to-day operations of PON in those early days and to fuel its expansion ever since. Today, PON serves as the preeminent source for interdisciplinary research on organizational and legal conflict resolution and has helped thousands of mid-career and senior professionals master the basics of conflict resolution and more.

PON's website lays out the premises on which its work has always been based:

> There will always be conflict. In fact, many remark ruefully that conflict is a "growth industry." Knowing how to negotiate to solve problems, make deals, build consensus, avoid violence, and manage intractable disputes is a competency that is vitally needed in the world.
>
> Through different lenses, including law, business, government, psychology, economics, anthropology, the arts, and education, members of the PON community seek to better understand negotiations. Why did a deal not close that would have benefited both companies? Why did one country resolve differences peacefully, while another fought a bloody civil war? Why are some divorcing couples able to mediate their separation amicably, while others fight painfully and expensively in court?[4]

By the end of the decade, most American law schools were offering courses in mediation and negotiation. Some even had specialized programs in alternative dispute resolution. Most focused on what I called **transactional** conflict resolution in chapter 1 in which a single agreement could make a significant difference, perhaps even ending a conflict altogether.

With the publication of *Getting to YES*, the conflict resolution community was able to build itself around a series of principles that guided professional mediators and others and still structure that part of the field today. Figure 1.2 gave you an overview of the basic logic underlying them. Now, you have seen enough about transactional conflict resolution to see those principles in more depth.

Seek outcomes that benefit everyone. Victories that end up with winners and losers are often hollow, because the "loser" is still bitter and may even be angrier than ever. Instead, try to find solutions that benefit everyone, because one-sided victories typically lead to even more conflict in the medium to long term.

Reframe issues to expand the number of options for the parties to choose from. Win-win outcomes rarely materialize if the parties continue to negotiate around fixed positions. Normally, they have to get creative and explore new alternatives that may seem off the wall at first glance. This is why mediators often use brainstorming and other techniques for getting fresh ideas onto the agenda. Most people who read *Getting to YES* for the first time are surprised that they rarely (if ever) use the terms **win-win** or its academic equivalent, **positive-sum**. Instead, they talk about finding pathways toward mutual gain through which all parties to the dispute benefit.

Use third-party neutrals. Parties to a dispute can rarely do that on their own. Therefore, professionals who work in this tradition stress the role of **facilitators**, **mediators**, and other **third-party neutrals** who can help all sides see those new options, keep them on task, and prevent discussions from getting overheated.

Focus on interests rather than positions. We often get "stuck" defending rigid positions. If we step back and focus on our broader, underlying interests, it is usually easier to envision alternative options that could lead to more satisfactory outcomes for all concerned.

Do not demonize your opponents. Avoid stereotyping or engaging in what psychologists call the image of the enemy. Once people start blaming the other side for causing or perpetuating a dispute, solutions are all but impossible to find.

Trust is an outcome of success. Do not assume you can trust your adversary when negotiations begin. In fact, doing so can be catastrophic, especially when the stakes are particularly high or the divisions particularly emotional. Trust tends to get built on the basis of success when each side begins to see how it can count on the other to hold up to its end of the bargain.

Always have a BATNA. Not all negotiations work. So, you should always be prepared to walk away if no agreement is in sight. This position is almost always referred to using the acronym Fisher and Ury coined—having a **BATNA**, or a better alternative to a negotiated agreement.

There has been a steady growth in this kind of conflict resolution work since PON and similar programs were created. We have gotten better at using these kinds of skills, albeit without making the kinds of major new breakthroughs that we will see in other aspects of conflict resolution and peacebuilding. Still, we should not scoff at this progress. In addition to the tangible results you will learn about in the rest of this book, terms like win-win have found their way into mainstream culture in ways we almost take for granted. Conflict resolution specialists now have jobs in places one could not have imagined when *Getting to YES* was published—human relations departments of most major companies, the Internal Revenue Service, the Transportation Security Administration, leader-

CONFLICT LAB 4.2

You and the other members of your "mapping team" should pick a conflict that you have dealt with personally, if you can identify one. If you cannot, pick one that affects your community. Ask yourselves how applying the principles on the previous page would have helped:

- Can you identify one or more possible win-win outcomes?
- How could you have reframed the issue?
- How could a third party have helped out?
- What are the underlying interests that transcend the specific positions the parties take?
- In what ways does demonizing or stereotyping the other side get in the way?
- What was the role of trust—and the lack thereof—in the discussions?
- What could or should have been your BATNA?

ship and management training companies, police departments, the armed forces, software development, and even professional sports leagues.

Beyond the Law Schools

The publication of *Getting to YES* and the creation of programs like PON were not the only ways that cooperative problem solving entered peace and conflict studies during the 1980s. In fact, new programs at places like Harvard Law School alone could not have created today's peace and conflict studies programs either in academia or in the "real world" of political life.

That required the emergence of a number of policy entrepreneurs whose backgrounds did not lie in either contentious politics or alternative dispute resolution. Because their impact is easier to see in their practical work, I will put off dealing with them until the end of chapter 5, when you will see how conflict resolution and peace studies began to come together. At that point, you can see the beginnings of a field that combines conflict resolution with peacebuilding in a reasonably coherent way.

LINGERING TENSIONS

As I suggested in beginning this chapter, the historical material in parts 2 and 3 may not be all that important for understanding conflict resolution and peacebuilding today, per se. However, two key takeaways from this chapter are still at the heart of this field more than thirty years later.

The first is the fact that virtually every practitioner you will encounter in the rest of this book is committed to nonviolence. There may have been times and places some of my colleagues sympathized with movements that reluctantly used violence. However, to the degree that we helped produce lasting social and political change, it was because we used the tools of nonviolence, especially those introduced in this chapter.

The second theme does not build on that kind of common ground but on an ongoing tension. Some of us draw primarily on the bridge-building side of the field, whose roots can be traced back to *Getting to YES* and a variety of movements you will encounter in the next two chapters. Many of us also draw on the more assertive models of social change that are epitomized by Tilly and Tarrow's notion of contentious politics.

The two do not always pull us in incompatible directions. But sometimes they do, as is the case as the second decade of the twenty-first century draws to an end. We will return to these ongoing tensions from time to time in the rest of this book.

KEY TERMS

Concepts

agape, 78
alternative dispute resolution (ADR), 76
BATNA, 85
broker, 82
capacities, 82
contentious politics, 76
facilitators, 85
image of the enemy, 78
mediators, 85
nonviolence, 77
opportunity structures, 82
pacifism, 77
positive-sum, 85
scale, 82
third-party neutral, 85
transactional, 84
win-lose, 84
win-win, 85
zero-sum, 84

People

Gandhi, Mohandas, 77
King, Martin Luther, Jr., 77
Sharp, Gene, 81

Organizations, Places, and Events

Project on Negotiations (PON), 84

DIG DEEPER

Fisher, Roger, and William Ury. *Getting to YES: Negotiating Agreement without Giving In*. New York: Penguin, 1981. Still the most important book in the field.

Lum, Grande. *The Negotiation Fieldbook: Simple Strategies to Help You Negotiate Everything*. New York: McGraw-Hill, 2010. A more up-to-date version of and expansion on *Getting to YES*.

Sharp, Gene. *The Politics of Non-violent Action*. 4 vols. New York: Porter Sargent, 1973. The bible of nonviolent but coercive protest.

Tilly, Charles, and Sidney Tarrow. *Contentious Politics*. 2nd ed. New York: Oxford University Press, 2015. Not an easy read, but the most systematic and complete book on aggressive forms of protest.

NOTES

[1] The relevant portions of that book are reprinted in Cornell West, ed., *The Radical King* (Boston: Beacon Press, 2015), 39–55.

[2] Charles Tilly and Sidney Tarrow, *Contentious Politics*, 2nd ed. (New York: Oxford University Press, 2015), 12. In the interests of full disclosure, I studied with Tilly, and we later became friends who argued about the role of violence in social change until Tilly's death.

[3] Gene Sharp, *The Politics of Non-violent Action*, 4 vols. (New York: Porter Sargent, 1973).

[4] www.pon.harvard.edu/about/.

CHAPTER 5

Do the Russians Love Their Children, Too?

THINK ABOUT IT

During the 1980s, many in the peacebuilding and conflict resolution community resisted efforts to go beyond the issues of the day to talk about paradigms, modes of thinking, and root causes. Why do you think that was the case? How did it limit what activists and scholars of that generation did?

CORE CONCEPTS

Getting to YES—title of a book that came to symbolize win-win conflict resolution

mode of thinking—values and assumptions that make up one's personal paradigm

Nuclear Freeze—campaign against nuclear arms race during the 1980s

public judgment—consensus in public opinion about an overarching opinion

Believe me when I say to you, I hope the Russians love their children, too.

—*Gordon Matthew Thomas Sumner (aka Sting)*

STUDENTS TODAY ARE OFTEN SURPRISED to learn how important young people's fears about a nuclear war were in giving rise to today's conflict resolution and peacebuilding movements. Their surprise does make sense. The threat of annihilation in an all-out nuclear war has not been a major concern since the Cold War ended thirty years ago. Nuclear weapons do make the news when tensions with North Korea or Iran flare up. Nonetheless, most young people—as well as the rest of us—properly spend more time worrying about climate change, which has replaced nuclear war as the danger that could destroy human civilization.

That was not the case in the early 1980s. The Cold War had heated up again. A new nuclear arms race was underway. While there were plenty of other issues on the global political agenda, the nuclear arms race was the issue that launched the academic programs, activist movements, and global NGOs you will encounter in the rest of this book.

That is also why I chose the words from Sting's first solo hit for this chapter's title and epigraph. It makes more sense to ponder the song's message at the end of this chapter, because you need to see everything else in it before you can fully understand its significance. At this point, it is the song's backstory that should help get us started.

In the early 1980s, Sting was visiting a friend in New York who could watch Soviet television. After a Saturday night on the town, the two of them started watching. It was then Sunday morning in Moscow, so they had to watch cartoons. As the father of a four-year-old, Sting was struck by the amount of love that had gone into making Soviet children's television which showed through loud and clear even though he didn't speak Russian.

That got him thinking about Russians, love, children, politics, and his fears for his son's future. "The Russians" was the result. The song is a musical tour de force. However, it rose to the top of the charts because his words struck a chord, which I also know from firsthand experience.

Shortly after the song came out, I took a group of students on a study tour of the Soviet Union. We were taken to a disco. None of us wanted to go, because we had all heard about how bad Russian rock and roll was. Not this disco. Somehow, the DJ had access to bootlegged copies of the latest Western hits.

After some Madonna, Hall and Oates, and Tears for Fears, he played "The Russians" and announced that there was a delegation of American students in the house that night. When the song ended, there wasn't a dry eye in the room. When our discussions that evening ended, we had done our tiny bit to end the Cold War.

THE NEW COLD WAR

When the 1980s began, few would have predicted that a new peace movement would be born, let alone that it would play a part in bringing to an end the worst threat humanity had ever faced. Indeed, when the 1970s ended, things looked pretty bleak as far as the peace movement was concerned. American hostages were held in Iran. Arms control talks had ground to a halt after President Carter announced plans to base a new generation of medium-range nuclear weapons in Europe. The Soviets invaded Afghanistan. Conflicts festered in South Africa, South America, Southeast Asia, and beyond. **Ronald Reagan** (1911–2004) seemed likely to win the 1980 presidential election in the US.

Somehow, by the time the decade ended, the Berlin Wall had come down, marking the symbolic end of the Cold War, even though the Soviet Union itself would survive for another two years.

Rediscovering the Bomb

In the 1980s, memories of the war in Vietnam were fresh in many people's minds. It therefore wasn't hard to mobilize Americans, Europeans, and others to protest the new arms race. The new peace movements, however, were much smaller and less militant than those of a generation earlier. What's more, there were few signs that they would lead to anything like modern conflict resolution and peacebuilding.

As a result, we can dispense with them quickly here before turning to the policy entrepreneurs I mentioned in chapter 4 who added the new idea of win-win conflict resolution to the age-old desire for peace.

Europe. Europeans had long assumed that World War III would begin somewhere on their continent. Adding new intermediate-range missiles only heightened popular fears about nuclear war and set off protest movements throughout Western Europe especially in the countries where the new weapons were to be based, which presumably made them some of the first targets.

Antiwar movements had sprung up throughout Europe in the 1950s. For example, the British Campaign for Nuclear Disarmament had held annual marches protesting against what we now call weapons of mass destruction since the 1950s, during which time it adopted the now-universal peace symbol.

The 1980s European peace movement did not take off immediately after Carter's announcement. It took the election of conservative leaders, most notably Margaret Thatcher in the UK and Helmut Kohl in what was then West Germany to galvanize a new generation of protesters into action. At that point, public opinion shifted dramatically. By the early 1980s, a majority of the voters in most European countries opposed deploying the new weapons. Demonstrations attracting hundreds of thousands of people were held throughout Western Europe. Protesters, for example, began camping out on Greenham Common in the United Kingdom which is adjacent to the air force base where the weapons were located.

The best lasting evidence of the change in public opinion came with the 1983 German election when the **Green Party** won seats in the Bundestag, or parliament, for the first time. Subsequently, green movements won seats in most European legislatures after running on platforms based on **deep ecology** that stressed the interdependence of all political issues, including nuclear weapons and the environment, which had a lot of parallels with systems thinking as presented in chapter 3.

Few echoes of these movements remain. Those, organizations like the green parties that do still exist have lost their radical edge. Nonetheless, they did give rise to a new generation of scholars and activists who became the architects of the NGOs and political movements that are at the heart of the conflict resolution and peacebuilding world to this day.

The United States. The renewed Cold War had a similar impact in the US, especially given liberal opposition to almost everything the Reagan administration did after it took office in 1981. That made the American protests against nuclear weapons somewhat different from those in Europe, however.

The larger and more successful American organizations did not have many links to earlier peace movements. At the time, analysts paid the most attention to activists who protested against the new administration's arms buildup, most notably the **Nuclear Freeze** movement. Its basic goal was simple enough. Randall Forsberg and her Institute for Defense and Disarmament Studies literally called for a freeze or halt in the testing, production, and deployment of nuclear weapons.

The technical complexity of the weapons themselves made negotiations complicated and hard for average citizens to follow. Once the new administration began making comments about fighting and winning a nuclear war (see chapter 6), the very simplicity of the freeze allowed the movement to take off. Public opinion polls showed widespread support for a bilateral freeze. Close to a million people demonstrated in New York in mid-1982. That march ended when a petition bearing over two million signatures was delivered to the UN. Almost two hundred Vermont communities endorsed the freeze at their annual town meetings that year. Many religious denominations endorsed the freeze. Some went even further, like the US Council of Catholic Bishops which issued an encyclical questioning whether there could ever be a just use of nuclear weapons.

As you will see in chapter 6, the freeze and other campaigns did not sway policy makers. There can be little doubt, however, that it and related movements in Europe and North America did go a long way toward building a public consensus that we should never fight in a nuclear war, a consensus that continues to this day despite the divisions over the nuclear programs in Iran and North Korea.

A more lasting impact came from what seemed like an unusual place. At the time, few of us thought of doctors as being particularly politically active, especially on the left. However, many of them ended up playing a pivotal role not only in creating the movements of the 1980s but in pointing them in directions that led to today's peacebuilding and conflict resolution communities.

A small group of doctors had formed **Physicians for Social Responsibility** in 1961 and had consistently warned about the dangers associated with nuclear energy and weapons. In the late 1970s, its incoming president, the Australian **Helen Caldicott**, helped breathe new life into the organizations by sending doctors around the country to educate their colleagues, often by graphically illustrating the nuclear threat through a video, *The Last Epidemic*, which is still worth watching today.

www.youtube.com/watch?v=omj5oEE_AdU

Others, led by Dr. Bernard Lown, began reaching out to the prominent Soviet physician Evgeni Chazov, with whom he formed **International Physicians for the Prevention of Nuclear War**, which won the 1985 Nobel Peace Prize.

Broadening the Field

In the process, European Greens, activists like Forsberg, and doctors like Caldicott, Lown, and Chazov expanded what working for peace meant. Having worked with some of their colleagues at the time, I know that none of them had anything like today's peacebuilding in mind. Nonetheless, they led us to begin thinking in three broad ways that began manifesting themselves in the initiatives to be discussed in the second half of this chapter which also remain on our agendas today.

Despair and personal power. Perhaps the most distressing and surprising evidence from this period was not the opposition to nuclear weapons per se. Rather, it was the fact that poll after poll showed that fears of a possible nuclear war skyrocketed during the decade. Books and articles bore titles like "no reason to talk about it" or "scared stiff or scared into action." Psychotherapists began holding sessions to overcome the widely felt "despair" about the state of the world. Although research on their effectiveness was limited, the sketchy evidence suggests that these workshops may not have had a lasting impact on their participants. Nonetheless, they helped convince some middle-class parents, for example, to become involved because of the worries their children talked about.

That, in turn, led some of my colleagues to begin thinking about our broader mind-sets or personal paradigms. As you will see toward the end of this chapter, those fears added to the "gloom and doom" feel of both the academic and practical sides of peacebuilding work and led me to dig deeper into those psychological dynamics and redirect my teaching and activism around possible solutions that could empower people rather than heighten their despair.

Citizen diplomacy. The doctors and others began to take what best-selling author Jonathan Schell called the fate of the earth into their own hands by engaging in citizen or **Track II diplomacy**.[1] Technically, the term Track II refers to the work of individuals who are not government officials and can explore issues and connections that people in foreign ministries would have a hard time including in their formal discussions. As we will see in part 3, Track II diplomacy has played a role in a number of the peace agreements reached since the end of the Cold War. Here, we will limit our attention to grassroots efforts, because they illustrate the diversity, creativity, and, in many cases, naïveté of the new peace movement.

Because Track II was such a new concept, it should not come as a surprise that these initiatives were all over the map. Few of them had much of an impact on the kinds of policy issues we will consider in the next chapter. Nonetheless, these efforts contributed to shifts in public opinion that, no doubt, indirectly contributed to the end of the Cold War. Emphasis on *indirectly*.

- "Sister" city projects in which people in the West decided to build connections to communities in the Soviet Union. Waterville, Maine (where I lived at the time) paired itself with Kotlas, which we discovered was so far north that it only had a forty-five day growing season which meant that you couldn't even raise radishes there. Boulder, Colorado partnered with Dushanbe in what is today's Turkmenistan. The mayor of Dushanbe was able to convince the city of Boulder to send old computers to his city. Dushanbe sent an entire tea house, which was reassembled and converted into one of Boulder's best restaurants.
- The ten-year-old Samantha Smith sent letters to Soviet leader Yuri Andropov and President Reagan urging them to end the arms race. She got a lot of publicity after Andropov invited her to visit the Soviet Union. Tragically, she got a lot more attention after she was killed in an airplane crash shortly thereafter.
- Exchange programs were established in which groups of Westerners visited the Soviet Union and a smaller number of Soviets came West. Farmers went. So did musicians. Students. Religious leaders. Former astronauts and cosmonauts created the Association of Space Explorers, which still exists today.

The collapse of communism. Many people make the case that everything covered in this chapter so far was irrelevant. As they see it, these protests had little or no impact on public policy. Instead, they believe that the Cold War really ended because unexpected events in Eastern Europe led to the sweeping changes that ended this first phase in the peace and conflict movement's history.[2]

I will defer dealing with events in the Soviet Union and Eastern Europe until chapter 6, because they had little to do with the emergence of modern peace and conflict studies, which was almost exclusively a Western phenomenon.

FOUNDING THE FIELD(S)

It is no coincidence that Harvard's Project on Negotiations is housed in a law school or that we have seen a dramatic expansion in programs that specialize in transactional disputes. It has always been easy to see the benefits of getting at least close to yes in everything from labor-management negotiations to getting a refund from eBay (which, of course, had not been invented in the 1980s).

In practice, however, the major intellectual progress on what we later called transformational conflict resolution came from new academic programs that were not housed in law schools. The first American peace studies program was created in 1948 at Manchester University in Indiana as an outgrowth of that school's affiliation with the Church of the Brethren, which is one of the so-called **peace churches** or denominations with a commitment to pacifism. Over the next four decades, other peace studies programs were created at schools affiliated with other faiths with a strong tradition of working for peace, including the Quakers (Society of Friends), Mennonites, Roman Catholics, and the Soka Gakkai community in Japanese Buddhism.

The real breakthrough came when broader programs were created at universities that focused on graduate and professional education. As noted in chapter 1, the first was located at George Mason University in the Virginia suburbs of Washington, DC. GMU was not even fifteen years old when the veteran Australian diplomat and scholar John Burton brought a team to campus and created what is now the **School for Conflict Analysis and Resolution**.

The GMU curriculum was different from those used in the original peace studies programs. Indeed, Burton always rejected using that term, and the program still has very few explicitly peace-related courses to this day. Rather, Burton focused on conflict resolution because he was convinced that disputes occur when people's **basic needs** were not being met. The school's founders also started by offering master's degrees in conflict analysis and resolution, making it the first university in the world to do so. Within a few years, it began offering PhDs as well. In the early 2000s, it added an undergraduate major, making it one of the few programs in the world to offer degrees at all three levels.

Within a decade, a number of other universities joined George Mason. The William and Flora Hewlett Foundation provided funds for the creation of what it called theory centers at GMU and other universities that had also created interdisciplinary graduate programs. Several dozen other colleges—beyond those with faith-based origins—created undergraduate majors and minors in peace and conflict studies.

A new kind of activist organization, the **nongovernmental organization (NGO)** was created, too. The word itself is a new addition to the English language that came into use with the establishment of the UN. Its charter invented the term to describe organizations other than nation-states that enjoyed an official, consultative status with the UN. Today there are probably a million NGOs or **civil society organizations (CSOs)**, as they are often known, throughout the world.

Until the 1980s, few NGOs dealt explicitly with peacebuilding or the kinds of conflict resolution discussed so far in this book. That changed in 1983 when **Search for Common Ground** was formed and was followed by dozens of similar organizations, most of which had their headquarters in the industrialized democracies in what is today referred to as the Global North.

While the term common ground is so widely used today that it often seems trite, it was a novel idea at the time. When John Marks created Search as it is commonly known, he made it clear that it was not going to be part of the traditional peace movement. Instead, he intended to stress the values embodied in its name. Rather than simply opposing war, Search literally searched for common ground along the very lines Fisher and Ury talked about.

Like many of the other groups created in the 1980s, Search for Common Ground initially focused on building bridges between American and Soviet leaders. Perhaps because he had spent a few years as a foreign service officer in the US State Department, Marks sought to create a new and more cooperative form of diplomacy. Marks is best known, however, for his use of television and radio in peacebuilding work, which led him to begin making recordings of Soviet and American thought leaders, which he distributed using a then novel piece of technology, the video cassette.

TOWARD PEACEBUILDING 1.0

I do not want to mislead you.

The Cold War was not the only problem that peace and conflict activists worried about during the 1980s. Protesters took to the streets on a number of other issues, many of which were also at the heart of what was covered in peace and conflict resolution courses at the time.

At the top of any such list were the struggles against apartheid in South Africa and opposition to the American-led wars against leftist revolutionaries in Central America. Environmental issues also grabbed our attention, most notably when the same models used to predict what a nuclear winter would be like began hinting at what we now know as climate change.

However, few of these initiatives had much of an impact on the way the field evolved after the 1980s. So, although we will deal with them later on in this book, we can put them on the intellectual back burner for now and consider other initiatives that suggested where the field would head once the Cold War ended.

To see that, focus on a subtle shift that began to take place during the second half of the 1980s that led some—but by no means all—of the activists and academics to think in terms of what I have called Peacebuilding 1.0. Nobody actually used that term during the 1980s. They couldn't have, because the idea of thinking in terms of this and that x.0 was a product of the information technology revolution that began in the 1990s.

More importantly, very few of the 1980s activists thought that they were creating an entirely new academic field or political movement anchored in the convergence of conflict resolution and peacebuilding. Instead, as you saw in the first half of this chapter, the organizations they formed and the courses academics taught grew in large part because their activists and teachers relied on what George Lopez called Gloom and Doom 101.

By the time he gave that talk in 1988, some of us were beginning to think in terms of both the deeper causes of and the potential alternatives to the status quo that bubbled to the surface with the kinds of initiatives I just mentioned. I am going to present the Peacebuilding 1.0–like ideas through my own experience during those years first in the classroom and then through my work in the Beyond War movement.

Therefore, this entire section probably deserves an Out on a Limb box, because very few of the people I worked with shared this approach to peace and conflict resolution at the time. The Beyond War movement, for example, rarely gets more a few footnotes in histories of the period. I include it in the text that follows rather than in what would have to be an overly lengthy box, because the themes I will be exploring in the rest of this chapter became common denominators of Peacebuilding 2.0 and 3.0.

The World Is Messed Up: Discuss

Even before I heard Lopez's speech, I had begun changing the way I taught all of my classes because of an unexpected encounter with a student. During the previous semester, I had team-taught an introductory course in comparative politics at Colby College. My colleagues and I could not agree on an essay question to ask in the final exam. So, we took the cowardly way out. At the beginning of the last class, I asked students to suggest questions. We would then choose the best one and use it on the exam. On my way out of the room, one of the students tapped me on the shoulder and said that the question was obvious: "The world is messed up. Discuss."[3] He was right on target. So, on the day of the final, I walked into the classroom, wrote those six words on the board, and handed out the bluebooks. The students wrote the most insightful set of final exams I have ever read.

It was obvious, too why the essays were so good.

During the semester, the students had learned what we were teaching all too well. They heard us lay the blame for the world's problems on a set of institutions, ideologies, and leaders that reflected the global distribution of power at the time.

It was also easy to read between the lines of what the students wrote and see that many of them were frustrated by our negativity and wanted a reason to be hopeful about the future. Some even wanted us to help them find ways in which they could do their part in making things better.

This is exactly what Lopez had in mind when he criticized the content of our classes and, by implication, the political movements that were being organized against the new nuclear arms race, American intervention in Central America, or the apartheid regime in South Africa. We were teaching negative courses and organizing oppositional movements that emphasized everything that was going wrong and all but ignored progress that was being made on dozens of issues all over the world.

That led me toward two decisions that reshaped my own career in way that, more importantly, are typical of the changes that led to Peacebuilding 2.0 and 3.0.

First, I realized we had to expand our audience. At the time, I knew that a majority of my students had voted for Reagan. I also knew that a lot of them shared the fears about nuclear war and the other concerns raised by the peace movement, yet were reluctant to adopt my way of thinking because they assumed that you had to be on the left to actively work for peace.

I have already pointed out that there is no logical reason why peace and, especially, conflict resolution have to be identified with the left. Indeed, you will encounter Evangelical Christians, business leaders, and even military officers who have joined forces with people who were part of this first wave of conflict resolution and peacebuilding initiatives.

In fact, there already were signs that we could have expanded our support beyond the left even at that time. Many of the leading peace organizations were faith based. Some, like the Catholic Pax Christi, had the obvious potential to reach people who had not been associated with the **new left** of the 1960s and 1970s. More generally, public opinion research conducted by Ronald Inglehart and his colleagues suggested the significant numbers of upper-middle-class young people held what he called postmaterial values that left them predisposed to support the peace, women's, and environmental movements even if they came from upper-middle-class homes and had conservative parents.[4]

Before I changed the way I taught, any hope that peacebuilding could appeal to people who did not identify with the left was little more than an abstract idea. To my surprise, my students were giving me tangible signs that we could do just that as one more story from those days attests. Even more than is the case today, Birkenstock sandals were something of a left-leaning fashion statement. Or, as the *New York Times* once put it, wearing "the sandal to represent the pushier side of liberalism is a long-running joke."[5] However, many of my cool, hip, environmentally conscious, peace-loving, feminist, and postmaterialist Republican students wore them. In fact, one day, when I was presenting Inglehart's research and using footwear as an indicator, a normally quiet student suddenly stood up, walked to the front of the room, took off her sandals, and yelled, "Hey, Chip, Republicans can wear Birkenstocks, too!"

Second, Lopez wanted us to see that Gloom and Doom 101 kept us focused primarily on what Johan Galtung called **negative peace**. Frankly, only a few of us talked or wrote about **positive peace** or **stable peace**. Scenarios that projected plausible futures did exist. We just didn't talk much about them either in our classrooms or in our grassroots organizing efforts.

To see what we were missing, consider a single, simple example that fell across my desk at about that time. An in-flight magazine from a now defunct airline carried an article on how the trillion dollars a year the world's governments then spent on the military could be used in the six-state region its flights served. I'll leave it to you to recalculate the numbers from those 1986 estimates:

> With that amount of money, we could build a $75,000 house, place it on a $5,000 plot of land, furnish it with $10,000 worth of furniture, put a $10,000 car in the garage—and give this to each and every family in Kansas, Missouri, Iowa, Nebraska, Oklahoma and Arkansas. After having done this, we would still have enough out of our trillion dollars to build a $10 million library for each of 250 cities and towns through the six-state region. After having done all that, we would still have enough money left out of our trillion to put aside, at ten percent annual interest, a sum of money that would pay a salary of $25,000 per year for an army of 10,000 nurses,

> the same for an army of 10,000 teachers, and an annual cash allowance of $5,000 for each and every family throughout that six-state region—not just for one year but forever.[6]

For good or ill, very few of my academic or political colleagues even considered the potential for organizing new supporters that was embedded in statements like this one.

Expanding the Personal

In the end, taking the peace and conflict world beyond those limits required adapting one of the key lessons from Fisher and Ury's work—reframing the terms of the debate away from Gloom and Doom 101. Again, relatively few activists or scholars did so at the time.

Beyond War did, perhaps because of its unusual origins. Its leaders had not been active in the new left in the 1960s. Instead, they had joined a spiritual and personal growth organization, Creative Initiative, which had been founded by Harry Rathbun, who was simultaneously a professor of business, engineering, and law at Stanford, and his wife, Amelia.

Creative Initiative was designed to help people take just those kinds of steps in their personal lives. Few of the organization's thousand or so active members fit anyone's stereotype of a left-wing activist. Most were successful Silicon Valley entrepreneurs or professionals in related industries who had been drawn to Creative Initiative by the Rathbuns' unique blend of science and spirituality. Many outsiders, in fact, viewed Creative Initiative as one of the many new age cults that were springing up in places like Palo Alto.

Its members had experimented with a number of other issues in the 1970s, including the environment, youth empowerment, feminism, and more before they stumbled onto nuclear weapons. In 1981, a number of them attended a conference at which Dr. Jack Geiger made the presentation mentioned on page 91. At that point, they ended all of Creative Initiative's other projects and created Beyond War as an attempt to blend ideas on the nuclear threat, interdependence (which we would now call globalization), conflict resolution, and personal responsibility for the planet and take them to the American public. Within a year, they had created a three-evening "orientation" to a world beyond war and in-depth curriculum for people who wanted to pursue those ideas further.

Shortly thereafter, seventeen families decided to give up their jobs for at least two years (yes, many of them were quite well-to-do) and move to eleven states to get the movement off the ground outside of California. It was at this point that I got involved and spent the next five years running orientations, doing broader outreach work, developing advanced curricula, and spending a sabbatical year on the organization's national staff.

Beyond War's approach set it apart from the mainstream peace movement in three ways. First, it (mistakenly) decided that it did not have to spend a lot of time trying to influence decision makers in Washington. Instead, it wanted to build networks of local activists who internalized the lessons about dealing with conflict in the nuclear age and applied them in their daily lives at home, at work, and in their communities in ways that anticipate today's emphasis on local peacebuilding. Second, given the leaders' background in Silicon Valley, Beyond War groups around the country started their efforts by reaching out to local leaders in Rotary Clubs and other networks that were rarely associated with the political left. Finally, Beyond War started using new technologies, including satellite dishes for global television transmissions, sharing video tapes with material facilitators could use in the orientations, and even using the then revolutionary tool—email. Remember, this was at a time before the modern internet existed, satellite dishes cost more than three thousand dollars in today's terms, and live video conferencing was all but unheard of.

The three hundred thousand or so people who went through the orientation had a six-hour introduction to the kinds of issues we will be covering in the rest of this book. During these sessions, people were introduced to principles of conflict resolution drawn largely from *Getting to YES* and interdependence as reflected both in spiritual traditions and simple versions of systems theory. By the end of the third evening, they would have been asked to make five key commitments that built on the principles of **nonviolence** discussed in chapter 4. The discussions went deep enough for participants to see both how these principles would change the way they dealt with conflict in their personal lives and how hard they would be to live up to:

- I will resolve conflict.
- I will not use violence.
- I will not preoccupy myself with an enemy.
- I will maintain a spirit of goodwill.
- I will work with others to build a world beyond war.

Like Search for Common Ground and the faculty members at S-CAR, Beyond War saw the connection between the kinds of conflict resolution raised by the likes of Fisher and Ury and what we later would call peacebuilding. In the process, they also got at the role that personal paradigms or mind-sets play in the way individuals respond to conflict at all levels.

Despite the breadth of its ideas, Beyond War, as such, did not survive the end of the Cold War. It had become so identified with nuclear weapons and superpower relations that it could not find a way to pivot and effectively work on other issues. Early in the 1990s, it returned to its origins as a personal growth organization with a social conscience and, as its senior leaders aged, decided to cease all operations in the early 2010s.

Yet Another Exercise

Beyond War also deserves our attention here because it asked its ten thousand most committed volunteers to delve into intra- as well as interpersonal conflict. That was the case for two reasons. First was its concern with personal growth, which long antedated its interest in nuclear weapons. Second was its focus on modes of thinking as reflected in the statement by Albert Einstein that I used to develop the idea of a paradigm shift in chapter 2 and which served as an early bridge to the field's evolution over the last thirty years.

I led a group of Beyond War volunteers in developing one more exercise that you can incorporate in the Conflict Labs in the remaining chapters of this book. It was designed to help students and workshop participants see the importance of modes of thinking or cultural norms in the ways they approach conflict. The exercise allows them to begin seeing alternatives to the status quo at everything from the interpersonal to the global level.

I have used versions of this in a variety of settings ever since. Like the exercise I used to begin this book, you can do this one on your own, but it leads to far more interesting (and unpredictable) insights when done in a group with a facilitator, so I will describe it that way here.

I first divide the participants into groups of three or four people. I ask them to discuss a global intractable conflict and focus on why we have made so little progress in solving it. After no more than five minutes, I ask each group to report out and list the reasons its members had discussed.

I have never worked with a group that had any trouble coming up with long lists of causes. I also have never had any trouble dividing their lists into two clusters which I put in separate columns. The objective issues that gave rise to the conflict in the first place go on the left side of the board. The more subjective values, attitudes, and assumptions the participants mention go on the right.

Then, I do the same for a conflict that is unfolding in their own country. The groups report out again, and I add new items to the chart from the first round. The substantive issues go on the left side next to the ones that emerged in the international discussion, and there rarely is much overlap between the two lists. That is not the case with the subjective ones. Some of the values and assumptions are new, and they get added to what is now an expanded list. However, versions of some of the subjective causes mentioned in the first round crop up again, such as fear of the other side or miscommunication. In that case, I put an asterisk next to the related term that had appeared in the first round.

Finally, I ask the small groups to have a short discussion about an interpersonal conflict, though this time I let the participants choose the one they want to talk about. After a few minutes, they report out again. As I write their ideas on the board this time, the participants begin to see that the subjective causes can be collapsed into a handful of clusters that apply at all three levels and are summarized in the left-hand column of table 5.1. Together, they give us a good first glimpse at the values underlying our personal and political paradigms regarding conflict today. The discussions do not always produce the same exact list, but something like it emerges almost all of the time, no matter who is in the audience.

The people who have taken part in this exercise over the years assume that the parties to the dispute are all trying to get their share of those scarce resources or at least to prevent the other side from doing so. We also see ourselves as independent or separate actors who pursue our self-interest in competing for those scarce resources. Table 5.1 presents that as putting "me" first. However, "me" is a metaphor that covers not only me personally but the groups I belong to and identify with. In that sense, we assume that conflict always involves an ingroup and an outgroup.

Although it does not have to turn out this way, we often demonize our adversaries by using what I have called the **image of the enemy** several times already. By doing the exercise, the participants realize that we all have a tendency to do this, which is one reason why conflict (and hence politics) can feel like a life-or-death struggle.

It is hardly surprising that we also assume that our dispute will have a **zero-sum** outcome, in which only one side can win and one side has to lose. Under the circumstances, winning matters, but not losing matters even more.

Under those circumstances, we have little choice but to think of power in the way I defined in chapter 1—"my" ability to get "you" to do something you

TABLE 5.1 Contrasting Values and Ways of Thinking

Current Values	New Thinking
Scarce resources	Scarce resources
Separate	Interdependent
Short term	Long term
Self-interest = "me" first	Self-interest = good of the whole
We versus they, image of the enemy	We with they thinking
Power over	Power with
Power = force and violence	Power = cooperation and working together
Conflict is bad	Conflict can be good

otherwise wouldn't do. As you saw on a number of occasions already in this book, we assume that the use of power will involve at least the threat, if not the actual use, of force. That force doesn't have to be physical. It can be as simple as a dean's threat to suspend students who cheat on exams—a threat I frequently hear about when I work with undergraduates!

After this often depressing discussion of our modes of thinking, I put the participants back into their small groups. This time, I ask them to think about disputes that had better outcomes.

This time, I reverse the order and start with interpersonal issues, because frankly, it is hard for people to identify examples of the kinds of bright spots we discussed in part 1 at the national or global level. Most of them, however, have seen interpersonal conflicts in which things turned out well. Many have been parties to one or more disputes of that nature.

As with the first half of the exercise, they have no trouble realizing that there are "objective" issues that gave rise to the dispute over which they have little or no control. However, they also come up with a list of "subjective" factors that stand in sharp contrast to the ones that emerged in the first half of the exercise and that end up looking like the right-hand column of table 5.1.

When I ask them to consider a national or global issue that also turned out reasonably well, they have a hard time coming up with examples. But, once they do, they again have no trouble identifying the objective causes of the dispute. More importantly, they have no trouble making a list of predispositions, values, and assumptions that allowed these conflicts to have a happier ending.

That list, too, starts with competition over scarce resources, but after that, the two differ all but completely in part because when people operate using the values in the table's right-hand column, they are already thinking in something like systems terms, even if they aren't aware of it—which is why my colleagues and I invented the exercise in the first place.

These conflicts worked out "better" because the parties to the dispute treated them as if they were part of an interconnected whole, whether that whole was an entire country or a family. In an interdependent world, it makes sense to think of our differences as something we share as well as something that divides us. That is the case because anything I do affects you and vice versa, as figure 2.4 suggests. And, if I exert power over you and force you to do what I want (and you don't), the odds are good that you will eventually react in a way that comes back to haunt me and could well do us both harm.

People tend to act in ways that are consistent with the right-hand column when they see a shared or common interest in doing so. When that happens, our goal—and often the outcome we reach—is the kind of **win-win** or **positive-sum** outcome that benefits everyone involved, including ourselves.

To that end, the technology and organizational behavior expert Clay Shirkey asks us to think about such mundane events as picnics rather than politics to help us see that we tend to cooperate whenever a group of people decide that it is in their common interest to do something like share a meal outdoors.[7] If he is right, it becomes easier and easier for people anywhere to cooperate once they see that they share common interests and problems and act accordingly. The challenge is to carry those skills over to divisive conflicts.

From this perspective, the often gloomy assumptions we make about human nature should not be taken for granted. Yes, we all have a self-interested side that leads us to try to assert power over others *some* of the time in ways that are hard-wired into our brains as a by-product of our biological evolution, a point I will return to in part 5.[8]

But we also have other built-in motivations that include a desire to cooperate and do good things for others, especially if we do well ourselves in the process, which is what win-win outcomes are all about. Under these circumstances, power itself takes on a new meaning. Power is now also something I exert *with* you. In fact, in French, the word for power (*pouvoir*) simply means to be able when used as a verb. In that sense, we can talk about empowering or enabling others to accomplish things.

From this perspective, conflict can actually even be a good thing. Rather than the vicious cycles that grow out of the traditional paradigm as a result of dealing with problems using the left-hand column of table 5.1, our actions can lead to what complexity theorists refer to as virtuous circles in which success builds on itself and progress gets taken to scale.

What's more, thinking this way can take us back to Friedman's fork in the road and Keltner's redefinition of power that you saw in chapter 2. If I'm right, we really can rethink what we mean by power and use it to take a hopeful fork in the road.

The exercise also has an even deeper pedagogical lesson—assuming your version of it turned out the way mine usually does—which I have depicted in figure 5.1. In particular, you will see that these first-generation peacebuilding groups—especially groups like Beyond War—did not pay that much attention to the questions in the bottom half of this figure. In particular, we simply assumed that if we produced a paradigm shift in the way people thought, which led them to live according to the principles discussed on page 99, we would address the root causes of the issues that gave rise to the conflict.

FIGURE 5.1
Modes of Thinking

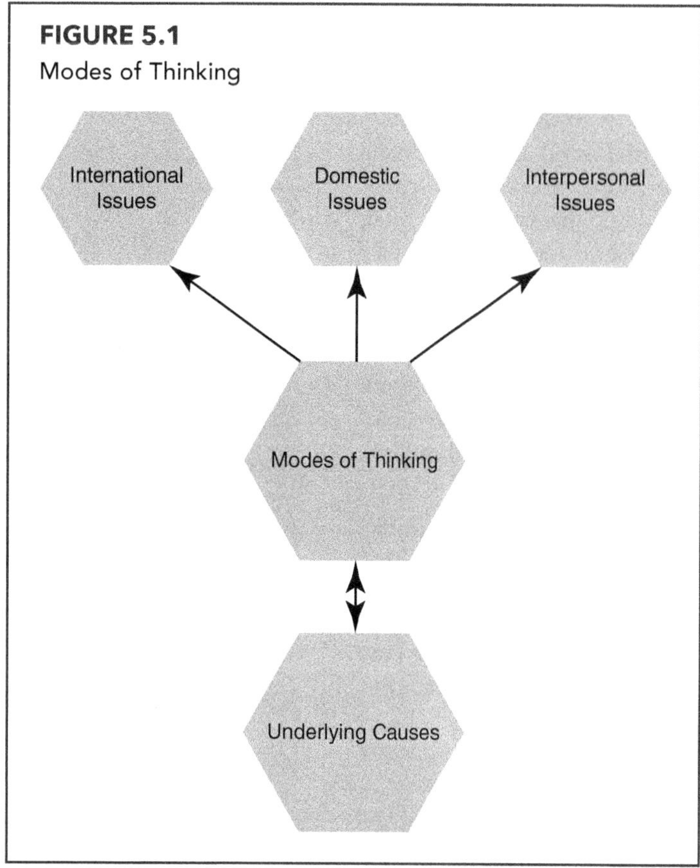

Put simply, we were wrong on that front. Or maybe just naive. Questions of power will occupy intellectual center stage more and more as this book wears on.

Figure 5.1 does not suggest that the underlying causes of a dispute that showed up in the left-hand column of my whiteboard are irrelevant. They are, indeed, the root causes of the disputes because they reflect, for example, what John Burton referred to as unmet human needs. However, the ways we react to the dispute are determined largely by our modes of thinking, which is another way of referring to our personal paradigms.

Even more importantly, the second half of the exercise suggests that those modes of thinking are not set in stone. Later chapters will explore ways in which my colleagues have helped people address their personal mind-sets which could then become the first steps in a broader paradigm shift. For now, it is enough to see how the Beyond War exercise opens the door to a theory of change that includes and often emphasizes the role of the individual in larger-scale social and political transformations.

TOWARD PUBLIC JUDGMENT

This chapter covered a decade-long period that began with heightened Cold War tensions and ended with the collapse of the Soviet Union. After the red flag was lowered from the Kremlin for the last time in 1991, the issues that preoccupied us in the 1980s all but disappeared from the global agenda. Totally different ones took their place, including quite a few we should have paid more attention to at the time.

Before leaving that decade's grassroots peace movements behind, however, there is one last idea to consider, because it, too, will feature prominently, especially in part 5 where we will consider the future of peacebuilding, including your role in it.

In the late 1980s, the pollster and philosopher Daniel Yankelovich wrote about the difference between public opinion and **public judgment**. After thirty years as a pollster, he knew that public opinion can be fickle. Most people do not pay much attention to the details of public policy debates. As a result, their attitudes about most issues tend to change with the times and are often all over the political map.

Occasionally, however, something else happens. Attention gets riveted on a particularly important issue at a particularly difficult time. As that happens, community leaders begin talking about that issue and then take action on it, as happened in the 1950s and 1960s with civil rights in the US. At that point,

CONFLICT LAB 5

The personal or local conflict you chose to discuss in chapter 1 may not have existed during this first period. If it had, it certainly would have played itself out quite differently than it does today. Still, it is worth asking how people at the time would have dealt with it, given the peacebuilding and conflict resolution tools they had at their disposal in the 1980s.

Do a quick version of it using the exercise outlined on page 99. Do take note of the objective divisions that gave rise to the dispute in the first place and made it hard to resolve. However, focus on the ways our personal paradigms or modes of thinking about conflict shape our responses as well.

a population can very quickly reach a new consensus or public judgment on at least this one issue.

We probably reached something akin to public judgment on nuclear weapons during the 1980s. We can see that indirectly in the way popular culture changed during that decade.

In the early 1980s, the American and Soviet media were filled with shows that depicted the other side as evil empires—to use Reagan's term for the USSR. By the end of the decade, there were still plenty of anti-Soviet and anti-American shows on their respective televisions. Nonetheless, activists like Samantha Smith became household names. Gorbachev was named *Time* magazine's man of the decade for the 1980s—an award it had never given before. Shoddily made Soviet goods became trendy and were sold in some of New York's leading stores. Films like *Threads* in the UK and *The Day After* in the US filled the airwaves.

Nothing reflects the uncertainties of the day or the shifting public attitudes toward nuclear war than Sting's song.

www.youtube.com/watch?v=wHylQRVN2Qs

Based on music by the Russian composer Sergei Prokofiev, Sting crystallized the fears that were rumbling around in the heads of millions of people around the world and reflected the emerging public judgment of the time.

> Mister Khrushchev said, "We will bury you"
> I don't subscribe to this point of view
> It'd be such an ignorant thing to do
> If the Russians love their children too

Much of the world also reached something like a public judgment about one set of issues underlying the superpower rivalry—Marxism, communism, and the political movements they inspired. For good or ill, they disappeared as goals that could inspire social change activists or their more conservative opponents. That change was so sweeping and so unexpected that some analysts echoed Presidents Gorbachev and George H. W. Bush, who spoke evocatively about the birth of a new world order.

We may have reached public judgment on nuclear weapons and communism, but we certainly have not on the broader set of issues that give rise to the kinds of disputes you discussed in doing the exercise that led to figure 4.1. That is what parts 3 through 5 are all about. Especially part 5.

KEY TERMS

Concepts

basic needs, 93
civil society organizations (CSOs), 94
deep ecology, 90
image of the enemy, 99
negative peace, 96
new left, 96
nongovernmental organization (NGO), 94
nonviolence, 98
peace churches, 93
positive peace, 96
positive-sum, 101
public judgment, 102
stable peace, 96
Track II diplomacy, 92
win-win, 101
zero-sum, 99

People

Caldicott, Helen, 91
Gorbachev, Mikhail, 93
Reagan, Ronald, 89

Organizations, Places, and Events

Green Party, 90
International Physicians for the Prevention of Nuclear War (IPPNW), 91
Nuclear Freeze, 91
Physicians for Social Responsibility, 91
School for Conflict Analysis and Resolution (George Mason), 93
Search for Common Ground, 94

DIG DEEPER

Cortright, David. *Peace Works: The Citizen's Role in Ending the Cold War.* Boulder, CO: Westview, 1993. Written by a leading activist in those days and now, this book focuses on the freeze and related movements.

Lofland, John. *Polite Protesters: The American Peace Movement of the 1980s.* Syracuse, NY: Syracuse University Press, 1993. The best analysis of the 1980s protests in the United States.

Macy, Joanna Rogers. *Despair and Personal Power in the Nuclear Age.* Philadelphia: New Society, 1982. Obviously dated, but her exercises can easily be updated for today's events.

Michnik, Adam. *Letters from Prison.* Berkeley: University of California Press, 1987. The best analysis of what happened in Eastern Europe. Jonathan Schell's introduction is also worth reading.

Schell, Jonathan. *The Fate of the Earth.* New York: Knopf, 1982. The best book on what nuclear war would be like.

NOTES

[1] Jonathan Schell, *The Fate of the Earth* (New York: Knopf, 1982).

[2] For more detailed information, see Charles Hauss, *Comparative Politics: Domestic Responses to Global Challenges*, 10th ed. (Belmont, CA: Cengage, 2018), part 3.

[3] In fact, he used a different adjective beginning with *f*, which my editor asked me not to use in this book.

[4] The best source is Ronald Inglehart, *The Silent Revolution: Changing Values and Political Styles in Western Publics* (Princeton, NJ: Princeton University Press, 1977).

[5] Coelli Carr, "Thank You for Insulting My Sandals," *New York Times*, March 12, 2006, www.nytimes.com/2006/03/12/fashion/sundaystyles/thank-you-for-insulting-our-sandals.html. Also Charles Hauss, *Beyond Confrontation: Transforming the New World Order* (Westport, CT: Greenwood, 1996), 188.

[6] Harry G. Shaffer, "A Trillion Dollars," *Republic Airlines Magazine*, May 1986, 24.

[7] Clay Shirkey, *Cognitive Surplus: How Technology Makes Consumers into Collaborators* (New York: Penguin, 2011).

[8] Nicholas Christakis, *Blueprint: The Evolutionary Origins of a Good Society* (Boston: Little, Brown, 2019).

CHAPTER 6

Far from the Grown-ups' Table

THINK ABOUT IT

This will be one of the shortest chapters in *From Conflict Resolution to Peacebuilding* because neither conflict resolution professionals nor peacebuilding activists had much of an impact on the momentous events that shook the world in the second half of the 1980s. That said, there are four key questions to ask about what they did accomplish during these years:

- Why weren't we at the grown-ups' table? Or, in more conventional terms, why did most activists treat the state as an adversary, and how could Western leaders pretty much ignore us?
- Why did some activists choose to become what we call polite protesters, while others followed a more adversarial path?
- If you accept the argument that the peace movements of the 1980s had at most a limited effect on the events of those years, why did the Cold War end?
- How did the events of the 1980s set the stage for the peace and conflict studies initiatives of later years, or is this chapter largely an exploration of bygone and largely irrelevant events?

CORE CONCEPTS

contentious politics—involves the use of disruptive tactics to change state policy

grown-ups' table—a metaphor for our access or lack thereof to major public policy making circles

polite protesters—the notion that protesters limit themselves to what 1960s activists used to call "inside the system" activities;

public policy—the process by which governments at all levels determine what they will do

self-limiting revolution—the notion that protesters would end or limit their revolution if and when they felt the need to run violent

Don't worry, if there's a nuclear war, if there are enough shovels to go around, we're all going to make it.

—*T. K. Jones*

THIS CHAPTER STARTS WITH a paradox. On the one hand, conflict resolution and peacebuilding professionals demanded dramatic policy changes during the 1980s. On the other, they had next to no chance of turning those demands into reality, because they were mostly ignored by the powers that be.

In some cases that was our own doing. Many mediators and other conflict resolution professionals have always shied away from getting involved in what they see as divisive political issues. With good reason, they feared that doing so would compromise their neutrality.

That caveat aside, most of us would have loved to have steered public policy on the arms race and other issues of the day in another direction. While we tried, we failed to do so.

To begin seeing why, recall Julia Roig's concern that we did not have a place at the grown-ups' table when key decisions involving national or global security were made, which I introduced in part 1. There, I also noted that she was probably right when describing these early years. Now, you will see why that was the case.

And that the world changed anyway.

WHAT GROWN-UPS' TABLE?

Obviously, Roig was not thinking about a physical grown-ups' table at a holiday dinner party. Instead, she had an imaginary one in mind that she used as a metaphor while lamenting the fact that policy makers in Washington and other national capitals did not include us when they made the decisions that shaped people's lives.

I agree with Roig. The peacebuilding community does need a more prominent place at that "table" today. We will see in parts 3 and 4 that we have inched closer to the grown-ups' table and—to continue to use her metaphor—are now sometimes invited to at least have a snack at it.

Wherever we stand (or sit) vis-à-vis that table today, Roig certainly was right about the 1980s. Virtually all of the activists and intellectuals discussed in chapter 5 were on the outside looking in when policy makers around the world were considering what Jonathan Schell ominously called the fate of the earth. Two examples, which will probably strike you as absurd today, illustrate just how weak we were.

With Enough Shovels

The first starts with the statement by T. K. Jones that begins this chapter. Jones was a little-known physicist who was serving as a deputy undersecretary of defense in the Reagan administration when he included this sentence in an interview with a reporter from the *Los Angeles Times*. Needless to say, the small antiwar movement seized on his words and used them to build support for their protests against the renewed arms race.

Reading the interview thirty-five years later, it is hard not to laugh at Jones's naive belief that we could build enough shelters for a majority of the American (or Soviet) people to survive an all-out nuclear exchange as such a war was euphemistically known. In fact, statements like his made as little sense then as claims that climate change might not be the result of human activity do today.

As absurd as his common might seem in retrospect, Jones was very much part of the national security mainstream at the time. He may have been a bit more colorful and a bit more outspoken than other members of the administration—but not by a lot. After all, Reagan had won the 1980 presidential election in large part because he promised to update the American nuclear arsenal and, more generally, build what conservatives at the time called peace through strength.

Statements like these may have filled the ranks of the newly rejuvenated peace movements discussed in chapter 5. At the same time, those activists realized that the likes of T. K. Jones were not about to listen to them.

In other words, they knew that there was no place for them at the grown-ups' table. Even if peace activists of the day somehow got the chance to sit down with policy makers, everyone assumed that their relationship would be testy—at best.

Patting the Warheads

In 1984, Harvard and MIT invited forty-eight liberal arts college faculty members who were interested in teaching about the arms race to attend a two-week seminar. I was one of them, but it was Carol Cohn's reaction to what we learned that shows just how isolated we were and how out of place we would have felt if we did have a seat at the table.

As a feminist scholar, Cohn was initially flabbergasted by the absence of women on the seminar's teaching staff. As the seminar wore on, other things bothered her even more, including the often dehumanizing language the instructors used and what it told us about elite-level national security policy making.[1]

Cohn was on target in that respect (pun intended). The weapons experts we heard truly spoke in a language of their own that was filled with bizarre acronyms that they then tried to pronounce and assumed the participants would understand. Submarine-launched cruise missiles became SLCMs and then Slick 'ems. When launched from the ground, of course, their equivalents became GLCMs and Glick 'ems.

These weapons of mass destruction somehow became little more than commodities that you could trade like baseball cards. Though Cohn doesn't mention it in her own articles, I remember being shocked when a faculty member pulled a special slide rule (page 108) out of his briefcase and showed how it could calculate the damage that would be done by a nuclear bomb of a certain size that exploded at a particular height over a city with a given population and a specific set of weather conditions.

Cohn was particularly concerned when the group went to the nuclear submarine base in New London/Groton, Connecticut, which also happens to be

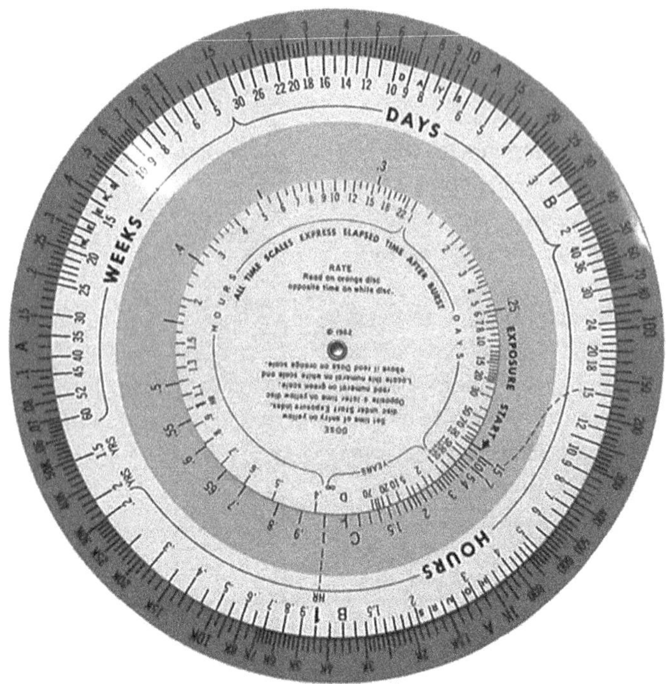

A Nuclear Weapons Slide Rule

my hometown. While there, one of the experts said that the main reason we were deploying GLCMs in Europe was so that our allies could "pat" the missiles.

Cohn knew that the men who taught the course were not warmongers. Most believed in some form of arms control and were critical of the more aggressive policies then being proposed by the Reagan administration. But even here, they made it clear how much distance there was between the kinds of positions advocated by the Freeze Campaign and what they, the experts, were willing to endorse. Thus, George Rathjens, a physicist who worked on the original atomic bomb, pointed out that we would have had to eliminate about ninety-five percent of the world's nuclear weapons to reach a point that a war would not endanger civilization as we knew it. They wanted to make certain that critics like Cohn (and me) knew that that was not about to happen.

Theirs was a world in which diplomatic and military expertise mattered. Trust was in short supply, as Sting's song "The Russians" suggested (see the end of chapter 5). Agreements were all but impossible to come by. Confidence in the other side's motivations was low, as reflected in President Reagan's famous line "trust, but verify."

What a Difference a Decade Makes

The world looked very different by the time the decade ended. Leaders like T. K. Jones were long gone. The Cold War was over and took the threat of an all-out nuclear war with it for the next thirty years—and counting. The missiles and the scientists that Cohn worried about were still around, but they didn't seem as frightening.

That does not mean, however, that peacebuilding and conflict resolution activists made all that happen. Historians still debate how and why the superpower rivalry ended and whether the world is better off as a result. We are rarely mentioned in their accounts.

The *most* we could say about our role is that we had an impact on the margins. The changes in norms and public opinion discussed in chapter 5 did help set the stage for the remarkable events of the second half of the 1980s. But frankly, the changes you are about to read about occurred as a result of decisions made at grown-ups' tables around the world that did not have a place for us.

TENTATIVE STEPS TOWARD THE TABLE

I introduced the idea of **theories of change** in chapter 3 and suggested that it only entered our work in this century. Even though no one used the term, per se, in the 1980s, activists and academics alike made certain assumptions about how they should try to affect the policy-making community. Before we get to that discussion, we do have to add a new concept.

I have intentionally been vague about what we mean by policy or decision makers, let alone the grown-ups' table. Critical here is the political scientist's understanding of the **state**, which also became an important topic in scholarly research during these same years for reasons that had nothing to do with peace and conflict studies.

The generation of political scientists who came of age at that time drew a distinction between the formal governmental institutions and the state, which, they held, was where real power resided. They drew on the earlier work of Max Weber who claimed that the state included all actors who exercised the legitimate use of force in a given territory. In other words, the state includes most government institutions, but it also encompasses corporate leaders and even officials of international governmental organizations that played a role in making those decisions.

We also realized that it is difficult, if not impossible, to measure the impact that the peace movement or anyone else actually has over the state. At a time when social scientists in general were becoming increasingly quantitative, we found ourselves struggling to find ways of systematically measuring that impact. That was especially true when it came to the kinds of issues we would later call wicked problems. Still, even for the seemingly simpler issues facing a bipolar world, it was hard to determine how much any one set of actors contributed to any one set of decisions, including one as important as ending the Cold War.

That said, it is safe to say that most peace and conflict resolution activists assumed that they were in the opposition. They did not agree on how best to act on their disdain for the conservative politics of the day. Still, they fell into two broad camps, which we will see first in the relatively tame protest movements in Western Europe and the US and in the nonviolent revolutions that swept the Soviet bloc.

Polite Protesters

Despite the swing in public opinion that we saw in chapter 5, it is hard to make the case that the protest movements in Western Europe and North America had much to do with ending the Cold War. The shift away from détente actually began before **Margaret Thatcher** (1925–2013) and **Ronald Reagan** took office in 1979 and 1981, respectively. The SALT II treaty failed to get the votes needed for ratification by the US Senate. By the time that happened, both the US and the Soviet Union had begun deploying the new short- and medium-range missiles Cohn objected to, which reduced the time between launch and detonation of a warhead to as little as nine minutes, whether that weapon was fired from European land bases or a new generation of submarines.

The 1980s did not get off to a good start as far as peace activists and their allies were concerned. Thatcher and Reagan did not owe their victories to their foreign policy stands alone. To the degree they did, however, they won because a series of events—including the OPEC oil embargos, civil wars in Central America, and the overthrow of the Shah and the hostage crisis in Iran—eroded support for cooperative initiatives in foreign policy. More generally, the conservative leaders reflected the newfound popularity of what are often referred to as **neoliberal** policies at home and abroad. Meanwhile, the Soviet-American détente of the late 1960s and early 1970s deteriorated when it became clear that neither side was willing to budge on key issues that held up arms control negotiations. Thing got even worse after Soviet troops invaded Afghanistan at the end of 1979.

Then as now, there was no single or unified peace movement. The many competing organizations lacked a clear consensus either about what the issues were or on strategies for addressing them. If the movement(s) agreed about anything, it was their focus on what Johan Galtung called negative peace. Rarely did activists get beyond their anger and fear to propose anything that looked even vaguely constructive and realistic. It would be another decade before analysts and activists took the positive side of the peacebuilding equation seriously.

Most of the new activists who opposed that rightward drift chose to become what John Lofland called **polite protesters**. As is always the case, the new peace movement of the 1980s did not emerge out of political thin air. As I suggested in chapter 5, these protests helped breathe new life into a number of arms control and other movements that had grown out of early "ban the bomb" efforts, most of which had been eclipsed by the civil rights and antiwar protests of the 1960s.

Whether in the streets or in the halls of Congress, these were polite protesters indeed. Millions of people may have opposed the arms buildup and renewed tensions with the Soviet bloc; however, fewer than two hundred people were arrested as a result of their participation in demonstrations in the US in any year during the 1980s.

Thus, no one was surprised when organizations like the Arms Control Association or the Council for a Livable World along with the movements discussed in chapter 5 failed to sway the new generation of conservative leaders. They had no trouble amassing evidence that showed how the arms buildup that Reagan and Thatcher pushed through would worsen superpower relations.

For instance, they developed models that suggested that the likelihood of accidents would grow as the time between the launch of a weapon and its impact was reduced because it also shortened the amount of time leaders would have to verify that an attack actually was—or was not—taking place.

Then, in the middle of the decade, climate scientists developed plausible models of the long-term effects of a "nuclear winter" even in places where no bombs landed. Ironically, these hypotheses were based on research tools that would later be used in today's cutting-edge models regarding climate change. Last, but by no means least, many members of the aging generation of scientists that built the first bomb became strident opponents of the arms race and rallied to organizations like the Federation of Atomic Scientists and its famous nuclear clock, which all of a sudden started reading five, four, or three minutes to midnight. In short, whether you looked at the demonstrations in the streets or congressional hearing rooms, the evidence in support of arms control and slowing down the arms race seemed overwhelming.

Yet, the new organizations discussed in chapter 5 also found themselves far from the grown-ups' table. The academics largely stayed on the sidelines. If they got involved, it was in the movements of polite protesters. Beyond War decided not even to try to influence policy makers. None of its founding families moved to the Washington, DC, area, because its leaders mistakenly assumed that shifts in public opinion would automatically result in a corresponding shift in **public policy**, which did not happen. Even Search for Common Ground, which did engage in Track II diplomacy, enjoyed little success in convincing the Reagan administration that change was needed.

For good or ill, Reagan, Thatcher, and the other newly elected conservative leaders proved popular enough to withstand those protests. What looked like a conservative blip in 1979 and 1980 became a generation-defining electoral tidal wave that largely continues to this day. Despite the protests in the US, Great Britain, and Germany, not only were the GLCMs, SLCMs, and other new weapons systems deployed but conservative leaders were reelected with record levels of support. Even France's newly elected socialist government showed little interest in supporting a fresh approach to either nuclear weapons or the Cold War in general.

If anything, incumbent leaders treated the opposition with disdain. A single example should suffice. Secretary of state George Schultz publicly dismissed Helen Caldicott's critiques because she was a woman and therefore could not possibly be as well informed as the diplomats and other supposed experts who were, of course, men. Highly publicized events like that were just the tip of the iceberg. Peace activists were rarely listened to even by academics, who filled new institutes created to study arms control and other "inside the system" responses to the arms buildup.

What little impact the peace movement had peaked in the middle of the decade and then began to decline. Green members were elected to the German Bundestag (parliament) in 1983. However, support for the American and European peace movements evaporated because they had not been able to develop what internet analysts today call **stickiness**. They could get people to turn out for the occasional demonstration and even donate some money to the cause. However, few of them succeeded in recruiting and retaining activists who made the kind of long-term commitment that a paradigm shift would require.

The Collapse of Communism

Events on the other side of the Iron Curtain were far more surprising and had a much bigger impact than anything that happened in Western Europe or the US. In little more than a blink of a historical eye, dissidents overthrew what seemed like permanently entrenched communist regimes. In other words, unlike the peace movements in the West, they not only got to the grown-ups' table, but they threw the previous occupants out of the dining room in the process.

The events that destroyed communism in Eurasia after 1985 had little to do with the peace movements in the West. However, they had a huge impact on the way our field evolved because they dramatically changed the political world we operated in. As you will begin to see toward the end of this chapter and then will explore in much more detail in parts 3 and 4, we shifted our attention to the rest of the world, which, in turn, required moving beyond "simply" reaching win-win outcomes and addressing the underlying root causes of conflict.

The Soviet bloc countries were governed by all-powerful communist parties when the 1980s began. Protesting against regimes that dominated almost all aspects of people's lives was dangerous and seemed fruitless. Yet, before the decade was out, nonviolent revolutions swept those regimes from power. A mere two years later, the Soviet Union itself was gone.

How and why that happened is still the subject of academic and political debate. However, there can be no doubt that the protest movements we are about to see helped produce one of the most dramatic shifts in global politics in centuries and did so in ways that had equally dramatic implications for peacebuilding and conflict resolution.

To get a taste of the events and their longer-term implications, consider how Rachel Kleinfeld described them in her recent book on political turmoil:

> Ordinary people brought down the totalitarian empire. Young people wanting to wear jeans and listen to rock and roll, families wanting more for their children's futures, and apparatchiks who could no longer believe in the crushing gray system they served ended an evil regime. You did not need to be a superhero to change history. You did not need to be a politician. Peaceful protest could make a difference.[2]

Gorbachev and new thinking. The fireworks began shortly after **Mikhail Gorbachev** (1931–) became secretary general of the Communist Party of the Soviet Union in 1985. That title might not seem like much today, but at the time, holding that office meant that Gorbachev was the all but unquestioned leader of one of the two seemingly invincible superpowers.

The Soviet Union and its allies no longer were the totalitarian countries many in the West had labeled them a generation earlier. Still, anyone who spoke out against the regime or its policies ran risks that included everything from a ruined career to time in prison.

Revolutionary change did not seem to be in the cards. In fact, when I led a student group to the USSR in early 1986, we met plenty of young people who wanted to buy our jeans and listen to American music. However, we saw no signs that the country was on the verge of falling apart.

Gorbachev was a generation younger than the men he replaced and there were signs that he was something of a reformer even before he reached the top. Still, when Gorbachev came to power, he was still a dedicated Marxist and led the most powerful politician in the second most powerful country on earth.

In short, no one knew what to expect. So, the outside world watched attentively when Gorbachev made his first trip abroad as heir apparent to the ailing leader, Konstantin Chrernenko, in December 1984.

Serge Schmeman, the *New York Times* bureau chief in Moscow, put those uncertainties particularly well in his coverage of that trip. He began his report with Gorbachev's departure. Dressed in a somber gray suit, Gorbachev shook the hands of his equally somberly dressed colleagues who had come to see him off at the Moscow airport. Out of public view his wife Raisa walked up the back ramp onto the plane. When they arrived in London, however, they emerged from the airplane together, wearing colorful Western-style clothes, and enthusiastically greeted the crowd.

Which one, Schmeman wondered, was the real Gorbachev?

It didn't take long for us to find out.

Mikhail Gorbachev and Ronald Reagan at the 1986 Reykjavik Summit

Gorbachev is better known today for the way his ill-conceived domestic reforms helped destroy his country than for his bold moves at home and abroad. Members of his leadership team quickly discovered that they had no choice but to act decisively because their country lagged dramatically behind the West on almost every indicator imaginable. After a few months spent fruitlessly experimenting with incremental political changes, he and his colleagues opened up their political system and started doing the same in the economy, all of which unleashed decades of pent-up resentment. Soon that dissent would tear the country apart and doom not only the reforms but the Soviet Union itself.

As a result, we tend to forget that his team went further and enjoyed plenty of success in foreign policy. At what everyone assumed would be a minor summit in Reykjavik, Iceland in 1986 Gorbachev proposed a dramatic cut in both sides nuclear arsenals. The two leaders came surprisingly close to reaching an agreement before Reagan's aides convinced him not to accept the offer. Still, the momentum in the relationship between the superpowers had suddenly swung toward peace. The two sides soon reached an agreement to reduce the number of those intermediate-range nuclear weapons that had inspired the new peace movement in the West. In ways we do not need to go into here, the superpower relationship continued to improve to the point that you could almost say that Reagan and Gorbachev had become friends by the time the American president left office in January 1989.

We should not, however, lose sight of the fact that Gorbachev's analyses and policy proposals were sweeping enough for some of us to think of them as a paradigm shift in the making, which is how I presented them to my classes at the time. In fact, he referred to his work as ***perestroika***, or "new thinking." While those terms were used primarily to describe his failed economic reforms, Gorbachev himself thought of them as shorthand for everything he tried to accomplish as he made clear in his book of the same name.

He pulled those ideas together in ways that anticipate systems thinking in the peacebuilding community in his remarkable address to the UN in 1988, just as President Reagan was about to leave office and his own "empire" was beginning to collapse:

> Further world progress is now possible only through the search for a consensus of all mankind, in movement toward a new world order. We have arrived at a frontier at which controlled spontaneity leads to a dead end. The world community must learn to shape and direct the process in such a way as to preserve civilization, to make it safe for all and more pleasant for normal life. It is a question of cooperation that could be more accurately called "co-creation" and "co-development." The formula of development "at another's expense" is becoming outdated. In light of present realities, genuine progress by infringing upon the rights and liberties of man and peoples, or at the expense of nature, is impossible.[3]

Gorbachev, of course, was not the only prominent person who thought along these lines. German (and other) Greens, for instance, spoke of deep ecology. Still, he was the first national leader to use these terms, which gave rise to much of the discussion of a **new world order** during the next few years—the collapse of which we will turn to in part 3 and, especially, part 4.

Revolution in Eastern Europe. Although it was not obvious at the time, the political momentum was also shifting to Eastern Europe, where the Soviet Union had imposed regimes very much like its own after World War II. Soviet leader Josef Stalin assumed that the Soviet Union needed these countries to protect it from an invasion that he assumed would be launched from western Europe and lead to World War III. Once the Cold War solidified, Western observers began to call these countries Soviet satellites.

Unlike the Soviet Union itself, Eastern Europeans periodically protested against communist rule, most notably in East Germany (1953), Hungary and Poland (1956), and Czechoslovakia (1968). Each time the USSR was able to reimpose its control and each time it did so, resentment continued to build.

Few observers realized just how deep the resentment was until protesters occupied the Lenin shipyards in the Polish city of Gdansk in 1979. This time, the workers organized themselves into a formal union, **Solidarity**, that was supported by a network of intellectuals known as KOR (Workers Defense Committee). Poland was also the one communist country in which farmers owned their own land. It also had a reasonably independent Catholic Church whose leader, Karol Wotyla, had just been named the first non-Italian pope in centuries.

To make a long story short, Solidarity became the first independent organization that the authorities allowed to operate openly in any communist country. Its leader, **Lech Walesa**, became a fixture on the nightly news around the world, as did footage of average Poles sending food to support the workers who were occupying the shipyard. Then, to the surprise of people around the world, the protests spread across the country.

Solidarity continued to grow until Soviet leaders feared it might actually pose a threat to the Polish regime—and conceivably to their own. At the end of 1981, Marshal Wojciech Jaruzelski imposed martial law, almost certainly after the Soviet leadership demanded that he do so. Most opposition leaders were arrested and sentenced to lengthy prison terms. More than ninety protesters were killed. Although military rule only formally lasted for two years, Jaruzelski continued to run the communist party and, hence, the government until the regime collapsed.

In retrospect, one key to this period was Adam Michnik's notion of a **self-limiting revolution**. Solidarity had always committed itself to nonviolence. However, there were fears that it would not be able to keep its pledge when and if the authorities cracked down and imprisoned dozens of Solidarity leaders, including Michnik. Sympathetic guards started smuggling his letters out of prison. In them, he made it clear that Solidarity had willingly suspended its contentious activities because continuing the movement would have required meeting the state's violence with violence of its own. It had not given up, but it would regroup underground so that it could have an even bigger impact when it could act openly again.

They did not have to wait long. A new wave of protests broke out in 1988, this time starting in Hungary. The hard-line communist rulers there that had been put in power after the Soviet invasion of 1956. Some of the country's younger leaders had begun experimenting with reforms that introduced market principles into the economy that also challenged communist party hegemony. Demonstrations then broke out against the aging, hard-line communist leadership in East Germany. These developments came to a head when Hungarian officials began dismantling the barbed wire fence that made up most of the Iron Curtain in 1989, allowing thousands of East German "tourists" to escape to the West. Protests spread to Poland and Czechoslovakia and then culminated in the destruction of the Berlin Wall on November 9, 1989, as depicted in the photograph at the beginning of this chapter. Two years later, the Soviet Union itself disintegrated.

There were lots of remarkable things about the end of the Cold War. High on any list of them has to be the commitment to nonviolence. In Poland, Hungary, Czechoslovakia, Bulgaria, and East Germany, only a single person was killed in 1988 and 1989—and that was an accidental drowning. There was violence towards the end of the uprising in Romania, but almost none of that was initiated by the protesters.

The protest movements accomplished many things, including bringing nonviolent regime change back onto the world's political agenda. Such movements had led to independence in India and had inspired the American civil rights and antiwar demonstrations in the 1960s. However, the end of the Cold War built new support, in particular, for the ideas developed by **Gene Sharp** (1928–2018), which would go on to inspire other nonviolent insurgencies in authoritarian regimes.[4]

As we will see in the part 3, there was a civil war in Yugoslavia, although it had little to do with the protests that swept communism from power in the rest of Eastern Europe. And the current governments of Hungary and Poland have distanced themselves from nonviolence and the other values that shaped their revolutions barely a quarter of a century ago.

Still, the revolutions in Eastern Europe did set the stage for much of what was to follow, as we will see in the rest of this book.

CONFLICT LAB 6

Take the national or global conflict you discussed in the exercise in chapter 1. In all likelihood, it did not yet exist during the 1980s, at least in its current form. The concepts covered in this chapter should still be able to help you understand it. So, ask yourself these two sets of questions:

- What kind of "polite protest" tactics have been used to address that conflict? How successful have they been? Why have they been less successful than their participants wanted?
- Which contending groups are trying to exert pressure on the state or states involved? Have they had to make a choice about using violence? If so, what did they decide to do, and why did they decide to do it? Whatever tactics they chose, have they been successful? Why (not)?

What About South Africa? And Beyond?

You could properly ask why I did not include the transition to a multiracial democracy in South Africa in this section. After all, the wave of protests that undermined apartheid reached a peak in the late 1980s, and Nelson Mandela was released from prison in 1990, more than a year before the Soviet Union collapsed.

The Cold War did have a lot to do with events in South Africa, and its end did dim the already fading staying power of the White government. However, it makes more sense for our purposes to think of the South African struggle as the first example of the highly visible identity-based conflicts that defined the second period in the history of conflict resolution and peacebuilding.

South Africa, of course, was not the only place where conflict raged during the 1980s. They, too will appear in later chapters, because my goal in part 2 was to get you to see how modern conflict resolution and peacebuilding came together to form this field during that decade. Those other issues and other places were important, but they would have taken us away from the core narrative.

Don't worry. We will get to them. Soon.

MISSING LINKS AND LURKING IDEAS

We should not end part 2 without considering two things that happened in the 1980s, that did not fit into either this chapter or the previous one, but which will figure prominently in the pages to come.

The United Nations

It may have surprised you that the **UN** did not feature in this chapter. After all, it was created in 1945 to provide an alternative to war. Yet, we could ignore it here for one simple reason: Cold War tensions between the US and the Soviet Union made the UN and the international community in general all but irrelevant. Whenever one or the other superpower determined that its interests were being threatened, it used its **veto power** in the UN **Security Council**, thereby preventing the UN from acting decisively during most the crises during the Cold War years.

The UN was not totally paralyzed. The US and its allies did take advantage of a Soviet absence to authorize sending UN troops for what became the Korean War. Similarly, UN peacekeepers were deployed when it was either in the interests of both superpowers or when neither of them had much "skin in the game." That was the case, most notably, when UN peacekeepers were sent to the Sinai Peninsula after the 1956 war between Israel and its Arab neighbors. As a result, we can defer talking about the UN in any depth until parts 3 and 4, because it was only after the end of the Cold War that then secretary general Boutros Boutros-Ghali laid them out in a systematic manner.

United States Institute of Peace—The Exception That Proves the Rule

Peace activists did score one major victory in the US, although many of my colleagues scoffed at it at the time. In 1983, President Reagan bowed to pressure and signed into law a bill creating the **United States Institute of Peace (USIP)**.

The United States Institute of Peace, Washington, DC

Beginning in the early 1970s, a group of activists began lobbying for the creation of a National Peace Academy that would be the equivalent of the existing military academies. Frankly, the idea never got much support either among policy makers or even in the peace movement until its advocates made common cause with a group of World War II combat veterans who were then serving in Congress. To make a long story short, the broadened coalition convinced a reluctant Reagan to sign a bill creating a very different kind of institution that would not have either the prestige or the resources of the army, navy, or air force academies.

Most peace activists were skeptical. USIP's president and board of directors were to be appointed by the president. Its budget was tiny and almost completely dependent on annual congressional appropriations. It had to be strictly nonpartisan and could not work on any issue that involved domestic politics in the US.

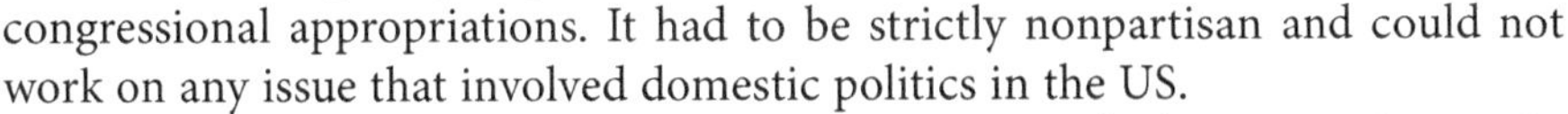

USIP opened its doors in 1986 with an initial staff of three professionals. Later it moved into two floors in a nondescript office building. It was only in 2011 that it moved into its own flashy building on the Washington Mall that sits across the street from the State Department.

Still, its work began to take off almost immediately after retired ambassador Samuel Lewis was named its president and it awarded the first group of Jennings Randolph fellowships to distinguished academics who spent a year in residence at the institute and normally produced a book, which its new press published.

It may not have been what the original advocates of a national peace academy wanted. Nonetheless, by the end of the 1980s, USIP was well on its way to establishing two niches that it continues to occupy today:

- Its own staff and visiting scholars played a key role in defining the intellectual parameters of the field, some of which you have already seen, most notably Michael Lund's chart tracing a conflict's life cycle, which was developed while he was a Jennings Randolph fellow.
- A reputation for being one of the few places in Washington where people on the left and right as well as academics and practitioners could meet and avoid the rancor of the rest of political life.

USIP has always faced a degree of skepticism. Given the United States' role in almost all of the world's major conflicts since its creation, it could hardly be otherwise. Similarly, left-wing critics complained that its budget (which has never reached $100 million in any year) is too small to be taken seriously.

Nonetheless, it was the first institution created by a major world government that even acknowledged that peace was a national public policy goal that was worth institutionalizing. Since then, a number of other countries and the EU have created similar bodies that give peacebuilding at least a glimmer of political support. And, as you will see in the next six chapters, USIP also helped pave the way for the creation of a number of UN offices as well as its 2018 report on peacebuilding which the UN wrote to the World Bank and was cited on a number of occasions in part 1.

KEY TERMS

Concepts

neoliberal, 110
new world order, 114
perestroika, 113
polite protesters, 110
public policy, 111
self-limiting revolution, 114
state, 109
stickiness, 111
theory of change, 108
veto power, 116

People

Gorbachev, Mikhail, 112
Reagan, Ronald, 109
Sharp Gene, 115
Thatcher, Margaret, 109
Walesa, Lech, 114

Organizations, Places, and Events

Security Council (United Nations), 116
Solidarity, 114
United Nations, 116
United States Institute of Peace (USIP), 116

DIG DEEPER

Cortright, David. *Peace Works: The Citizen's Rule in Ending the Cold* War. Boulder, CO: Westview, 1993. The best single book on the period written by a veteran scholar who had been a leader of the freeze campaign.

Gorbachev, Mikhail. *Perestroika: New Thinking for Our Country and the World*. New York: HarperCollins, 1987. Written at the height of his popularity at home and abroad, this book lays out his plans for restructuring the USSR and the planet. Still an amazingly interesting read.

Gromyko, Anatoly, and Martin Hellman, eds. *Breakthrough: Emerging New Thinking*. New York: Walker, 1988. The first jointly written book by Soviets and Americans in the social sciences. Covers a lot of the ground in all of part 2, not just this chapter.

Lofland, John. *Polite Protesters: The American Peace Movement of the 1980s*. Syracuse, NY: Syracuse University Press, 1994. More systematic evidence than Cortright provides. Perhaps less useful to read today.

NOTES

[1] Cohn wrote a lot about these issues at the time. In retrospect, the best version for seeing both her insight and her wit is one of her shorter articles, "Slick 'Ems, Glick 'Ems, Christmas Trees, and Cookie Cutters: Nuclear Language and How We Learned to Pat the Bomb." *The Bulletin of the Atomic Scientists*, June 1987, 17–24.

[2] Rachel Kleinfeld, *A Savage Order: How the World's Deadliest Countries Can Forge a Path to Security* (New York: Pantheon, 2018), 135.

[3] https://digitalarchive.wilsoncenter.org/document/116224.

[4] Gene Sharp, *The Politics of Non-violent Action*, 4 vols. (New York: Porter Sargent, 1973).

PEACEBUILDING 2.0

CHAPTER 7

Identity and Intractable Conflict

THINK ABOUT IT

We shift gears again with the beginning of part 3. In particular, you will see how the entire field had to make a huge pivot so that it could come to grips with identity-based issues and the conflicts they spawned.

Therefore, ask yourself the following questions:

- Why did so many identity-based conflicts seem to erupt in the 1990s? Which did they reflect more—"ancient hatreds" or contemporary issues?
- Why did issues like reconciliation become more central to our work?
- How do new ideas like appreciative inquiry and scenario planning fit into peace and conflict studies?
- Why did contentious politics largely disappear from the scene during the 1990s?

CORE CONCEPTS

During the 1990s, we added more new ideas to both our analytical and practical work, including:

cultural sensitivity—the requirement that conflict resolution be in line with a community's cultural norms
empathy—the ability to put oneself in the "shoes" or mind-set of someone else, especially one's adversary
identity—the often emotional ways we define ourselves along racial, religious, gender, ethnic, linguistic, and other lines
intractable conflict—a conflict that has multiple causes and consequences that cannot be settled quickly or easily
reconciliation—the process whereby parties to a dispute restore their relationship after it has ended
transformational—a form of conflict resolution in which the underlying causes of a dispute are addressed and the relationships involved are literally transformed

There is an old joke: A Jewish man stopped on the street in Belfast and is asked whether he is a Protestant or a Catholic. When he responds that he is Jewish, the rejoinder comes: "Aye, but a Catholic Jew or a Protestant Jew?"

—Feargal Cochrane

ENDING THE COLD WAR did not end conflict.

Far from it.

In the heady days after the Berlin Wall came down, there was a lot of talk about a **new world order**. Political leaders like **George H. W. Bush** (1924–2018) and **Mikhail Gorbachev** (1931–) eagerly envisioned an international system in which countries would work out their problems without taking up arms.

Almost immediately, the euphoria of 1989 and 1991 gave way to pessimism as old conflicts intensified and new ones broke out. Within a matter of months, it became clear that it might make more sense to speak of a new world disorder instead. One of the leading academic realists, John Mearsheimer, actually wrote a widely cited and very persuasive article in which he argued that we would come to miss the Cold War because the rivalry between the superpowers had kept other conflicts from getting out of hand.

All of a sudden (or so it seemed), some long-standing conflicts intensified, while others appeared on the global radar screen for the first time. Instead of Moscow and Washington, our attention shifted to some familiar places such as Northern Ireland, South Africa, or the Middle East, while a lot of us discovered new hot spots like Rwanda, Yugoslavia, or East Timor.

What's more, the conflicts themselves seemed different. Now, they were about **identity** rather than traditional national security issues that had dominated the Cold War and the academic study of international relations.

And many of those conflicts were horrific. To see why, just look at the photograph that begins this chapter. It depicts just a few of the skulls kept at the Nyamata Genocide Memorial in Rwanda. As you will see, more than eight hundred thousand people died in a single two-month period, fifty thousand of whom are buried at that single site.

Like everyone else, the peacebuilding and conflict resolution community had a hard time adjusting to these new realities. Some, like the Beyond War movement which I had worked in, failed to adapt and saw their influence decline or disappeared altogether.

The NGOs that did survive had to adapt to these new kinds of conflict and develop new strategies for working in new places. In the process, conflict resolution and peacebuilding became even more closely intertwined in the work of organizations like Search for Common Ground and academic programs like the one at GMU. Even more importantly, hundreds of new organizations were formed, the vast majority of which specialized in dealing with these identity-based conflicts.

By the end of the decade, both the academics and the practitioners had homed in on five main emphases that will be at the heart of part 3.

- We continued to integrate resolving conflict with building peace.
- Our geographical focus shifted to conflicts in what was then referred to as the **Third World** and is now more commonly called the **Global South**.

- We concentrated on grassroots efforts, albeit without neglecting political elites as we will see in the next chapter. Still, almost all of us soon realized that conflict resolution and peacebuilding had to start with the bottom of Lederach's triangle (see figure 3.2) and build upward until it led to policy change.
- We realized that the kinds of transactional outcomes at the heart of our work in the 1980s were not going to be enough. We would have to transform the nature of the conflict and the relationships that gave rise to it.
- Few of those initiatives were anchored in contentious politics.

There was more to the story which I will get to by the end of this chapter. Mediation and other forms of transactional conflict resolution took root in the US and many of the other advanced industrialized democracies. New ideas developed outside of peace and conflict studies began to gain an audience. However, focusing on them now would take you away from the core narrative, which is the pivot we made away from the superpower rivalry to conflicts over identity.

A (NOT SO) NEW KIND OF CONFLICT

To be honest, there rarely is much to laugh about about in our work. I am not entirely sure why that's the case. Part of it, though, has to do with the fact that the topics we deal with in peace and conflict studies often seem deadly serious—pun intended.

Yet, people in the "real world" routinely turn to dark humor as a way of expressing their frustration with unjust regimes and seemingly unsolvable problems. To that end, one of the best ways for a young person today to understand the absurdity of the Cold War arms race is to watch Stanley Kubrick's comedy about a looming nuclear apocalypse, *Dr. Strangelove*.

But the humor that emerged in the 1990s was different because the conflicts were different. Unlike the Cold War, they revolved around identity issues that boil down to questions such as "who am I?" Answering that kind of question tends to lead people to identify with some kinds of people, while excluding everyone else, which leads us to think in terms of what social psychologists call **ingroups** and **outgroups**. Needless to say, thinking in those terms rarely lends itself to humor.

That takes us to Feargal Cochrane's joke, which appears in the first few pages of his book on the Troubles in his native Northern Ireland. You won't be surprised to learn that there aren't a lot of Jews in Northern Ireland. There is only one synagogue in Belfast, which has about eighty members. No one knows for sure, but there probably aren't a thousand Jews in the entire province.

Their small numbers only make Cochran's joke all the more absurd—and revealing. When he grew up in Northern Ireland in the 1970s and 1980s, the population was split into two antagonistic communities—Catholic and Protestant. In those charged circumstances, asking the absurd question if someone is a Catholic Jew or a Protestant Jew might not have seemed all that absurd.

Everyone "had to be" either Catholic or Protestant. Even the Jews.

Joking aside, Cochrane's story tells us a lot about the conflicts that have preoccupied us since the 1990s. Unlike the Cold War, they weren't over territory that could be separated by Berlin Walls. Even more importantly, they weren't about formal ideologies like Marxism and capitalism.

The new and not so new conflicts of the 1990s were about identity and "pushed" lots of deeply rooted and highly emotionally charged "buttons." National boundaries and formal ideologies were of little significance. Compromise was hard to imagine. Fights to the death became the norm.

I don't want to minimize the Cold War or underestimate the severity of its divisions. After all, if it had turned hot, it could have ended civilization as we know it.

Still, the US and the Soviet Union were able to deter each other from "pushing the button." At times, they reached compromises that reduced the risk of nuclear war. Also, the Cold War revolved around the control of territory, and that was the kind of issue that international relations experts and diplomats thought they knew how to deal with. Last but by no means least, what had started as an ideological dispute that pitted adherents of incompatible belief systems against each other had turned into more of a conventional power struggle in which commitment to communism or democracy served largely as a veneer, especially on the Soviet side.

Now, all of a sudden, most of the conflicts were over race, religion, language, or ethnicity. These issues brought deeply held emotions to the surface and led people to despise their adversaries with an intensity we rarely encountered during the Cold War.

To see how and why things were different, think back to Sting's song which I discussed at the end of chapter 5. It certainly makes an emotional appeal. However, he does so by asking people to be rational and use their "common sense."

As you are about to see, it was a lot harder to do that when people asked if someone is a Protestant Jew or a Catholic Jew. It can be all but impossible when what social psychologists call the "other" lives in your community and maybe even on your own block.

Those are the kinds of conflicts that burst on the scene in the 1990s. Because they hit so close to home—however you chose to define close to home—we had to change, too.

The New World Disorder

It is hard to overestimate how optimistic people were when the 1990s began. It wasn't just national leaders like Gorbachev and Bush. Mainstream analysts on the left and right were convinced that we had put a dark and dangerous period behind us. None got more publicity than **Francis Fukuyama** (1952–), who had served in the State Department under Bush and then wrote a book entitled *The End of History*. On one level, Fukuyama knew that history had not literally come to an end. However, he was convinced that the defeat of communism had removed the last great ideological division in human history.

The end of the Cold War also seemed to make progress on other conflicts possible. In yet another surprising move, President F. W. De Klerk took to the podium in the South African parliament on February 11, 1990, and announced that the ANC was no longer banned and that Nelson Mandela would be released from prison later that day. Peace talks had also begun in Northern Ireland, Israel/Palestine, and other hot spots.

However, it wasn't long before people understood that that the new world order wasn't going to be all that orderly. Fukuyama, for one, soon realized that conflicts broke out for reasons that had little or nothing to do with Cold War era issues. New and seemingly more difficult kinds of conflicts engulfed much of the Global South. The first fighting broke out in Armenia and Azerbaijan and magnified the ethnic divisions that had led to the Soviet Union's collapse. Then, Yugoslavia splintered into six constituent republics with bloody civil wars being fought in Bosnia, Serbia, and Croatia. In ten weeks, more than eight hundred thousand Rwandan **Tutsis** were killed in genocidal violence. The list goes on and on.

Although I have called these a new kind of conflict, there was little new about many of them. As you will see, in most cases, their roots were centuries old. What changed was the global political context that both put them on everyone's radar screen and helped us see ways we could address them. That new context made conflict in the 1990s anything but traditional or amendable to transactional solutions.

Identity

Analysts like Fukuyama did get one thing right. World politics no longer centered on the conflict between Marxist inspired socialism and western capitalism and democracy. Unfortunately, for those who had spoken so glowingly about a new world order or the end of history, the new identity-based conflicts did not readily lend themselves to the kinds of geopolitical alternatives that had been at the heart of Cold War.

On one level, these were old conflicts that long antedated the Cold War. Serbian nationalists, for example, liked to dredge up memories of the Battle of Kosovo Polje—which took place in 1389, long before there was anything like modern-day Serbia, Bosnia, Croatia, or Kosovo. The conflict in the Middle East set Jews against Arabs (most but not all of whom were Muslims) in part over control of Jerusalem, which is a holy city to Muslims, Jews, and Christians alike. The animosity in Northern Ireland can be traced back at least to the "plantation" in the sixteenth and seventeenth centuries when the English government sent thousands of Protestants to Ireland, who seized land Irish Catholics had farmed for centuries.

Others were a by-product of classical imperialism. Europeans from the British Isles, France, Belgium, the Netherlands, Germany, Italy, Spain, and Portugal ended up controlling virtually all of the Americas, Africa, and Asia. Only Ethiopia, China, and Japan escaped being colonized outright. But even there, the impact of imperialism loomed over everything.

In the case of South Africa, it led to the creation of what turned out to be two antagonistic immigrant communities made up of English and Afrikaner settlers. By the end of the twentieth century, of course, they could trace their South African roots back at least two centuries and had long thought of themselves as Africans. In places where there was no large settler population that remained after independence, the colonial powers had drawn boundaries in ways that forced historically antagonistic groups to live in the same countries.

The conflicts spawned by the end of imperialism took on new significance precisely because the Cold War ended. From the 1940s until the 1980s, the superpower rivalry had shaped the way most of these conflicts played out, including the independence movements that freed most of these countries from formal colonial rule by the 1970s. In some cases, including Southeast Asia, the Middle East, and Central America, the Cold War essentially turned regional disputes into proxy battles between the US and the Soviet Union. In Eastern Europe, the Soviets were able to paper over the ethnic, religious, and linguistic disputes that had roiled the region for centuries. Even when those disputes erupted around what looked like local issues as in South Africa, it was easy for leaders on all sides to cast them in Cold War terms.

Many of these long-simmering disputes now burst into the open with unexpected fury, in some cases even before the Cold War had definitively come to an end. Historians and conflict specialists were not all that surprised, but politicians and average citizens alike were shocked when they saw footage of violence in these faraway places that had rarely been on the public's radar screens before.

Analysts struggled to make sense of what was happening, which led some of them to see these conflicts as reflections of what some called ancient historical hatreds. Fukuyama's PhD advisor, **Samuel Huntington** (1927–2008), gave a lot of support to this interpretation of identity conflict in a 1993 article and subsequent book about what he called the clash of civilizations.[1] Huntington agreed with his former student that the age of classical ideological divisions was over. Unlike Fukuyama, he was convinced that other cultural divisions would take their place and that we would be facing new kinds of disputes.

Imagined Communities

Most peacebuilders did not agree with either Fukuyama or Huntington, because we thought that their arguments were historically flawed and culturally biased—especially Huntington's fears about a clash of civilizations. From this perspective, what he saw as deeply ingrained civilizations and their seemingly unshakable norms could better be thought of as **imagined communities**—a term coined by **Benedict Anderson** (1936–2015).

Anderson was as different from Huntington as two academics of their generation could have been. Huntington was born in New York, educated at Harvard, and spent almost his entire adult life in those two communities. By contrast, Anderson was born in China, where his father worked for a local government. His family fled China to escape the Japanese invasion on the eve of World War II. After graduating from Cambridge with a degree in classics, he came to the US and did his first scholarly research on Indonesian independence. After a distinguished career at Cornell, Anderson returned to Indonesia, where he died shortly before his eightieth birthday.

Both his scholarly research and life experiences led him to the conclusion that the conflicts of the postimperial world were not largely the result of hatreds that had festered for centuries. Rather, like his contemporaries who wrote about modernity (see chapter 2), Anderson was convinced that the values Huntington worried about reflected imagined communities that humans had invented rather recently and could therefore uninvent. What's more, he was convinced that they could not have existed in an earlier age when few people could read, write, or travel and otherwise learn about the rest of the world.

Although he focused on nationalism when writing *Imagined Communities* in 1983, people began applying his three main points to identity issues in general, which is how we will use them here:

- Intensely held, identity-based beliefs are new phenomena. People may have thought of themselves as Bosnians or Muslims in earlier centuries.

However, it was only with the spread of the nation-state and the modern mass media that people began to define themselves primarily in terms of national, racial, ethnic, or any other kind of identity.

- That led people to think more in terms of ingroups and outgroups in ways that often lead to stereotypical thinking and conflict.
- Identities can be based on powerful emotions, including those that lead people to make amazing sacrifices for their group, at times including their own lives.

Intractability

Differences over race, religion, language, and ethnicity proved to be even harder to address than those over territory or economic goals that had preoccupied international relations scholars and practitioners during the Cold War. Toward the end of the 1990s, Guy and Heidi Burgess of the University of Colorado convened a large group of specialists (including me) to write an online handbook for the field, which we ended up entitling Beyond Intractability. **Intractable** was a good term to use in describing the conflicts of the day because most dictionaries define such problems as unmanageable, uncontrollable, difficult, awkward, troublesome, and burdensome, while intractable people are stubborn, obstinate, inflexible, headstrong, willful, uncooperative, perverse, and pigheaded. One medical dictionary added "unstoppable," as in unstoppable diarrhea.

At one of our first meetings, we concluded:

> As we see it, intractable conflicts are those that lie at the frontier of the field—the conflicts that stubbornly seem to elude resolution, even when the best available techniques are applied.
>
> These conflicts are not hopeless, and they most certainly are worth dealing with. But they are very different from more tractable conflicts, such as most labor-management conflicts, some family conflicts, many workplace conflicts, and even many international conflicts that can be successfully resolved through negotiation or mediation. Intractable conflicts need a different, more multi-faceted, and more prolonged approach. (www.beyondintractability.org)

That leads to a simple proposition that underlies everything that follows in this chapter. Conflicts became intractable because people, organizations, and governments made choices which made them extremely hard to solve. To use an admittedly awkward phrase, some became less intractable and even came close to disappearing because people, organizations, and governments chose to move in other directions.

In other words, if we learned anything during these years, it was that no conflict is permanently intractable. Some, like the one between Israel and the Palestinians may be harder to deal with than others. However, even there, the evidence shows that progress can be made if, as one of my students once put it, you can make the stars align. As she understood that metaphor, doing so can be difficult indeed, but it is never impossible.

Ignoring the Home Front?

As our attention turned to the Global South, the problems facing the wealthier countries dropped off our agenda. We knew that they faced social and political problems. Some NGOs did try to address them, as did Search for Common Ground when I worked there at the turn of the century. I will spend some time in chapter 9 on our effort to create a US Consensus Council, but few of these projects had much of an impact, including what we did at Search.

As a result, I will not spend much time on them in this chapter.

Atrocity Prevention

During the 1990s, the peacebuilding community and to a lesser degree our colleagues in conflict resolution also came face-to-face with a kind of conflict many of us had hoped humanity had left behind—**genocide** and other forms of **mass atrocity**. As noted above, the worst example came during an eight-week period when as many as eight hundred thousand Tutsis and others were killed in Rwanda. It wasn't just Rwanda. Most of the conflicts that made the world's headlines had some form of mass violence that evoked memories of the Holocaust.

The conflict resolution and peacebuilding community obviously had to find ways of responding to these humanitarian disasters and live up to the phrase that best sums up the Jewish community's response to the Holocaust, never again.

As odd as it may seem, the antigenocide and peacebuilding communities did not have all that much in common at the time, and their different approaches to the problem continued to keep them from regularly working together into the 2010s. Both communities emphasized the need for atrocity prevention as the very term, never again, suggests. However, that community also focused on achieving justice by punishing the perpetrators of any crimes against humanity. Peacebuilders focused more on reconciliation as we will see later in this chapter. We typically focused on bringing the two sides together to heal the wounds after the killings ended.

Not surprisingly, the two communities talked past each other and are just now finding ways to work together to identify warning signs that crimes against humanity might occur (the peacebuilder's strengths) and, together, find ways of creating what I will call an architecture for prevention in part 4.

PEACEBUILDING TAKES OFF

Not surprisingly, these unexpected and dramatic events ushered in an equally unexpected and dramatic shift in what conflict resolution and peacebuilding professionals did.

That started with where we worked. Some academic programs and activist groups had paid attention to places like Cyprus, Israel and Palestine, Colombia, and South Africa during the 1980s. Now, they were home to just about the only kinds of disputes we worried about. There were a few exceptions, including the former Yugoslavia and Northern Ireland. On balance, however, our attention shifted to the Global South.

We also changed how we worked. The new initiatives drew on key ideas, such as win-win conflict resolution, that only a few of the peace movements of the 1980s had paid much attention to.

But, as you are about to see, they lent themselves to these new kinds of conflicts only if we added to the kinds of tool kits suggested by the likes of Fisher and Ury. As you will also see, we relied on institutions like truth and reconciliation commissions or encounter groups that made it easier for people on both sides to get to know each other and which led to unprecedented and unexpected progress in places like South Africa and Northern Ireland. Meanwhile, win-win conflict resolution and the like gained a toehold in many corporations and courtrooms.

During the Cold War, people in all wings of the peacebuilding world tended to be **reactive** rather than **proactive**. That is to say, elites in Washington, Moscow, and other world capitals largely set the agenda, and peacebuilders determined what they would do in response. During the 1990s, however, we spent more time planning for the future we wanted to build.

However, as you will also see in the next two chapters, not everything we tried worked. Grassroots peacebuilding efforts led by NGOs headquartered in the Global North were not always based on a solid cultural or historical understanding of the places we worked in. In chapter 9, you will see that that was even more true of national governments and international bodies. Similarly, many of our colleagues who worked on the resurgence of genocide and other mass atrocities rejected the very idea of trying to forge win-win and other cooperative outcomes for one simple reason. They were convinced that the perpetrators of crimes against humanity had to be held legally accountable for their actions. Still, you will have no trouble seeing how the field matured during a single decade and ended up adopting analytical and practical tools that were surprisingly close to those I outlined at the end of part 1.

Conflict Is Normal

Because the main parameters of modern peacebuilding were set during the 1990s, I will spend a fair amount of time here deepening the discussion of many of the key concepts introduced in part 1.

That starts with the realization that conflict is a normal part of our lives. That was not earth-shattering news to our colleagues who came to this work as mediators, especially the lawyers. Their professional *raison d'être* is to help clients solve disputes. By adding mediation and other ADR procedures, they were able to offer cheaper, faster, and better ways of solving many legal disputes.

Realizing that conflict is a fact of life had a bigger impact on those of us who came out of the peace movement. Most of us became activists because of a particular war that we found unacceptable and, by implication, abnormal.

As we headed into the 1990s and began dealing with conflicts around the world, we, too had to deal with the fact that conflict was an integral part of the human experience. In and of itself, that did not come as much of a surprise.

Three of its implications did, however, which led us to make conflict resolution a more central part of peacebuilding.

First, the identity-based disputes reinforced our understanding that conflict resolution had to be transformational and would take a long time to reach fruition. Still, knowing that intractable conflicts had their roots in imagined communities reinforced the key point that analysts like Johan Galtung and the Bouldings had been making for years. We had to address the root causes of the conflicts that were an outgrowth of our social identities and the institutions we created to reinforce them, which also were the ones that produced the structural violence that Galtung, in particular, had drawn our attention to.

Second, the fact that we were now dealing with dozens of conflicts in hundreds of places meant that we had to start looking for patterns among those causes, trajectories, and consequences. Of course, all conflicts are unique. However, as organizations like Search for Common Ground started working in places as different as Burundi, Beirut, and Buffalo, they began looking for what was common in common ground.

Third, most—but by no means all—of the leading peacebuilders at the time started with an assumption that paralleled Einstein's notions of modes of thinking (see chapters 2 and 3). Although few of us actually used his words, per se, we all worked on the assumption that cultural norms were a major underlying cause of most conflicts. Even where they weren't, we stood the greatest chance of changing the way people acted toward each other if we started by helping them change the way they thought about each other. .

Our Position(s) on the Lund Curve

Critical here was our growing reliance on tools like Michael Lund's conflict curve which helped us see what those patterns were and how we were best placed to address them (see chapter 3). As we did so, one thing became clear very quickly. As much as they may have wanted to do so, few of the new NGOs were active in countries that were going though conditions that would be mapped near the top of Lund's curve. Many would have liked to be on the ground in Bosnia or Rwanda to help stop the fighting. In reality, it was too dangerous for NGO workers to be deployed in active conflict zones. In the few cases where they were on the ground as was the case in Israel/Palestine, their work was effectively limited to areas and periods of time in which NGO workers faced little immediate danger. When they were able to maintain an ongoing presence in a conflict zone as the Community of Sant'Egidio did in Mozambique (see chapter 9), they were only effective when they worked in the national capital and a few other places where their staff members did not have be preoccupied with their own security.

Instead, NGOs tended to focus on activities that were concentrated in the two "tails" of the curve. While those activists may have had a win-win outcome in mind, their work in the short run had to unfold in other ways that might make a win-win outcome possible at some point in the future, such as:

- de-escalating tensions to **prevent** conflict from turning violent and going "up" Lund's curve
- preparing the way for reaching multistage agreements through which more peaceful conditions gradually take root

- working toward reconciliation and trauma healing after the fighting stops, so that all sides can address the root causes of the conflict and keep it from turning violent again

The Third Side

The first tangible expansion of our work again came from Harvard's PON. Toward the end of this chapter, you will see how it helped institutionalize mediation and ADR (alternative dispute resolution) in the US. Here, it is more important to focus on a less well known breakthrough made by William Ury. Recall from the discussion of *Getting to YES* that Fisher and Ury had stressed the importance of reframing the conflict as an important step in finding and agreeing on new ways of settling a dispute. Now, Ury redefined what it meant to be a **third-party neutral**, something he found he had to do as his own work expanded to include more intractable conflicts from more parts of the world.

Instead of focusing on neutrality per se, he now included it as one of as many as ten roles that people on the **third side** could play. It had not been hard to see how a strictly impartial mediator could stay above the fray in many intense disputes. There were others, however, in which the conflict resolution professional would favor one side over the other or otherwise have skin in the game. To cite but one example we will consider in detail in chapters 8 and 9, virtually every conflict resolution professional who worked in South Africa assumed apartheid had to end. They may not have fully supported the ANC, but they certainly opposed the policies enacted by the National Party governments before Nelson Mandela's release in 1990.

Ury agreed that mediators and other conflict professionals had to keep enough distance to facilitate discussions between adversaries that could, in time, lead to win-win outcomes. However, he was now arguing that third siders do not need to strictly neutral and could even be a party to the dispute as long as they sought to:

- understand all sides of the conflict
- encourage everyone to seek a cooperative solution
- support a solution that met the needs of the entire community

CONFLICT LAB 7.1

Ask yourself the following questions about how—and if—the conflict resolution principles covered in the first half of this chapter apply to the disputes you have been mapping since chapter 1:

- To what degree are identity issues involved in them? How did identity issues shape their origins? How do they stand in the way of making long-term progress?
- The approaches discussed in this chapter are based on the assumption that we make the most progress when norms and other cultural values change first. Once that has happened, changed forms of behavior will follow. Does that line of reasoning make sense for your conflicts? Why (not)?
- Which of the tools and techniques discussed in the first two-thirds of this chapter seem to hold out the most promise for making progress on those conflicts? Why did you reach that conclusion?

Emotional Steps along the Way

If nothing else, we learned that emotions are at the heart of any conflict that revolves around identity. If you need to be convinced of that fact, think back to the exercise on the relationship between modes of thinking and conflict I asked you to do near the end of chapter 5.

In trying to understand that connection, we drew on a number of theories which we borrowed from social psychologists. All were well established ideas that were routinely covered in Psychology 101 courses. Now, they seemed relevant to the kinds of conflicts we were interested in. Several of them came to structure peacebuilding projects in the 1990s—and continue to do so today.

Hierarchy of needs. Recall from chapter 3 that John Burton had drawn our attention to the role that unmet human needs played in causing conflict. During these years, many scholars and activists went further and added ideas associated with **Abraham Maslow** (1908–1970) and his theory about a **hierarchy of needs** to our list of the psychological causes of conflict. As the term hierarchy suggests, Maslow argued that we all have basic needs including food, clothing, shelter, and security. Once we can take those for granted, we would have more time and energy for what he referred to as higher-level needs, including love, belonging, emotional security, and self-actualization. The higher one moves "up" the hierarchy, the easier it was to deal with conflict, concern oneself with morality, and worry about national or global issues.

Contact theory. Most of the concrete interventions to be discussed below had their roots in **contact theory** which can be traded back to Gordon Allport's landmark study on the nature of prejudice which was published in 1954. He and others who have followed after him argue that enhanced contact between antagonistic groups can reduce tensions between them and, hence, lead to a more peaceful relationship. I emphasized the word *can* in the previous sentence because more contact does not always lead to improved relationships. People who use contact theory today, like Italy's Rondine community (see the cover of this book and chapter 11), not only bring people from both sides together but prepare them for the emotionally difficult challenges that are inevitably part of working with the other when they return home to their conflict zone.

Right relationships. This next point starts with a truism. Problematic relationships are at the heart of any conflict. I asked you to do the exercise in chapter 5 so that you could see that any conflict that turns nasty includes at least one failed relationship, whether that is between you and your partner or between the US and North Korea. There may be times when a relationship doesn't matter that much and its failure has few—if any—negative consequences. However, conflict and peacebuilding professionals are drawn to disputes in which those relationships deteriorate and have lasting implications because the conflict turns truly nasty—however you want to define either truly or nasty. Again, that holds whether you are talking about divorced parents who have to continue co-parenting their children or about the US and Iran who have to navigate their places in a VUCA world. By the end of the 1990s, some of us (but by no means all) began talking about **right relationships** in which people and social groups find ways of settling their disputes without the nastiness that characterizes so much of the world today.

Surface negative emotions. We also learned that negative or hostile feelings get in the way of any kind of successful conflict resolution. Many people—including a surprising number of professionals in this field—act as if they can avoid conflict by suppressing and denying the existence of powerful emotions. However, by the middle of the 1990s, most programs were built on the assumption that those underlying feelings had to be brought to the surface and addressed before the parties to a dispute could move toward any kind of construction solution.

That grows out of the human tendency to divide the world into ingroups and outgroups, which I have already referred to a number of times. What matters here is how we treat members of those outgroups.

Using the same kind of reasoning you saw with imagined communities or Sting's song "The Russians," psychologists also suggest that we create those images and can unlearn them if we first bring them to the surface, talk about their roots, and try to deal with the anger that lies behind them. Thus, in 1998 and 2000, I was asked by PASSIA, an NGO based in East Jerusalem, to help lead a seminar on conflict resolution for young Palestinian professionals. I was by no means the leading expert in the field. However, my colleagues at PASSIA knew that I was both Jewish and critical of Israeli government policies at the time. They hoped that I would be an effective third sider who would both be proud of my Jewish heritage and be open to hearing Palestinian grievances.

Among other things, we spent a lot of time talking about our mutual stereotypes of each other in ways that were often hard to sit through. By the end of the seminars, each of us understood the other better because we took the time to truly listen to each other's deepest fears. I suspect I did a reasonably good job, since many of the attendees went on to spend the first years of their careers actively working for the two-state solution that still eludes us today.

Empathy. At the time, empathy had not yet become the buzzword it is today. Nonetheless, this first generation of global conflict resolution specialists understood that developing the ability to put oneself in another person's mental shoes had to be a central part of our work in at least two ways.

First, it is hard for people to see beyond their negative attitudes about another individual or group unless they can also see why people on the "other side" think and act the way they do. One way to foster a sense of empathy fairly quickly and easily is through the use of a "walk through history," which was first developed by retired US diplomat Joseph Montville who was also the first person to use the term Track II diplomacy. When working with a group of Israelis and Palestinians, Montville would put pieces of paper with a series of key dates in a row on the floor. 1948, 1956, 1967, 1974, 1988, and so on. Then, he would ask one or more participants from each side to walk along the paper path and have them talk about wheat each year meant to members of his or her community. It is amazing how much one can learn about the other side's perspective in a two-hour session in which each side "walks" through a common history and talks about the different things they take away from the same past. They probably will not agree any more than they did before the walk began. They will, however, understand the other side's perspective a lot better.

Second, the facilitator or other person playing one of those third-side roles also has to have that sense of empathy. That's certainly true when a Jewish person like me works with a group of Palestinians. It is never an easy thing to do so. In my case, developing a sense of empathy was made easier by the fact that I could point out during the introductions that the young woman sitting next to me the first time I visited was the spitting image of my own sister when she was in her early twenties. I told her so. I doubt that she had ever thought that she might have a Jewish doppelgänger. At first, she just smiled. Later, we built a friendship that lasted for years.

Facilitators can't always draw that kind of personal connection with one side or the other. Still, we have learned that the more third siders can empathize with the people they are working with, the easier it is to get people on both sides to do the same.

Build trust. Trust is one of the first casualties once we begin to think in terms of enemies. "We" assume that we are totally trustworthy, but that "they" are not, a feeling that President Ronald Reagan evoked when he claimed that the US should "trust, but verify" any agreement it reached with the Soviet Union. What he was really saying, of course, was that the Soviets were not to be trusted.

As Reagan knew, trust is one of the most important ingredients in any negotiation because its absence can make success all but impossible to achieve. Our work increasingly came to be based on the assumption that people could learn to trust each other if they got to know each other and discovered that someone whom they had thought of as an enemy could actually become trustworthy. Your adversaries may not become people you like or agree with. But, you can learn to trust them because they have earned your trust.

How that can happen becomes clear if you consider a basic definition of the term trust developed by business school professor and conflict resolution specialist Roy Lewicki, who claimed that trust is the:

> confident positive expectations regarding another's conduct.[2]

In other words, I tend to trust you if I can predict how you will behave and you live up to those expectations.

Lewicki's most important contribution lay in his notion that trust and the mistrust that Reagan and almost everyone else worry about are different phenomena. When we trust, we are hopeful about the future and are willing to give the people we trust some leeway.

Mistrust, by contrast, leads to fear and makes me want to protect myself against whatever it is I fear you might do. The more mistrust there is, the harder it becomes to achieve anything resembling a win-win outcome.

Since the 1990s, conflict resolution specialists have increasingly come to agree that trust can thus best be seen as the outcome of a successful relationship rather than a precondition for starting a discussion or a negotiation. In documenting success stories, they have rarely turned to politics, where Reagan-like doubts are the norm. Instead, they have looked to interpersonal disputes and, especially, the corporate world. Indeed, it is no coincidence that Lewicki studies companies and not Congress or the UN.

Practical Pathways/Changed Behavior

The sheer number of themes developed so far in this section suggests just how much our work expanded during the 1990s. Indeed, so many new projects were started that I could not hope to cover them all here. I decided not to include pathways that led to intellectual or practical dead ends and those that proved to be little more than fads that did not last long before falling out of favor. In the end, several of those tools have stood the test of time and were at the heart of the initiatives I will consider in more detail in the rest of this book.

Dialogue. Just about every conflict resolution and peacebuilding NGO has had some version of dialogue at the heart of its work. As a result, there are dozens of definitions of what a dialogue or other such discussion should be like. I am particularly drawn to the one offered by the late pollster and philosopher Daniel Yankelovich, which I first alluded to in chapter 4 "a discussion that is so charged that it leaves neither party unchanged."

Problem-solving workshops. Those dialogues often took the form of what the social psychologist **Herbert Kelman** (1927–) and his protégés called **problem-solving workshops** which soon became a generic term used to describe any attempt to bring citizens from both sides together. Whatever form they take or name they use, facilitators bring carefully selected members from all sides to a dispute together. Such workshops rarely have a set agenda. Instead, the facilitators help people from the two communities first get to know each other. Then, and only then, do they move on to consider specific responses to specific conflicts as you will see in many of the interactions between Israelis and Palestinians in the next two chapters. What's more, these approaches deepen the progress made in the Track II encounters between Americans and Soviets discussed in chapter 6 precisely because they make creating and then strengthening the relationships among the participants a top priority.

Faith-based peacebuilding. As should already be clear, religious divisions led to some of the most divisive identity-based conflicts of the 1990s and beyond. At the same time, many—but by no means all—conflict resolution and peacebuilding professionals draw on religious or spiritual ideals. In that sense, they draw on another key theme in religious history that goes back to the Latin origins of the word itself which combines *ligare*, which is also the root of the word ligament, which tie bones together, and re, which means again. In short, religious peacebuilders stress the importance of reconnecting people or restoring broken relationships. Best known in this respect are the so-called peace denominations, including the Society of Friends (Quakers), Mennonites, and Brethren among Christians and the Sokka Gakai among Japanese Buddhists. While we will talk about plenty of movements they inspired, we will see some surprising entrants here, including Evangelical groups like Relational Wisdom 360 and the Arbinger Institute, whose roots lie in the Church of Jesus Christ of Latter Day Saints (Mormons). Thus, while this may come as a surprise to many readers, Ken Sande, the founder of Relational Wisdom 360, cites four biblical themes underlying his work that also apply to most secular initiatives covered in this book:

- Love your enemies.
- Take initiative in resolving conflict.
- Admit your own faults and mistakes.
- Make conflict an opportunity to witness, or, as we would say in secular terms, to grow.[3]

During the course of the 1990s, we also began to focus on what we wanted to achieve as well as the problems we wanted to overcome. The shift here was subtle, but important nonetheless.

We continued to work *against* hatred, intolerance, inequality, and everything else that gave rise to the destructive conflicts of the 1990s. At the same time, we began paying more attention to what we were working *for*. When I introduced terms like **positive peace** and Peacebuilding 2.0 in chapter 1 they undoubtedly seemed way too vague. That should have been clear even from figure 1.3 which AfP developed to use in describing Peacebuilding 2.0. The image of petals on a daisy did not take us very far toward defining what the future would look like let alone how we could get there. Nonetheless, we began making progress in that direction in four more ways which are still at the cutting edge of our work today.

Conflict transformation. The distinction I drew earlier between transactional and transformational conflict resolution may have seemed abstract and resembled splitting clichéd hairs. Now, it became clear to us that you could not realistically resolve intractable conflicts using the kinds of transactional tools developed by Fisher and Ury alone.

As you will see most clearly in the case of Israel and Palestine, progress could be made by taking piecemeal or incremental steps. However, no single agreement could put an end to what we would later call a wicked problem that manifested itself in just about every area of Israeli and Palestinian life, ranging from the right of refugees to return to their homeland to the composition of football (soccer) teams.

As a result, more and more of us began talking in terms of transforming rather than resolving a conflict. While wicked problems cannot realistically be solved once and for all, we can change the ways in which people approach them and, in turn, help them set off in a more constructive direction. For good or ill, however, this change in the way professionals understand conflict has not carried over into public discussions, where most people still think in terms of conflict resolution, a point I will return to in laying out the challenges we are likely to face in the future in part 5.

Human security. Peacebuilding 2.0 rests on the assumption that our work cannot be divorced from addressing other pressing issues which is one of the reasons why we adopted the daisy-like image in figure 1.3. Adding those substantive issues allowed us to see that conflict resolution and peacebuilding were both important in and of themselves and that they also allowed us to reach broader goals.

The UN gave that second reason for supporting conflict resolution and peacebuilding a boost when it introduced the concept of **human security** which challenged the then dominant assumption that security was defined largely in national and geopolitical terms. This expanded definition first appeared in the UN Development Programme's annual report in 1994, in which its lead author, Mahbub ul Haq, made the case that:

> the world can never be at peace unless people have security in their daily lives. Future conflicts may often be within nations rather than between them—with their origins buried deep within socio-economic deprivations and disparities. The search for security in such a milieu lies in development not in arms.[4]

Since then, ul Haq's sense of "deprivations and disparities" has been expanded to include the environment, development, gender, and the other issues in figure 1.3. In particular, they were developed further when the UN defined its Millennium Challenge Goals at the end of 1999. However, I will defer discussing them until part 4, where I will focus on the more recent Sustainable Development Goals, which the UN adopted in 2015.

Reconciliation. Research has shown that at least half of the peace agreements reached since the 1990s broke down within five years. As a result, we had little choice but to focus on what happens after a conflict *seems* to end. I emphasized the word seems in the previous sentence because we also quickly realized that what may have looked like conflict resolution was often little more than a temporary quick fix.

To try to understand why only some peace agreements last, we began paying more attention to the right-hand end of Lund's curve, because it covered the period when the parties to a conflict were most likely to suffer their equivalent of an addict's relapse. Perhaps because of the South African experience, which we will consider in the next two chapters, much of that attention focused on a single concept, **reconciliation**.

Dictionaries define reconciliation in two main ways—as the restoration of friendly relationships and as making one point of view compatible with another. As such, it is hard to imagine Jews and Nazis reconciling during the 1930s or Blacks and Whites doing so in South Africa as long as apartheid remained in force.

Those reservations aside, adding reconciliation as the ultimate or long-term goal of any conflict resolution or peacebuilding process was a huge step forward,

Management? Resolution? Transformation? Engagement?

Academics have a habit of arguing over the way words are used. Often, those arguments seem to make intellectual mountains out of molehills. Occasionally, however, terminology does matter. In this case, the four words we often use after "conflict" tell you a good bit about how this field has evolved:

- People whose work is most explicitly based on Fisher and Ury's tend to talk about conflict **management** because they are convinced that that is the best we can do.
- Others talk about conflict **resolution** because they stress the underlying values and needs that give rise to the conflict in the first place and seek deeper and more long-lasting agreements than the term management implies.
- Some practitioners prefer the term **transformation** because they don't think resolution goes far enough. From this perspective, to truly end a conflict, the issues that give rise to it need to be dealt with once and for all so that the relationships among the individuals or institutions involved are permanently changed for the better.
- Still, others who are less optimistic about what we can hope to accomplish refer to conflict **engagement**, in which they assume we will remain involved in a dispute for an extended period of time and can, at best, hope to nudge it in a more productive direction.

because it forced us to focus on what **John Paul Lederach** thinks of as its four key components:

- peace
- truth
- justice
- mercy

The first, not surprisingly, is peace, defined here as the end of fighting. But note that Lederach goes further and talks of seeking truth or learning about what happened, providing justice for victims and perpetrators, and demonstrating mercy for all involved.

Although you will have to take it as a leap of faith (yes, reconciliation often has religious overtones) for now, it is hard to imagine achieving his last three goals without also addressing the roots causes of the conflict. In other words, reconciliation does not involve forgetting the conflict or, as the cliché would have it, sitting around a campfire and singing "Kumbaya."

Instead, reconciliation requires hard work in which all parties to a dispute come to grips with what happened and find ways of solving long-term social, economic, political, and identity-based inequalities. Despite the successes you will see in South Africa and elsewhere, reconciliation never happens quickly or easily, as that country's continuing conflicts suggest.

Restorative justice. Related to reconciliation was our new interest in **restorative justice**. Until recently, most legal systems revolved around principles of retributive justice in which guilty parties would be punished for their crimes. That is no longer always the case.

There may be times when the world is better off if guilty parties are punished. It would have been hard, for example, not to have held the Nazi leaders legally accountable for their role in the Holocaust.

In many other cases, it makes just as much sense to rebuild the relationship that was damaged by the commission of a crime. That can take the form of lighter sentences or even the absence of jail time altogether.

More importantly, restorative justice programs attempt to literally restore a damaged relationship. That can include something as simple as a thief returning stolen property or someone who insulted a friend issuing a sincere apology. More often, it involves helping all parties to a dispute—including the perpetrator and the victim—create a healthier relationship, however the formal legal case is decided. Thus, we have seen new interest in programs as different as advice on co-parenting for divorcing couples, prisoner reentry programs, or finding ways for victims and perpetrators to work together to prevent future instances of the criminal episodes they experience.

There is no single model of restorative justice. All, however, share a commitment to determining:

- who has been harmed
- what their needs are
- who is responsible for the injustice
- why it occurred
- who else has a stake in the outcome of the legal process
- how can we best meet all of the stakeholders' needs, which may include the imposition of a fine or prison time

Naming and Shaming

There was—and still is—one exception to the rule that conflict resolution and peacebuilding practitioners all had some version of win-win outcomes as their goal. The thousands of activists who protested against genocide and other crimes against humanity in places like Bosnia and Rwanda had a hard time accepting any outcome that did not lead to the condemnation and prosecution of those responsible for the violence.

Many found the very notion of sitting down and talking with—let alone reconciling with—what the Rwandans called the *génocidaires* to be morally repugnant or worse. In the name of peace and justice, they were more inclined to condemn the perpetrators and engage in what some peacebuilding activists pejoratively referred to as naming and shaming them. Most, too, assumed that they would have to engage in some form of contentious politics that would lead to some form of traditional, punitive justice.

Those tensions have not yet been fully resolved, although you will see some hopeful signs on that front when I discuss architectures for prevention in part 4.

THE HOME FRONT

As you will see in the next two chapters, most of these conceptual breakthroughs grew out of our work in the Global South. While we tended to overlook the problems facing the countries and communities closer to home, three new ideas expanded the scope of what the transactional or ADR wing of our field worked on. They did not have much of an impact on our global efforts at the time and therefore will not play much of a role in chapters 8 and 9. Still, they are worth mentioning here because they were a product of the 1990s even though they did not enter mainstream political work until the 2000s.

Conflict Styles

The conflict resolution side of the field became far more professional during these years. Mediators built and expanded practices to the point that ADR was commonly used by major law firms, schools began instituting conflict resolution programs, and police departments began introducing training in violence reduction and restorative justice. This work, frankly, did not move the field as a whole forward very far, since it was focused on transactional rather than the kinds of transformational tools the divisive issues of the day seemed to call for.

There was one exception to that rule. Early in the decade, Kenneth Thomas and Ralph Kilmann developed a way to measure an individual's **conflict management style**. They discovered that people do not deal with conflict in the kind of rational, strategic way that Fisher and Ury seemed to take for granted. Instead, we each have at least five ways of dealing with conflict which I will describe here and then ask you to reconsider in this chapter's second Conflict Lab.

The first style they mention is one that most people who go into this field try to avoid—**compromise**—in which everyone gets "a piece of the pie" but no one is really happy. I rarely encounter anyone who says anything like "Whoopie, we just reached a compromise!" However, we often assume that it's the best we can do.

Thomas and Kilmann suggest that we can think of four other ways people deal with conflict that lead to very different kinds of outcomes, not all of which are desirable. Their model can get quite complex, but it really boils down to the ways we deal with conflict along two dimensions as reflected in table 7.1. From their perspective, the dimensions are better thought of as continua along which you ask how cooperative you are. For the purposes of an introductory text and Conflict Lab 7.2, it is good enough to think of them in either/or terms.

Thus, you can be assertive, which means that you tend to push your own point of view, or unassertive and usually let others take the lead. Similarly, you can be cooperative and see the value of working together with others, or you can be uncooperative, which means that you prefer to handle things on your own. Taken together, we end up with four main conflict styles:

- **Avoidance.** Some people simply do not like conflict and try to avoid it or engage in denial when and if it appears. Peacebuilding and conflict resolution professionals often jokingly refer to themselves in these terms.
- **Accommodation.** Other unassertive people do not engage in conflict denial but tend to be willing to go along all with their adversaries in order to minimize the conflict's negative consequences.
- **Competitive.** These individuals thrive on solutions that lend themselves to win-lose outcomes, including competitive sports and election campaigns.
- **Collaborative.** By contrast, people who are predisposed to work cooperatively want to see their views prevail, but understand that they have to take those of the other parties to the dispute into account.

As conflict resolvers and peacebuilders, we want people to be as collaborative as possible. That said, it is also important to know where the parties to a dispute all fit in this table and plan the negotiations accordingly. To take the obvious example from the news as I was writing this book, it would be a mistake to enter a negotiation with Donald Trump without knowing that he tends to be one of the most assertive and least cooperative leaders in the world today!

Two Ideas from Business

As odd as it might seem, the most important progress made in the advanced industrialized world during these years came from the business world.

TABLE 7.1 | Thomas–Kilmann Conflict Styles

	Unassertive	**Assertive**
Uncooperative	Avoidance	Competitive
Cooperative	Accommodation	Collaborative

CONFLICT LAB 7.2

It helps to know you own conflict style because you will be dealing with conflict for the rest of your life even if you don't pursue a career in peace and conflict studies. Our conflict styles do vary from issue to issue and from time to time. Nonetheless, figure out which of the Thomas–Kilmann categories you fit into most of the time. You can pay to have your style measured using their questionnaire. However, if you watch this video, you should be able to place yourself in one of the categories in table 6.5.

www.kilmanndiagnostics.com/catalog/thomas-kilmann-instrument-one-assessment-person

Tom Peters, for example, developed tools managers could use to reduce the conflict that came from hiring a more diverse work force. Clayton Christensen conducted pathbreaking research into the way new technologies disrupted entire industries.

In retrospect, however, the biggest contribution came from initiatives that were not directly aimed at resolving conflict but ended up having a lasting impact on the way we think about the subject today. Two of them are worth considering here.

Scenario planning. The better known approach has two seemingly unlikely sources—the US military and the Royal Dutch/Shell. Military planners first started using scenarios during World War II and later employed them to devise strategies for fighting and surviving a nuclear war. By the end of the 1990s, scenario work had been taken up by Shell, spawned a number of consulting groups, was widely used by Silicon Valley start-ups, and was beginning to find its way into some peacebuilding processes.

Fisher, Ury, and other pioneering conflict resolution thinkers emphasized reframing an issue because it helped the parties to a dispute widen the options they could choose from, often creating the seeds of a win-win outcome in the process. This new breed of planners used scenarios to expand the number of options even further to the point that they bordered on the kind of thinking involved in envisioning paradigm shifts.

Before exploring what scenario planning is all about, I should clear up one common misconception. They do not predict the future. Rather, they outline a number of plausible futures. They know that none of those futures will unfold exactly along the lines anticipated in any of the scenarios, but by exploring each of them, it becomes easier to choose between different forks in the road and identify those that are most likely to lead to a more peaceful outcome.

Scenario planning is also based on the assumption that our **mind-sets** or personal **paradigms** shape the decisions we make, often without our being aware of it. Working with scenarios was, thus, designed to help bring those often unspoken assumptions to the surface so that decision makers could question them and seek alternatives. In fact, with the exception of Beyond War and a couple of other organizations I did not have time to consider in part 2, the scenario planners were the first to explicitly bring paradigms and mind-sets into conflict resolution and peacebuilding.

The basics of scenario planning, however, are quite simple. As one of its leading proponents, Peter Schwartz, put it:

> a scenario is a tool for ordering one's perceptions about alternative future environments in which one's decisions might be played out. Alternatively: a set of organized ways for us to dream effectively about our own future. The end result is not an accurate picture of tomorrow, but better decisions about the future.[5]

Shell's planners understood that we all have a tendency to expect a future that looks a lot like the present. When and if we are forced to deal with unexpected events, we are rarely at our best. At these times, we tend to be surprised, act reflexively, and miss the opportunities that the unexpected events might offer if we viewed them more creatively. That is why they set out to help leaders expand the number of options they could choose from, especially when their decisions can carry price tags that reach billions of dollars.

In essence, the planners create descriptions of between two and ten alternative futures. They start with things we can predict with near certainty, such as the aging of the American population now that many baby boomers are entering their seventies. Then, they take other trends that they know will still be important, but whose evolution is far less predictable. Today, that would include the development of new information technologies, global trade patterns, migration, and the like. Next, they do extensive research on each of these trends and the most plausible ways they could evolve over the next fifteen to twenty-five years.

At that point, they become a lot like a novelist or screen writer and develop "plot lines" that would take those driving forces forward in a number of plausible directions. Like a good novel or movie, the scenarios have to be credible because the planners want their clients to take each of them seriously. The scenarios help participants see some of the reasons why the company is having trouble in ways that make it easier to reshape their priorities and business plans. Similarly, considering a number of plausible scenarios also leaves participants more likely to see early signs that major shifts could be underway.

In the early days the scenarios were presented as written narratives. Today, they can take other forms, including homemade videos that look like television news programs, computer simulations, and skits. Whatever form the scenarios take, the planners ask their clients to consider what they would do if the world headed in each of those directions. In the process, they help participants question their assumptions and, in the process, lead them to see that they have more options than they might have thought before the scenario building process began.

Sometimes, the planners will actually help their clients develop their own scenarios. In fact, this is how I first encountered this work in an off-the-record session on threats to American security in 2000 at a workshop run by Peter Schwartz, who then ran the Global Business Network (GBN). He had convened a diverse group of foreign policy wonks who ended up envisioning a surprise attack on the American homeland that looked eerily like the events of 9/11. None of us came to the workshop with that scenario in mind. Yet, as we considered the driving forces that weren't likely to change along with the uncertainties of life as we headed into the new millennium, we began thinking about the possibility of large and flashy terrorist attacks. We got there because the facilitators helped us pay more attention than we otherwise would have to changing long-term political dynamics, technological advances, and the options open to angry people who wanted to harm the US and its allies.

We were by no means the only people to think of massive, surprise terrorist attacks. What's relevant, instead, is that the scenario building process led us to think of the political forces affecting the world at century's end in a new light in much the same way that Fisher and Ury talked about reframing the terms of a dispute but, in this case, in a far more expansive and creative way.

In other words, scenario planning lets decision makers see some of the implications of their assumptions and realize that they do have options. When scenarios are well planned, decision makers discover that they have a number of new options they can choose from and are less likely to fall into the trap of creating what Schwartz calls the "official future."

During the 1990s, scenario planning was used in peace processes in both Colombia and South Africa. Here, it is easier to see their potential by exploring an example that might seem a bit off task, at least at this point in the book.

Scenario planning had a lot to do with the way American military leaders first thought about climate change and with the way much of the public as a whole later began to see global warming as a threat to peace and security. When the first serious evidence that oil prices were unstable and that the climate might be changing in dangerous ways, the Department of Defense was concerned. If nothing else, the Pentagon is the single largest energy consumer in the US. Its Office of Net Assessment, which focuses on long-term threats, hired Schwartz's Global Business Network to explore what all of this might mean for the country's security.

GBN developed a number of scenarios about the effects of sudden, dramatic changes in the world's weather patterns. After doing research on such periods in the earth's geological past, they developed a number of scenarios, the most plausible of which anticipated the kinds of climate-related impacts that almost all scientists accept today. The Pentagon took notice, and senior officials started making the Defense Department more energy efficient and environmentally conscious.

The scenarios and their report to the Office of Net Assessment were not classified, and the media soon learned about some of their more dramatic conclusions including the possible disruption of the Gulf Stream. It even inspired the first popular docudrama on climate change *The Day after Tomorrow* which aired on Fox (of all places) in 2004.

The scenario work by no means created a consensus on what climate change policy should be. Nonetheless, a not very expensive report had ripple effects that included bringing concerns about climate change closer to mainstream American political life.

Appreciative inquiry. The second approach is **appreciative inquiry (AI)** which was the brainchild of **David Cooperrider** (1954–) and his team at Case Western Reserve University's Weatherhead School of Business. Its principles are even simpler than those underlying scenario planning. When used effectively, they also lead participants to see alternatives to the status quo and help them take steps toward realizing those goals.

Cooperrider was one of the first analysts in either management or conflict resolution to suggest that we should not dwell on the problem. If you do, you will only ask questions about the problem, take steps to address the problem, and may actually end up making the problem worse.

Instead, appreciative inquiry starts by literally appreciating what works in your system, which its developers refer to as the productive core in figure 7.1. That may strike you as an odd place to start given the intractability of many of the conflicts discussed so far in this book. After all, there wasn't much to be positive about in the relationship between Whites and Blacks in South Africa or Jews and Arabs in Israel and Palestine.

FIGURE 7.1
Appreciative Inquiry: The Basics

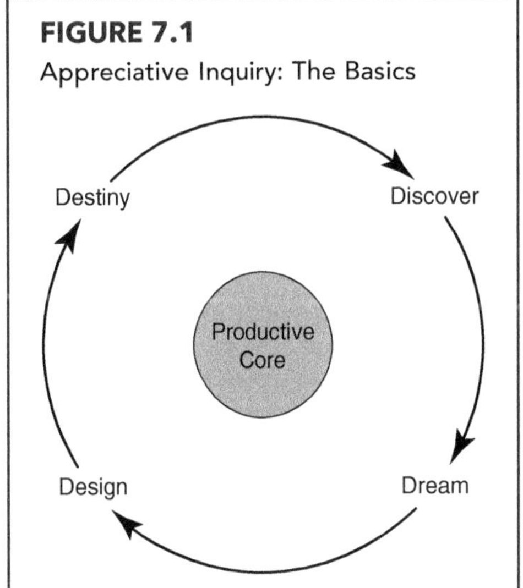

But remember that appreciative inquiry was developed for businesses that had enjoyed at least a modicum of success at some point in the not so distant past. As such, its advocates thought of appreciative inquiry as a tool that existing organizations could use to revitalize themselves.

As Cooperrider and Diana Whitney put it:

> appreciative inquiry involves systematic discovery of what gives life to an organization or a community when it is most effective and most capable in economic, ecological, and human terms. AI involves the art and practice of asking unconditionally positive questions that strengthen a system's capacity to apprehend, anticipate, and heighten positive potential.[6]

By starting with what it calls discovery, an appreciative inquiry team enlists as many of an organization's employees as possible to interview each other and concentrate on what is working or has worked in the past rather than on its problems. This kind of information gathering alone can go a long way toward pulling an organization out of the vicious cycles that got it into trouble in the first place.

If Cooperrider and others are to be believed, the discovery process opens the door to a very different and more productive version of the typical brainstorming session which they call dreaming. They bring the entire team together to set goals that link its day-to-day work with its broadest aspirations which may have already been laid out in the organization's mission statement but which typically gets ignored when the going gets tough.

As is the case with all forms of organizational planning, dreaming, too, is never enough. Therefore, the AI process helps the group design specific goals that explicitly tie the organization's productive core together with the dream the team has developed. In the original formulations of the methodology, facilitators would help their clients deploy those new practices and procedures. In recent years, however, appreciative inquiry developers have begun using the term destiny instead, because they want their clients to see that their challenge won't end with a single campaign. Appreciative inquiry has to become part of

CONFLICT LAB 7.3

Scenario planning and appreciative inquiry can still be useful for understanding conflict today. So, take both your grassroots and policy-level conflicts and ask yourself:

- Identify anywhere between two and six scenarios that show how the conflict could unfold over the next five to twenty years. Did thinking in terms of scenarios help you both better understand the underlying causes of the conflict and see constructive steps that could be taken? Why (not)?
- Apply the logic of appreciative inquiry to both of the conflicts. What are the positive features of the systems you considered? How could building on those broaden the options for addressing the conflict in the future?

the organization's "DNA" so that its stakeholders live up to the principles and goals the process surfaced long after the problem that led someone to try AI has passed.

Not surprisingly, appreciative inquiry did not gain a lot of support among the organizations whose work I will be profiling in the next two chapters. Its most impressive accomplishment during these years came, instead, from its work with a new organization, the United Religions Initiative (URI), which was created using AI principles.

In 1995 William Swing was serving as the bishop of the Episcopalian Church in California. The UN asked him to organize a meeting of world religious leaders in San Francisco (where the UN's first meetings had been held) to mark its fiftieth anniversary. Swing asked an even bigger question. Why couldn't the world's religions unite in the same way(s) that the UN had brought together the world's national governments together.

Over the next five years, Swing's team used AI tools and a team of AI facilitators to help bring as many of the world's religious leaders together as possible, which was no mean feat. More than twenty-five thousand people from all faiths and from all over the world took part in a series of interviews and meetings which led to the signing of a common charter in 2000. Despite the differences between the faith traditions, the URI team agreed to a charter that covers not just conflict resolution but environmental protection and economic development. Even more importantly, AI helped Swing and his team develop a decentralized, self-managed structure of national teams which has guided URI's work ever since.

THE LIBERAL PEACE

We began to at least get a few glimpses at the policy-making grown-ups' table because our own conceptions of war and peace aligned more with the ways mainstream students of international relations (IR) in what I briefly referred to as theories of a **liberal peace** in part 1.

Until the 1990s, academic international relations had been dominated by debates over **realism** or the theory that states rationally pursue their national interests in an anarchical world. While we do not have time to consider the intricacies of those academic debates, or their real world implications here, you should note that some political scientists began to consider other models that paid more attention to emotions, values, and the like in ways that paralleled what we have already seen in this chapter.

What matters here is that our own views changed and began to converge with the emerging consensus among policy makers. Despite the fact that many of us had been on the left in the 1960s and 1970s and despite the fact that we rarely explicitly decided to do so, we began to take the parameters of the existing world order more or less for granted.

Unlike everything else you have seen so far in this chapter, no peacebuilder I know of ever explicitly said that she or he accepted the premises of the liberal peace. Nonetheless, we took its two key parameters for granted even when we had ethical qualms about them for one simple reason. Even if we did not go as far as endorsing Fukuyama's ideas about the end of his history the West had "won" the Cold War, socialism had been removed as a viable alternative to the now-dominant liberal order.

That meant that liberal democracy suddenly became the rhetorical goal political leaders around the world at least said they wanted to reach. At the very least, American scholars began talking about a third wave of democracy in which free elections and the rule of law could now spread around the world.

Furthermore, economic liberals (again, in the European sense of the term) do not support the kind of welfare state or egalitarian economic policies we Americans associate with the term. Instead, given their intellectual roots in laissez-faire economic thought. The end of the Cold War meant that market capitalism had also won—again at least at the rhetorical level. Liberals now began calling for the removal of state control over what should be free markets.

They used their control over multinational companies, global sources of investment and other funds, and the **World Bank**, **International Monetary Fund** (IMF), and the new **World Trade Commission** to all but force governments in the Global South to adopt what they saw as market-friendly policies. Under what became known as structural adjustment, or the Washington Consensus, they insisted that these states impose austerity measures, bring inflation under control, and enter the global marketplace on their terms.

In part 4, we will see that the World Bank's position has evolved in the last few years. In the 1990s, however, it eagerly supported structural adjustment and all it entailed for global conflict resolution—or the lack thereof.

At first glance, this economic side of the liberal peace might not seem to have much to do with the topic of this book. However, austerity and these other new policies often exacerbated the identity-based conflicts.

International Society

British scholars took the idea of a liberal peace one step further by blending it with the idea of **international society** in ways that also came to the fore in the 1990s. The roots of the **English school** of international relations actually lie in the writing of Australian-born **Hedley Bull** (1932–1985) who mounted one of the first systematic critiques of realist theory.

Bull and his colleagues agreed that international political life is anarchical, but only up to a point. There obviously is no functional equivalent of a Weberian state that can enforce its policies and keep the system in order. However, they drew our attention to a middle ground where some of the functions that states perform domestically exist internationally as well.

In particular, they point to what scholars call international **regimes** in which national governments and other agree to a series of **norms** that are implemented through institutions of various sorts. Even without a world army, police force, or even a set of legally sanctioned international treaties, states and other actors do increasingly abide by certain rules many of which have been codified since the end of the two world wars. Indeed, the strength of international regimes covering everything from telecommunications to crimes against humanity has a lot to do with the broader arguments about the declining use of violence made by Steven Pinker and so many others.

Bull himself died in 1985, but his intellectual heirs have shown how the institutions and values of international society contributed to conflict resolution and peacebuilding in unprecedented ways in many parts of the world. To be sure, theirs was a liberal peace in the sense I used that term in the previous section. In other words, international peacebuilding took place within the framework of the emerging world capitalist order which meant that they rarely addressed issues that dealt with the distribution of wealth or the political power exercised by the private sector at home or abroad.

But make no mistake. As you will see in detail in the rest of part 3, international society or, to use a twenty-first-century term, the international community, became an integral part of just about every peacebuilding and conflict resolution effort since the 1990s.

Domestic Politics

That takes us to the final point in this section. As far as peace and conflict studies scholars are concerned, the most serious flaw in the realist argument lies in its mistaken assumption that states are unitary actors which act as one in pursuit of the national interest. That got enshrined in American political folklore when US senator Arthur Vandenberg claimed that "politics stops at the water's edge" at the beginning of the Cold War.

Anyone who pays any attention to American politics will know, no government ever acts as a single-minded entity. What goes on inside the "black box" of the state matters. Otherwise, the US and other countries wouldn't suffer from gridlock because politicians frequently can't agree on what to do.

Some international relations specialists, known as **constructivists**, have brought domestic politics into international relations. They did so in order to show why leaders have a hard time following the kind of purpose-driven approach to policy making that realists expect. Although, that may not have been their primary goal, they also have helped us see how ongoing political dynamics can contribute to as well as hinder the reaching of agreements that foster peacebuilding, conflict resolution, or both.

Very few of the world's major powers ended up putting peacebuilding goals near the top of their agendas during the 1990s. Still, you will see that some national leaders on the right as well as on the left were able to propel their countries—and at times the larger world—in a more constructive direction. In fact, that had occurred in the 1980s as well, but it was only in the 1990s that peace and conflict studies scholars began paying explicit attention to leadership, political and otherwise.

CONTENTIOUS POLITICS

Despite what you might have concluded from this chapter so far, not everyone in the field abandoned contentious politics. Individuals and organizations that preoccupied themselves with human rights or genocide prevention found it impossible to break away from political strategies that ended up pitting one side against the other. Power was always at the heart of their agendas. By contrast, members of the new conflict resolution and peacebuilding communities tended to steer away from taking stands on controversial issues out of fear that doing so would hinder their efforts to work with all sides. In fact, it was only in the 2010s that AfP changed its bylaws so that it could become an advocate and take stands on specific issues in the US and beyond.

There was little open antagonism between what were now almost two separate fields. However, people who focused on atrocity prevention were more inclined to engage in contentious politics. As they put it themselves, they often focused on "blaming and shaming" people who commit genocide and were highly critical of conflict resolution professionals who thought they had no choice but to work with the perpetrators, who are often referred to using the French term *génocidaires*.

In the last few years the two communities have begun finding ways of working together. However, that is another one of the developments we will have to put off until part 4.

KEY TERMS

Concepts

appreciative inquiry (AI), 142
compromise, 138
conflict management style, 138
constructivists, 146
contact theory, 131
engagement, 136
English school, 145
genocide, 127
hierarchy of needs, 131
human security, 135
identity, 121
imagined communities, 125
ingroups, 122
international society, 145
intractable conflict, 126
liberal peace, 144
mass atrocity, 127
mind-set, 140
new world order, 121
norms, 146
outgroups, 122
paradigm, 140
positive peace, 135
prevent, 129
proactive, 128
problem-solving workshops, 134
reactive, 128
reconciliation, 136
regimes, 146
resolution, 136

People

Organizations, Places, and Events

DIG DEEPER

Anderson, Benedict. *Imagined Communities: Reflections on the Origins and Spread of Nationalism*. London: Verso, 1983. This book has led two generations of scholars to rethink history and the role of identity-based conflicts, as well as nationalism.

Cooperrider, David, and Diana Whitney. *Appreciative Inquiry: A Positive Revolution in Change*. San Francisco: Berrett-Kohler, 2005. The best short introduction to a field that has gained a lot of traction in corporate circles.

Lederach, John Paul. *Building Peace: Sustainable Reconciliation in Divided Societies*. Washington, DC: United States Institute of Peace Press, 1998. The best short introduction to reconciliation by an author we will encounter many times in this book.

Lund, Michael. *Preventing Violent Conflicts*. Washington, DC: United States Institute of Peace Press, 1998. The source of the Lund curve and the first book to take prevention seriously.

Rothman, Jay. *Resolving Identity Based Conflict in Nations, Organizations, and Communities*. San Francisco: Jossey-Bass, 1997. Although focused on Rothman's ARIA method, the book is also a good overview of the entire field of identity-based conflict.

Schwartz, Peter. *The Art of the Long View: Planning for the Future in an Uncertain World*. New York: Crown, 2012. Originally published in 1991, this readable book explores the basics of scenario planning and includes some intriguing scenarios for the evolution of the world from those days until the present.

Ury, William. *The Third Side*. New York: Penguin, 2000. Far more nuanced than *Getting to YES*, this reflects the next phase of Ury's work, when he was involved in conflicts in which he had more of a stake and realized he could be more than just a third-party neutral. And that he should be more than a third-party neutral.

NOTES

[1] To be fair, Fukuyama's and Huntington's arguments were far more nuanced than their critics alleged. In Fukuyama's case, it led him to set his career off in two new directions. First, he examined cultural norms, focusing especially on trust. Then, he wrote a massive two-volume study of the way the world's great civilizations had evolved since the dawn of recorded history. That work received a lot less attention—and a lot less criticism.

[2] Roy J. Lewicki, "Repairing Trust," in *Negotiator's Desk Reference*, ed. Christopher Honeyman and Andrea Kupfer Schneider (New York: DNR Press, 2017), 218.

[3] Ken Sande, *Resolving Everyday Conflicts* (Ada, MI: Baker Books, 2012), 31.

[4] United Nations Development Programme, *Human Development Report: 1994* (New York: UNDP, 1994), http://hdr.undp.org/sites/default/files/reports/255/hdr_1994_en_complete_nostats.pdf.

[5] Peter Schwartz, *The Art of the Long View: Planning for the Future in an Uncertain World*, Kindle ed. (New York: Crown, 2012).

[6] David Cooperrider and Diana Whitney, *Appreciative Inquiry: A Positive Revolution in Change* (San Francisco: Berrett-Koehler, 2005), 7–8.

CHAPTER 8

Going Global

THINK ABOUT IT

You can start by revisiting the questions about identity I posed at the beginning of chapter 7 to which you can then add the following ones:

- Why did so many identity conflicts seem to erupt in the 1990s? Which did they reflect more, "ancient hatreds" or contemporary issues?
- Of the tools discussed in chapter 7, which were the most effective in dealing with the conflicts covered in this one? Why did you reach that conclusion?
- Why was major progress made in resolving some conflicts but not others?
- Why did contentious politics largely disappear from the scene during the 1990s?

CORE CONCEPTS

bright spot—outlying example that "works" however you choose to define works

civil society—a term referring to the network of voluntary social organizations in a society

mutually hurting stalemate—a situation that arises when both sides can continue fighting but realize that the costs of doing so have gotten too high

reconciliation—the process of overcoming past emotional differences

ubuntu—southern African term meaning a person is a person through another person

Why should I be a minority in your country when you can be a minority in mine?

—*Anonymous Bosnian Serbian nationalist*

GIVEN WHAT YOU JUST SAW, it will not come as a surprise that this chapter will be quite different from its equivalent in part 2. Between the late 1980s and the late 1990s, the conflict resolution and peacebuilding fields continued to merge. More importantly, our work became global in scope. All of a sudden, new organizations sprang up to deal with the emotionally laden intractable conflicts that seemed to be breaking out all over the world.

That is why I chose this statement and this photograph to begin chapter 8. The statement was made by an ethnic Serb who lived in Bosnia-Herzegovina and who fought in that country's civil war, in the hope of having his part of Bosnia united with Serbia, which, of course, was dominated by his fellow Serbs. As you will see, he became part of a genocidal campaign.

As you will also see, what we increasingly called the **international community** struggled to keep up with the wave of new and recently reignited conflicts. By the end of the decade, NGOs and some national governments had developed tools that would help them prevent conflict or deal with its aftereffects. Still, the history of the decade is one in which survivors built too many memorials like the one in Rwanda shown at the beginning of chapter 7 or this one of the war memorial in Tuzla, Bosnia. Toward the end of this chapter, I will have some kind words for the citizens of Tuzla. The fact of the matter is, however, that we will remember the 1990s more for the outrages such memorials somberly recall.

My challenge is to get you to see how conflict resolution and peace-builders responded to that violence and made some progress along the way-despite the proliferation of memorials.

PRINCIPLES IN ACTION

In this chapter and the next one, you will see how my colleagues began to put the principles discussed in chapter 8 into practice. In the process, you will see that the line between micro and macro level efforts began to blur which means that I have had to include some policy-level material here so that you can make sense of what happened at the grass roots.

South Africa

When the Berlin Wall came down, the White-dominated **apartheid** regime in South Africa was already in serious trouble and may well have eventually collapsed of its own accord. Still, the end of the Cold War gave both sides more room to maneuver while also depriving each of them of a lot of the financial and ideological support that had come from the two superpowers and/or their proxies.

The original dispute between the ruling White minority and the rest of the population had nothing to do with the Cold War since its roots could be traced to the arrival of the first Dutch settlers in 1652. To make a long story short, three hundred years later, South Africa was as racially divided as any country in the world because a White minority dominated a Black majority and did so with an iron fist (see table 8.1).

Opposition to White domination began before all of South Africa was unified under British rule. The **African National Congress (ANC)**, in particular, organized a first round of protests while Mohandas Gandhi was starting his career as a leader of the South African Indian community in the last quarter of the nineteenth century. Like its Indian namesake, the ANC was initially committed to nonviolence. In the early 1960s, however, **Nelson Mandela** (1918–2013)

TABLE 8.1	Events in South Africa
Year	**Event**
1949	National Party begins implementing apartheid laws
1964	The ANC is banned
	Start of guerilla war
	Mandela sent to prison
1986	Creation of United Democratic Front
1990	Mandela released
1994	Transition to democratic rule
	Creation of Truth and Reconciliation Comission
1999	Mandela leaves office

and his colleagues reached the conclusion that a nonviolent campaign could not topple the apartheid regime. They reluctantly chose to take up arms after the White minority government outlawed (or banned, as South Africans put it) the ANC and sent Mandela and dozens of his colleagues to prison. In response, the ANC leaders who stayed out of jail by going into exile launched Mkhonte we Sizwe (Spear of the Nation [MK]) to wage an underground, guerilla war against the regime.

MK does not deserve much of the credit for bringing the regime down, however. The decisive pressure came from South African activists and (eventually) foreign governments which found the regime's racism morally unacceptable. Global pressure was actually slow to build because the apartheid regime succeeded in portraying itself as an ally of the capitalist West against an ANC that received support from the Soviet Union. Far more important for our purposes was the growing opposition to the regime that came from trade unions and other organizations that formed the United Democratic Front that was largely controlled by the ANC's exiled leaders.

Although few of us were aware of it at the time, South Africa had begun moving toward a peaceful solution in the late 1980s. Mandela started holding secret discussions with his jailers and then the senior leadership of the Whites-only National Party that ran the government. Meanwhile, courageous business leaders and even a few Afrikaner clergy members began bringing ANC and National Party leaders together, first outside the country and later in secret discussions held inside South Africa itself.

In the end, the apartheid regime fell because the ANC was able to challenge the regime in three main ways that will remind you more of contentious politics than of the techniques discussed in chapter 7.

First, there was a noticeable change in elite opinion. White moderates helped mobilize foreign opposition to apartheid, especially in Great Britain and the US. Unlike their radical colleagues, journalists like David Wood or politicians like Helen Suzman could be portrayed as liberal reformers who demonstrated that apartheid was a violation of human rights and that there was a nonrevolutionary alternative to it.

Opposition to apartheid also gained support from Black religious leaders and from a handful of their White colleagues. As in the American South during segregation, one of the few professions an educated Black man or woman could aspire to was the clergy. Key among them was **Desmond Tutu** (1931–), who was named Anglican archbishop for South Africa in 1989 after winning the 1984 Nobel Peace Prize. The very appointment of a Black to head the Anglican Church, of course, was a political act. Add to that the fact that Tutu is a remarkable and charismatic man who would have been seen as one of the world's great leaders of our time had he not had to share the limelight with Mandela.

Second, grassroots opposition to apartheid grew out of an ever-escalating cycle of protests and crackdowns. Throughout the 1980s, the government was able to defeat the protesters—or so it seemed. In the longer term, however, that repression only deepened opposition to apartheid at home and abroad.

In retrospect, it is somewhat surprising that the government allowed groups affiliated with the **Black Consciousness** movement to organize openly and legally because of the ways it was able to galvanize opposition in the African community in South Africa itself. It was inspired by a medical student, Steve Biko (1952–1977), and burst on the political scene in 1978. He was part of a generation of students educated at segregated universities who were unwilling to put up with apartheid and who sought to organize younger, less-educated people in the townships.

An uprising in Soweto, the most famous of the segregated townships, proved to be an important turning point in this early period. It began on June 16, 1976, and was led by high school students who protested against a new rule that made Afrikaans the language of instruction in Black schools, which next to none of them either spoke or wanted to learn. The police fired on the crowd, killing twenty-three people according to the official figures, which was almost certainly an underestimate. More protests broke out around the country in which nearly six hundred died. The next year, Biko was arrested, tortured, and killed, which gave the opposition yet another martyr and more evidence of how repressive and corrupt the regime had become.

Despite being banned, the ANC's support continued to grow through two legal organizations it for all intents and purposes controlled. In 1983, it helped form the Union of Democratic Forces (UDF), a coalition that eventually numbered nearly six hundred organizations. Although the UDF was not able to coordinate everything at the grassroots level, the fact that it was dominated by the ANC increased support for the banned party and its exiled leaders. Perhaps even more important were the trade unions, especially the Congress of South African Trade Unions (COSATU), which is still affiliated with the ANC and which successfully organized industrial workers after multiracial unions were legalized in 1985.

Finally, the apartheid state faced growing pressure from abroad as you will see in more detail in chapter 9. Here, it is enough to note that the regime found itself increasingly isolated while Mandela, Tutu, and their colleagues saw their international reputations soar.

CONFLICT LAB 8

In this chapter, I'm giving you a "vacation" from the conflicts you have been tracking since chapter 1, because I asked you to deal with them in chapter 7's Conflict Lab. Here, take any two of the key concepts from chapter 7 and ask yourself if and how they might have made a difference had they been used from the beginning of any of the conflicts discussed in this chapter.

Once the cracks in White rule widened, apartheid collapsed. Dramatic change had now become possible because key leaders realized that they had reached what scholars call a **mutually hurting stalemate**. They knew that they could continue to fight and might conceivably win someday. However, the costs of doing so would exceed any conceivable benefits they could gain if, in fact, they did win.

A Typical Protest against Apartheid

Unlike the case in other countries you will be considering, the stalemate laid the groundwork for meaningful change because remarkable leaders, most notably Mandela and President **F. W. de Klerk** (1936–), took the political risk of bringing the ANC and the National Party together. As Mandela himself put it:

> it was clear to me that a military victory was a distant if not impossible dream. It simply did not make sense for both sides to lose thousands if not millions of lives in a conflict that was unnecessary. It was time to talk.[1]

As far as the outside world could tell, the government appeared more willing than ever to crack down on dissent in the late 1980s. However, behind the scenes negotiations were taking place between Mandela and the authorities which led to de Klerk's surprising announcement at the opening of the new parliamentary term on February 11, 1990:

> The prohibition of the African National Congress, the Pan Africanist Congress, the South African Communist Party and a number of subsidiary organizations is being rescinded. The government has taken a firm decision to release Mr. Nelson Mandela unconditionally.[2]

Mandela was released later that day and gave this amazing speech to a massive audience, none of whom had seen his image or heard him speak since he was sent to prison in 1964.

www.youtube.com/watch?v=M6U_QeIgepI

At this point, the ANC and White leaders entered into serious negotiations that led to the transition to democratic rule four years later, which I will deal with in more detail in the next chapter.

Opposition activists were free to organize. And they had to do so, because Mandela's release only heightened tensions and led to an upsurge of violence in most parts of the country.

Negotiations progressed slowly while violence between Blacks and Whites and within the Black community continued. After a difficult year of negotiations, the White and Black leaders agreed to the **National Peace Accord**. It largely left the formal negotiations to the politicians but sought broader cooperation between what we would now call **civil society** and the political leaders who were in charge of the transition.

At the grassroots level, the Accord led to the creation of consultative bodies that engaged White business leaders in economic reconstruction and provided a venue for average citizens to raise issues involving policing. Even more importantly yet, it helped people work together to address the violence that marred what turned out to be a four-year transition.

Meanwhile, Rev. Theuns Eloff, a leader in the Dutch Reformed Church who had taken part in some early discussions with ANC leaders, denounced apartheid. He also understood that Blacks and Whites would have to live together whatever the outcome of the formal negotiations and wanted to make the transition away from apartheid as smooth as possible. In order to make that happen, he created a network of business leaders (all White to begin with) who saw the need for a smooth transition. They then reached out to the multiracial South African Council of Churches and to the ANC. Soon, Blacks and Whites began making plans to integrate everything from the country's biggest businesses to its still segregated soccer, rugby, and cricket teams.

Far better known is the **Truth and Reconciliation Commission** that was a critical component of the overall peace process. Its creation was one of a series of policy compromises the ANC and the National Party reached which made it relatively easy for the latter to give up political power. For students of peace and conflict studies, however, it marks one of the world's first and, still, most important attempts to implement the principles underlying restorative justice.

Traditionally, the winning side in a protracted, bloody conflict punishes its adversaries. In restorative justice, by contrast, the emphasis literally is on recreating the conditions of the victims before the crimes occurred to the degree that it is possible. The TRC alone could not do that. However, it could begin the process by allowing South Africans to confront their past in a way that might begin healing a few of the wounds.

The TRC was created by a 1995 law and chaired by Archbishop Tutu. The truth side of its work revolved around documenting offenses that occurred between the Sharpeville Massacre in 1960 and the transition to democracy thirty-four years later. For the next three years, the commission held hearings around the country at which victims and perpetrators alike told their stories. The results were mind boggling because many people were hearing systematic accounts of apartheid era atrocities for the first time.

When all was said and done, South Africans learned as much as they could have about what had happened. Although the security services destroyed thousands of documents in the early 1990s, the commission was able to uncover evidence about a period when authorities thought it was perfectly acceptable to torture and kill their opponents. After wading through the evidence of twenty thousand witnesses, much of which is published in the thirty-five-hundred-page report, the commission minced no words about apartheid.

The country learned that the cabinet and, almost certainly, de Klerk himself knew about a shadowy "third force" of vigilantes who terrorized Blacks and their allies. There was no doubt that the White authorities committed the overwhelming majority of the crimes which allowed the ANC and the rest of the resistance to occupy the moral high ground.

There was also no doubt that some of the insurgents used unjust means toward just ends on numerous occasions. As Tutu himself put it, "Atrocities were committed on all sides. I have struggled against a tyranny. I did not do that in order to substitute another. That is who I am." Most notable here was the president's former wife, Winnie Madikizela-Mandela, who had to answer to charges that she had been involved in human rights abuses, including eight murders. Although she refused to testify about any specific allegations, she acknowledged her involvement and guilt and, like many others who appeared before the commission, expressed remorse for her actions. The commission, however, still found that the Mandela United Football Club that she headed was a "pure vigilante unit."

Because it was a truth *and reconciliation* commission, its main goal was to use the truth about apartheid to begin healing the wounds it had created. The TRC was allowed to grant amnesty to people who committed explicitly political crimes, publicly acknowledged what they had done, and expressed remorse for their actions. The assumption underlying its work was that learning the truth and beginning to build bridges across communal lines was far more practical than prosecuting tens of thousands of wrongdoers and deepening tensions further as a result.

Television viewers got to see hundreds of people who committed some of those crimes make public confessions and ask for amnesty. To the surprise of many observers, the TRC only granted amnesty to 849 of the 7,112 people who applied as of January 2001. It rejected more than five thousand applicants because the actions were not linked to the kind of political causes specified in the authorizing legislation. Individuals who were not granted amnesty are still subject to criminal prosecution, though as of this writing more than a decade later, it is clear that such prosecutions will be few and far between.

Any focus on prosecutions also misses the most important point. The commission's primary task was to establish the truth and then use it as a first step toward reconciliation. As Tutu saw it, that first step was a hard one because it required bringing the horrors of South Africa's past into the open, but it was also a necessary one. As he put it in the final report:

> reconciliation is not about being cozy; it is not about pretending that things were other than they were. Reconciliation based on falsehood, on not facing up to reality, is not reconciliation at all.
>
> We believe we have provided enough of the truth about our past for there to be a consensus about it. We should accept that truth has emerged even though it has initially alienated people from one another. The truth can be, and often is, divisive.
>
> However, it is only on the basis of truth that true reconciliation can take place. True reconciliation is not easy; it is not cheap.[3]

The TRC was not perfect. No political institution is. However, progress on race relations over the last quarter century in South Africa has been remarkable, at least some of which can be attributed to the commission. According to a 2010 poll for the Reconciliation Barometer, two-thirds of the population think a

Ubuntu

Ubuntu is a word found in a number of southern and eastern African languages. There is no way we can demonstrate how big (or how small) a role it played in the South African transition. However, it has become a key meme used in building support for conflict resolution, peacebuilding, and reconciliation throughout the world.

The term even has found its way into other parts of our lives. For years, the Boston Celtics said it in unison while breaking their huddle after a time out. It has been used as the name of movie characters and as the title of a documentary about orphans in Malawi that was made by Madonna. Finally, it has also given its name to a computer operating system based on Linux. The owner of that company is a White South African.

It is critical for conflict resolution and peacebuilding because it brings relationships onto center stage. After all, how can I be a person through another person without making certain that I make that relationship work as smoothly as possible, especially when we disagree?

racially united South Africa is a definite possibility. The same proportion of the population talk to someone of a different race at least weekly, although only about one in five socialize with members of another group. Nine out of ten people of all races believe that apartheid was a crime against humanity. Three-quarters affirm that the country needs a work force that is representative of all racial groups. Half approved of interracial marriage. Two-thirds would be comfortable living in a mixed neighborhood. The same number would be comfortable working for a person of another race.

In many ways, the logic behind the TRC and reconciliation in general lies in a word found in many southern African languages—***ubuntu***. It can be translated in many ways, the most useful of which for our purposes is that "a person is a person through another person." In other words, I define who I am in part through my relationship with you. If those interpersonal relationships are out of balance, so are those within a society as a whole.

No one is under any illusion that race relations in South Africa are perfect. Therefore, reconciliation work continues, but it is largely carried out behind the scenes by research companies like the Reconciliation Barometer and NGOs like the Centre for Conflict Resolution.

Nonetheless, the continuing effort to promote reconciliation continues to have a very public and visible face. Ever since 1995, the country has celebrated an official national holiday, Reconciliation Day, December 16, to mark the transition away from apartheid on a day that is of symbolic significance. Coincidentally, December 16 also happens to be the date on which White South Africans took the vow that they believed led them to victory over the Zulus at Bloemfontein in 1838 and is therefore a day filled with pride for Afrikaners but is also the day that the ANC decided to take up arms against the White regime more than a century later.

Northern Ireland

Events in Northern Ireland followed a similar trajectory. As in South Africa, it is hard to argue that the kinds of ideas discussed in chapter 7 played much of a role in reaching the 1998 **Good Friday Agreement (GFA)**. However, it is easy to make the case that they have helped the agreement survive and contributed to the improved relations between Catholics and Protestants.

The roots of the conflict stretch back at least to the seventeenth century, although we can simplify things and begin our account with the partition of the island which took place in a series of steps between 1920 and 1922. The overwhelmingly Catholic Irish Republic took control of most of the island, while the Protestant-dominated Northern Ireland (known to Protestants as Ulster) remained a part of the UK.

After most of the island gained its independence, the conflict subsided until the start of the so-called **Troubles** in the late 1960s. At that point, Catholic activists, who were part of a largely impoverished minority in the north, began a civil rights campaign in opposition to long-standing practices that reinforced economic inequality and Protestant political domination. The discrimination was real and led most of the rest of the world to sympathize with the Catholic cause in part because it was hard to miss the parallels with civil rights movements elsewhere, especially the US and South Africa.

Unionists controlled the provincial government and met the protests with violence by giving at least tacit support to the creation of Protestant **paramilitaries**. Meanwhile, the British government openly sided with the Protestant leaders in Belfast.

Despite what many people believe today, the **Irish Republican Army (IRA)** was quite weak when the civil rights movement began. It only gained strength and radicalized because of its justifiable outrage against the violent policies of the provincial government. It became even more radical—and violent—once the British imposed direct rule and suspended local autonomy after its soldiers killed dozens of Catholic protesters in Derry on what is known as **Bloody Sunday**.

At that point, what had been a violent dispute between Catholic and Protestant paramilitaries turned into an armed insurrection. More than ten thousand bombings and other acts of violence were to take more than three thousand lives in Northern Ireland and the British mainland over the next twenty years.

Although the conflict never moved all the way "up" Michael Lund's curve to become a full blown civil war, the attacks provoked the kind of widespread fear terrorists hope to instill, especially after one bomb almost wiped out Margaret Thatcher's British government in 1984. Critical to the conflict were the respective Nationalist (Catholic) and Unionist (Protestant) paramilitaries whose campaigns resembled those of today's terrorists or street gangs. Perhaps nothing is more evocative of the fear the bombing produced than the fact that the British removed all trash cans from train stations because the IRA had placed bombs in so many of them.

It might seem surprising that an antiwar movement did not form all but immediately in either Northern Ireland or the UK mainland given the global politics of the 1960s and 1970s. Most observers are convinced that it was slow to develop because the British and American media were reluctant to cover anything resembling antiwar activities. In fact, the publicly owned BBC (British Broadcasting Corporation) was legally barred from carrying statements made by or do interviews with anyone associated with the IRA. In order to report on the IRA, the networks had to use actors who spoke the Irish leaders' words.

To complicate matters further, the most important political groups in the province and beyond were themselves parties to the dispute. That included Protestant and Catholic political parties in Northern Ireland, the British and Irish governments, and the Irish-American diaspora, some of whose member provided vital direct and indirect support for the Nationalist cause.

Gradually, public opposition to military rule did grow. A series of official and unofficial inquiries showed that the British army and Protestant officials had authorized the use of torture on Catholic prisoners. Others revealed that the authorities had lied about what happened during such key events as Bloody Sunday itself.

Still, Northern Ireland did not seem to be a good candidate for even the kind of problem-solving workshops you will see when we turn to the Middle East. Instead, most Catholic and Protestant activists remained convinced that they were in a life and death struggle with each other and that it would be heretical for them to talk.

Things did begin to change in the late 1980s, however. Oddly enough, the take-over by London indirectly made that possible. By removing Protestant politicians from office in Stormont palace, direct rule created "space" for new civil society organizations to form, many of which were focused on peace even if they did not refer to themselves as peacebuilders. Just as importantly, more and more people understood that the conflict was moving toward a mutually hurting stalemate in much the same way that it had in South Africa.

During the 1980s and early 1990s, activist groups did build support for an as yet ill-defined peace process. Many of them were started by family members of people who had been killed in the fighting. Others formed groups that gathered members of both communities together ostensibly for other purposes, such as Belfast United which encouraged Catholic and Protestant teenage boys to learn how to play basketball together, but really wanted to give them practice at living together Existing interfaith organizations like the Corrymeala community redoubled their efforts to bring members of the two communities together.

Perhaps the biggest impetus for change came from an unlikely source—the Irish American community. More than thirty million Americans claim some degree of Irish descent. The Irish diaspora was nowhere near as involved in life "back home" as the American Jewish community is with Israel. Still, a number of Irish Americans formed NORAID which ostensibly provided humanitarian aid to all sides but funneled a good bit of money (and, some claim, arms) to the IRA.

Then, in the 1990s, something remarkable happened. A few key members of the diaspora decided to work for peace. Leading Irish-America politicians put pressure on the new Clinton administration to do something about the Troubles. It responded by allowing **Gerry Adams** (1948–) and a few other Sinn Fein leaders to visit the US. Clinton himself visited Northern Ireland in late 1995, making a point of publicly meeting with both Unionist and Republican leaders during his brief but widely reported stay. Most importantly of all, he appointed the prominent former senator **George Mitchell** (1933–) to be his special envoy to Northern Ireland. As we will see in more detail in the next chapter, Mitchell deservedly gets much of the credit for leading the negotiations that produced the Good Friday Agreement. Here, it is enough to note that it ended the fighting, removed border barriers with the Republic of Ireland, and established power sharing institutions in Northern Ireland.

If you could put yourself back in 1998, you probably would not have been optimistic about the future of the GFA. The deadliest bombing in this history of Northern Ireland actually took place after the agreement was signed. The paramilitaries failed to keep their commitment to disarm. Delay after delay prevented the creation of the new political institutions. No one even mentioned a truth and reconciliation commission.

Yet, what began as at best a fragile peace continues to hold. There are lots of reasons why that's the case that involve the dramatic expansion of the intercommunity work that had begun before GFA was signed, most of which is still going on to this day. I do not have enough space in this chapter to cover them all, but these three examples suggest how those efforts continue to reinforce the peace.

The International Fund for Ireland. The American and European commitment continued after the agreement was signed. Much of the impetus came from the business community, especially Charles Feeney, who made billions as the inventor of duty-free shopping. He led a group of philanthropists and investors who funded successful reconciliation efforts. Much of this has involved the creation of new businesses, including, surprisingly, a peace tourism industry (see the section on Kabosh below). Many of the investors have included reconciliation between Catholics and Protestants as an explicit part of their business plans.

None have been more important than the **International Fund for Ireland**. The fund itself antedates the GFA. Created in 1986 by the British and Irish governments on the assumption that funds would come from countries with large Irish diasporas, the fund did little until 1998. Since then, with the backing of Feeney and other wealthy members of the diaspora, it has invested more than a billion dollars in over one hundred projects that are designed to boost the Northern Irish economy by funding initiatives that involve cooperation between Catholics and Protestants.

It promotes reconciliation in lots of ways that were probably not envisioned by the negotiators who signed the GFA. It focuses on young people in economically disadvantaged areas where the fighting during the Troubles took their heaviest toll precisely because the next generation will be key to the province's economic and political future. For instance, it has helped people both take down the bizarrely named peace walls that were built to keep Protestants and Catholics apart at the start of the troubles and replace the vicious graffiti that used to adorn buildings like the one depicted on this page that stood in the predominantly Catholic, working class Ardoyne neighborhood of Belfast.

A Typical Mural Warning Catholics Not to Collaborate with the British, Ardoyne, North Belfast

TABLE 8.2	Events in Northern Ireland
Event	**Year**
1922	Partition
1969	Start of civil rights movement
1972	Bloody Sunday
1994	IRA cease-fire
1998	Good Friday Agreement

Kabosh. By far the most entertaining of the three Irish examples (and perhaps of this entire book) is a Belfast-based theater company that explicitly takes on historically divisive topics. Founded in 1994, Kabosh puts on many kinds of performances in many kinds of locations. Under the leadership of the charismatic Paula McFetrdige, it "creates engaging narratives using local stories and histories to create plays that chart the way Northern Ireland is evolving in the belief that the politics of theatre transform lives." Its most explicitly political production follows the work of one Ulster and one Republic of Ireland police officer as they patrol the border at the height of the Troubles. My favorite, though, is "Belfast Bred," which is a play and walking tour of Belfast's pubs and grocery stores woven around the history of Barney, who was a chef on the Titanic (built in Belfast) who returns from his watery grave replete with a lobster dangling from his hat. Every Saturday morning, he guides locals and tourists alike through the eateries of the divided city as he ostensibly plans his emigration to North America. "Belfast Bred" was funded in part by the Belfast Tourism Board which is trying to build a peace tourism business. It and several other Kabosh plays come with an app which allows people to go on the tours on their own and see links to historical events that are reenacted if you pay $30 and see Belfast Bred live.

www.youtube.com/watch?v=3M30RD8vM2

Brexit. Ironically, the best evidence of the progress made in Northern Ireland lies in the UK's biggest crisis so far in the twenty-first century—Brexit. Although it was still not clear exactly what would happen when I put the finishing touches on this book in early 2019, the UK was still scheduled to withdraw from the EU later in the year.

Most people in Northern Ireland had voted to stay in the EU for a number of reasons, not the least of which was the fact that the border between the province and the rest of the island had been open since 1998. Long gone were the border check points and the hassles that came with traveling from Ulster to the Republic and vice versa. Now, most observers were convinced that leaving the EU would

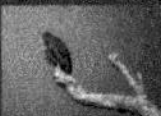

OUT ON A LIMB

A Note of Caution to American Readers (and Others)

Many observers take the people and politicians of Northern Ireland to task for their reluctance to "get over" the Troubles and the rest of their troubled past. There is plenty to be critical of regarding the often glacial pace at which progress has been made, if it has been made at all. However, we in the US are 150 years removed from our own Civil War. As we have seen with the controversies surrounding the renaming of Confederate memorials and the broader turmoil surrounding the Trump presidency and the legacy of racism, the raw emotions that lead to intolerance and violence never disappear quickly or easily, because they are, indeed, among the most wicked of problems.

require creating new border crossing points because the frontier between the two marked the dividing line between the UK and the EU.

No one wanted to turn back those clocks.

Northern Ireland is far from a bastion of peace. Fighting could easily break out again, especially if Brexit goes badly. However, consider the words that Feargal Cochrane uses toward the end of his book on what he calls the reluctant peace. And remember that this is the same author whose quip about Protestant and Catholic Jews began chapter 7:

> There is plenty of evidence to suggest that Northern Ireland is moving forward as a society to a point where the history of political violence becomes decoupled from contemporary political debate. It is likely to take several more generations for the pain and bitterness of the conflict to fade, but in time, it [could become] clear that Northern Ireland has begun to cast off the shackles of identity politics.[4]

Bosnia

We cannot paint anything like that rosy a picture about Bosnia today. The bloody civil war there did end with the 1995 Dayton Accords, but it is hard to argue that the former Yugoslav republic has taken any significant steps toward stable peace.

That story changes if we focus on the single city of **Tuzla** whose residents came together in ways that allowed them to avoid the worst of the fighting. Tuzla stood out because people acted like the third siders William Ury described even though none of them had ever heard of Ury or his ideas.[5]

A little background is in order before I get to Tuzla itself.

That starts with Bosnia's geography, which is why I have included a basic outline map of the former Yugoslavia on the next page. Created after World War I, post–World War II Yugoslavia was divided into six republics and two autonomous regions, each of which had a dominant ethnic group. None of them, however, was close to homogeneous. A bit more than half of Bosnia's population was made up of Muslim descendants of Slavs who had converted to Islam after the Ottomans took control of the region in stages from the fourteenth through the sixteenth centuries.

Yugoslavia was a fragile country throughout its brief history as a unified state. After a rocky first twenty years, it splintered while occupied by the Nazis

The Former Yugoslavia

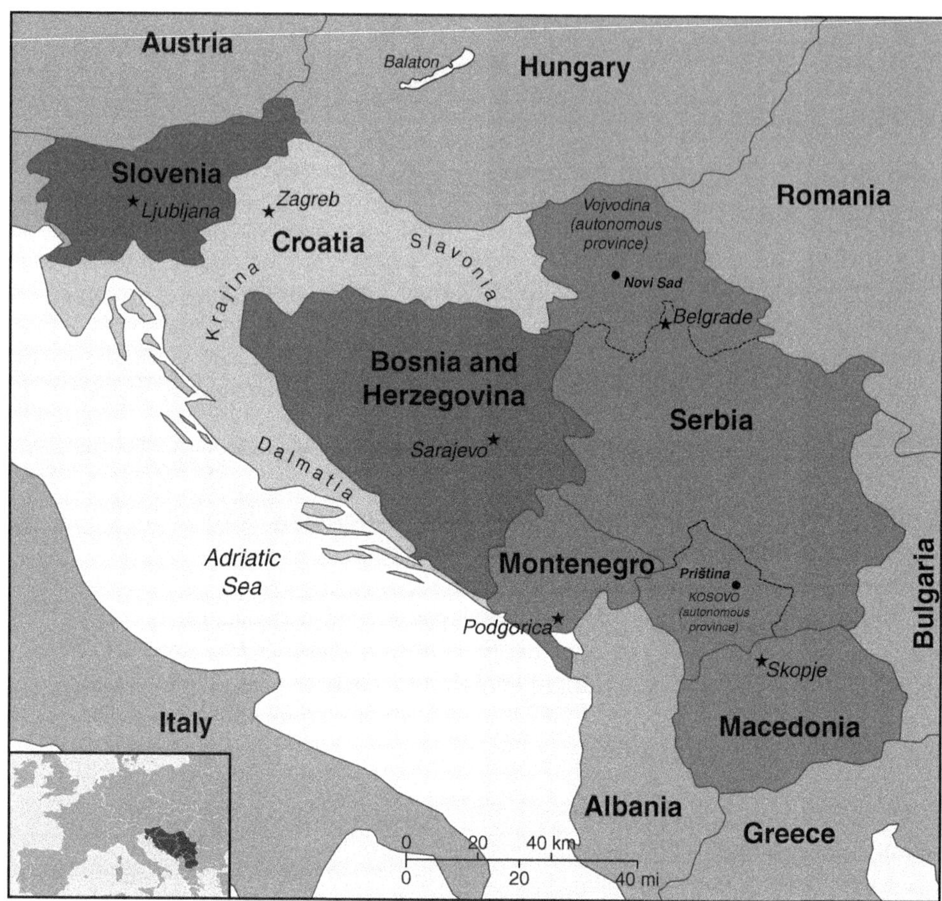

during World War II. It was successfully reunited by the anti-Nazi resistance led by the charismatic communist leader, Josip Broz Tito.

Tito and his colleagues were able to keep the country politically united if not emotionally unified. Yugoslavia successfully weathered its expulsion from the Soviet bloc in the late 1940s after which it followed an independent path in both its domestic and foreign policy.

After Tito's death in 1980, his less than charismatic successors had a hard time holding the country together as nationalist forces in each of the six republics began to surface. The end of the Cold War destroyed whatever national unity Tito and his colleagues had forged. The westernmost republic, Slovenia, declared and won its independence with a minimum of fighting. Everywhere else, the country's break-up produced the worst fighting Europe had seen since 1945.

The fighting was particularly intense in **Bosnia-Herzegovina**. To make a long and complicated story short, Serbian leaders in **Serbia** proper and in Bosnia-Herzegovina launched a civil war that destroyed much of Bosnia and most of the other former Yugoslav republics. Between 1991 and 1995, something on the order of 250,000 Bosnians were killed and another half million turned into refugees simply because they spoke the wrong language, belonged to the wrong ethnic group, or practiced the wrong religion.

The fighting brought talk of mass atrocity and genocide back to Europe less than half a century after the Holocaust. So many women were attacked that the Bosnian conflict gave new momentum to the successful campaign to include rape on the list of internationally recognized war crimes. Diplomatic efforts initiated by the EU and others all failed. The carnage seemed to go on and on.

Except in Tuzla.

In essence, Tuzla will be our first concrete example of a bright spot or outlier which I first mentioned in part 1.

Bosnia's third largest city is nestled near the borders of both Croatia and Serbia. Ethnic Bosniacs made up almost half of the population, but the city also had significant Croatian and Serbian minorities along with almost as many people who defined themselves simply as Yugoslavs.

It had been an unusual city for decades. Tuzlans had been at the forefront of opposition to Ottoman rule—even though a majority them were Muslims. The city was a key hub in the resistance against Nazi occupation during World War II. In addition to its history of resistance to outside rule, it developed a strong local culture of tolerance among its three main ethnic groups.

Tuzla did not completely escape the fighting. The city was besieged for almost two years. More than twelve hundred people, or about one percent of its total population, died in the fighting or from famine and disease that resulted from the siege. Another twenty-five thousand people fled, becoming either displaced persons in one of the former Yugoslav republics or refugees elsewhere.

Still, the fact that Tuzlans largely opted out of the Balkan civil war comes as a surprise to most outside observers and reflects the impact third siders can have. Before describing what they did, do note that their efforts ran against the grain of what happened elsewhere and required a lot of courage on the part of the city's leaders and average citizens alike.

The city's mayor, **Selim Beslagic** (1942–), gets much of the credit for what happened, including a richly deserved Nobel Peace Prize nomination. Before, during, and after the siege, he played a number of third sider roles. He single-handedly made it clear that individual Serbs were not the problem. Serbian nationalism was. After Croatian (Catholic) extremists kidnapped the city's Mufti, he was the broker who secured the man's release and strengthened ties between the two communities. Time after time, he found ways to help Tuzlans take what he called the "citizen's option" and put the interests of the entire city over those of its component groups.

Beslagic was not alone. Ten thousand residents joined the Forum of Tuzla Citizens which organized everything from public discussions to interethnic band concerts during the siege. Its members also led the healing process after seventy-one young people were killed in a mortar attack while they were celebrating the local team's victory in a basketball tournament. The mayor helped create a Unified List political party whose candidates were all committed to ethnic and religious harmony. Similarly, the miner's union, which represented the largest occupational group in the city, supported these efforts. So, too, did some—but not all—of the city's clergy, the local radio station, and the women's health collective.

Not everything worked perfectly in Tuzla as the number of casualties and refugees attests. Moreover, the city government was not able to resolve all of the interethnic disputes despite the personal authority wielded by Mayor Beslagic. Perhaps most importantly of all, no one in Tuzla paid much attention to what could be done to expand what they accomplished to the rest of the country—which I will refer to as a cumulative strategy in chapter 12.

TABLE 8.3 | Events in Bosnia

Year	Event
1980	Tito's death
1991	Separatists win Bosnian election
1992	Independence declared; civil war begins
1995	Massacre at Srebrenica; Dayton Accords signed

Still, the Tuzlan example is worth raising for two reasons, both of which will be important in the rest of this book. First, Mayor Beslagic and his colleagues experimented with and adapted key conflict resolution principles until they found something that worked. Second, it draws our attention to something that probably should have been obvious a lot earlier. If you want to build what I will later call peace writ large, it is a good idea to start by considering cases in which people defied expectations and created more cooperative institutions albeit only at the local level (see table 8.3).

Israel and Palestine

The Middle East in general, and relations between Israel and the Palestinians in particular, are often properly held up as examples of how futile peacebuilding work can be. Indeed, any conflict between two communities who share a single land has the potential to become intractable. That should not keep you from seeing the grassroots-level progress that was made during the 1990s.

As with Bosnia, some background first. The modern conflict in the region began when Zionists began arriving in Palestine towards the end of the nineteenth century, when it was part of the disintegrating Ottoman Empire. After its collapse during World War I, the League of Nations turned Palestine into a British mandate, and it is safe to say that British rule contributed to the deepening tensions between Palestinians and the growing Jewish population.

Everything intensified after the end of World War II with the arrival of even more Jewish settlers and the creation of Israel in 1948, which Palestinians to this day refer to as *al-nakba* or the catastrophe. Many Palestinians fled Israel, although Palestinians still make up about twenty percent of the population inside of its 1948 borders. Wars followed in 1967 and 1974 which led to Israel's occupation of the West Bank and Gaza.

By that time, opposition to Israeli policies had led to a peace movement involving activists on both sides as well as the more widely known armed resistance led by the **Palestine Liberation Organization (PLO)** and later, Hamas. Hopes for peace languished until the end of the Cold War. At that point, opportunities opened up, and the region became home to some of the most creative Peacebuilding 2.0 initiatives.

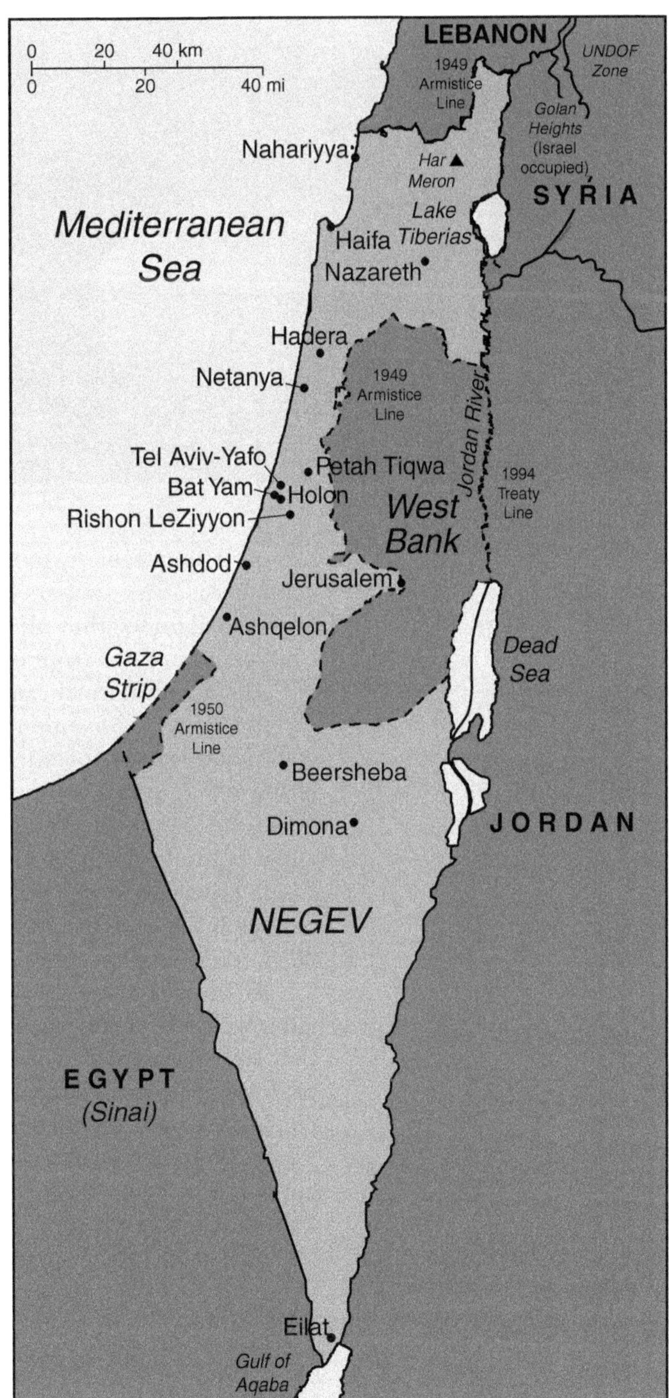

Israel and Palestine

In fact, the Israeli/Palestinian conflict was on peacebuilders' radar screens even before the Cold War ended. To cite but one example, Search for Common Ground took a group of Soviet and American intelligence officers it had worked with in the late 1980s on a tour of the Middle East to see how their experiences could be applied in that other troubled region (see table 8.4).

By the end of the 1990s, there were literally hundreds of initiatives underway. Since we cannot cover them all here, three will have to serve as illustrations of the ways the techniques discussed in chapter 7 were used.

Problem-solving workshops. As noted earlier, these off the record, informal discussions became quite the rage around the world and were especially important in the Middle East because many of the idea's pioneers had a personal interest in the region. They were used at all levels, including in the Track II negotiations that led up to the **Oslo Accords** which we will focus on in the next chapter.

Here, it is enough to see how they operated at the grassroots level. Typically, a trusted third party would invite a group of Israeli and Palestinian professionals to a meeting in some convenient location just outside of the region, like Cyprus. There, trained facilitators would help the participants get to know each other personally and politically and help them come up with concrete proposals they could begin putting into practice when they returned home. Thus, Search for Common Ground brought Israeli and Palestinian journalists together in a series of meetings that ultimately led to the creation of Common Ground News, a service that initially wrote and curated articles on peaceful approaches to the Arab–Israeli dispute and now covers a much wider range of issues.

Neve Shalom/Wahat al-Salaam. The Oasis of Peace was created in 1970 by Bruno Husser, who, intriguingly, was a nonpracticing Jew from Cairo who converted to Catholicism when he was a student in France and subsequently became a priest. His order sent him to Israel to create a center for Jewish studies at which point Hussar became convinced of the need to promote interfaith dialogue and respect. Eventually, he was able to lease 120 acres of desolate land along the 1967 border between Israel and Jordan that became Neve Shalom/Wahat as-Salaam.

The House of Silence at Neve Shalom/Wahat al-Salam

By the end of the 1990s, it had sixty resident families, half of whom were Israeli, half of whom were Palestinian. It gained legal recognition from the Israeli government and has been organizing intercultural projects ever since. These include running its own school, writing curricula for joint Arab–Israeli education, and the like. More importantly, it has gained global recognition as one of the few places where Israelis and Palestinians can meet on what is literally common ground.

Seeds of Peace. Most of these grassroots efforts took place in the region. An exception to that rule is the Seeds of Peace summer camp in Otisfield, Maine. On one level, Seeds of Peace is a conventional summer camp for fourteen- to sixteen-year-olds. On another, it is unlike any other camp because its campers hail from some of the world's most violent conflict zones. Originally, they all came from Israel, Palestine, and Egypt, although campers now come from other troubled regions.

Along with normal camping activities, the teens learn to live together and are encouraged to continue interacting with each other after the summer is over. There is little doubt that the lives of the Seeds (as the campers are known) changed during their four week stay in Maine. However, doubts have been raised about the long-term effectiveness of the experience since the camp does not—and really cannot—prepare the teens for the inequalities and injustices they will continue to experience after they return from their month in the woods. Still, this one camp alone has more than three hundred young "graduates" each year, many of whom have gone on to become leaders in the broader peacebuilding process.

By the end of the 1990s, it had become clear that these kinds of projects alone would not bring peace to the Middle East. Criticism began to surface that they failed to account for the power imbalances that made it hard for Seeds of Peace "veterans" to continue their relationships after they returned to the region. Even worse, whatever empathy or sympathy the camping experience fostered began to evaporate as soon as the Palestinian participants confronted abusive Israeli border guards or Israeli peacebuilders dealt with incidents of Palestinian violence.

And, most importantly of all, it was hard to sustain the momentum created at the camp when the overall political situation deteriorated as it did following the outbreak of the Second Intifada in 1998. For good or ill, we will have to defer exploring that until we consider the broader policy situation in the next chapter (see table 8.4).

THE HOME FRONT

I could include other places and other conflicts here, including Macedonia, East Timor, Rwanda, Cyprus, and Colombia among others. But, frankly, they would not add much to your understanding of what we accomplished during this period above and beyond what I have already covered.

TABLE 8.4 | Events in Israel/Palestine

Year	Event
1948	Israel declares independence; first Arab–Israeli war
1956	Second Arab–Israeli war
1967	Six Day War
1973	Yom Kippur War
1987	Start of First Intifada
1993	Oslo Accord

Instead, it makes more sense to shift our attention to the one geographic region in which very few of these programs were even attempted—the US and the other advanced industrialized democracies. That isn't to say that these countries did not have their share of problems, as you will see in part 4. However, the kinds of NGOs you just encountered just didn't pay much attention to them.

There was one notable exception to our reluctance to take on tough political questions at home. During the 1990s, reproductive health was as divisive an issue as it is today in the US. Even the words you choose to call it are problematic. In fact, I could not find a more descriptive but politically neutral term to use instead of reproductive health! Each side ended up choosing a term that its leaders believed put it in the most favorable light. Pro-choice was coded language for supporting abortion; their opponents preferred calling themselves pro-life rather than anti-abortion.

In the early 1990s, the conflict reached a fever pitch the likes of which it has not seen since. Protests outside clinics where abortions were performed were common. Confrontations between pro-choice and pro-life demonstrators were routine. On occasion, the protests turned violent. After one of those episodes in Buffalo, New York, local activists on both sides asked Search for Common Ground to help. It put together facilitated discussions on life v. choice issues that brought activists together in ten American cities. Meanwhile, the Public Conversations Projects (now Essential Partners) hosted a series of conversations in which three pro-choice and three activists pro-life met around someone's kitchen table for a dozen or more heartfelt and facilitated discussions.

Neither project solved the problem, of course. However, each demonstrated that the two sides could agree on some things, most notably on the shared goal of reducing the number of unwanted teen pregnancies. More importantly, the projects demonstrated that people who disagree with each other on one of the most intractable conflicts in the world today could engage in useful and productive dialogues. In the Boston case, the six women went out of their way to say how much they had come to enjoy each other's company—even though they still disagreed as vociferously as ever on the issue of abortion.

In short, the two teams built trust, empathy, and a common understanding even if they didn't reach agreement on abortion itself. In the last twenty years, we have seen a resurgence of this kind of activity which we will return to in chapters 11 and 12. However, relatively few of the initiatives seeking to bridge left and right in the US have been based on as deep an understanding of conflict resolution practices as these two were. As we will also see, today's dialogue projects have not all helped bridge the divide as a result.

THE BOTTOM LINE

In short, the peace and conflict studies community ended the twentieth century on a high note. We may not have prevented many of the world's conflicts, but we had developed tools and established programs that could deal with many of them.

It was also at this point that I joined Search for Common Ground's staff as it began creating a project on peacebuilding and conflict resolution in the US. My colleagues and I were enthusiastic because we thought it would be easy to bring what we had learned in places like South Africa, Northern Ireland, Bosnia, and the Middle East and apply them at home. We also assumed we could build off of the policy successes that I will discuss in the next chapter.

Then, of course, 9/11 happened, which threw us all for a loop. Before seeing how and why that was the case, we first have to explore the progress we made on the policy front during the 1990s.

KEY TERMS

Concepts

apartheid, 150
Black Consciousness, 152
bright spot, 163
civil society, 154
international community, 150
mutually hurting stalemate, 153
paramilitaries, 157
problem-solving workshops, 165
reconciliation, 155
ubuntu, 156

People

Adams, Gerry, 158
Beslagic, Selim, 163
De Klerk, F. W., 153
Mandela, Nelson, 150
Mitchell, George, 158
Tutu, Desmond, 152

Organizations, Places, and Events

African National Congress (ANC), 150
Bloody Sunday, 157
Bosnia-Herzegovina, 162
Good Friday Agreement (GFA), 156
International Fund for Ireland, 159
Irish Republican Army (IRA), 157
National Peace Accord, 154
Oslo Accords, 165
Palestine Liberation Organization (PLO), 164
Serbia, 162
Troubles (Northern Ireland), 157
Truth and Reconciliation Commission, 154
Tuzla, 161

DIG DEEPER

Cochrane, Feargal. *Northern Ireland: The Reluctant Peace*. New Haven, CT: Yale University Press, 2013. A great and balanced introduction to the peace process.

Gerner, Deborah. *One Land, Two Peoples: The Conflict over Palestine*. Boulder, CO: Westview, 1994. Surprisingly, still the best introduction to the crisis.

Marks, Susan Collin. *Watching the Wind: Conflict Resolution during South Africa's Transition to Democracy*. Washington, DC: United States Institute of Peace Press, 2000. Not the best overall book on South Africa, but the best on peacebuilding during the transition. Written by a participant observer.

Silber, Laura, and Brian Little. *Yugoslavia: The Death of a Nation*. New York: Penguin, 1997. One of the best narrative accounts of the disintegration of Yugoslavia and the wars that followed.

NOTES

[1] Cited in Waldmeir, Patti, *Anatomy of a Miracle* (New York: W. W. Norton, 1997), 94.

[2] Cited in Allister Sparks, *The Mind of South Africa* (New York: Knopf, 1996), 213.

[3] From the text of the Truth and Reconciliation Commission's report, www.doj.gov.za/trc.

[4] Feargal Cochrane, *Northern Ireland: The Reluctant Peace* (New Haven, CT: Yale University Press, 2013), 296.

[5] This section draws heavily on Mary Anderson and Marshall Wallace, *Opting Out of War* (Boulder, CO: Lynne Rienner, 2013), chapter 7, and Joshua Weiss, "Tuzla, the Third Side, and the Bosnian War," which is available at www.thirdside.williamury.com.

CHAPTER 9

A Glimpse at the Grown-ups' Table

THINK ABOUT IT

During the 1990s, the peace-building community only had a limited impact on national level decision making. Therefore, ask yourself

- Why did the enthusiasm reflected in Gorbachev's speech to the UN evaporate so quickly?
- How and why did the international community get involved more than it had during the Cold War years? How can you account for our successes and failures?
- Why did contentious politics largely disappear in the Global North during the 1990s? How did that affect whether we did or didn't have a seat at the grown-ups' table?

CORE CONCEPTS

We actually saw most of the concepts that are critical to understanding the material in this chapter in part 1. Now, however, they enter center stage.

consensus—a form of decision-making in which unanimity or something close to it is required

international society—the belief that national governments can and do cooperate through shared norms, informal organizations, and international regimes

liberal peace—a definition of peace that also includes a commitment to liberal democracy and market capitalism

multitrack diplomacy—informal negotiations carried out by people without diplomatic status

peacebuilding—processes that lead to stable or positive peace

peacekeeping—processes that prevent former adversaries from returning to war

reconciliation—the restoration of positive relationships

spoiler—individual or institution who can and wants to jeopardize a fragile agreement

trust—the ability to count on and/or predict the behavior of another

Today, peace means the ascent from simple coexistence to cooperation and common creativity among countries and nations. Peace is movement towards globality and universality of civilization. Never before has the idea that peace is indivisible been so true as it is now. Peace is not unity in similarity but unity in diversity, in the comparison and conciliation of differences. And, ideally, peace means the absence of violence.

—Mikhail Gorbachev

IF YOU THOUGHT THERE WAS a disconnect between parts 2 and 3 after reading chapter 8, you are going to see that the changes were even more dramatic when it comes to public policy making. This time, rather than the rapid growth you just saw, you will find that we were met with failure and frustration.

The 1990s began amid great hopes, which arguably the most important world leader of the day—**Mikhail Gorbachev** (1931–)—summed up in the epigraph that begins this chapter. There was good reason to be optimistic about the prospects for what he and many of his fellow leaders called a **new world order**. But, that optimism soon evaporated in the new and rekindled conflicts in the Global South.

Peacebuilders were actively involved in just about every conflict of any consequence that took place anywhere in the world. Closer to home, conflict resolution practices like mediation were increasingly finding a niche in the mainstreams of American and European life.

When it came to actually making public policy at the national and international levels, however, the record was rather mixed. There were clear examples of success. South Africa and Northern Ireland headed the list of countries that took enduring steps toward ending generations of violent conflict. The **United Nations (UN)** and the **European Union (EU)** assumed a more prominent role in all aspects of international life, including conflict resolution.

Although peacebuilding had made it onto the global **public policy** agenda in ways no one could have anticipated even a decade earlier, we fell short in two key respects.

- Some key conflicts defied resolution, most notably the one between Israel and the Palestinians.
- We did not get a regular seat at the policy-making grown-ups tables in the key northern capital cities which is where most of the important decisions were made.

These two shortcomings led me to this chapter's title. Unlike the 1980s, we did get a glimpse at the grown-ups' table. In some countries at some times, we actually had a seat at it.

But on balance, it was only a glimpse. What's more, we did not try particularly hard to get a seat in bodies like the US National Security Council. Indeed, when AfP was created in 2004, its bylaws explicitly prohibited its staff from engaging in policy **advocacy**, because many of its founders felt it could not do so and maintain its status as a **third-party neutral**. What's more, in cities like Washington, Ottawa, or London, national governments were, at the best of times, vaguely sympathetic to our goals and, at the worst, actually hostile to peace processes.

THE UNITED NATIONS

The most progress was made at the UN although the peacebuilding community had next to nothing to do with it. However, because this book covers all aspects of conflict resolution and peacebuilding, we have to start our narrative there.

You undoubtedly noticed that the UN and other **international governmental organizations (IGOs)** played next to no role in part 2 because Cold War tensions made it all but impossible for them to have any noticeable impact on the conflicts of the day. With only a handful of exceptions, the US or Soviet Union used their veto power in the Security Council to keep the UN out of the kinds of conflict zones that we considered in earlier chapters.

The end of the Cold War changed all that. All of a sudden, the UN was at the heart of most major peacebuilding initiatives. No one claimed that its efforts brought world peace to our clichéd doorstep. Nonetheless, imperfect as they were, they did show us how IGOs could make a difference.

As you will see in part 4, while the UN's ambitious have continued to grow, its ability to act effectively in dealing with crises has not kept pace with demand for its services. Therefore, the 1990s in some ways marks the high point as far as the UN's influence on global conflict is concern.

UN Basics

Although the UN was given more powers than its predecessor, the League of Nations, no one ever expected it to be a world government for one simple reason. As realist international relations scholars regularly remind us, **sovereignty** would still reside in the member states. In other words, the UN cannot intervene to assure world peace whenever or wherever its leaders want to. Under most circumstances, it has to have the consent of the countries involved. And even when they want to act, the UN's leaders also have to overcome some important internal hurdles of their own. Still, its founders assumed that it would play a far more important role than the League of Nations had in preserving the peace.

Cold War tensions mostly kept it from meeting those expectations until the 1990s. That was the case because real decision-making power on questions of war and peace lies with the **Security Council** and the UN offices it supervises. The Security Council has fifteen member states. Ten of them are chosen on a regional basis and serve two-year terms. The five main victorious allies from World War II have the other seats and are known as **permanent members**—the US, the UK, France, Russia, and China.[1] Each has a veto power, which means that it can prevent the council from taking action. All of them—but especially the US, the Soviet Union/Russia, and China—have done so often enough to keep the UN on the sidelines in dozens of crises when it might have made a difference.

The United Nations Security Council

Before the Cold War fully took hold, the UN did get involved in some of the world's hot spots. It sent missions to the Middle East to help resolve the first Arab–Israeli war and to the border between the new countries of India and Pakistan. Like almost all of the missions that followed, these early UN missions

And the Rest of the UN?

Most of what the UN does has little or nothing to do with peacebuilding. Its "family" of organizations, normally referred to by their acronyms (UNICEF, UNESCO, etc.), do not have responsibility for peace and conflict issues. As a result, they will not feature prominently in this chapter. The same holds for the **General Assembly**, which includes all of the member states but has little real power when it comes to questions of war and peace in any particular part of the world.

were made up of lightly or completely unarmed soldiers, police officers, and civilian administrators.

Soon, however, it became all but impossible to deploy even that kind of mission. By the end of the 1940s, the Soviet Union and the US were willing to use the veto power to block the creation of these kinds of missions wherever either felt its vital national interests were at stake. At the height of the Cold War, that meant just about everywhere.

As a result, the UN was rarely able to summon the votes needed to send even lightly armed blue-helmeted peacekeeping forces (called that because of the distinctive color of their headgear) to maintain a fragile peace. It had even fewer levers to use on those rare occasions when it was called on to actually stop the fighting in any of the world's trouble spots.

The one apparent exception to the rule shows just how much the Cold War hamstrung the UN's peacekeeping efforts. In 1950, the US asked the UN to send troops to South Korea in response to a Chinese-led invasion from the North. Because the Nationalist government on Taiwan still held the Chinese seat, it was not about to cast a veto. However, the Soviet Union, which backed the North's invasion, would have vetoed the American resolution had it cast a vote. Because the Soviet Union was boycotting Security Council sessions at the time, it did not cast its expected veto. UN troops led by the US were then deployed to Korea where they still remain today, since the war was never brought to an official end.

After that, one of the five permanent members either threatened to or actually cast a veto whenever the UN might have intervened in a major world crisis. UN troops and peacekeepers, thus, were not sent to Vietnam, Afghanistan, Algeria, and most other places where fighting raged.

Peacekeeping before 1989: The Case of Cyprus

There were limits to what those few missions could do that were summed up by their very title, **peacekeeping**, whose scope was far less ambitious than I have in mind when I use the term peacebuilding. While I will define these and other related terms later in this section on the UN, it is enough to see two things at this point. First, the few UN missions that did get deployed were not expected to do all that much. Second, UN leaders used the window of opportunity provided by the end of the Cold War to dramatically expand its goals as you will see in the rest of this section.

Most of them were sent to countries where the parties to the dispute had agreed to a cease-fire, although in many cases, the peace was fragile at best. Most of the blue helmets were unarmed and were deployed primarily to monitor the degree to which the parties were living up to their agreements. The first few missions in the Middle East and South Asia had been small and had limited mandates. The first large mission in what is now the Democratic Republic of Congo (DRC) had about twenty thousand soldiers, but its rules of engagement put very strict limits on when and how they could use their weapons. And as we know from the history of that country since the 1960s, the UN was the first of many organizations that failed to end the ongoing fighting in the DRC.

The UN occasionally enjoyed a modicum of success that it could build upon after 1989 as you can see by examining its mission in Cyprus which is still in place. Cyprus is an island off the southern coast of Turkey. Roughly eighty percent of the 1.2 million people who live there, however, are of Greek origin and identify as such. Despite its location, only about two hundred thousand of them are Turks.

The island's history is complicated because it had long been a geopolitical ping pong ball that shifted back and forth between Western (essentially Greek and Orthodox) and Ottoman (Turkish and Muslim) rule until 1878 when it became a British colony for reasons that need not concern us here. From then on, the Greek population dreamed of a (re)union with Greece known as *enosis* while the Turks wanted the island partitioned so that their portion could become part of nearby Turkey.

After World War II, the British began planning for Cypriot independence. As was the case in most of its colonies, that planning only deepened ethnic antagonisms. In 1960, Britain granted **Cyprus** its independence under a constitution that called for a single government but protected Turkish minority rights. Those arrangements broke down in December 1963 when the country's president, Archbishop Makarios III proposed constitutional amendments which many Turks believed were designed to remove provisions that protected their rights. Rioting broke out in the capital city, Nicosia, and soon spread around the country.

In part because this conflict raised a few Cold War–related issues, the Security Council was able to send what became the lightly armed **UNFICYP** (United Nations Forces in Cyprus) in May 1964 to keep the two sides from fighting again. Since then, the UN's **good offices** have also been used to bring the two sides closer together but has not yet been able to forge a lasting peace.

UNFICYP did not succeed on either front at the time, but not for a lack of trying. The UN sponsored negotiations came close to reaching a power sharing agreement for governing the island nation but failed to reach a successful conclusion. Then, after a military coup in Greece, the Turkish army invaded Cyprus in 1974 and gained control of the northeastern third of the island which led to the creation of the Turkish Republic of Northern Cyprus. In all, about one-fifth of the population was forced to move with Turks heading north and Greeks south so that by the end of that year, the population of the island lived in what amounted to two ethnically homogeneous enclaves that were separated by a UN-controlled **green line**.

Even though the UNFICYP forces are mostly unarmed and have a total budget of under $60 million today, their presence has kept armed forces from the two sides apart. More importantly, life has returned to something like normal in the two parts of the island. The Greek half is now quite prosperous given its membership in the EU and its role as a place for Russians and others from the former communist world to invest, bank, and live. The Turkish half of the island is not as well to do, but its regime is secure and enjoys widespread popular support even if it is not recognized by most of the world's other governments.

At first, it was all but impossible for Greeks and Turks to visit the other's side of the island. Now, it is fairly easy for people cross the border, at least in cities like Nicosia that straddle the Green Line. Few choose to do so, however.

FIGURE 9.1
Map of Cyprus Showing the Green Line

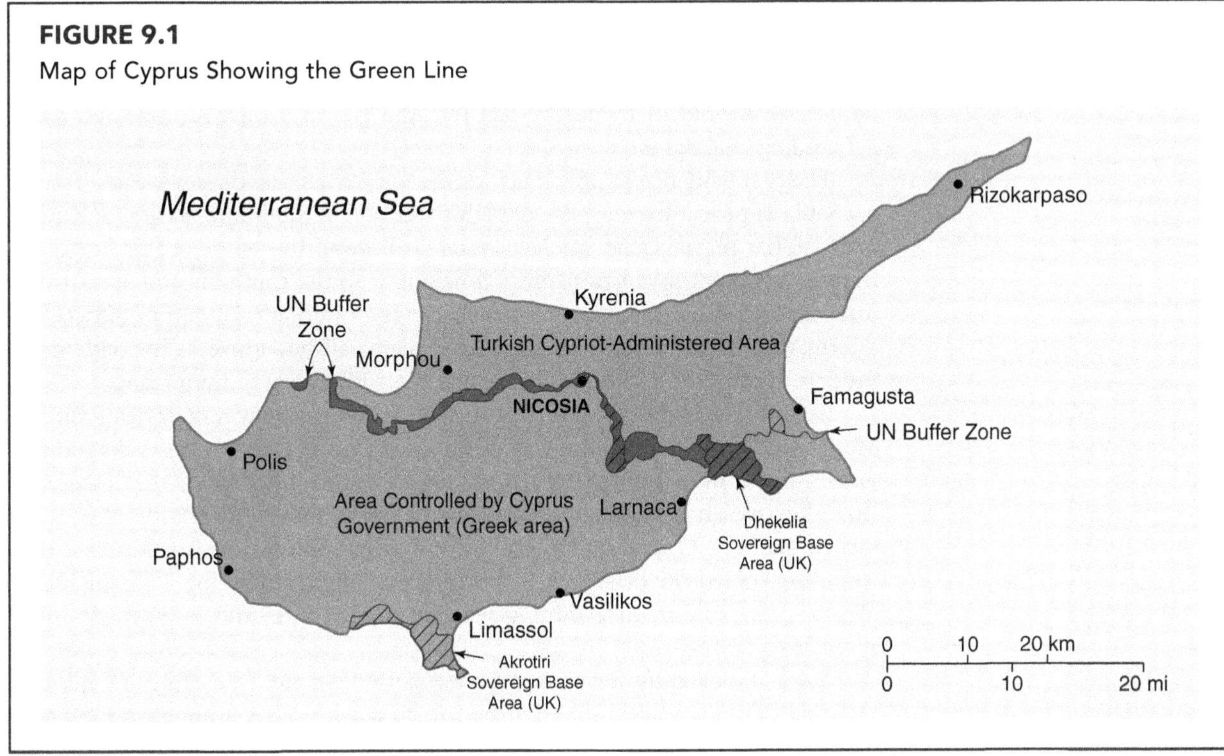

The UN has not been able to get the two sides to find a permanent resolution to the dispute, although most leaders agree that there should be a federal government that gives both communities autonomy over its own affairs. The two governments did reach an agreement along those lines in 2004, but the Greek side overwhelmingly defeated it in a referendum.

Each peace process is, of course, unique. However, the case of Cyprus does suggest some common denominators shared by all UN-brokered peacekeeping missions, especially those that began in its early years:

- The UN can rarely compel the parties to a dispute to put down their weapons.
- Because most of its missions are at most lightly armed, the UN has a hard time imposing an agreement that we will call peacemaking in the next section.
- The UN succeeds to the extent that people on all sides accept its moral authority and legitimacy.

UN Peacekeeping in the 1990s

All of that changed between 1989 and 1991. Because the US and Russia (which replaced the Soviet Union as a permanent member of the Security Council) no longer saw every conflict in zero-sum terms, there was a veritable explosion in the number of missions the UN deployed. Between 1945 and 1980, it sent a total of eighteen missions. In the 1990s alone, it mounted thirty-nine more.

Some were unarmed and simply monitored dangerous situations in places like Tajikistan. Some were traditional peacekeeping missions, for instance, in Haiti or the Central African Republic. Some went further than anything the UN had even contemplated before and tried to prevent war or pick up the pieces after the fighting stopped, as you will see in a few paragraphs in Bosnia and Rwanda.

For our purposes, the key is not simply that there were more UN missions. Rather, we should focus on the fact that the UN also took on new and more demanding challenges.

The best evidence of how much things were changing does not come from a particularly peaceful example—the UN's reaction to the Iraqi invasion of Kuwait in 1990. For reasons that would take us far beyond the scope of this book, the Iraqi government invaded its oil rich neighbor to the south, on the pretext that Kuwait was really its nineteenth province. The international community (itself a term that came into use during these years) all but universally condemned Saddam Hussein's regime and demanded the withdrawal of Iraqi troops.

Because the Cold War was over and the Soviet Union was in its death throes, Moscow did not stand in the way of President George H. W. Bush's decision to force Iraq out of Kuwait. It did not always cooperate, but neither the Soviet nor, later, the Russian government vetoed any of the resolutions that authorized what turned out to be Operation Desert Storm. In this context, it is worth noting that while the US led the brief war, it was officially approved by the UN which also played a key role in determining what happened after the Iraqi government agreed to a cease-fire.

More importantly for the purposes of this chapter, the UN now became the organization peacebuilders turned to first when they wanted the international community to help build peace. But it did so without having updated the UN's procedures and mandates in light of the the growing importance of identity-based conflict. Not surprisingly, the deployment of lightly armed troops with **rules of engagement** that restricted their use of force got many of these missions in trouble, which is what I will focus on by considering two of its most ambitious efforts and important failures of the decade—Bosnia and Rwanda

Bosnia. As you saw in chapter 8, Yugoslavia was created out of the ashes of World War I and included an ethnic hodgepodge of Slavs whose rivalries could be traced back for centuries. We can ignore many of them here other than noting that its six constituent republics and two autonomous regions were all ethnically mixed, although one group dominated each of them.

Many people at the time argued that the fighting that broke out in 1992 was the result of what they referred to as "ancient racial hatreds." While it is true that the differences between Serbs, in particular, and other Slavic ethnic groups can be traced back at least to the fourteenth century, the outbreak in the 1990s was actively promoted by politicians who played the "ethnic card," especially in Serbia.

The newly independent Bosnia started out with plenty of problems. Its government was corrupt. The economy was mired in a prolonged slump. As a result many Bosnians relied on the remittances they received from family members who lived and worked abroad. In other words, Yugoslavia as a whole, and Bosnia in particular, suffered from a classic collection of wicked problems, which made it easy for politicians to stoke the political fires by making identity-based claims.

The fighting started elsewhere, but when the war did finally reach **Bosnia**, it was truly gruesome. At least two hundred thousand people died and ten times that many had to flee their homes. So many women were raped that the international community declared it a war crime. Terms like **ethnic cleansing** were coined to describe the return of genocide to Europe, less than half a century after the

Holocaust. The fighting continued for three years, culminating in the massacre at Srebrenica, where more than eight thousand Muslim boys and men had gathered in what they thought was a safe haven. Instead, they were slaughtered by Serb paramilitaries while UN forces watched, powerless to do anything to stop the carnage.

The UN could not do much even though there were plenty of requests for it to intervene. Early on, Bosnian President Alija Izetbegovic asked the UN to send peacekeepers, but the international body determined that it could not do so until a cease-fire was declared. The EU also tried to find a negotiated settlement without success.

In late 1992, the UN did authorize **UNPROFOR** (United Nations Protection Force for the Former Yugoslavia) to try to limit the fighting in all of the former republics other than Slovenia which was already independent and reasonably stable. With about twenty thousand troops, it was the largest United Nations mission to date. However, given its terms of engagement, aggressive UN military action was out of the question. Meanwhile, the EU and UN continued their diplomatic effort while the war continued and the Bosnian capital city of Sarajevo was besieged for more than three years.

In the end, it took the active intervention of the United States to end the fighting. Under the leadership of Richard Holbrooke, the US was eventually able to get all of the sides to the negotiating table at Wright-Patterson Air Force Base, where they hammered out the **Dayton Accords**.

The agreement essentially divided Bosnia into three largely ethnically homogeneous and autonomous regions. It also authorized the deployment of sixty thousand **IFOR** (International Force, later SFOR or Stabilization Force) to keep the sides from fighting again. Although authorized by the UN, IFOR and SFOR were actually NATO operations.

In the end, it is hard to be anything but critical of the UN's role in Bosnia. The best we can say is that its difficulties contributed to the expansion of the international community's mandate for dealing with all forms of conflict, which we will turn to after we see the UN's even more tragic failure in Rwanda.

Rwanda. The genocide in **Rwanda** was even worse than the one in Bosnia. Like the former Yugoslavia, Rwandan politics had long been shaped by ethnic differences whose origins are centuries old. However, it was only during Belgium's colonial rule in Rwanda and neighboring Burundi that the differences between Hutus and Tutsis became identity-based powder kegs.

For reasons that are not important here, the Belgians turned the differences between the two groups into the defining characteristic in Rwandan society, often forcing individuals to define themselves as one or the other for the first time. They also favored the Tutsi minority, leaving them atop most hierarchies when the country gained its independence in 1962 thereby embittering many Hutus.

The new Rwandan regime was never particularly stable. By the early 1990s, the majority Hutus were in power when Tutsi rebels based in neighboring Uganda launched a surprise attack and took control of much of the country. Many feared a full-blown civil war would ensue until international mediators convinced the two sides to accept the 1993 Arusha Accords which called for a degree of power sharing. The agreement also created a traditional UN peacekeeping and observation force, **UNAMIR** (United Nations Assistance Mission for Rwanda).

Meanwhile, Hutu extremists began plotting against their own leaders and preparing to wipe out the Tutsis. On the night of April 6, 1994, an airplane carrying the presidents of Burundi and Rwanda back from a negotiating session in Arusha was shot down as it approached the airport in Rwanda's capital city, Kinshasa. The Hutu government, its radio station, and others called for revenge against the Tutsis, whom it blamed for the attack on the airplane. The genocide began the next day. Between April 7 and the following July, somewhere between five hundred thousand and one million Rwandans were killed. Most of them by machete.

People were slaughtered, including many who had taken refuge in churches and hospitals. One of the worst atrocities occurred at a technical school in Murambi where sixty-five thousand Tutsis went seeking refuge after being assured that French troops would protect them (see the photograph at the start of chapter 7). Instead, Hutu extremists attacked and killed forty-five thousand of them on the spot. Most of the few who escaped were killed a few days later after seeking safety in a church which was, itself, attacked. The French soldiers who were supposedly protecting the victims ended up digging mass graves into which their bodies were thrown. Today, the school is home to one of five sites commemorating the genocide and is best known for its rooms full of skulls including the one in that photograph.

In assessing the UN's role in the tragedy, we have to return to the onset of the crisis and note that the Canadian general heading UNAMIR, **Roméo Dallaire** (1946–), had warned his superiors in New York that a genocide was immanent and that he could prevent it if he had a few thousand more troops and a mandate that allowed him to use force. That authority never came because world leaders were not willing to authorize it. Besides, UNAMIR had been deployed with the consent of all parties to the dispute, and the Hutus certainly would have rejected any greater use of force. Dallaire and his team tried to broker a truce, but they were hamstrung by the terms of their deployment under chapter VI of the UN Charter which prohibited them from using force.

The genocide only ended when the Tutsi rebels gained control of the entire country. Even that didn't end the carnage, since as many as two million Hutus fled to neighboring countries where hundreds of thousands remain to this day.

And, remember that there were only eight million Rwandans when the crisis began.

The UN Rethinks Its Role

Scholars and practitioners understood that traditional UN peacekeeping missions could only reduce the likelihood of violence *under the right circumstances.* I emphasized under the right circumstances in the preceding sentence because the circumstances obviously weren't right in Bosnia and Rwanda.

Given the upbeat mood of the early 1990s, the mixed results did not deter the UN's leaders who soon began to rethink *and expand* the organization's agenda in five key ways. None of them have been fully implemented because of the UN's own structure and the continuing rivalry among its most powerful member states. Nonetheless, including them even as rhetorical goals demonstrates the degree to which the entire international community saw its peacebuilding role expand during the 1990s. In reading about those goals, keep in mind that most of them were adopted late in the decade. Then, when the UN faced new pressures early in the twenty-first century, most of them were not fully implemented. Still, they define the international community's expanded aspirations as far as peace and conflict resolution are concerned. At some future point when superpower rivalries do not keep the UN hamstrung, they may live up to the promise many of us anticipated a generation ago.

Agenda for Peace. The UN made it clear that it was broadening its agenda when Secretary General **Boutros Boutros-Ghali** (1922–2016) issued the Security Council's *Agenda for Peace* in 1992. He pointed out that the UN had gone far beyond the kinds of peacekeeping and monitoring missions you saw in Cyprus. The UN's policies therefore had to catch up with the new reality by including the following kinds of interventions, all of which remain on its agenda today:

- **Peacemaking**. Where fighting was taking place, as in Bosnia or Rwanda, the international community would have to engage in **peacemaking** or impose peace over the heads of the warring parties and even national governments.
- **Peace enforcement**. Once fragile cease-fires are in place, UN soldiers, police officers, and others would be called on to engage in **peace enforcement** and maintain law and order or physical security so that fighting did not break out again.
- **Peacekeeping**. There would still, of course, be a need for the traditional missions, many of which were deployed in less volatile parts of the world during the 1990s.
- **Peacebuilding**. The UN would have to be involved in efforts to address the root causes of the conflict in ways that began merging peace with the UN's other traditional initiatives involving education, health, development, gender, the environment, and so on.

This fourfold breakdown was not only important for the UN. Much like Michael Lund's curve (see chapter 3), they showed us that peacebuilding is a complicated, multidimensional phenomenon. The people I worked with then and now gravitated toward the peacebuilding end of Boutros-Ghali's continuum. However, we also came to realize that we can't do that work unless someone else has already made, enforced, and kept the peace. To the surprise of many, that "someone else" often turned out to be the military, which few of us had ever thought of as a potential partner before—a point I will return to frequently in the rest of this book.

R2P. Before the 1990s, UN intervention was usually seen as a last resort to be considered only after everything else had failed—and then only if the obstacles posed by the superpower rivalry could be overcome. In other words, when the UN did get involved, it reacted to an existing human disaster.

By the end of the decade, UN officials were beginning to think proactively, arguing that humanitarian law and basic morality compelled them to act in what came to be called the **Responsibility to Protect (R2P)**. Earlier interventions had been made using what is known as chapter VII authority which focused on conflicts between states and made respecting their internal sovereignty a top priority. Now, Boutros-Ghali and his successor, Kofi Annan, declared that the UN had an obligation to prevent genocide, war crimes, and ethnic cleaning from occurring in the first place even if that meant violating an offending government's national sovereignty.

The mere fact that the UN was willing to even consider R2P was significant because it called into question not only the underpinnings of the UN but also of realist theory. Earlier attempts to provide food, clothing, medical supplies, and other forms of humanitarian relief to people suffering in combat zones had often been stymied when states refused to allow the UN to operate in its supposedly sovereign territory. Now, Annan made case that the UN had to act.

> If humanitarian intervention is, indeed, an unacceptable assault on sovereignty, how should we respond to a Rwanda, to a Srebrenica—to gross and systemic violations of human rights that offend every precept of our common humanity.[2]

It was only in 2005 that the General Assembly formally adopted these principles. It should also be noted, they have been used sparingly in large part because one or more of the permanent Security Council members found reasons to object to them and invoked their veto power as the Russians and Chinese did when the US wanted to obtain UN approval for its 2003 invasion of Iraq.

The International Criminal Court. Many of us thought humanity had learned its lesson after the Holocaust. The UN and its member states adopted a series of human rights conventions and took other steps to strengthen international law so that we could live up to one of the most powerful pleas made by Holocaust survivors and their supporters—never again.

The genocides of the 1990s demonstrated that international legal system did not go anywhere near far enough. Rather than "never again," mass atrocities had become an all too common occurrence as we first realized in the killing field of Cambodia in late 1970s. Now, Rwanda, Bosnia, and more brought the question of war crimes and genocide back onto the global agenda. In particular, international legal activists wanted to create permanent, standing institutions that could be used to held perpetrators accountable.

International law, of course, antedated our current concern with crimes against humanity. As the realists are quick to point out, however, the relevant courts were rarely able to enforce their decisions, could only hear cases involving states, and often functioned only if the states that were party to a dispute agreed to submit a case to their jurisdiction. That changed a bit after World War II when the Allies established ad hoc courts to deal with German and Japanese war criminals. Of the two, the Nuremberg trials were the more famous because they resulted in the execution of most surviving Nazi leaders.

For good or ill, attempts to create a permanent international court that had real enforcement power foundered until the number of genocide and similar atrocities in the 1990s. Initially, the UN created ad hoc tribunals to hear cases for those accused of crimes against humanity in Rwanda and the former Yugoslavia. These were the first war crimes trials since those held after World War II and built moment for the creation of a permanent **International Criminal Court (ICC)**, which would have jurisdiction over the kinds of crime covered by R2P. The General Assembly approved a treaty to create the ICC in 1998. It went into effect after sixty countries had ratified the treaty and opened its doors in 2002.

Note, however, that a number of countries voted against its creation, never ratified the treaty, or both and do not come under its jurisdiction. That includes the US, Russia, China, and India. In other words, to the degree that the Court has had an impact, it has not involved the major powers, including three of the five permanent members of the Security Council.

Still, the ICC's creation was certainly a starting point that later generations might be able to build on.

Human security. Traditional realists—including most diplomats—would have defined national security in geopolitical terms in which traditional questions of war and peace were all that mattered. Leaders like Gorbachev and some cutting edge scholars started expanding that definition when they began talking about common or collective security in the 1980s.

The UN Development Programme annual report in 1994 broke new ground when it referred to human rather than "just" national security. Its lead author, Mahbub ul Haq made the case that what we mean by security had to be expanded given the events of the preceding half-century:

> The world can never be at peace unless people have security in their daily lives. Future conflicts may often be within nations rather than between them—with their origins buried deep within socio-economic deprivations and disparities. The search for security in such a milieu lies in development not in arms.[3]

In the twenty years since then, ul Haq's sense of "deprivations and disparities" has been expanded to include the environment, development, gender, and the other issues that have been at the heart of the UN's work ever since. More importantly for the purposes of this book, it got peace and conflict studies experts to begin thinking holistically which eventually led us to emphasize systems thinking when we developed Peacebuilding 3.0. At this point, it is enough to see that the premises and promises of human security allowed us to portray Peacebuilding 2.0 using metaphors like the daisy in figure 1.3 that conceptually and explicitly connected peace to other socials and economic concerns for the first time.

The Millennium Development Goals. The UN leadership also realized that statements like ul Haq's were important because they defined key new goals. They were, however, lofty aspirations and it would take a coordinated and global effort to turn those dreams into reality. It began to do so by adopting a series of measurable targets for the first fifteen years of the new century in the **Millennium Development Goals (MDGs)**. As is the wont of the UN, its leaders went back and forth in determining what should be on that list and made a number of compromises along the way, including not mentioning peace in any of the goals. Still, the MDGs would serve as benchmarks for measuring the progress the international community as a whole made in achieving human security.

On one level, the MDG, too, seemed like little more than another list of pie-in-the-sky ideals that would be honored in the breach, including:

- eradicating poverty and hunger
- universal primary education
- gender equality
- reducing child mortality
- improving maternal health
- combating HIV/AIDS
- environmental sustainability
- creating a global partnership for development

But the MDGs were different because they contained plausible, specific subgoals for each of the main categories. There is no reason to detail all of the MDGs here, but three of them should show how practical—and achievable—the goals were:

- halve the number of people living in extreme poverty, which it defined as living on the the equivalent of $1.25 a day
- reduce the number of children who die before reaching the age of five by two-thirds
- improve the living conditions of at least one hundred million slum dwellers

Needless to say, progress toward reaching the goals was uneven, as you will see in chapter 12 when I discuss the SDGs that came into effect in 2015. For now, it is enough to see that however imperfect the goals and their implementation might have been, they did mark an important step forward, because they committed the international community to tangible changes in policy areas that had not even been on the global agenda a few short years earlier.

THE OTHER INTERNATIONAL INSTITUTIONS

Although their impact paled in comparison with the UN, I should at least mention the expanded role of a few other international organizations. They are best known for expanding their impact in policy areas that do not involve conflict resolution or peacebuilding. Nonetheless, they did set the stage for these organizations to play an expanded role in the next century, which means that they are worth at least a cursory look here.

The European Union. The 1990s were boom years for the EU. It took on new powers, expanded its membership, and prepared to launch the world's first multinational currency, the euro, which went into circulation in 2002.

Here, it is worth noting that the EU also took tentative steps toward becoming more than an economic community. Thus, as we have already seen, it was a key player in the early efforts to end the fighting in Bosnia. Similarly, the Treaty of Maastricht (which also created the euro) anticipated the creation of a common security policy as one of the EU's three "pillars" or centers of power.

NATO. The **North Atlantic Treaty Organization (NATO)** is a military alliance and therefore rarely finds its way into books on peacebuilding or conflict resolution. Created in 1949 to contain the Soviets, many in the peacebuilding community wanted to abolish it after the end of the Cold War. For good or ill, NATO leaders ended up redefining the alliance's mission in two key ways instead. First, along with the EU, it helped define new responses to security threats within its own region, as it did in nominally spearheading the SFOR and IFOR missions in the former Yugoslavia. More importantly (although less peacefully), it began to expand its footprint to cover most of the world, with its support for the ouster of Iraq from Kuwait in what became known as the first Gulf War.

African Union. Of the other regional bodies, the African Union (AU) is the most important for our purposes. It was formally created in 2002, replacing the earlier Organization for African Unity. Even before it formally came into existence, the OAU and some of its member states played an active role in trying to end conflicts, especially in the aftermath of the genocide in Rwanda.

The International Financial Institutions. The **World Bank**, the **International Monetary Fund**, and the **World Trade Organization** are informally referred to as the **International Financial Institutions (IFIs)**. They did not have peacebuilding on their initial agendas. If anything, the IMF was seen as "part of the problem" because of its insistence on free trade and structural adjustment policies that tended to exacerbate rather than ease identity-based conflict in much of the Global South.

However, as it became clear that intractable conflicts were inhibiting development, their leaders gradually came to the conclusion that they had to include peacebuilding as part of their mission. As we will see in part 4, these bodies only began taking that work seriously in the last decade or so. Still, they began to consider peace and conflict issues when they touched on trade and development as certainly was the case with the MDGs.

Perhaps most importantly of all for analyzing global conflict, the IFIs were at the heart of sustaining the **liberal peace**. The World Bank has explored alternatives to northern domination of a world capitalist order in the last decade or so which has turned it into one of the most innovative peacebuilding institutions in the world today. However, you will have to wait until part 4 to see that.

MULTITRACK DIPLOMACY

It is now time for peacebuilders themselves to enter the discussion. Don't, however, expect them to be major players.

In fact, the story that will unfold in the rest of this chapter comes close to being the mirror image of the one you saw in chapter 8. There, I documented an explosion of activity by peacebuilding NGOs based in the North who worked primarily in the Global South. You will see a period of growth here as well. But now, most of the leverage came from the international organizations we just discussed and from the countries facing the conflicts themselves. Northern governments were obviously part of all of the global peacebuilding initiatives during the 1990s. However, the peacebuilding NGOs rarely had a "piece of the action."

In fact, most of the organizations discussed in chapter 8 did not even try to get a seat at the grown-ups' table in the advanced industrialized democracies. Many assumed that their position as a third-party neutral meant that they should avoid supporting one side or the other in political disputes. Others were convinced that they would not be taken seriously by established foreign policy communities.

That does not mean that we avoided all political engagement. In countries that were wracked by conflict, any solution would have to have a public policy component. Similarly, reaching the Millennium Development Goals would require action on the part of the world's governments as well as the UN itself.

Still, our impact on the political life of the advanced industrialized democracies was limited. Interaction, the network of American-based NGOs in the development and humanitarian space, was already effectively pressing governments to provide more funding for humanitarian relief and development aid. Peacebuilders did the same, while also trying to convince the American, British, Canadian, German, and other governments to adopt policies that would be more conducive to peace in the world's hot spots. But, we mostly avoided getting involved in major policy debates. That changed dramatically after the turn of the century, but in the 1990s, we rarely had a place at the policy-making grown-ups' table in part because we still assumed that "they" would not take us very seriously.

You briefly encountered the one "exception" to this "rule" in part 2—informal or **Track II diplomacy**. There, I presented it as a set of tools used by relatively powerless actors (e.g., the sister cities movements during the Cold War) or as grassroots efforts (e.g., people to people initiatives between Israelis and Palestinians). Now, you will see how similar initiatives made a difference at far higher, policy-making levels.

By the time the Cold War ended, people inside and outside of governments were already using the term which had been coined by Joseph Montville when he was one of those State Department officials who had to work with what most of his colleagues thought of as well-intentioned amateurs. Montville was one of the few career diplomats who appreciated the fact that "amateurs" could do things that their "professional" colleagues could not, something he has himself continued to do since he retired from the American foreign service in 1994.

Technically, Track II activists refers to efforts by people who were not themselves in office (hence the idea of a second track), but were close to the men and women who were. Montville and others argued that those informal discussions could then lead to agreements by officials who did have the authority to make binding public policy. By the end of the 1990s, the term was used to cover a wide variety of activities, including the problem-solving workshops discussed in chapter 8.

If nothing else, Track II activists could meet with people who were off limits to official diplomats as was the case both in Israel/Palestine and South Africa. In short, they could take risks and explore new issues that conventional diplomats could not easily address. Sometimes, their efforts went nowhere. More often than realists expected at the time, they laid the groundwork for breakthroughs that formal officer-holders ultimately got the credit for.

It also turned out that Montville was not alone. Senior officials in the US and other Western governments came to see the value of informal diplomacy. As you are about to see, some were professional diplomats whose frustrations with normal channels led them to be willing to experiment with new techniques. Some were career politicians who transferred their ability to forge unusually broad coalitions at home and started using them in the international arena. By the end of the decade, there so many different initiatives along these lines that we began calling them **multitrack diplomacy** as you can see by (re)considering three examples we have already encountered.

Israel and Palestine

Although it may be hard to believe today, there was a time when it looked like the conflict between Israel and the Palestinians might end with the adoption of a **two state solution**. The odds were always stacked against it for reasons Deborah Gerner put her finger on in her aptly titled book *One Land, Two Peoples*.[4] Two antagonistic communities laid claim to the same territory. As she and other authors demonstrated, the two sides had been at logger heads ever since a significant number of Zionist settlers arrived in what was then an out of the way corner of the Ottoman Empire in the late nineteenth century. Skirmishes broke out almost immediately and turned into full scale wars in 1948, 1956, 1967, and 1974. While there has not been a traditional war since then, the region remains a violent conflict zone because it is a hotbed of both terrorism and mass protests.

Professional diplomats have made their share of peace proposals over the years. A few, like Henry Kissinger's "shuttle diplomacy," were important enough to be included in many international relations courses to this day. Others even made some progress, including the establishment of formal diplomatic relations and the creation of an initially shaky peace between Israel and Egypt that has been in place since the late 1970s.

However, it is highly unlikely that conventional diplomatic efforts alone could ever have led to a breakthrough. That was certainly true in the early 1990s which opened in the aftermath of the first **Intifada** or protests by young Palestinians angered by forty years of what they saw as Israeli oppression. The demonstrations typically pitted stone-throwing Palestinian youths against well-armed Israeli soldiers and police officers. Before the protests lost their momentum, about one thousand protesters had been killed, and the size of the demonstrations made it clear that the **Palestine Liberation Organization (PLO)** no longer spoke for all of the Palestinians in the West Bank, Gaza, or Israel proper.

Amid this turmoil, there was one reason why peace advocates were more optimistic than they had been at any point since the first Arab–Israeli war in 1948. The end of the Cold War made peacebuilding more attractive, including the use of Track II diplomacy. For reasons we don't have time to get into here, this was one of the regional conflicts that was most closely tied to the superpower rivalry. From the 1960s onward, the Soviet Union had given the PLO lots of aid, financially and otherwise. All of a sudden, that support disappeared which led **Yasir Arafat** (1929–2004) and other PLO leaders to become more open to discussions with Israel. The situation became even more fluid as a result of the first Gulf War in which the PLO sided more or less openly with Iraq which led the George H. W. Bush administration to explore new options in the Middle East writ large.

During these years, academic observers began seeing the shortcomings in the argument William Zartman and others had made about how a **mutually hurting stalemate** was a necessary precondition for ending a long-standing armed conflict. As you are about to see, the existence of such a stalemate itself does not always lead to effective negotiations let alone to a lasing and equitable agreement. Nonetheless, once leaders on both sides decided that the costs of continued fighting would far outweigh any plausible benefits, they often become more open to talking with their adversaries. One could make the case that such a stalemate had existed for years—if not decades—between Israel and Palestine, but that no one had yet found a way to seize on the opportunities such an impasse potentially provides.

This is where one of the world's most famous Track II initiatives took place. Recall from chapter 8 that Israelis and Palestinians were routinely meeting in dialogues that addressed any number of pathways toward more peaceful relations between their two communities. Some of them involved prominent Israelis and Palestinians who had close ties to the current leadership, but were themselves private citizens. All were held in secret, and most took place outside of the Middle East.

Things sped up on that front in the early 1990s. The end of the Cold War removed Soviet hostility toward Israel and the US from the equation. Bill Clinton's election to the presidency in 1992 ushered in a new administration that promised to be more flexible in its own policies toward the region.

These global events might not have amount to much if someone other than **Yitzhak Rabin** (1922–1995) had become prime minister of Israel. Despite a distinguished military career and having been in charge of putting down the intifada in the previous government, Rabin let it be known that he, too, would be more flexible as more and more Israelis and Palestinians came to say at least privately that they had reached a mutually hurting stalemate.

Meanwhile, the Norwegian sociologist who initiated the talks that led to the **Oslo Accords**, Terje Larsen, informed the Israeli and Palestinian authorities that his research institute was willing to host informal talks. It did not hurt that Larsen's partner was a senior foreign service officer who reported to the Norwegian foreign minister. Larsen and his team began discussions with Yossi Beilin, a leader of Rabin's Labor Party, and Abu Ala, one of Arafat's closest confidants.

In early 1993, the Israeli parliament lifted its ban on direct contacts between Israelis and members of the PLO. Larsen then held an initial meeting in London that went well enough that he was able to get the Norwegian foreign ministry (in other words, his partner convinced her boss) to organize a session in Oslo under the guise of an academic seminar, That turned into the Norway round.

Over the next six months, seven key negotiators held a series of secret meetings. In fact, the talks were so confidential that most key decision makers in Washington did not even know they were taking place until a few days before the Accords were announced.

Firsthand accounts of the sessions reflect the same kinds of interpersonal dynamics we saw with grassroots activists in chapter 8. As the men (they were all men) got to know each other, ignorance, antagonism, and stereotypical thinking began to evaporate.

Once it became clear that the two sides were nearing a breakthrough, the PLO and the Israeli government sent more senior officials, who had the authority to speak for their respective leaderships. They could not reach a sweeping agreement, but they did do something that had eluded traditional diplomats for forty years. Their Declaration of Principles was issued in August 1993 and consummated with a famous session on the White House lawn that included the public handshake between Arafat and Rabin which you can see in the photograph at the beginning of this chapter.

Three of the agreement's provisions are important here. First, Israel recognized the PLO, while the Palestinians acknowledged Israel's right to exist, neither of which had been politically possible before. Second, Israel accepted the Palestinians' right to self-government in the West Bank and the Gaza Strip, both of which it occupied during the 1967 war. Third, the agreement called on both parties to continue negotiating until Israel withdrew from most of the occupied territories. The agreement also held out hope for what has since been called a two state solution in which Israel would recognize the existence of a Palestinian state that would have sovereignty over most or all of the West Bank and Gaza.

Those negotiations never reached their hoped-for conclusions, as anyone can see by glancing at the news today. The failure to finish the Oslo process to bring the kind of stability you will see in the next section on Northern Ireland was not purely the fault of the Accord or its negotiators. They understood that Oslo had the makings of what political scientists call an **orphaned agreement** that dies on the vine because negotiators fail to seize on the momentum coming out of the original deal.

In this case, the failure to do so doomed the negotiations and went a long ways toward creating the impasse the region finds itself in today. Indeed, the Oslo Accords were never meant to be anything more than a provisional agreement and were based on the assumption that further and even more complicated negotiations would follow. At the time, hopes were high that the two sides could reach broader agreements as the Palestinian Authority gained control over more of the West Bank, and Israel eventually withdrew its troops from Gaza.

However, once the initial enthusiasm died down, the situation deteriorated. Rabin was assassinated by a right-wing Jewish extremist. Tensions ounted as Israel continued to build settlements and imposed its rule on parts of the West Bank that made any prospects for creating a viable Palestinian state diminish. Meanwhile, a second intifada broke out in 2000, hardening Israeli resistance to making further concessions. Then came 9/11, after which divisions within each community deepened and we returned to the seemingly unbridgeable impasse we are at today.

In the process, another concept was born—the **spoiler**—which refers to leaders or groups who act as troublemakers who undermine an agreement (see the box on the next page). A wide variety of individuals and organizations did their best to do just that after Arafat and Rabin's famous handshake. That starts with Rabin's assassin. But, there were other Israelis, including the conservatives who came to power shortly thereafter and have dominated political life there ever since. On the Palestinian side, the Second Intifada, Hamas's rise to power in Gaza, Arafat's death, and other events made it hard for the PLO to continue negotiating as the sole representative of the Palestinian people. And, for reasons that historians have yet to fully sort out, foreigners lost the ability to effectively bring Israelis and Palestinians together in ways that could lead to further agreements.

Northern Ireland

Most accounts of the other classic example of Track II diplomacy in the 1990s concentrate on what **George Mitchell** (1933–) and his team accomplished in Northern Ireland. In reality, Mitchell was not a classical Track II negotiator who only had limited ties to his own government. What's more, he was only

CONFLICT LAB 9.1

Most of the tools and techniques discussed so far in this chapter are still used today. Therefore, it makes sense to ask how each of them could be used for the national or global conflict you have been following since chapter 1:

- multitrack diplomacy
- the use of outside mediators
- faith-based peacebuilding
- avoiding spoilers

Spoilers

The Stanford political scientist Stephen Stedman was one of the first academics to talk about the ways spoilers and other troublemakers can derail peace agreements. It wasn't just Israel and Palestine. Every agreement faced opposition from people on one side or the other who could have derailed it. And it wasn't just global peace agreements. A negotiated agreement to any conflict can be disrupted by spoilers. To see why, think about the subnational conflict you have been following in the Conflict Labs.

Stedman argued that peacebuilders have to pay attention to at least four aspects of the threat posed by all of which came into play in one or more of the cases considered in this chapter.

- **Position**. Are there potential spoilers who took part in the negotiating process?
- **Number**. How many potential spoiler groups are there, and how much support could they attract?
- **Type**. How entrenched is their opposition, and what lengths are they willing to go to in voicing their opposition?
- **Power base**. What kinds of resources do spoilers have at their disposal?

If there is a lesson to be learned from conflict resolution in general and not just from the cases covered in this chapter, it is that few leaders spend enough time worrying about spoilers.

able to get the Catholics and Protestant leaders to reach the **Good Friday Agreement** in 1998 because his team capitalized on the work of a host of grassroots and other Track II initiatives. And, unlike what we just saw with the Oslo process, much of what Mitchell's team did played itself out in front of the world's television cameras.

Still, it is hard to imagine how British and Irish officials could have ended the **Troubles** on their own. Traditional diplomatic efforts did yield some results during the 1980s. The British government, for instance, acknowledged that the Republic of Ireland would have to be involved in finding or approving any solution. However, progress toward a lasting peace was glacial well into the 1990s. At that point, a number of Sinn Fein and IRA leaders (who were often one and the same) realized that there was next to no chance that they could unite Ireland and began signaling that they were open to an agreement that fell far short of that goal.

The Conservative government in London stuck to its rhetorical guns and refused to negotiate with the IRA/Sinn Fein or the extremist Protestant paramilitaries until they agreed to a cease-fire and began to disarm. Tentative cease-fires were reached during the mid-1990s that seemed to suggest that some kind of negotiated agreement was possible, but each time one was declared, it ended with a new bombing. In short, the Northern Ireland conflict had arrived at its mutually hurting stalemate, but, in this case, it was hard to see how the deadlock alone could lead to an agreement *unless and until* one or both of the parties decided to budge.

That left the door open for Mitchell and his team of third-party mediators. President Clinton broke with American political tradition when he met with Gerry Adams and other Sinn Fein leaders in Washington shortly after he assumed the presidency in 1993. Later in that year, he paid a brief visit to Northern Ireland and made a point of publicly meeting with leaders from both sides. including Adams. More importantly, he named Mitchell his special envoy for Northern Ireland and made him available to help lead the talks once they began.

It took a while before Mitchell's team gained much traction. At first, Protestant leaders balked on the assumption that he was a Roman Catholic and, they assumed, beholden to the Irish lobby in the US. In fact, he is a Maronite of Lebanese extraction. Gradually, the fact he was not "Ted Kennedy's stooge," as Protestant hard-liner Ian Paisley put it, sunk in. Still, progress was hard to come by until the 1997 British election brought the Labour Party and Tony Blair to power. Unlike the Conservative Party that had been in office since 1979, Labour had few ties to the Protestant community in Northern Ireland, had the support of most English Catholics (many of whom were of Irish origin), and included a number of leaders who were personally committed to finding a peaceful outcome in Norther Ireland.

Critical here was Marjorie (Mo) Mowlam, who was the minister for Northern Ireland in Blair's first government. Always known for her feistiness and sense of humor, Mowlam played a pivotal role at key points during the negotiations. Shortly after the talks began, she was diagnosed with a brain tumor. She continued working despite radiation treatments that made her hair fall out, leading her to start wearing a wig. When negotiations got particularly testy, Mowlam was known for taking off the wig and throwing it around the room in frustration—but also getting a laugh from the otherwise tense people sitting around the negotiating table. Similarly, in one of her more courageous acts, she visited the (in)famous Maze prison where members of the various paramilitaries were incarcerated, took off her wig, bummed a cigarette from one of the most hardened fighters, and sat down for what apparently was an intense and productive discussion.

Still, one cannot underestimate the role that Mitchell and his international team played in coaxing the parties in Northern Ireland and the governments in London and Dublin toward an agreement. Just as importantly, Mitchell had an even greater personal impact than Mowlam in part because he was even better at tugging on the heart strings of the Irish negotiators. To cite but the most obvious example, Mitchell recessed the talks so that he could go back to New York for the birth of his child. He then had his staff send a note to the Catholic and Protestant negotiators asking them why the fifty-one children born on that day in Northern Ireland shouldn't have the same opportunity to live in peace as his son Andrew would.

Mitchell could also be a tough negotiator. Here, too, a single example will do. He set the symbolically important date of Good Friday 1998 as a make-or-break deadline for reaching an agreement. After a flurry of shuttle diplomacy between London, Belfast, and Dublin, the agreement was finally reached early the next morning and announced that same day.

Like the Oslo Accords, everyone understood that the Good Friday Agreement would not settle everything. It opened the border between Northern Ireland and the Republic. All sides would disarm. A new provincial government would be created at Stormont, the palace that served as the de facto capital building. Unlike the previous government, which had been dominated by the Protestants, all parties would share power and hold cabinet offices, which meant that Unionists and Nationalists would have to govern together.

There was already some opposition to the agreement. The more extreme Unionists, led by Ian Paisley, urged voting against the agreement in the referendum that was held in May that passed with a majority of the vote in both communities (though note that Paisley's party currently shares power with Sinn Fein). Some hard-line Catholics not only refused to support the agreement but were responsible for one of the most egregious bombings in the town of Omagh.

In other words, there was a good chance that spoilers might wreck the agreement. But enough key leaders in London, Dublin, and especially Belfast, kept at it in the ways discussed in chapter 8.

It took years, but the IRA and the Protestant paramilitaries finally disarmed. The new institutions at Stormont have never functioned as intended. However, as you also saw in chapter 8 the Good Friday Agreement did not become orphaned like the Oslo Accord in large part because its negotiators committed themselves to going further and created "spaces" for grassroots activists to do so.

As Patrick Madden Keefe's book, which came out as I was finishing this chapter, demonstrates plenty of tough questions were still unanswered twenty years after the Good Friday Agreement was signed, including Adams's own alleged participation in the killing of "touts" or Catholics who collaborated with the British. However, the Sinn Fein leaders, the unionists (now led by Ian Paisley's son), and the other parties always found ways to keep the spoilers under enough control so that they could not undo the still fragile peace.

Sant'Egidio in Mozambique

I almost did not include this final example because Mozambique has never been big enough or important enough to get much outside attention. Yet, the role that the **Community of Sant'Egidio** played in ending a fifteen-year-long civil war there raises so many of the issues that will be at the heart of the rest of this book that I couldn't leave it out. Experience has shown me that few people know much about Mozambique and even fewer have heard about Sant'Egidio. Therefore, it makes sense to briefly describe the country and what the community did before turning to its broader lessons about peace and conflict studies.

The community is a lay Catholic order with a mission to help the world's poor. It was created in 1968 by Italian high school students and took its name from the church in Rome that serves as its headquarters. Today, the order has about fifty thousand members in seventy countries around the world, including the US. Unlike denominations like the Quakers or the Buddhist Soka Gakkai, Sant'Egidio does not make peacebuilding its highest priority. Instead, it focuses on spreading the Gospel by caring for the world's underprivileged.

Sant'Egidio has always worked to forge dialogues across social and political dividing lines. In their case, much of the work builds off a single slogan and goal—seeing "that which unites us." I have no reason to believe that the members of Sant'Egidio had even heard of Appreciative Inquiry (see part 2), but they did share its key principle of starting with the ideas and values that people share, in this case pride in Mozambican independence.

Mozambique gained its independence in 1975 after five centuries of Portuguese rule at which point it was one of the poorest countries in the world. Its situation deteriorated when a civil war broke out two years later between the Marxist FRELIMO government that had won independence and the opposition RENAMO which represented minority ethnic groups but also had the support of the US and of South Africa's apartheid-era government. To the degree that Mozambique made the news at all in those fifteen years, it was because the conflict between FRELIMO and RENAMO was one of dozens of places where the superpower rivalry played itself out at the expense of the local population.

As the 1980s wore on, Sant'Egidio realized that it could do something to break the bloody logjam. The community has always had lay leadership and is independent from the official Catholic hierarchy, although its members have close ties to liberal leaders at the Vatican. During the 1970s and 1980s, it had created beachheads in much of the Global South, including Mozambique where Italian businesses had invested heavily for decades.

Perhaps because of its work with the poor, the Italian community in Mozambique, and the local clerical leadership, Sant'Egidio found itself in the unusual position of being able to build relationships with both sides. Despite its religious inspiration, the community started with the Marxist and often antireligious FRELIMO government. Along with the Polish born and anticommunist Pope John Paul II and, ironically, the leadership of the then powerful Italian Communist Party, the community built ties with President Samora Machel's government that continued after his death in an airplane accident. Signs that things could change became clear in 1989 when the supposedly atheist FRELIMO party invited the religiously observant founder of Sant'Egidio to address its annual conference.

Meanwhile, the community reached out to the RENAMO guerillas through some of its supporters in the Mozambican diaspora in Italy and Germany. Gradually, its leaders, too began to see the community as what mediators would call a third-party neutral whose main interest was to improve the conditions of the Mozambican poor on both sides of the dispute.

At about the same time, countries like Mozambique began to feel the effects of what was happening in superpower relations. By removing the Soviet Union as FRELIMO's main funder the end of the Cold War opened up new possibilities for peace in Mozambique. Still, an attempt to hold negotiations in Kenya in 1988 went nowhere. As you saw in chapter 8 and will see again below, change was already afoot in South Africa, which was RENAMO's leading funder along with the US.

All the pieces came together in 1990 when senior representatives from both sides invited Sant'Egidio to host peace talks which took place over the next two years at the community's headquarters in Rome. The community drew on what it knew about the bitterness between the two sides which had been at war for almost fifteen years in defining its mediation strategy. There was little of the informal getting-to-know-you time that had worked so well in Oslo. Instead, its leaders created a more structured process in which the two delegations were housed separately and rarely came together except for formal negotiating sessions. As is often the case in tough negotiations, even the structure of the room mattered. In this case, the room had a horseshoe shaped table at which the Sant'Egidio and other Catholic officials sat in the curved section that both kept the two sides apart but also linked them together.

After two years of private meetings, the sides announced an agreement on the Rome General Peace Accords on October 4, 1992. The negotiations never went smoothly but progressed step by step. Early on, the community helped the delegations from the warring factions see one thing that they shared—pride in the Mozambican nation. Gradually, they helped them build enough trust in the mediators and in each other to reach agreements that would end the fighting, create a single national army, grant something akin to amnesty, and turn warfare into peaceful, electoral competition between two political parties.

On balance, the Accords and subsequent agreements have worked. Mozambique's economy has boomed by African standards. Political violence never completely disappeared but it was reduced dramatically. In 2013 some RENAMO members decided that twenty years of peace had not brought enough progress and took up arms again. At this point, they are little more than a minor irritant in a country which is far more peaceful than most of its neighbors.

Broader implications. I did not include this much material on Mozambique or Sant'Egidio because of their importance, per se. Rather, their success leads to at least eight conceptual conclusions that have been at the heart of peacebuilding since the 1990s:

- **Faith matters**. Sant'Egidio is one of many faith-based organizations at the heart of peace and conflict studies.
- **It's all about relationships**. Perhaps because of their religious roots, organizations like Sant'Egidio stress the belief that building peace starts with fostering powerful and constructive human relationships. That includes how peacebuilders themselves deal with conflict, a point I will return to at length in part 5.
- **Trust has to be built**. As you already know from relationships in your own life, you cannot enter a conflict and assume you can trust the other side. Trust is an important outcome of a peacebuilding process. It almost never exists when any kind of tough negotiations begin. It has to be constructed. Indeed, building trust usually has to be explicitly included as part of the process.
- **Politicians can rarely build peace on their own**. You are about to see some examples of political leaders who did take bold initiatives that led toward peace. They are very much the exception. For reasons any political scientist can explain, political leaders have a hard time seeing beyond their own interests and values, or those of their constituencies.
- **Resolving conflict and public peace takes time**. It took years for conflicts to turn ugly and/or violent. It will also normally take years to resolve them. Sant'Egidio spent fifteen years working in Mozambique before forging a limited agreement. That extended time period should remind you of a point I made in chapter 1. There are no magic wands.
- **Conflict resolution has to be holistic**. If you want to build some version of positive or stable peace, you eventually have to address all of the issues that gave rise to the dispute in the first place. In the case of Mozambique, the Rome Accords addressed more than just the political issues separating FRELIMO and RENAMO that started the fighting. And, they set the stage for further reforms.
- **Reconciliation has to be in the mix**. Mozambique did not create a form of truth and reconciliation commission. However, Sant'Egidio and the two parties all understood that they would have to confront all of the emotional issues that went along with the dispute if they had any hope of building on "what unites us."
- **Our work has to be context specific**. Sant'Egidio was among the first groups of experienced peacebuilders who explored the implications of the fact that no two conflicts are alike. That is true at the interpersonal level. It is even truer when you consider the complex conflicts that give rise to wicked problems in an entire society. To repeat another theme from chapter 1, there are no simple roadmaps that can guide our way toward transformational conflict resolution or peacebuilding.

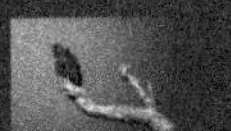

OUT ON A LIMB

The eight bullet points that ended the section on Sant'Egidio and Mozambique are not shared by everyone in peace and conflict studies. In particular, individuals and organizations who focus on mass atrocities, social and economic inequality of all kinds, and the shift toward authoritarian governments tend to argue that the kinds of tools discussed in this chapter may not be what we should turn to first. They argue convincingly that there are times when taking a stand against racism, sexism, xenophobia, and other affronts to human dignity is more important—not to mention more ethical.

Given the politics of the times, these issues were not at the forefront of most peace processes in the 1990s.

They are today, and I will spend much of parts 4 and 5 exploring how we are trying to find common ground between approaches to peace that stress building bridges and those that emphasize taking a stand against injustice.

DOMESTIC POLITICS

I finished writing this book in early 2019. To be honest, it was hard to feel hopeful about what was happening at the grown-ups' tables anywhere in the world at the time. As an American, I worried about polarization, the Trump presidency, racial discord, and the potential threats to American democracy. As a comparative political scientist, I realized that most of the countries I write about found themselves in difficult circumstances, too.

The optimism in Gorbachev's statement that began this chapter was long gone. As a result, many students and others I work with today find it hard to believe that as recently as twenty years ago, many of today's deeply divided societies were making progress on a number of fronts, some of which have ramifications for today's troubled world.

Two sets of those initiatives are worth considering here. The first, in South Africa, will not come as much of a surprise given what you have seen in the first eight chapters. The fact that the others took place in the US and Western Europe, will probably seem more unusual, but their unexpected nature also point us toward the kinds of initiatives peacebuilders are working on today.

South Africa: *Tomorrow Is Another Country*

Allister Sparks entitled his 1996 book *Tomorrow Is Another Country* to reflect just how dramatically his country had changed in the first six years following **Nelson Mandela**'s release from prison. In his writing since then, Sparks has become more skeptical about the new South Africa's accomplishments. Nonetheless, as you saw in considering the **Truth and Reconciliation Commission (TRC)** in chapter 8, its transition from apartheid to a multiracial democracy comes as close to a success story as you will find in the world of transformational conflict resolution and peacebuilding.

That success involved more than just the TRC as discussed in chapter 8. In fact, a number of steps had to be taken by national leaders before anything like the TRC became possible. I will use two of those steps in illustrating the kind of constructive role political officials *can* play in leading their countries in new directions.

I emphasized the word can in the previous sentence, because South Africa has been an outlier when it comes to transforming a society after an initial agreement to stop the fighting was reached. More often than not, the leadership that helped end the fighting evaporates once tensions resurface after an agreement is signed and we end up with orphaned agreements or worse. South Africa demonstrated that a combination of effective leadership and grassroots organization can carry peacebuilding momentum far beyond any initial—and therefore partial—agreement.

In so doing, the South African example helps illuminate one of the most important concepts in conflict resolution and peacebuilding which few practitioners mention because it is so abstract—reaching a **superordinate goal**. As social psychologists see it, such a goal can only be reached if all or most of the people involved find ways of cooperating with each other. Pursuit of their individual self-interest or that of their social, economic, or other such group will never be enough.

You have seen hints of superordinate goals and the need for cooperation already, for instance, in Sting's song "The Russians." For practical purposes, however, superordinate goals and the ideas underlying them only became part of the peacebuilding lexicon as a result of the South African transition.

Two anecdotes. The South African transition is full of stories that analysts and participants alike tell in explaining why it worked as well as it did. As is always the case with political folklore, observers tend to sugar coat what happened and exaggerate its importance. In this case, we do know that both events actually occurred and that each played at least a symbolic role in bringing blacks and whites together.

The first involves two of the most prominent figures in the first stages of the transition. The country's current president, Cyril Ramaphosa, was then head of COSATU, the Congress of South African Trade Unions which was all but officially a wing of the ANC (African National Congress). Rolf Meyer was a rising star in the governing National Party and in the Afrikaner community. They were scheduled to meet at one of the first informal discussions involving leaders from both sides who lived in South Africa rather than in exile.

The men had already discovered that they each liked to fish. So, they agreed to meet for a few hours of fishing before the formal sessions began. Meier somehow got a fish hook embedded in his wrist. Since they were in the middle of nowhere, there was no hospital nearby. Because the wound might have been life threatening, he had no choice but to rely on Ramaphosa and his wife, who happened to be a nurse. After a strong shot of whiskey, one or the other of the Ramaphosas (the story does differ on this front) pulled the hook out, possibly saving Meyer's life. Whatever actually happened, Meyer has publicly stated on any number of occasions (including once when I asked him) that this was one of a number of life changing moments that led him to shift from being the apartheid government's heir apparent to becoming the leading white architect of the transition.

The second involves an event that occurred early in Mandela's presidency and was more or less accurately portrayed in the 2009 film *Invictus*. Before turning to the event, you should know that most South Africans love sports, especially their national teams that play against global soccer, cricket, and rugby competitors. During the apartheid years, those teams were segregated. Rugby, in particular, was almost exclusively played by members of the Afrikaner community.

Because they were legally segregated, South African teams had been banned from international competition in the 1980s and were only readmitted after Mandela assumed the presidency. In recognition of the transition, World Rugby awarded the 1995 World Cup tournament to South Africa. Many in Mandela's entourage advised him to skip the games because the team would be virtually all white (one black eventually made the squad) and its, captain, François Pienaar was rumored to be hostile to what was now being called the Rainbow Nation. Not only did Mandela reject that advice, but when the beloved Sprinboks won the tournament despite being seeded ninth, the president showed up at the finals and presented the trophy to Pienaar and the rest of the team. In a stroke of symbolic genius, he wore a replica of Pienaar's uniform shirt in a scene that was even more tear jerking in real life than it was in the film (in which Morgan Freeman played Mandela and Matt Damon portrayed Pienaar).

President Mandela Hands François Pienaar the Trophy after South Africa Won the 1995 World Cup in Rugby.

Building a democratic South Africa. Recall from chapter 8 that President **F. W. de Klerk** surprisingly freed Mandela and ended the ban on the ANC in early 1990. That by no means guaranteed that South Africa would become a viable multiracial democracy or heal its racial wounds. Potential spoilers and other obstacles to a smooth transition were there for all to see, ranging from militants on the left who wanted to destroy apartheid and all it stood for to hard-line Afrikaners who resisted any change to the status quo.

As hard as it may be to believe in today's polarized world, a reasonably successful transition did take place, although it did not come easily. It succeeded because a diverse group of political leaders was able keep the superordinate goal of a multiracial South Africa in mind when making a series of tough choices. They did not explicitly draw on Sant'Egidio's idea of focusing on what united them nor were they able to draw on a team of outside mediators to help them make most of the hard decisions that South Africa faced after Mandela's release. In some ways, that makes their success all the more remarkable.

As you saw in chapter 8 the transition actually started while Mandela was still in prison. To make a long story short, Mandela began talking with government leaders as early as 1985 when he was hospitalized. Because he had learned the language of his oppressors while in prison, he normally held these discussions in Afrikaans to show his respect for his captors. Meanwhile, Meyer and others began meeting with other ANC leaders outside the country's borders and then later in South Africa itself (at which point the famous fish hook incident occurred). Mandela was transferred to prisons on the mainland to make it easier for the two sides to meet—and presumably to make it harder for anyone else to find out that they were meeting.

A key turning point came in 1989 when Mandela met the hard-line President P. W. Botha and his wife for tea. Not only did Mandela talk to them in Afrikaans but he offered to pour Mrs. Botha her tea. The Bothas never endorsed the transition or abandoned their support for apartheid, but Mandela's graciousness at their afternoon tea quickly became another tale that has become a part of South African political folklore.

More importantly for our purposes, Botha suffered a stroke in January 1990 and resigned as president a month later. In part because leaders like Meyer knew that change was inevitable, the National Party surprisingly turned to then little-known F. W. de Klerk, who came from a hard-line family but who also personally knew that change was inevitable. Mandela's release came two months later.

Even then, the situation was tense. The regime's supporters wanted to retain some form of apartheid. Many ANC leaders wanted revenge. Perhaps most importantly, despite the euphoria surrounding Mandela's release, there actually was a significant increase in intercommunal violence during the four years in which the country's leaders desperately tried to manage the transition.

To make another long story short, the people around Mandela and those around de Klerk both realized that a peaceful, democratic South Africa was in everyone's long-term interest which turned a smooth transition into a classic superordinate goal. Most white South Africans had long lost any real ties to Europe and therefore knew they would remain in the country after the black majority took power. Meanwhile, many ANC leaders realized that the country's wealth was a by-product of the apartheid system and that any immediate demand for economic equality would doom hopes for continued prosperity.

Realizing this, the two sides reached a de facto compromise which neither fully acknowledged in public. The country would adopt a one person one vote system which meant that it would have a majority black government. At the same time, the ANC agreed that it would seek restorative justice through the TRC but would not undermine the white community by taking over the commanding heights of the economy.

All of this would be implemented during a transitional period in which the ANC and the National Party would actually govern the country together. As expected, the ANC and Mandela won the country's first democratic election in 1994. As few expected, de Klerk and the National Party agreed to serve as junior members of an all-party government. And since symbolism is always important in peacebuilding, the world was treated to the amazing spectacle of President Mandela and the first Vice President de Klerk standing side by side at Mandela's inauguration and singing the country's new national anthem. If you watch the video, you will have no trouble seeing how uncomfortable de Klerk was, but the fact of the matter is that he was there singing in all five languages—including Afrikaans—in which it is written.

www.youtube.com/watch?v=RtHLCw4rYI0

The transition was not an unqualified success. De Klerk and the National Party left the government in 1996. Some extremists on both sides resisted the compromises that led to the TRC, the retention of a basically capitalist system, and a commitment to a very gradual redistribution of income and wealth from the white minority to the black, colored, and Asian communities which together make up over eighty percent of the South African population.

***Ubuntu* and the National Peace Accord.** The transition would not have proceeded as smoothly as it did had it only involved the elites. In fact, the South African leaders on both sides realized that it had to have a bottom up as well as a top down component—a theme I will return to frequently in part 4. Peace processes that do not have strong grassroots support tend to end up with the kinds of orphaned agreements you saw in the Middle East—or worse. In this case, however, South Africa became one of the first countries to give **civil society** pride of place in its peace process.

South Africa was lucky in this respect, too. While violence that threatened to destroy the transition swirled all around them, the major stakeholders agreed to the National Peace Accord in 1991. In addition to the negotiations taking place in Johannesburg and Cape Town, it called for the creation off eleven provincial and two hundred local peace committees which eventually trained about fifteen thousand peace monitors.

In so doing, the leaders were able to tap into the large activist networks that had been created during the fifty years of apartheid rule. Some of these were already interracial, including the organizations the ANC helped create while it was officially banned. The committees also were able to draw on some members of the Afrikaner Broderbond which is a dense social network that had supported the National Party during the apartheid years. It included organizations that you would expect to find, including the conflict resolution groups that had already sprung up around the country. But they also included the police and business leaders who had been part of the old system which they were being asked to help dismantle.

Not all of them functioned effectively, nor did all of their members agree on everything. Nonetheless, they all rested on a common assumption that Susan Collin Marks, who was an active participant, summed up as "we turn and face the problem as a *joint* problem."[5] As they did so, they were able to draw on an African term which I have referred to several times already, ***ubuntu***, which usually gets translated as "a person is a person through another person."

What they did varied from place to place. Everywhere, however, members of those committees sought to build bridges that crossed racial and other dividing lines. Even more importantly, they realized that they had to be the living proof that a nonracist South Africa was possible. As Marks summed it up,

> slowly, we learned that peace had to start with each of us, that the only way to be a peacemaker in tis troubled world is to be a peacemaker within, working to resolve the turmoil of our hearts and souls, and our personal conflicts with others.[6]

In fact, the local peace committees anticipated many of the themes we will focus on in part 4 including:

- intervening and often physically standing between potential combatants, which you will see again when we consider Cure Violence's work in American cities
- incorporating the police and other symbols of authority from the old regime
- explicitly training other activists in peacebuilding and conflict resolution skills

As Marks so eloquently put it in the statement quoted above, the committee members realized that they had to work on themselves and what we would today call their implicit biases every bit as much as they had to work with other groups in South African society. In so doing, they adopted principles very much like I started using when I worked with Beyond War in the 1980s (see chapter 5).

Since 1999. The South African transition has experienced more setbacks than progress in the twenty years since Mandela retired in 1999 for reasons that go far beyond the scope of this book. In all probability, had South Africa not gone through the kind of peace process that promoted elite cooperation around a common set of goals that rested on increasingly shared cultural norms, its democracy would not have survived the corrupt and weak leadership of his two successors as president.

Consensus Policy Making

Despite my earlier statement that conflict resolution and peacebuilding specialists largely ignored divisive issues at home during the 1990s, the advanced industrialized democracies will now make a cameo appearance to end this chapter. Were this a book in comparative politics, the two examples you are about to see would warrant a footnote at most. However, they are both fraught with implications for conflict resolution and peacebuilding in ways I will return to more in part 5 than in part 4 because we have not yet done much to take advantage of the possibilities they would seem to offer.

Political scientists, as well as average citizens, tend to equate democratic politics with majority rule. There are times when it makes sense to pass a law even if it can only win a bit more than half of the votes. In other cases, there really isn't any other option, most notably in elections which, by definition, result in winners and losers.

However, as British or American readers will certainly understand, narrowly won, zero-sum victories can make things worse. A bare majority of the vote in the 2016 referendum sent the UK on the perilous and divisive route toward Brexit. Under the Obama and Trump administration, American legislation routinely passes with the votes of only one party in Congress (if it passes at all), leaving the members of the minority even angrier and more suspicious of the majority than they already were.

In other words, because majority rule often lends itself to boastful winners and angry, resentful leaders, it is rarely a good way to solve the kinds of disputes considered in this book. As a result, policy makers in some of the established democracies have begun experimenting with alternatives in which some kind of supermajority or even **consensus** is required before major policy changes are adopted, This kind of policy making reflects the importance of superordinate goals, although I am not aware of any major political scientist who explicitly uses that term.

Strictly speaking, achieving consensus means that all parties to a dispute have to agree before a decision is made. Some religions manage their internal affairs using that strict definition, most notably the Quakers. Other faith-based groups do not put as much emphasis on consensus building, per se. However, it is easy to see the connection between reaching consensus as a goal and the emphasis on reconciliation, dialogue, and shared values that are at the heart of the Community of Sant'Egidio's work.

Critics properly point out that it is all but impossible to reach anything like unanimity when you have to work with large and heterogeneous populations, whether you are thinking about an entire country or merely a major metropolitan area. It is therefore hard to imagine reaching a consensus on the kinds of tumultuous issues we have been considering here if it requires universal agreement on any policy initiative. Instead, policy makers are beginning to explore decision-making procedures that emphasize cooperative problem solving with the goal of reaching what political scientists would call supermajorities as was the case with the referenda that ratified the Good Friday agreements in 1998.

Without that kind of widespread support, the initiative will lack the buy-in needed to carry it forward through the rough periods that inevitably follow agreements like the GFA. Two examples should illustrate why the conflict resolution and peacebuilding communities—if not most political scientists—are beginning to pay attention to these kinds of policy making procedures.

The US Consensus Council. In 2000, I joined Search for Common Ground's new team that focused on conflict resolution and peacebuilding in the US. That made us the first global NGO that tried to apply the lessons learned around the world to problems we faced "back home." As the dust settled from that year's contentious presidential election, we were approached by people who had worked at the highest levels of the Bush and Gore campaigns. All had been willing but reluctant participants in the legal battle that followed after the disputed results in Florida were announced. During those tension-filled weeks, they realized that they wanted to avoid a repetition of that contest's ugly outcome that had ultimately been decided by the Supreme Court. All the signs were that the Bush presidency would be as divisive as anything the US had seen since the Vietnam era when the members of our team were all college students.

One of the Bush campaign's leaders, Marc Racicot, had created a consensus council when he was governor of Montana, which helped policy makers make policy decisions with a minimum of acrimony. Racicot and former Democratic Secretary of Agriculture Dan Glickman agreed to head a committee to create such a body at the federal level.

We worked with them to assemble a team of policy-making veterans who would draft authorizing legislation and build support for a US Consensus Council. The plan closely resembled similar bodies that had been created in North Dakota, New Mexico, and Delaware, as well as Montana. Meanwhile, Search's staff experimented with consensus building principles with working groups it assembled on a number of issues, ranging from prisoner reentry, President George W. Bush's Faith-Based Initiative, health care coverage, and HIV/AIDS.

Search's prototypes were based on the principles that would be mirrored in the official US Consensus Council when and if Congress passed a law creating it. We carefully chose leaders who represented all of the major positions on a given issue and asked them to participate in a series of off the record discussions which we facilitated. Most of the participants either did not know each other at all or, if they had met, it had been at congressional hearings or media events in which they typically talked past each other—or worse.

Much like Track II negotiations, holding closed door meetings made it easier for our staff and the political leaders to build trust and for the policy makers to identify and explore potential areas of agreement. Sometimes they found enough common ground that they reached consensus on major policy initiatives. Sometimes, they even discovered that they actually liked each other.

In particular, we made significant progress in building agreement on criteria that could be used in granting federal funding to faith-based social service groups, some of which made it into law. The health care group reached agreement on many of the issues that would later end up in the Affordable Care Act. Not every working group we tried was a success. Indeed, the HIV/AIDS project collapsed before it got off the ground.

We also failed to get the Council itself created. Legislation was introduced to create it as a stand-alone agency funded by Congress, much like the United States Institute of Peace. Congress itself would refer issues to the Council for consideration. If the Council agreed to take the issue on, it would convene a series of meeting that would unfold in much the ways that Search's prototypes had. Because its recommendations would have the support of almost all of the key interest groups, the assumption was that legislation would then pass fairly easily.

In 2003 a version of the bill was passed by the relevant Senate committee. However, one senator exercised his right and put a "hold" on the bill, effectively killing it.

The idea of a consensus council did not die with the legislation. Instead, Search's team (without me—I had already moved to AfP) decided to go off on its own, creating the **Convergence Center for Public Policy**, which continues promoting consensus policy making as an alternative to the gridlock that has only deepened since the original bill died.

Corporatism in Germany. The second example might seem like an odd one to include here. Corporatist decision-making antedates the 1990s and comes from political science rather than peacebuilding. I include it here, because its conflict resolution implications surfaced during the research we did as part of the consensus council initiative.

Corporatism is one of the most controversial concepts in modern political science. Its origins lie in nineteenth-century Catholic thought. Later on, fascists used it to describe the sham legislatures they created that supposedly represented major interests or "corporations." In other words, when scholars first began using corporatism to describe close relationships between the state and interest groups, the very choice of words revealed their deep doubts about it.

Nonetheless, it has become a cornerstone of public policy making in a number of democracies, most notably Germany. Corporatism, per se, is not mentioned in Germany's constitution and only rarely appears in legislation. Nonetheless, it has been an integral part of economic policy making in Germany and most of the industrialized democracies that have enjoyed sustained growth over the last half-century.

Corporatist policy making also takes place behind closed doors and rarely involves either political parties or members of parliament. Rather, cabinet members and high-level civil servants help interest group leaders reach agreements which are then accepted by all key stakeholders.

Corporatist procedures initially made a difference when a neo-Nazi political party was on the verge of making an electoral breakthrough during the country's first post-war recession. Socialist and Christian Democratic leaders opted to form a Grand Coalition government in which both major parties held cabinet seats in a display of solidarity in the face of the antidemocratic threats. Among its first initiatives were so-called Concerted Action meetings at which business, government, and labor leaders together tried to come to grips with the recession. Over the next three years, the group met annually to hammer out agreements on wage and price increases, broad macroeconomic and social policy goals, and the landmark 1967 law on balanced growth. Once the immediate crises passed, the discussions became more acrimonious and less productive and were discontinued in 1977. Since then, corporatist decision-making has continued in a more informal—but no less important—way. Most ministries' planning staffs, for example, still cooperate with business and labor leaders in determining their goals for the next few years.

The Grand Coalition government also passed the Vocational Training Act in 1969 which expanded existing partnerships between business owners, the trade unions, and state and federal educational authorities. It, subsequent legislation, governmental decrees, and informal arrangements have created what is known as a dual system of secondary education which helps explain why youth unemployment in Germany is about half of what it is in the US.

After they turn sixteen, German students can choose between remaining in a conventional high school or enrolling in an apprenticeship program. Because most now wait until they finish secondary school before making the decision, the apprenticeship has also become an alternative to conventional universities.

Each year, about half a million young people start an apprenticeship that typically lasts three years. Students can choose from about 350 professions, which range from jobs in traditional manufacturing to the newest high-tech industries. During the apprenticeship, the young men and women split their time between conventional classrooms and on the job training. Typically, companies cover the costs of the training program and pay the apprentices stipends that are usually about a third of regular full time wages.

At the end of the apprenticeship, students take state-administered academic exams as well as professional certification tests which are administered by an employer or a trade association. About half of the graduates are offered jobs by the firm that supervised their training; the others have valuable credentials when they apply for jobs elsewhere. Almost a quarter of apprentices also gain admission to universities where they typically study applied fields like engineering or social work.

Dual education is not a panacea that will smooth Germany's transition to the next economy or solve all of its labor market problems. Those are both wicked problems that defy simple "one stop shop" solutions. Still, the apprenticeship program does suggest that Germany is an unusual industrialized democracy in that it often finds reasonably cross partisan and holistic solutions to the enduring problems it and other countries confront.

Germany's system of codetermination is also worth mentioning for that very same reason. Created as early as 1951 under a conservative government, it now gives unions half of the seats on boards of directors of all companies that have more than two thousand employees. Firms also have works councils that bring employees and management together to discuss job-related issues. The workers' representatives are not quite as powerful as those named by the ownership, because the law reserves one of the union seats for management employees and automatically gives stockholders the power to name the chair of the board.

CONFLICT LAB 9.2

I obviously don't know which issues you have been focusing on in the Conflict Labs—unless you sent them to me, that is. Normally, that has not made a difference because I was able to design Conflict Labs that applied to just about every conflict I could imagine.

That is not be the case with consensus policy making. There certainly are times when a community or society will not be able to reach anything approaching unanimity on a controversial issue. So, in this version of the lab, ask yourself:

- Might consensus policy making be useful in addressing the national or global conflict you have been following?
- If you don't think so, why did you reach that conclusion?
- If you do think consensus building might work, what would such a program look like, and why do you think it might succeed?

Corporatist policy making does have its problems. Although labor has fared rather well in Germany, it has only approached being an equal partner with business during the Socialists' first period of power in the early 1970s. Other groups have fared even less well. The consensus and the neocorporatist arrangements are used almost exclusively for economic policy making. Groups concerned with issues such as women's rights, the status of immigrant workers, and the growing elderly population have far less access to top decision makers. Corporatism also poses problems for democratic theory. Not only does corporatist policy making take place behind closed doors, it de-emphasizes the role of elected officials who can at least potentially be held accountable at the ballot box. Still, these corporatist policy-making processes are worth considering as we move forward and consider Peacebuilding 3.0—and beyond.

GLIMPSING THE GROWN-UPS' TABLE

This chapter has revolved around an unspoken contradiction involving its epigraph and title that I intentionally let lurk below the surface until now. Gorbachev's statement spoke of a hopeful future in which political leaders would build on the momentum of the late 1980s and create a more peaceful world in which they increasingly used cooperative methods for solving their problems.

Those dreams evaporated within a matter of months. Meanwhile, the events of the early 1990s forced conflict resolution and peacebuilding specialists to change the way they dealt with the new world (dis)order and its problems. Oddly enough, even though we spent less time focusing explicitly on public policy questions than we had during the 1980s, we ended up developing tools and techniques that allowed us to at least glimpse the grown-ups' table. In a few places, we even played a significant role in improving people's lives.

At the start of the decade, few of my colleagues in peace and conflict studies expected to routinely play that kind of a role. By the time it ended, a number of us had seen enough to make us want to be "in on the action" in Washington and

New York as well as in the problem-solving workshops and local peace committees in Cape Town.

It would take another wrenching change in the global political environment to begin getting us there.

KEY TERMS

Concepts

advocacy, 171
civil society, 197
consensus, 198
corporatism, 200
ethnic cleansing, 176
Good Friday Agreement (GFA), 188
good offices, 174
green line, 174
International Financial Institutions (IFIs), 183
international governmental organizations (IGOs), 172
liberal peace, 183
multitrack diplomacy, 184
mutually hurting stalemate, 185
new world order, 171
orphaned agreement, 187
peace enforcement, 179
peacebuilding, 173
peacekeeping, 173
peacemaking, 179
permanent members, 172
public policy, 171
Responsibility to Protect (R2P), 179
rules of engagement, 176
sovereignty, 172
spoiler, 187
superordinate goal, 194
third-party neutral, 171
Track II diplomacy, 184
two state solution, 184
ubuntu, 197

People

Arafat, Yasir, 185
Boutros-Ghali, Boutros, 179
Dallaire, Roméo, 178
Gorbachev, Mikhail, 171
Mandela, Nelson, 193
Mitchell, George, 187
Rabin, Yitzhak, 186

Organizations, Places, and Events

Bosnia, 176
Convergence Center for Public Policy, 200
Cyprus, 174
Dayton Accords, 177
European Union (EU), 171
General Assembly, 173
IFOR, 177
International Criminal Court (ICC), 180
International Monetary Fund (IMF), 183
Intifada, 185
Millennium Development Goals (MDGs), 181
North Atlantic Treaty Organization (NATO), 182
Oslo Accords, 186
Palestine Liberation Organization (PLO), 185
Quakers, 190
Rwanda, 177
Sant'Egidio, Community of, 190
Security Council, 172
Troubles, 188
Truth and Reconciliation Commission (TRC), 193
UNAMIR (United Nations Assistance Mission for Rwanda), 177
UNFICYP (United Nations Forces in Cyprus) World Bank, 174
United Nations (UN), 171
UNPROFOR (United Nations Protection Force for the Former Yugoslavia), 177
World Bank, 183
World Trade Organization, 183

DIG DEEPER

Boutros-Ghali, Boutros. *An Agenda for Peace.* New York: United Nations, 1996. The UN's first foray into defining what became peacebuilding.

Carnegie Commission. *On Preventing Violent Conflict.* www.carnegie.org/media/filer_public/b2/0e/b20e1080-7830-4f2b-9410-51c14171809b/ccny_report_1997_ccpdc_final.pdf. The definitive research study on conflict at the time.

Gerner, Deborah. *One Land, Two Peoples.* Boulder, CO: Westview, 1994. Still the best single volume on the origins of the conflict between Israel and Palestine.

Gourevitch, Philip. *We Regret to Inform You That Tomorrow We Will Be Killed with Our Families.* New York: Farrar, Straus, and Giroux, 1999. A gripping and depressing account of the genocide.

Holbrooke, Richard. *To End a War.* New York: Random House, 1999. By the main architect of the Dayton Agreement, which ended the war in Bosnia.

Keefe, Patrick Madden. *Say Nothing: A True Story of Murder and Memory in Northern Ireland.* New York: Doubleday, 2019. Another gripping tale, this time of the parts of the conflict that were not addressed all that effectively in the Good Friday Agreement.

Mitchell, George. *Making Peace.* New York: Knopf, 1999. The insider's look at what happened in Northern Ireland.

Sparks, Alister. *Tomorrow Is Another Country.* New York: Farrar, Straus, and Giroux, 1995. The most readable and optimistic book on the transition that led to a democratic South Africa.

Stedman, Stephen, Donald Rothchild, and Elizabeth Cousins. *Ending Civil Wars.* Boulder, CO: Lynn Rienner, 2002. The best single source on spoilers and other obstacles to building peace, especially during the 1990s.

NOTES

[1] The Chinese seat was held by the Nationalist government, which was in power at the end of World War II. It continued to hold it even after the Chinese Communist Party came to power in Beijing in 1949 and created the People's Republic of China (PRC). In 1971, the US allowed the PRC to assume the Chinese seat, and the Nationalist government (which had moved to Taiwan) lost its membership in the UN. Russia inherited the Soviet Union's seat after the USSR collapsed.

[2] http://unpan1.un.org/intraday/groups/public/documents/un/unpan000923.pdf.

[3] United Nations Development Programme, *Human Development Report: 1994* (New York: UNDP, 1994), http://hdr.undp.org/sites/default/files/reports/255/hdr_1994_en_complete_nostats.pdf.

[4] Deborah Gerner, *One Land, Two Peoples: The Conflict over Palestine* (Boulder, CO: Westview, 1994).

[5] Susan Collin Marks, *Watching the Wind: Conflict Resolution during South Africa's Transition to Democracy* (Washington, DC: United States Institute of Peace Press, 2000), 17.

[6] Marks, 68.

PEACEBUILDING 3.0

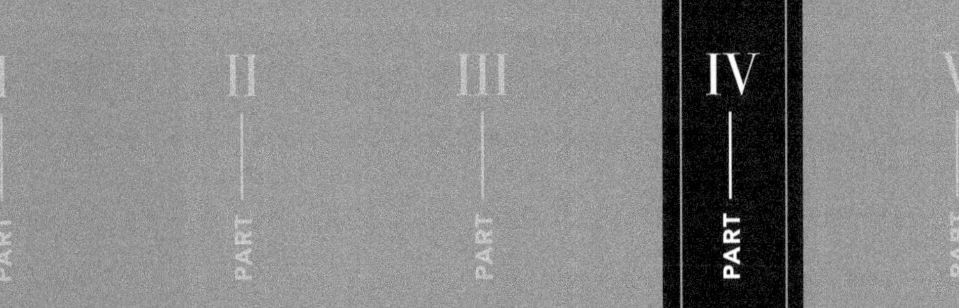

CHAPTER 10

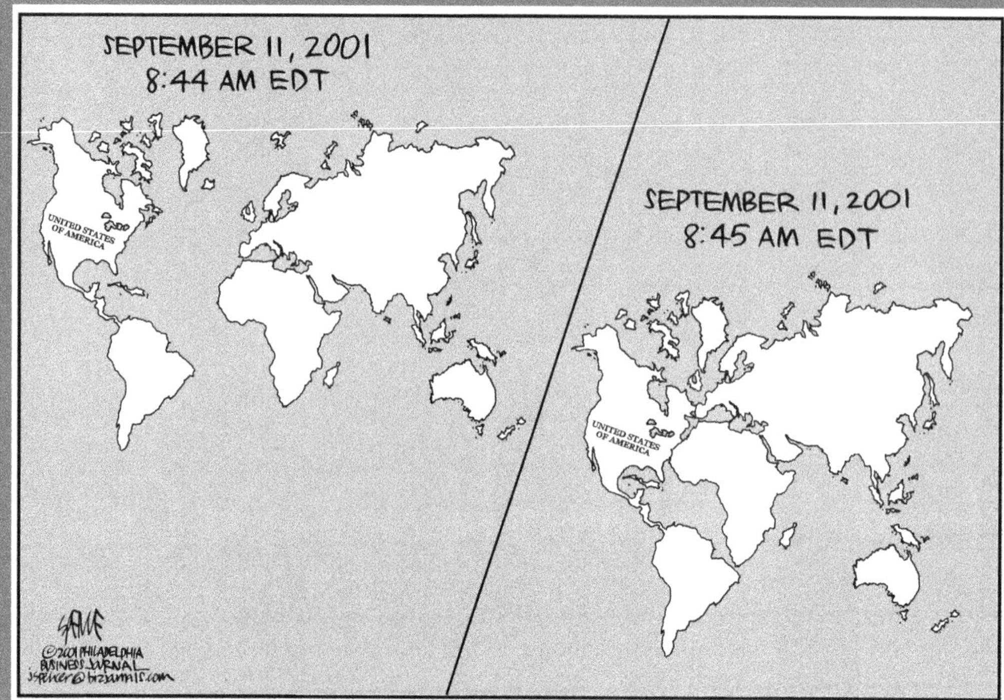

A World of Wicked Problems

THINK ABOUT IT

In filmmaking terms, we are nearing the climax of this book's story arc. Part 4 will tie up the narrative by looping back to many of the newest core concepts I first raised in part 1. The next three chapters, however, are not a refresher course in which I update them with more recent data. Rather, they are an opportunity to revisit questions you have been grappling with in the light of how the field has grown and is still growing.

For the purposes of this chapter, start with the following two questions:

- How have the events of the last twenty years or so changed conflict resolution and peacebuilding?
- Given what you have seen so far in this book, what have my colleagues and I missed?

CORE CONCEPTS

accelerating rates of change—when change in a phenomenon occurs at an ever greater rate; often referred to as an exponential rate of change or a power function

do no harm—for peacebuilders, our version of physicians' commitment to the Hippocratic Oath

intentionality—the conscious decision to seek a particular goal in response to a particular set of circumstances

local peacebuilding—the (as yet unproven) belief that lasting conflict resolution and peacebuilding have to be built from the bottom up

positive peace—occurs when people settle their differences constructively and their basic human needs are met

resilience—literally, the ability to bounce back or respond constructively to adversity

VUCA—volatile, uncertain, complicated, and ambiguous

wicked problem—issues that are so complicated that they can't be solved quickly, separately, or easily, if they can be solved at all

Prevention is about creating incentives for actors to choose actions that resolve conflict without violence [that] recognize and address group grievances.

—United Nations/World Bank

AS WAS THE CASE WITH the transition to Peacebuilding 2.0, a single, dramatic, and unexpected event shook up the conflict resolution and peacebuilding communities. This time, however, it brought grief and rather than joy and hope for the future. To see why, just consider the cartoon on page 206, which was published in the days following **9/11**.

The left panel depicts the world as we (thought we) knew it at on 8:44 on the morning of September 11, 2001. At 8:45, the first airplane hit one of the twin towers of the World Trade Center. Less than twenty minutes after that, another airplane crashed into the other tower. About half an hour later, yet another airplane struck the Pentagon. Shortly after 10:00, a fourth plane that had been hijacked and was also flying toward Washington was taken over by its passengers and crashed in rural Pennsylvania.

The world has not been the same since—including the world of conflict resolution and peacebuilding.

It took us a long time to figure out the implications of what had happened and to arrive at what AfP calls Peacebuilding 3.0. You could make the case that we are still trying to figure them out, since, unlike its first two versions, Peacebuilding 3.0 remains a work in progress. Indeed, I kept putting off finishing part 4 because new events kept me wanting to make more changes until my editors finally had to say "enough, already!"

Despite the world's uncertainties—not to mention my own—you should be able to see the following contours of Peacebuilding 3.0 by the time you finish chapter 12:

- We didn't get to Peacebuilding 3.0 quickly or easily. In fact, it was only in the early 2010s that we fully realized how much our work had to change.
- We shifted to a version of peacebuilding anchored in systems theory which requires a lot more than "just" getting to yes or dealing with identity. In addition, it forces us to anticipate the need for large-scale social change on a wide variety of fronts and perhaps even a paradigm shift.
- We can't ignore the Global North.
- It will take us a long time to achieve Peacebuilding 3.0—if we ever can get there.
- The dividing line between grassroots projects and public policy advocacy has blurred to the point that it is hard to separate the two.

THROWN FOR A LOOP

The attacks on 9/11 turned out to be a catalyst that sparked wide-ranging reflection that affected everything we thought and did. As you will see throughout part 4, we did not abandon what we had done in the previous generation. However, we reached new understandings, which led to a new set of initiatives, all of which were fed by a new sense of urgency.

9/11 and Its Legacy

The changes started with 9/11 itself, which sent shock waves through our community. We weren't alone, of course. Everyone was shaken by the events of that morning—to say the least.

The attacks forced us to deal with terrorism. Of course, we had known about it before 9/11—especially those of us who worked in places like Northern Ireland, the Middle East, and South Africa. Most of us, however, focused on other issues that we felt were more amenable to the kinds of tools discussed in the previous three chapters.

That wasn't going to be good enough anymore.

That point was driven home for me personally a mere two days later. I had long been scheduled to discuss my new book on peacebuilding at Search for Common Ground's office in downtown Washington on the night of September 13. To my surprise, Search's leadership decided to go ahead with the event. Needless to say, the mood in the room was somber.

But, by the time was over, I had begun to get a glimpse of some of the ways we would have to change. Those insights came from a surprising source. In the audience was someone I have known since we were in kindergarten. Unlike me, Dick O'Neill had spent nearly thirty years as a US Navy officer and was currently running a think tank to help the Pentagon think outside the box. We had reconnected in 2000 and had already been exploring a few common interests, which led me to invite him to the book launch.

I intentionally let him ask the first question, which, not surprisingly, dealt with how we were planning to respond to the attacks. My answer began a dialogue between the two of us on the role of force, cooperative problem solving, patriotism, and more. At some point, he told us that if he had still been on active duty, his office would have been on the direct flight path of the third airplane. Without fully thinking about what we were doing, we started responding to the rest of the questions together. By the end of the evening, the audience had a hard time figuring out which of us was the career peace activist and which of us was the career military officer for a simple, surprising reason. The two of us gave basically the same answers to every question.

That began a relationship between the two of us that has continued to this day both at AfP and at the Pentagon. More importantly, it was typical of discussions my colleagues began having once the shock of what happened on that Tuesday morning began to wear off.

As was the case with the people who assembled at Search's office that night, almost all of my colleagues recommitted themselves to their conflict and peacebuilding work. Little did we realize, however, how much the world of peacebuilding would change over the course of the next two decades. Little did we realize, too, that the events and their aftermath would convince us that we had to do a lot more than "just" adapt peacebuilding to the post-9/11 world.

As I suggested already, we did not abandon what we had done before 2000. Rather, we added new initiatives and finally got to some of the core principles involving systems theory that I introduced in the second half of chapter 3.

Meanwhile, we also began taking steps that would let us escape George Lopez's Gloom and Doom 101 trap. Despite the difficulties we had in crafting responses to what became the Global War on Terror, the general drift rightward, the Great Recession, the new populism, and more, we ended up shifting gears and took our obligation to build positive peace and address structural violence far more seriously than we had in the 1990s.

When all is said and done, we made that progress because we learned many of the lessons implicit in John Spencer's cartoon on page 206. The world has shrunk. Everything matters. Including what conflict resolution and peacebuilding professionals do. Some observers even make the case that civilization as we know it cannot survive without us.

We soon discovered that we could not come up with a simple answer to those questions that everyone in our community could support, which **John Paul Lederach** summed up at the time in a widely circulated note which he entitled *Quo Vadis*, which is Latin for "where are we headed?"[1] Even more importantly, we discovered that by digging into the root causes of terrorism, we began seeing the world as a whole in a new light that soon led us to systems analysis.

Before 9/11, most conflict resolution and peacebuilding professionals knew that terrorists *could* strike at what we now call the homeland. I emphasized the word could in the previous sentence because few of us actually expected anything like the events of that morning to happen.

To see why, consider yet another example that hits close to home. In 2000, I had been invited to a workshop organized by the Department of Defense at which a diverse group of foreign policy wonks were asked to predict the biggest threat to American security over the course of the next twenty years. We concluded that a sudden, surprise terrorist attack on a major American city would jar us out of our comfort zones. We even thought that an attack by hijacked and weaponized airplanes might set off an organized terrorist campaign against American interests.

None of us, however, really believed that anything like that would actually happen barely a year later. We certainly had no clue that such an attack would change the global geopolitical landscape as much as anything that happened anywhere on the planet since the Japanese bombed Pearl Harbor in 1941.

That was obvious within hours of the attacks. Just about everyone in American and European policy circles assumed that we had to strike back and destroy the organizations responsible for the attacks. Few of us in the peacebuilding community could come up with effective counterarguments at the time. Even if we had, we would not have been able to prevent the American government from going to war.

The jury is still out as to when that decisions was made. Most critics think that the Bush administration decided that it would have to fight back on September 11 itself. Even if you reject that interpretation, covert CIA and special forces operatives were operating in Afghanistan within two weeks. What became the **Global War on Terror (GWOT)** began on October 7 when the US and its allies launched an air campaign against both al-Qaeda and the Taliban government in Kabul that had at least given it safe haven.

Soon dubbed Operation Enduring Freedom, the coalition of allied forces and Afghan insurgents quickly toppled the Taliban. However, as we all know, toppling a government and establishing order—let alone peace—are not the same thing, since the war was well into its seventeenth year when I wrote these lines.

It wasn't just Afghanistan. Understandably, the American government and its NATO allies were worried that more attacks would follow and were convinced that terrorists would only respond to force. Peaceful alternatives were rarely considered, although some of us were brought in to talk with Pentagon officials about long term strategies for preventing the spread of twenty-first century terrorism.

As you also know, American attention soon turned to Iraq. The Bush administration and a dwindling number of its allies claimed that the Baghdad regime both supported al-Qaeda and continued developing weapons of mass destruction in violation of the agreements reached at the end of the first Gulf War in 1991.

This is not the place to rehash those arguments and the misleading evidence the administration used in making its case. It is enough to see that the administration overcame opposition from critics at home as well as many of its allies and invaded Iraq on March 19, 2003. Operation Iraqi Freedom's forces soon toppled Saddam Hussein and created a provisional government that would govern the country until a new Iraqi regime could be put in place. As you also do not need to be reminded, that war also continues to this day although virtually no American or other Allied troops are currently involved in major combat operations.

In short, the US and the rest of the Western world found itself in what felt like a permanent state of threat and a never-ending war. To that end, Rosa Brooks entitled her powerful 2016 analysis "how everything became war and the military became everything."[2] Afghanistan, Iraq, and other countries remain in turmoil. Terrorist attacks continue on a regular basis in Europe and North America as well as in the countries where conventional fighting is also taking place.

Terrorism or violent extremism as policy makers now call it, produced widespread fear and anger towards the "other," including Arabs and Muslims in general. Students of terrorism will tell you that this is exactly what al-Qaeda and its supporters wanted to happen. They know that they had next to no chance of defeating a country like the US on the battlefield. On the other hand, they hoped to instill enough fear to paralyze its government. To see one way in which they have succeeded, terrorism normally ranks near the top of the list of things the American public worries about even though drug overdoses, automobile accidents, and gun violence *each* kill far more people annually than al-Qaeda or ISIS could ever dream of.

To make matters worse, the world in general has grown more violent in the last few years in ways that go far beyond anything that could be attributed to terrorism. Two billion people live in countries where economic development is threatened by ongoing conflict. By contrast, only two percent of the world's people can be said to live in a country with fully open and democratic political systems.

As Brooks and so many other analysts have argued, we have reached an impasse. Despite the trillions of dollars that have been spent and the thousands of lives that have been lost, we are not much closer to defeating terrorism or securing our population than we were on that September morning when those airplanes flew into the World Trade Center and the Pentagon.

Broader Political Realities

The events of 9/11 and their geopolitical aftermath were just the tip of the clichéd iceberg, however.

It would be one thing if we only had to deal with these new global geopolitical challenges. Events since 9/11 have also forced us to confront conflict at home, too. The list of primarily domestic intractable conflicts is long, including economic, racial, and gender inequalities, climate change, and more. To complicate matters further, all of this is taking amid the unprecedented and unexpected growth in support for right-wing **populism**.

I assume that most readers of this book live and/or study in one of the established democracies which are clustered in Europe, North America, East Asia, and Oceania. So, I assume that you have seen this shift in public opinion first hand and that there is no need to go into populism and its causes in great detail here.

However it is worth thinking about the ways in which the WEIRD countries have gotten weirder, starting with the two ways I used the same word in this sentence. When I write about comparative politics these days, I use the acronym WEIRD as shorthand for countries like the US or the UK that are culturally Western, highly **e**ducated, **i**ndustrialized, **r**ich, and democratic, which in and of itself makes them unusual, if not literally weird. But they have recently gotten increasingly weird in the literal sense of the term as well.

As an American who has also lived in the UK and France, I pay the most attention to unsettling events in these three countries, including Trump's election, the Brexit referendum, and the combination of racism and terrorism in the streets of Paris and other cities. It's not just these three countries. No country is immune to the populist pressures, including Germany and Sweden, which arguably have among the most tolerant and progressive political cultures in the Western world.

The rise of populism to some degree reflects the fact that we are facing a large number of overlapping wicked problems that require some kind of policy response that might require us to question the dominant political paradigm(s). These systems-level responses are not forthcoming in part because policy makers have at least one thing in common with average citizens. They, too, increasingly live in their own "silos" or "filter bubbles," which make it hard to have meaningful and constructive discussions that cross ideological lines.

Democracy itself may be at risk, as so many of the world's leading political scientists think. While there is no a priori reason to assume that a peaceful society has to be democratic, the fact is that few nondemocratic regimes have been able to sustain the kind of stable peace you have been considering since chapter 1.

In short, these issues make it difficult for leaders to make effective public policy on all issues and not just those involving conflict resolution and peacebuilding. That said, they make the accomplishments covered in part 4 seem all the more impressive because the NGOs and others have faced surprisingly strong political headwinds when compared to the 1990s.

The Liberal Peace

At the same time, virtually every solution proposed by mainstream peacebuilding and conflict resolution NGOs takes the basic premises of the **liberal peace** for granted. Recall here the definition of this term revolves around acceptance of the basic capitalist economic and political status quo.

CONFLICT LAB 10.1

Even though this book focuses on approaches to conflict that lead to its resolution, it is worth your while to spend a few minutes answering that essay question I mentioned in part 2 that changed the way I taught.

The World Is Messed Up. Discuss.

It is worth revisiting that question here without returning to the "Gloom and Doom 101" issues that have long been at the heart of peace and conflict studies.

So, on the basis of what you have learned so far, ask if that statement is true at least for the two conflicts you have been considering since chapter 1. Explore why you reached those conclusions. The other Conflict Labs in part 4 will focus on how we could solve them.

Academic critics are quick to point out that we can only go so far in addressing the underlying drivers of conflict without questioning market capitalism as well. In particular, they point to the growing economic inequalities around the world and the continued discrimination against people of color, women, and others that led Galtung to talk in terms of structural violence. From this perspective, peacebuilding or conflict transformation efforts that do not address these built-in power relationships will not and cannot result in stable peace.

Still, the fact remains that most peacebuilding and conflict resolution NGOs who aspire to getting a seat at the grown-ups' table assume that they have to accept at least the basic contours of the liberal peace. That does not apply to my friends and colleagues whose strategies and tactics have their origins in contentious politics. While they will make an appearance at several points in this chapter, the fact of the matter is that those of us who want to work "inside the system" do take the liberal peace for granted.

Thinking the Unthinkable

At the same time, few prominent leaders seem willing or able to come to grips with the fact that we live in a world defined by accelerating rates of change and growing interdependence. Here, the work of Nik Gowing and Chris Langdon, which I first mentioned in part 1, is particularly compelling.

The research that led to the publication of *Thinking the Unthinkable* was originally commissioned by the Winston Churchill Foundation to serve as the empirical base for a brief study of leadership to commemorate the fiftieth anniversary of its namesake's death. Of course, Sir Winston is not normally known as a peacebuilder. Nor was Gowing who had just retired from a distinguished career as a television news presenter (or anchor to American readers). But, as Gowing began doing his interviews, he kept finding that political and corporate leaders were simply not prepared to deal with a world in flux. So, he brought Langdon onto his team, because he had spent years as a peacebuilder as well as a television news producer.

In the end, they interviewed about one hundred C Suite executives from both the public and private sectors who kept driving home a single point. None of them felt prepared to deal with technological disruption, political gridlock, climate change, and more. These were not people who normally cry wolf. Instead, they made it to the top precisely because they got things done.

Their research kept Gowing and Langdon busy for the next four years and culminated with the publication of *Thinking the Unthinkable*. The blurb on its cover tells us a lot:

> *Thinking the Unthinkable* is an investigation into why leaders have appeared more unable or unwilling than ever to anticipate the biggest issues of our time. In an era of "wicked problems," why are current leadership behaviours and culture apparently not fit for purpose? What are the causes of so many failures in policy and strategic forecasting? Are they human frailties? Or are they systemic failures to embrace smartly new realities?[3]

The image on the cover (reproduced here) says it all—blindfolded professionals wandering around trying to figure out where to go and what to do.

I was surprised that so many of the men and women they interviewed were willing to go on the record in saying how unprepared they and their colleagues were for the two overarching challenges that are now also squarely on the peacebuilding (if not the conflict resolution) agenda. While I introduced these terms, too, in earlier chapters, we did not spend much time thinking about them before 9/11:

- **VUCA**. VUCA (for volatile, uncertain, complicated, and ambiguous) is a term that we borrowed from the military. That peacebuilders started using that term reflects a key theme we will key theme in the rest of part 4—our willingness to work with new partners and allies. For now, it is enough to note that a VUCA world is characterized by accelerating rates of change which undermine established lines of authority and power are challenged.
- **Wicked problems**. The same holds for this other term, which we also borrowed from another field (urban planning) and I largely left hanging after introducing it in chapter 1. These problems are not called wicked because they are evil. Rather, the analysts who started using the term referred to problems whose causes and consequences are so inextricably intertwined that we can't solve them quickly, easily, or separately, if we can solve them at all. The issues that gave rise to 9/11 and its aftermath clearly fall into that category. But so do most of the other problems that seem to defy solution today, ranging from racism and sexism to climate change.

Thinking the Unthinkable

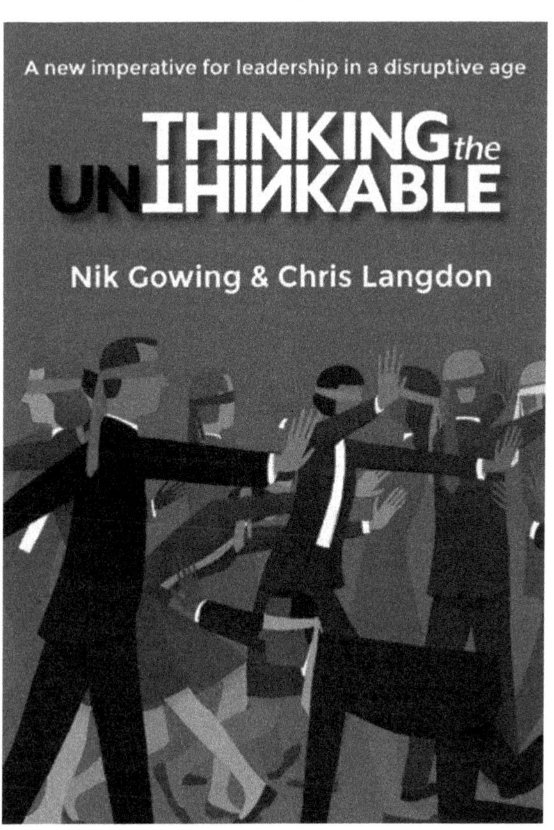

In the end, *Thinking the Unthinkable*, however, is not a book about gloom and doom. As they were finishing the book, Gowing and Langdon decided to form a small consulting group that would help leaders deal with the unthinkable.

They actually found a few prominent leaders who welcomed disruption and used it as an opportunity to try out new ideas. Many did so because they hired people from diverse backgrounds and gave them lots of leeway. Some discovered the importance of learning from their Millennial coworkers who have always lived in a world of constant change and for whom sticking with what worked in the past makes no sense at all.

OUT ON A LIMB

The Liberal Peace Again

Many people I know, like, and respect would make the case that trying to change the world using versions of the liberal peace comes close to meeting Einstein's definition of insanity—trying to do basically the same thing that hasn't worked over and over again on the assumption that it might just pan out the next time.

From that perspective, it is hard to see a way to build lasting peace without addressing the structural inequalities that analysts like Johan Galtung have been warning us about for fifty years.

On one level, I agree with them. On another, I have a hard time envisioning an alternative to the liberal peace and its acceptance of some version of modern capitalism gaining enough popular support to shift public policy and pave the way toward stable or positive peace.

Most of their examples come from the corporate world, including Safaricom, which brought cheap cell phone service and mobile banking to much of Africa, a Moroccan phosphate producer, and a bank in Singapore. But what they learned has implications for conflict resolution and peacebuilding as well.

NEW INSIGHTS

The first few pages of this chapter do not provide much evidence that we have been able to escape Gloom and Doom 101. Yet, we are beginning to do just that precisely because we had to go back to the drawing board which led us to a number of insights that I will be describing in the rest of this chapter and illustrating in the next two.

That started with a new concern with analytical rigor. At first, we set out to use data to counter the arguments being made to bolster spport for a violent response to 9/11. Gradually, however, we adopted new models using new sources of data that helped move us towards an emphasis on positive peace, five of which are important enough to include here. Just as important is the very fact that we started taking data seriously which marked an important step forward in our maturity as an academic discipline.

The Global Peace Index

To begin with, we started systematically measuring the problems we faced in a systematic manner. Among other initiatives, the Australia-based Institute for Economics and Peace first published its annual **Global Peace Index (GPI)** in 2009. For the last ten years, its database has ranked 163 of the world's countries on twenty-three indicators of conflict and peacefulness. Although it does not have enough data to compute its index for thirty UN member states, ninety-nine percent of the people on the planet live in those 163 countries for which adequate, reliable data exists.

The GPI is not without its critics. However, it is by far the most comprehensive such database, because it is based on three clusters of measures that cover almost all of the issues covered so far in this book:

- levels of societal safety and security
- engagement in ongoing domestic and international violence
- degree of militarization

The GPI has helped us see the financial costs of conflict, which is probably not all that surprising since it is produced by the Institute for *Economics* and Peace. The numbers are staggering. One could quibble with the specific indicators the Institute uses, but not with its basic findings. In the ten-year history of the GPI, global expenditure on violence and its prevention varied between a low of $12.62 trillion in 2010 and a high of $14.76 trillion in 2018.

That's trillion with a *t*.

That's the equivalent of more than twelve percent of the world's gross domestic product.

Or $1,988 for every man, woman, and child on the face of the earth.

Roughly forty percent of those dollars are spent directly on the military and its suppliers. More than a quarter of those funds are spent on the police and others responsible for domestic security. Seventeen percent of that total can be ascribed to the direct and indirect effects of homicide. If those figures weren't depressing enough, these expenditures accounted for a full forty-five percent of all economic activity in the ten countries most affected by violence in 2017!

Even though the GPI team intended to measure the factors that caused peace, it is best known for its findings about conflict itself. That starts with the countries that have scored at the bottom of the rankings—Somalia, Iraq, South Sudan, Afghanistan, and Syria in 2018. Four of those same five countries made the "bottom five" in the first list ten years earlier. Technically, Sudan made it rather than South Sudan, because the latter did not exist at the time. Syria was not in the first list because research for the first GPI was done before the beginning of the Arab Spring. Russia was on it instead.

The GPI's findings have confirmed a lot of what we had long suspected, but could not demonstrate on the basis of hard evidence. The most violent countries were among the world's poorest and least homogeneous. Few came close to being democracies. To make matters worse, the twenty-five least peaceful countries experienced a 12.7 percent decline in their overall GPI scores in that decade.

We should not ascribe too much meaning to those exact numbers since the GPI itself is a summary score based on twenty-three indicators which means that a lot of averaging and estimating takes place before the final result is calculated. Still, the GPI suggests that once countries get caught up in a cycle of violence, it can be hard for them to pull themselves out of it.

More surprising are some of the countries in the middle of the rankings, including most of the ones that have a major international footprint. They have also made the GPI controversial.

Nothing shows that more clearly than the US. Given its status as the world's remaining superpower, it is hard to imagine how the US could get a high score on the items measuring the size or cost of its military. However, the US has never scored higher than the middle of the pack. And, its overall ranking plummeted to 121st place in 2018. That's not only because of America's military involvement in Afghanistan, Iraq, and beyond. It scores so poorly, too because the GPI taps domestic measures of insecurity, including a country's homicide and incarceration rates, for which the US is in a league of its own.

The list of the most peaceful countries has never been all that surprising either. In 2018, Iceland, New Zealand, Austria, Portugal, and Spain topped the list. Ten years earlier, Japan and Finland made the list rather than Portugal and Spain. Whatever the annual fluctuations, the most peaceful countries tended to be small and isolated. At the Washington launch of the GPI the year that Norway topped the list, its ambassador quipped that the GPI also discovered that cold weather mattered, since any army that wanted to invade his country would have to buy a lot of parkas.

Pathways to Peace

Meanwhile, the **UN** and the **World Bank** have come to the realization that neither agency can reach its goals if dozens of conflicts remain unresolved in the poorest parts of the world. After the UN adopted its Sustainable Development Goals in 2015 (see chapter 12), the two bodies launched a research project that resulted in their *Pathways to Peace* report, which documented how violent conflict prevents societies from ending poverty or reaching just about any other social and economic goal.

We will explore the pathways themselves in chapter 12. Here, it is enough to see some of their insights about the new forms of conflict itself.

Unlike the GPI, which focuses on individual countries, *Pathways to Peace* explores the global patterns and reaches somewhat different—but equally gloomy—conclusions which they sum up with a bang at the very beginning of their report:

> There can be no sustainable development without peace and no peace without sustainable development. The Sustainable Development Goals cannot be attained without the attention to the effects of conflict.

That starts with the fact that the number and intensity of global conflicts have both surged after decades of decline. As has been the case most of the time since the end of World War II, there are next to no international wars being fought today. Still, the deadliest conflicts that have accounted for the largest number of casualties have involved the world's great powers—Afghanistan, Iraq, and Syria. In addition, there are between forty and seventy armed disputes taking place in the world today—the exact number depends on how you define armed dispute.

In some ways, these conflicts are more worrisome than those we've considered so far in this book. Many involve organizations that reject the norms and rules of conventional political life. To make matters worse, while most of these conflicts began in a single country, many have spread across their borders in three key ways. First, the fighting itself often spills over into neighboring countries. Second, the conflicts have led to the waves of literally millions of refugees and internally displaced persons who are so prominently in the news in countries like the US or Germany which are thousands of miles removed from the fighting. Last but by no means least, few of the conflicts in the world today show any sign of ending soon.

Better Angels and Minding Gaps

This is also where the line of of thinking that stresses the improvements in the human condition over the last few centuries that I also introduced in part 1 comes into play. Frankly, I did not expect those interpretations to make much sense at the time. They might now, because it has only been in the last twenty years that we have begun to blend the lessons about past successes with the problems of the present.

In the end, there are two paradoxical conclusions from this literature whose implications we are just beginning to incorporate into practical peacebuilding work:

- If you want to address intractable conflicts, you have to deal with all of its implications and not just those associated with negative peace.
- Sometimes you can do the most to advance peacebuilding if you tackle other issues first.

Better angels. As we saw there, the best-known (and most controversial) of those analysts is the evolutionary psychologist **Steven Pinker** (1954–). There is no need to repeat his conclusions in any detail other than to highlight two of them and then go on to consider the implications of the fact that he is an *evolutionary* psychologist.

First, simply remember the everyday events that have been all but eliminated in most parts of the world:

- burning witches
- most forms of slavery
- routine use of torture and the death penalty (at least outside the US)
- highway robbery (at least the literal kind)
- most public executions
- lynching

None have been completely eradicated. But we have made huge progress on these and dozens of other fronts.

Second, his data revealed what mathematicians refer to as a power law that is based on **accelerating rates of change**. Recall that I also used Pinker's work as one of the first of many examples of how rapid change has become a feature of modern life, as depicted in figure 2.2, which I have reproduced here as figure 10.1.

Recall that Pinker is part of a growing group of evolutionary psychologists, which brings me back to the idea of forks in the road, which I also introduced in chapter 2. These scholars explore how our physical and social histories have combined to create the kinds of value systems that we see in the world today. Pinker explored how those values have changed in the past. The idea of a fork in the road suggests that we now can make choices about our evolutionary future, too.

Put simply, little of the progress Pinker describes can be attributed to the ways we have evolved physically. Rather, we have evolved socially, which is now a theme that many in the conflict resolution and peacebuilding communities are applying to their own work as we contemplate the forks in the twenty-first century's road.

Minding gaps. That interest has led some of us to consider the work of **Hans Rosling** (1948–2017), which actually has more direct relevance to peace and conflict studies. Rosling followed a different methodological path in reaching similar conclusions about human progress. Trained as a physician in his native Sweden, Rosling shifted his attention to public health early in his career. Along the way, he developed a knack for presenting complex statistical trends in flashy

FIGURE 10.1
Accelerating Rates of Change: A Stylized View

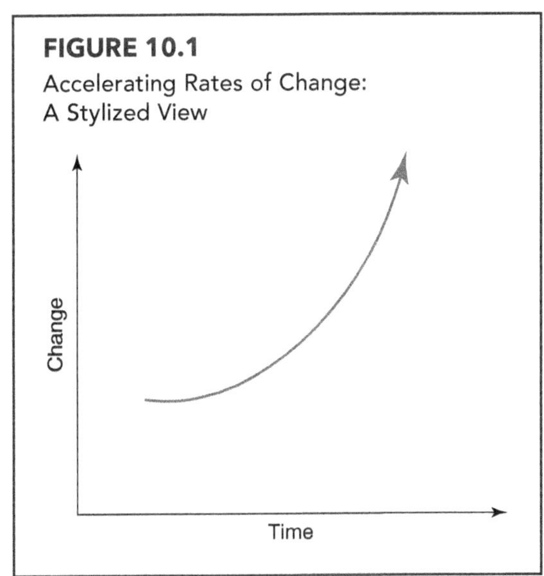

ways that included eye-grabbing and data-filled charts, stacked IKEA storage boxes, and the occasional toy Volvo.

Rosling did more than any other person of his generation to popularize the idea of human security, although he rarely used the term itself. Instead, he explored the interplay between economic growth, public health, family size, and consumption patterns to sketch out the challenges that we will face—and can overcome—in the rest of this century.

During the last twenty years of his life, he and his team developed powerful statistical and visual tools that showed just how much life has improved over the last two centuries. There are literally dozens of entertaining Rosling videos, but the best one for peacebuilders was his first TED talk that spent more time using IKEA boxes than his fancy digitalized data.

www.ted.com/talks/hans_rosling_on_global_population_growth

As you would expect from someone with his professional background, Rosling focused on indicators of health and welfare rather than the aspects of human security that involve war and peace. Nonetheless, his work is important here, because every video he made and the book his children finished after his death, *Factualness*, urged us to drop the mind-set in which we contrast a relatively peaceful and developed "West" and a much poorer, insecure, and violent "rest" of the world. As Rosling never ceased to remind us, because we get most of our information from the mass media and the unspoken assumption that "if it bleeds it leads" in determining what makes it onto the news, we miss the remarkable progress that has been made in the last thirty years or so that has rendered that kind of dichotomous thinking obsolete.

Toward Positive Peace

Ironically, the shift away from Gloom and Doom 101 brings us back to the Institute for Economics and Peace. Recall from my discussion of the GPI that the Institute was created to provide systematic evidence about the causes of peace, not war. However, as you saw a few paragraphs ago, the GPI's data led us to focus on the problem rather than any kind of solution.

After some soul searching as well as prodding from its partners in the peacebuilding world, the institute's researchers began exploring the drivers of what I have referred to as **positive peace** from time to time in this book. That led them collect data for a second scale, the **Positive Peace Index (PPI)**. Although there is a good bit of overlap between the two measures, they are not the same. The GPI focuses on the ways in which countries prepare for and engage in conflict. The PPI, by contrast, emphasizes the causes of the liberal peace and does so in ways that open the door to the kind of broader systems theory that undergirds much of what I will call Peacebuilding 3.0.

Recall, too, from earlier chapters that while the likes of the Bouldings and Johan Galtung did introduce the concepts of positive and stable peace, they did not do much to define what they are like in ways a social scientist would be happy with. As a result, we could not specify what positive and stable peace actually looked like, let alone chart paths for getting there other than explore the two end points on Michael Lund's curve (see chapter 3).

The PPI was created to fill that empirical gap by pulling together evidence about the attitudes, institutions, and structures that scholars have argued are most conducive to peace. The countries that have high scores on the PPI also tend to do well on the GPI, too. What makes the PPI more useful for our purposes here is that it also includes data on the eight factors that seem to contribute the most to stable and lasting peace as depicted in figure 10.2.

None of the issues raised in it had much to do directly with the identity-based conflicts discussed in part 3. However, countries that fell short on these indicators of positive peace also found themselves susceptible not only to identity-based conflicts but to the kinds of disruptions that have characterized life in the first two decades of this century. In developing Peacebuilding 3.0 in the rest of part 4, I will at least touch on three clusters of indicators that the PPI surfaced:

- **Governance.** This marked the first time that people in the field began paying serious attention to things like corruption or the state's ability to define and, especially, implement effective public policies.
- **Economics.** Oddly enough, the PPI researchers combine two seemingly contradictory conditions—a flourishing private sector and an equitable distribution of resources.
- **Information technology.** The researchers at the PPI refer to this as the free flow of information. Here, I will focus on the use of all forms of information technology, most of which were just coming on line as this century began.

Steve Killelea

Steve Killelea

It is only slightly ironic that one of the intellectual giants of contemporary peacebuilding is a high school dropout. After a number of years, in which he apparently spent most of his time surfing in his native Sydney, Australia, **Steve Killelea** founded Integrated Solutions, which made him a fortune by, among other things, creating software tools that allow ATMs "talk" to cardholders' banks and then release cash into their wallets.

By 2000, Killelea had become one of Australia's leading philanthropists. He soon realized, however, that a lot of the schools and hospitals he had funded were being destroyed in war. So he founded the Institute for Economics and Peace, which produces the GPI and PPI and, more generally, researches the social and economics drivers of conflict and peace around the world.

As you watch this short video, remember that you have spent more time in school than Steve did.

http://visionofhumanity.org/positive-peace/positive-peace-conference-2018/

FIGURE 10.2
Indicators of Positive Peace

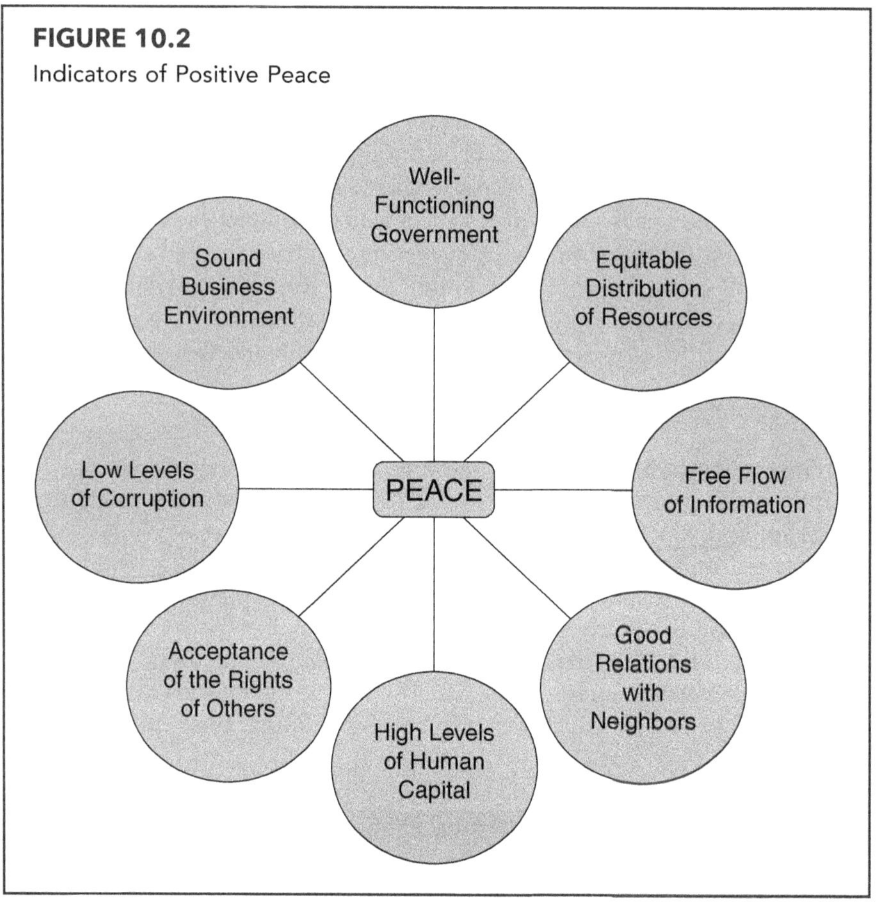

PEACEBUILDING 3.0

Psychologists and philosophers talk a lot these days about **intentionality** or the conscious decision to seek a particular goal in response to a particular set of circumstances. In that sense, our field has become a lot more intentional because we are finally beginning to think consistently and coherently about how our work can have the greatest impact at both the grassroots and policy-making levels.

It is high time that we did so.

The best we can say about the first decade of the twenty-first century is that the conflict resolution and peacebuilding community was in a holding pattern. Most organizations continued doing the kinds of projects they had begun before 9/11. How could they do otherwise? After all, the identity-based conflicts of the 1990s hadn't disappeared. If anything, they had become more intractable.

Still, I used the term holding pattern in the previous paragraph because it took us that long to begin developing something resembling a coherent set of responses to the needs of the post-9/11 world. Gradually, we pieced together a new understanding of the world based on those changed realities I just described and put together approaches to peacebuilding that took us in qualitatively different directions from the ones I emphasized in parts 2 and 3.

Do No Harm

Peacebuilding 3.0 focuses on positive alternatives to coercion, violence, and war. That said, the first new idea in its development is based on yet one more concept that is couched in the negative as this section's title suggests.

In 1999, the economic development specialist **Mary Anderson** added peacebuilding to her NGO's portfolio. In the process, she adapted a principle that had been at the heart of medical practice for more than two thousand years. When medical students take the Hippocratic oath, they pledge themselves to "do no harm." As Anderson examined the intersection between economic development funding and conflict in the kinds of countries considered in part 3, she discovered that efforts to spur economic growth often ended up hurting a country's chances for achieving peace and vice versa.

You didn't need to read the first nine chapters of this book to understand that we shouldn't do things that cause people harm.

However, it is actually far from obvious how one should go about doing work that doesn't cause harm in an age of rapid change and wicked problems. To see how and why that is the case, consider two examples I will come back to repeatedly in the rest of this book.

The first example is obvious now, but it was not at the time. After the American-led forces easily toppled Saddam Hussein's regime in 2003, they dismantled the Iraqi army and banned all members of the ruling Ba'ath party from holding office under the new regime. Few analysts in the West raised objections to what was referred to as the de-Ba'athification of Iraq.

It quickly became clear that the indirect effects of seeking traditional or punitive justice led to plenty of harm. As many as four hundred thousand Iraqis suddenly found themselves out of work. At least that many soldiers were sent home without handing over their weapons to the new authorities. Many of those former civil servants and former soldiers were far from happy. Some of them took up arms against the new regime that survived only because it had the support of the US and its dwindling number of coalition partners. In short, what looked like a battlefield triumph turned into the insurgencies that are still fighting the Iraqi regime today. Meanwhile, the ban prevented hundreds of formerly state-owned firms from reopening, further contributing to the misery—and anger—of even more Iraqis.

The second example is less obvious but involves a project that is near and dear to my heart. On August 11 and 12, 2017, a group of white nationalists held a rally in Charlottesville that drew global attention when one of the protesters struck and killed a counterdemonstrator. Even before that tragic end, the events had made the news because the protesters chanted slogans like "Jews will not replace us" and made it clear that they had chosen Charlottesville because it was a liberal enclave located deep in the former confederacy. Anger continued to mount after President Trump seemed to make light of what happened when he said that there were "good people on both sides."

The following spring, a new organization, Listen First, decided to hold an event that would bring all sides of the debate in Charlottesville together. As you will see several times in the rest of this book, I am personally involved in many such efforts. However, even members of the conflict resolution community who attended the event felt it did more harm than good.

The details are not all that important here, but the bottom line is something we all need to pay attention to. The event's leaders did not listen all that well to the residents of Charlottesville, especially to people of color who were offended by the notion that there were two sides, each of which had an equal right to be heard. It did not help that the Listen First team brought some speakers who were themselves closely affiliated with the Trump administration.[4]

The bottom line, however, was clear to almost everyone who attended. Despite the best of intentions, the two-day event drove the citizens of Charlottesville further apart. Harm was done.

Systems and Complexity

In these cases, harm occurred because American policy makers and Listen First organizers did not realize that not doing harm requires thinking about the longer-term and indirect consequences of our actions. Events such as these led peacebuilders and, to a lesser degree, conflict resolution professionals to adopt systems and complexity theory (see the end of chapter 3). The Beyond War movement, which I worked in during the 1980s, did think in terms of systems. However, we were very much in the minority as far as the overall peacebuilding community was concerned. It was only after 9/11 that more and more of us began to see the importance of such notions as feedback, ecosystems, and complexity.

Concretely, systems analysis has had its greatest impact on the way peacebuilders plan new projects. At least the larger NGOs now build in time and money to do the kind of systems mapping you have been doing in the Conflict Labs. That does not mean that we have fully learned all the lessons that are implicit in the scientific literature on complexity or the way it has been applied in corporate or environmental settings. Nonetheless, it is safe to say that most peacebuilding and conflict resolution organizations anchor their work in the ways of thinking that best handle VUCAness and wicked problems in three main ways.

First, we can't consider peacebuilding in isolation. The global conflicts we have to deal with today grow out of complex social environments with literally dozens of interconnected causes and effects. That's true of many of the disputes local and community-based mediators have to deal with as well.

Second, because no two systems are the same, we should abandon any hope of finding anything resembling a single road map to peacebuilding. Rather, to use the terminology of systems theory, individual projects have to be "context specific" with specific initiatives "emerging" out of what seems to be work in a continual process of experimentation. Here, we have learned a lot from **design thinking** with its emphasis on developing and testing rapid prototypes and building **cumulative strategies** in which we build on today's successes in charting tomorrow's initiatives.

Third, in a VUCA world filled with interconnected wicked problems, peacebuilding requires similarly interconnected and integrated responses. Organizations that had embraced human security and other elements of Peacebuilding 2.0 had already acknowledged that their goals had to be placed in a broader context. However, Peacebuilding 3.0 goes further. Peace and conflict resolution may not be the most important goal of a larger project. Indeed, if people like the Roslings or the Institute for Economics and Peace's researchers are correct, positive peace may well emerge as a welcome by-product of projects that focus on economic development or gender equality rather than peacebuilding itself.

To conclude this section, think about four guiding principles the Omidyar Group (see chapter 3) uses in designing peacebuilding and other projects based on its understanding of systems theory which they propose as alternatives to the ways we normally solve problems today:

- **Look for patterns**. Unlike appreciative inquiry (see chapter 5), systems theory does not work on the assumption that there always is a positive past reformers can build on. From their perspective, it makes more sense to look at the key patterns that structure the system, especially the most important feedback loops that produce either vicious circles of virtuous cycles.
- **Focus on improving the system's performance**. It is rare that you can claim victory in dealing with today's wicked problems. Given the logic developed in chapter 3, systems analysts to identify the changes that would help them perform better in ways that lead toward stable or positive peace.
- **Unlock the system's potential**. In this case, systems theorists do share a lot with appreciative inquiry practitioners. There is probably something about any system that is working well. As you will see in the case studies in the next two chapters, people on the ground are more likely to understand them than professional peacebuilders who have spent their lives and professional careers elsewhere. In short, the best paths toward peace build on what I have been calling the "bright spots" in a system.
- **Adapt and learn as you go**. We normally heap praise on people who define a clear goal that they doggedly pursue. Omidyar's systems theorists would not disagree given the way they incorporate north stars and guiding stars into their analyses. However, in a VUCA world, it almost never makes sense to define a grand strategy for pursuing a long-term goal and then rigidly stick to it, which is exactly how we designed most Peacebuilding 2.0 projects. Rather, like someone steering a sailboat, we have to constantly adjust our course given the peacebuilding equivalents of changing wind patterns or unforeseen obstacles we encounter on the way toward our destination.

Paradigm Shifts Get Put on the Table

Until recently, very few peacebuilders spent much time thinking about paradigm shifts. There were some outliers, again including the Beyond War Movement. But, as with thinking about systems, we were definitely outside of the peacebuilding and conflict resolution mainstream. That wasn't true of just conflict resolution and peacebuilding. In 2000, few average citizens would have even heard about paradigm shifts. Even today, it may not yet be part of most people's everyday conversations. Still, we rarely bat an eyelash when sports announcers talk about baseball's paradigm shift associated with the Sabermetrics revolution.

In our case, the 9/11 attacks, the subsequent Global War on Terror, the frustrations many of us felt with the conservative drift at home, and more convinced many peace and conflict studies practitioners that we needed to profoundly change the way we addressed the world's problems.

Thinking in terms of a paradigm shift is one thing. Making one happen is quite another. Indeed, we are just now pulling ourselves out of a trap many paradigm shift advocates fall into—myself included.

Once people learn about paradigm shifts, they usually assume that they occur in one fell swoop when a community intentionally adopts a new mind-set. Ironically, that is particularly true of people who were introduced to the idea through Thomas Kuhn's book which got this whole line of reasoning started when he raised the idea of scientific revolutions.

Although Kuhn spoke in terms of revolutions, paradigm shifts typically emerge gradually when a community makes a variety of incremental steps that lead to some sort of qualitatively different outcome. As the science writer Steven Johnson sees it, we are typically only aware that a paradigm shift has occurred after it has happened.[5]

Peacebuilding 3.0 Itself

Out of all this came Peacebuilding 3.0 which AfP presented in 2014 in a document that has guided its work ever since. Not many organizations have followed in our footsteps in adopting the Peacebuilding 3.0 label. However, more and more of them include its key provisions in their own work.

www.allianceforpeacebuilding.org/peacebuilding-3-0

The fact that they do so is actually more important, because AfP itself rarely gets involved in grassroots peacebuilding projects. As a result, I will have to use examples of projects other organizations have championed in the rest of part 4.

Nonetheless, our version of Peacebuilding 3.0's key points are worth quoting at some length. The first two sum up what we have seen so far and thus might seem redundant. However, they lead inexorably to the other three, which are the ways in which our community has set about building a more peaceful world, whether one uses the term Peacebuilding 3.0 or not.

In the process, note that we have moved beyond the fairly simplistic theories of change that you saw in parts 2 and 3 which typically took the form of "if peacebuilders do x, y is likely to happen." Now, because we have begun to view peacebuilding and conflict resolution as part of a more complex reality, the theories of change embedded in the final three bullet points are a lot more complicated, too.

- **Peacebuilding as the challenge of our age**. We have entered an era in which conflict is taking new forms and spreading in ways that are outstripping the power of the international community to respond.
- **Wicked problems**. Conflict today is understood as a wicked problem, a toxic brew of interconnected factors such as grievance, crime, climate stress, inequality, weak institutions, disease, and poor governance.
- **Disrupting narratives**. If peacebuilding were only about structure, we would have figured out a long time ago how to create durable peace. Peacebuilding also involves disrupting the dominant narratives surrounding political power and military force and creating new stories of peace that can form the basis of a new truth on the ground.
- **Networks and norms**. Peacebuilding is an elastic concept, encompassing a wide range of efforts by diverse actors in government and civil society at the community, national, and international levels, who all address the

immediate impacts and root cause of conflict before, during, and after violent conflict occurs. As global violence proliferates, a major challenge for us is to **network** peace—to interconnect the full spectrum of norms, institutions, informal and formal networks, and agencies that can manage conflict before it escalates into the full fury that poisons future generations.

- **Capable structures and networks for peace.** Peacebuilding has to be integrated in every sense of the word into the DNA of society in ways that are adapted to local conditions. A truly integrated peacebuilding system would stretch from grand strategy integrating ideas of human security and national and regional security policy to local peacebuilding structures that could prevent and mitigate conflict at a communal level.

PEACE WRIT LARGE

Despite the gloom and doom so far in this chapter, the peacebuilding community has become more holistic and ambitious when it comes to national and global policy making. Once again, Mary Anderson provides us with a phrase that captures the tighter link between grassroots and elite level peacebuilding in this third period. Recall from chapter 8 that her NGO had previously focused on economic development and added peacebuilding to its portfolio in the late 1990s.

Like many other NGOs at the time, what is now **CDA Collaborative** ran programs that represented the best of Peacebuilding 2.0. At that point, Anderson reached a troubling conclusion.

She could point to plenty of accomplishments in individual communities and on individual issues. She could not, however, claim anything like that kind of success at the national or the global level because we did not have enough support either in the general public or among political elites.

So, she began talking about **peace writ large** and exploring what it would mean for us to have the kind of impact we all yearned for that builds on the accomplishments of Peacebuilding 2.0 and what you have seen of Peacebuilding 3.0 so far. Anderson herself retired in the early 2000s, but as you are about to see, the efforts she sparked with those three small words continue to this day. In so doing, they also put the notion of a paradigm shift squarely on the table at the national and global levels.

Mary Anderson

A Job to Do

Curiously, the best way to see where peace writ large and similar ideas are taking us, is to take a step back from peace and conflict studies and add one more idea we have borrowed from business management. **Clayton Christensen** (1952–) is an expert on disruptive innovation at the Harvard Business School who has spent the last forty years studying how and why new products make it, ranging from sewing machines to digital cameras to automobiles to the personal computer.

Innovations succeed when entrepreneurs figure out what he calls their **job to do**, which really amounts to two jobs rolled into one. They have to create a product that fits a gaping unmet need. And, because potential customers aren't always aware that such a need exists, the entrepreneur has a second challenge. She or he has to create a market for that product. That means that the entrepreneur has to find a way to make the product attractive and affordable enough for consumers who may not even know that they want or need it.

One example should be enough to show what he means. When Apple set out to invent the iPhone and Google decided to build the Android operating system, next to no one demanded a computer that fit in your pocket, took photographs (let alone videos), surfed the web, got your email, tracked your exercise patterns, and, oh yes, made telephone calls. The pioneering companies had to make the product (job #1), and then they had to create the demand for it (job #2).

In the rest of parts 4 and 5, you will see how we are beginning to do both of Christensen's jobs and how they could lead to peace writ large. You will also see that we have plenty of work left to be done.

Historical Precedents

It is hard to be optimistic about our ability to overcome major conflict-related problems facing the world today because the problems themselves seem so daunting. Even more daunting are the findings that emerge from Gowing and Langdon's research. the leaders have serious blind spots when it comes to the kinds of issues covered in this book. The closer you get to people with the capacity to shape a country's or the planet's future, the less open they seem to be what Christensen thinks of as disruptive innovation.

While that sense of pessimism is easy to understand, it fails to take a key feature of the historical record into account. Time and time again, people and the states that govern them have overcome huge obstacles—including in the not so distant past.

If we step back from the kind of global data Pinker and Rosling use in the studies cited earlier and concentrate on specific policy areas, we do find examples of successful intentional efforts that had global payoffs. They may not amount to what I meant by a paradigm shift in earlier chapters. Nonetheless, they demonstrate how much and—sometimes—how quickly political systems can change when and if they summon up the political will to do so.

Here, too, the best examples come from Rosling's field of public health rather than peacebuilding or conflict resolution. In the last seventy years alone, we have all but completely eradicated two deadly diseases that used to kill millions of people a year. First, a global coalition of physicians and political leaders made certain that enough doses of smallpox vaccine reached enough people in enough places that we reached the point at which there were no more outbreaks of the disease anywhere in the world. Second, with the invention and now close to global use of the polio vaccine, there are no more than a handful of new cases a year, and each time a new one occurs, public health officials around the world bemoan the fact that eradicating polio completely still eludes their grasp.

Similarly, we have made major progress on a number of environmental issues, the looming danger of climate change notwithstanding. The accumulation of chlorofluorocarbons (CFCs) in the ozone layer threatened to cause massive and unpredictable damage to the atmosphere and could well have killed tens of millions of people. Then, a combination of scientific ingenuity that yielded alternatives to the use of CFCs and a global political consensus around what became the Montreal protocol put an end to that danger in a matter of years.

Those examples suggest three core common denominators that increasingly structure our work at all levels:

- We had to want to have that kind of an impact.
- We have to build broad coalitions that make it possible to reach any life-changing goal.
- Rosling and others who champion the progress we have made also emphasize the huge gaps that remain in a VUCA world that require a different kind of **theory of change** that brings our mind-set up to date.

In the end, much of the progress we made hinged on the adoption of systems approaches at two levels. We have made a lot more progress on the first one—using systems-based approaches to shape what peacebuilders themselves do. We have made less progress on the other—changing the norms and the narrative around which "conversations" at the grown-ups' table take place.

Advocacy

The first step to take in developing that kind of strategy can be found in grows out of the first bullet point above. It should also be obvious by now.

If we want a seat at the grown-ups' table, we have to ask for one. If my colleagues, who take contentious politics for granted, are right we may actually have to shove the people who currently sit at those metaphoric tables out of the way in order to get there.

That may well seem so obvious that it isn't worth making this point, let alone stressing it. However, the fact of the matter is that most conflict resolution and peacebuilding professionals didn't seriously try asking for any such seat before the 2000s for two main reasons, both of which I've hinted at before.

First, many of us were convinced that we should not take stands on controversial issues because it would jeopardize our standing as third-party neutrals. In fact, when I joined the AfP board of directors in 2005, our bylaws prohibited us from doing any kind of **advocacy** work. When we decided to change the rules, it produced the only contested vote in my fifteen years on the board.

Second, given our origins in the peace movements of the 1980s and, in some cases, in the new left of the 1960s, many of us assumed that the policy makers at the grown-ups' table would not be interested in talking to us. To see why, go back and look at the discussion of the nuclear weapons seminar at Harvard and MIT and Carol Cohn's reaction to it in chapter 6. Those preconceptions died slowly.

What you will see in the rest of this book is that we began to understand that we had no choice. We had to advocate for the kinds of public policies we wanted. Once we learned how to do so, at least some of the men and the increasing number of women at the grown-ups' table just might listen to us at least some of the time.

Norms and Narratives

The second bullet above did not lead us to give up on the kinds of projects discussed in part 3. Nonetheless, the desire to build broader coalitions did help us put our programs in a different and expanded perspective that included a desire to shift public policy everywhere in the world by changing the underlying **norms** that help determine how people deal with conflict.

There is considerable evidence that the kinds of community-based projects discussed in the next chapter have led to a shift in local or even regional norms in ways that help sustain peace. However, we have not done as good a job of creating what you might think of as **horizontal** linkages that spread out from a handful of localities to a country as a whole. To use today's terminological shorthand, we have not done a very good job of finding ways of making peacebuilding memes go viral. Or, to use the language of contentious politics as laid out in figure 4.1, we have not yet found the brokers who can create the opportunity structures in which those localized efforts can be taken to scale.

At the same time, there is evidence that it can be done. That happened in ways that I liked when I watched norms shift quickly until marriage equality became the law of the land in most of Europe and North America during the course of the last generation. It also happens in ways I did not particularly like, most notably when Donald Trump turned slogans like "Make America great again," "Build that wall," and "Lock her up" into memes that got him elected.

When peace and conflict studies researchers deal with this kind of material, they usually start with attitudes or beliefs on specific issues that could be placed in the box covering grievances in the USAID framework that I introduced in chapter 3. Occasionally, that is all we are interested in and the only thing we try to mobilize around. However, while a particular issue may be extremely important, the notion of creating shared understandings suggests that activists are usually interested in reshaping deeper and more lasting attitudes, including some that involve changing those aspects of a community's or a country's culture that have a bearing on how it deals with conflict.

When we think in terms of advocacy and social change, we often talk about the need to change the general **narratives** about conflict in general. In short, our challenge is to define a new narrative, which is also another word for a new paradigm. As we saw in the general discussion of paradigm shifts in chapter 2, its advocates then have to build broad-based support for it, while also focusing on those areas in which the cultural norms seem most amenable to change.

It is easy to look at an example like marriage equality and convince yourself that narratives and norms can be changed quickly and easily. As the growing body of research suggests, there may have been a **tipping point** at which support for marriage equality grew dramatically. We only got to that point, however, because the LGBTQ community spent year after frustrating year trying to build support around new norms and narratives. We will have to do the same thing in our own work, a realization that many of our colleagues are just now beginning to take seriously.

Adding Up to Peace

Far less attention was paid to the third bullet point and the **vertical** linkages that could turn popular demand for change into concrete policies in ways that would allow us to get at the points made in the third bullet point a few paragraphs ago. Here, the CDA Collaborative leadership team took

Mary Anderson's notion of peace writ large further in everything they did after her retirement.

Anderson and her colleagues went on what we would today call a listening tour to learn what peacebuilders were doing around the world. In that Reflecting on Peace Practices (RPP) project, they found a huge gap between our goals and our accomplishments in part because we did not take the long-term impact of our actions into account enough when we were planning those projects. Agreements often put a temporary end to the fighting but did not succeed in the long run because they failed to address the second of two goals which I have discussed earlier using terms like stable or positive peace. Diana Chigas and Peter Woodrow summed up this line of thinking in their appropriately entitled *Adding Up to Peace*:

> Peace Writ Large is a term [used] to describe changes at the macro level of society, comprising two basic goals which RPP found the wide array of program examined aimed to achieve:
>
> - Stopping violence and destructive conflict by working to end war and violence.
> - Building just and sustainable peace by addressing the political, economic, and social grievances driving conflict and forming the foundations for sustainable peace.[6]

The first bullet point in their statement should already be familiar because it has been a central theme throughout this book. As Anderson and her colleagues dug into the second one, they realized that building what they called a just and sustainable peace was no mean feat and, more importantly, that it couldn't be done without involving the government and other authorities which political scientists together call the **state**. You simply cannot "address the political, economic, and social grievances driving conflict" without taking on questions of power.

The RPP team was but one of a number of groups of applied researchers who came to the conclusion that the peacebuilding "job to be done" has to be anchored in systems-based approaches that commit practitioners and policy makers to solutions that can only be built over extended periods of time in what some call a cumulative strategy that builds toward—if not directly to—peace. Again, you should not be surprised that there are dozens of models of peacebuilding in the "marketplace" today. Still, most of them focus on three basic goals at the heart of *Adding Up to Peace*, as you will see in the rest of this chapter:

- **Create shared understandings.** Chigas and Woodrow stress the importance of developing common ways of analyzing a problem which, in turn, become what they call the intellectual backbone for broader peace processes. They do not make the case that everyone has to agree on everything. Still, they believe that agreement on the causes and consequences of the problems a country or community faces allows peacebuilders to find a common point of departure.
- **Identify networks**. As I first suggested in chapter 3, the key to understanding any system lies in the relationships between individuals and institutions or the **linkages** between them. That's why I put so much emphasis on exploring the meaning of the arrows you drew in the Conflict Labs. Now, in exploring how we can take the kinds of initiatives discussed in this chapter

to scale, I will emphasize the ways in which peacebuilding and conflict resolution professionals have turned their attention to the most important feedback loops in any conflict.

- **Expand leverage**. That leads to another key term that we have borrowed from systems theory which I hinted at as early as the first three pages of this book. Systems maps get very complicated very fast, which means that you can't realistically hope to intervene at every node or in every feedback loop. Instead, systems theorists in fields as different as engineering and management focus on what they refer to as key **leverage** points at which practitioners decide they can have the most impact on changing an entire system for an extended period of time and in ways that alter its "shape" in the process by addressing some or all of the root causes that gave rise to the conflict(s) in the first place.

GUIDE STARS AND NEAR STARS

You would not be off target it you reached two conclusions from this chapter. First, we have finally reached the point where our field has a degree of coherence that was made possible by the adoption of one form or another of systems theory that led us to focus on pathways toward what the Omidyar team called guide stars and near stars. Second, given what you have seen, it was far from obvious how we could and should chart those pathways.

That is what we turn to next.

KEY TERMS

Concepts

9/11, 207
accelerating rates of change, 217
advocacy, 227
cumulative strategy, 222
design thinking, 222
horizontal, 228
intentionality, 220
job to do, 225
leverage, 230
liberal peace, 211
linkages, 229
narratives, 228
network, 225
norms, 228
peace writ large, 225
populism, 211
positive peace, 218
state, 229
theory of change, 227
tipping point, 228
vertical, 228
VUCA, 213
wicked problem, 213

People

Anderson, Mary, 221
Christensen, Clayton, 225
Killelea, Steve, 219
Lederach, John Paul, 209
Pinker, Steven, 217
Rosling, Hans, 217

Organizations, Places, and Events

9/11, 207
CDA Collaborative, 225
Global Peace Index (GPI), 214
Global War on Terror (GWOT), 209
Positive Peace Index (PPI), 218
United Nations, 216
World Bank, 216

DIG DEEPER

Chigas, Diana, and Peter Woodrow. *Adding Up to Peace: The Cumulative Impacts of Peace Processes*. Boston: CDA Collaborative, 2018.

Gowing, Nik, and Christopher Langdon. *Thinking the Unthinkable: A New Imperative for Leadership in the Digital Age*. London: Catt, 2018. A remarkably readable book on a remarkably depressing topic.

Heimans, Jeremy, and Henry Timms. *New Power: How Power Works in Our Hyperconnected World—and How to Make It Work for You*. New York: Doubleday, 2018. Thought-provoking book on the changing nature of power.

Kuhn, Thomas. *The Structure of Scientific Revolutions*. Chicago: University of Chicago Press, 1962. Still the definitive book on paradigms and paradigm shifts.

Naim, Moises. *The End of Power: From Boardrooms to Battlefield and Churches to Why Being in Charge Isn't What It Used to Be*. New York: Basic Books, 2013. The best book on the fleeting nature of power.

NOTES

[1] This thought piece flew around the internet in the weeks after 9/11. It can still be found at www.mediate.com/articles/lederach2.cfm.

[2] Rosa Brooks, *How Everything Became War and the Military Became Everything: Tales from the Pentagon* (New York: Simon and Schuster, 2016).

[3] Nik Gowing and Christopher Langdon, *Thinking the Unthinkable: A New Imperative for Leadership in the Digital Age* (London: John Catt, 2018).

[4] https://deliberative-democracy.net/2018/05/07/considering-listen-first-in-charlottesville-reflections-of-frank-dukes/.

[5] Steven Johnson, *Where Good Ideas Come From: The Natural History of Innovation* (New York: Riverhead, 2010).

[6] Diana Chigas and Peter Woodrow, *Adding Up to Peace* (Boston: CDA Collaborative, 2018), www.cdacollaborative.org/wp-content/uploads/2018/04/ADDING-UP-TO-PEACE-The-Cumulative-Impacts-of-Peace-Initiatives-Web-Version.pdf.

CHAPTER 11

Toward Positive Peace

THINK ABOUT IT

The conflict and peacebuilding communities changed in unexpected ways in the aftermath of 9/11, which leads us to the following questions, none of which we have been able to fully answer. So, expect to be at least a bit frustrated and confused as you try to answer them:

- Why have 9/11 and terrorism in general been so hard for the peacebuilding world to respond to?
- Do systems approaches make sense in the post- 9/11world?
- How can you use systems analysis as developed in chapter 3 and here to incorporate globalization, climate change, and other issues into peace and conflict studies?

CORE CONCEPTS

accompaniment—in local peacebuilding, the notion that outsiders help or accompany grassroots activists and others

local peacebuilding—the notion that people on the ground have the best understanding of their conditions and therefore have the best ideas for building peace

resilience—the ability of an individual or organization to bounce back after adversity

wicked problem—problems that are so complicated that you cannot solve them quickly, easily, or separately

The McConnell peacebuilding program in Nepal will promote a peace culture building on respect for diversity, rights, and nonviolent response to conflict. The Foundation will support innovative and inclusive peacebuilding activities that increase dialogue and participation at all levels of Nepali society.

—The McConnell Foundation/John Paul Lederach

IN ENDING CHAPTER 10, I may have left you with the impression that we now have a handle on what conflict resolution and peacebuilding should be like. Conceptually speaking that may be true—at least until another earth shattering event shakes us out of our current mind-set. For the foreseeable future, we will be doing holistic projects that integrates the grass-roots with the elites and address the root causes of **wicked problems**.

There is only one problem with this line of reasoning.

It is very hard to design projects on such a grand scale. It is even harder to fund them and carry them out.

THE NEPAL PROJECT

In fact, I only know of one project that has tried to put the key conclusions from chapter 10 into practice—the decade-long **Nepal Project**. In 2003 Nepal was in the seventh year of what turned out to be a decade-long civil war. It pitted the traditional monarchy against Maoist insurgents with many mainstream politicians caught in between. By the time the fighting ended in 2005 more than ten thousand people had died and one hundred thousand more had fled their homes. As **John Paul Lederach** later put it, "a whole nation, already poor, was coming apart at the seams."

By that point, the **McConnell Foundation** was already funding projects in Nepal. It had not gotten involved there because of a long-standing commitment to peacebuilding. The Foundation has always focused on community building and had done most of its work in and near Redding CA where it is located. In fact, it had only branched out to do work in Nepal and Laos because there were significant immigrant communities from both countries living in their part of northern California. As the civil war was dying down, the foundation's leaders realized that they could make a commitment to lasting peace in Nepal as well as to economic development and the other issues that were already on their agenda.

Because they had never done peacebuilding work they decided to contact Lederach and William Ury (of *Getting to YES* fame), who are good friends, and neighbors in Boulder, Colorado. The McConnell team reached out to them because they specialized in aspects of peacebuilding that few Nepalese elites were familiar with—using outside mediators (Ury's forte) or empowering grassroots activists (Lederach's forte).

Ury decided not to work with McConnell after these first consultations because he was just too busy with his existing projects. Lederach had more flexibility in his schedule and was intrigued by the idea of working in Nepal. However, he was skeptical that another short term project that was funded by a foreign NGO could make much of a difference.

So, he asked for something that he assumed that the relatively small McConnell Foundation could not and would not deliver. He requested enough money to carry out a ten-year, integrated peacebuilding project in Nepal. Much to his surprise, the foundation's board decided to fund it as long as Lederach himself agreed to **accompany** the Nepalese peacebuilders for its entire duration, which turned out to be twelve years. They thus set in motion one of the most remarkable peacebuilding projects ever undertaken, which you can easily learn more about by reading his book (cited in the footnote a few paragraphs ago) which also shows off his photographic skills.

Lederach is one of the few rock star like figures in the peacebuilding world who is brought in to advise local peacebuilders and national leaders in conflict zones around the world. He is a remarkable man who has been a full-time grassroots peacebuilder since his undergraduate days and has spent about half of his adult life in conflict zones. He is able to combine a deep commitment to his Mennonite faith with the most sophisticated academic insights. He practices what he preaches. Humble beyond belief, he is among the best listeners I have ever met. When you talk with him, you know you have his undivided attention.

Those attributes carry over into his work in the field. During the course of the 1990s, he came to the conclusion that outside experts are never going to have "the answer" for a country they didn't know inside and out and which they will only visit a few times and then spend most of their time in the national capital. By the end of the decade, he was already arguing that local peacebuilders have the best understanding of what will work in their own societies. Unlike outsiders from an NGO or a national government who fly in and out, they have both deep roots in their communities and a real stake in the outcome. As he saw it, the outsider's role is literally to accompany people who are living in the conflict and, when appropriate, help them flesh out their own strategies and build on their own strengths.

From the beginning, the team did more than just commit itself for a decade. Among other things, it decided to:

- invest primarily in people and relationships rather than specific projects or outcomes, because if you don't get the relationships right, you won't have a chance of reaching your goals
- focus on building trust especially with key partners and others you will want to work with as circumstances improve
- be as transparent as possible
- proceed one step at a time and let the next one **emerge** (a key term in complexity science) after a rigorous evaluation of the previous one
- always remain flexible
- and humble

The entire logic of Peacebuilding 3.0 suggests that we have to resist the natural desire to find a single theory of change that provides "the" seemingly magic solution that will solve an entire problem. A conflict like the one in Nepal developed over a course of generations, if not centuries. It will take generations, if not centuries, to fully resolve those historically rooted disputes.

In the end, the Nepal Project set what you could think of as the gold standard for Peacebuilding 3.0 in ways that Lederach called "an almost perfect haiku" that is embedded in its mission statement. In other words, it covered just about every key goal I identified in chapter 10:

> Respect, diversity, rights,
> Nonviolent, innovative, inclusive,
> Dialogue, participation.[1]

Know the System

The Lederach/McConnell team did not draw the kind of systems map you have been working on in the Conflict Labs. In 2003 Lederach and his colleagues were like most peacebuilders. They had not much spent much time thinking in terms of systems theory. Still, everything Lederach and the McConnell team had done elsewhere had taught them two lessons that are at the heart of all systems-based approaches.

First, he shares the systems theorist's bias against reaching firm conclusions until you understand a culture's contours and complexities. You have to see the entire system and resist the natural desire to tackle the narrow slice of a problem you are most comfortable and familiar with. To use a cliché that is popular among this group of practitioners, "if a hammer is the only tool you have, everything tends to look like a nail."

John Paul Lederach in Nepal

Second, he also understood one of the paradoxes in systems theory. On the one hand, it lends itself to drawing the complicated maps like the ones you have been working on and to sophisticated mathematical modeling. On the other hand, as you will see in the discussion below about leverage and bright spots, using systems theory to guide practical projects requires giving the people who make up the system your highest priority, but they usually lack the analytical sophistication needed to use the tools discussed in chapter 3.

As a result, Lederach and his team did not arrive in Nepal with an agenda of projects they wanted to start. Instead, they took four months and carefully created a small advisory team that reflected the diversity of Nepalese society, respected each other, and shared an openness to experimentation. Few of their collaborators were part of the national elite other NGOs usually chose to work with. But, all were chosen because they exhibited a potential for personal growth. Indeed, by the time the project ended more than ten years later, all were still active in their grassroots movements, and half of them had also become part of the new political and social elite that was determining the country's future.

Leverage and Bright Spots

The main criteria the team used in determining where to focus their efforts reflect the degree to which their work was anchored in systems and complexity theory. Some grow out of earlier peacebuilding work, while others have their roots in other fields, ranging from the literature on public health in the Global South to what we know about successful start-ups in Silicon Valley.

A grassroots bias. When I write about comparative politics, I focus on national governments first. The Nepal Project is one of dozens of examples we can turn to in showing why that is not the right place to start if you want to understand and/or do something about the most intractable conflict.

To be sure, most peacebuilders, if not all conflict resolution practitioners, now assume that we will not succeed unless and until we have an impact on public policy. Therefore, many of my colleagues have also assumed that their work could and should focus on political decision makers at the national and international levels. Some of the best-known peacebuilding and conflict resolution specialoists, including Ury, are in the limelight largely because they have had a demonstrable impact at that level.

However, there is a growing consensus among practitioners that you should not focus only on elites. From this perspective, we cannot hope to have that kind of an impact unless we first build grassroots support for peace and then use it create credible demands for political change. Lederach wasn't the first peacebuilder to recognize this. A growing number of practitioners had learned the lessons of the Oslo Accords between Israel and the Palestinian Authority and other "orphaned" agreements that died in large part because there was not enough popular pressure on the leadership of either side to take them further.

Therefore, unlike some of the other, larger NGOs and international funding agencies, the McConnell team did not focus on decision makers in Kathmandu. They chose, instead, to begin by working in the rural regions near where the insurgency was based. Dozens of other NGOs around the world have similarly emphasized local peacebuilding, a theme I will return to frequently in the rest of this book.

Action research. The McConnell team tried to take advantage of the fact that they had an unusually long period of time to devote to Nepal by dividing their decade into three overlapping segments. The first three years were spent primarily in what Lederach called engaged learning.

In so doing, they relied on what is now a fairly commonly used tool known as **action research** which was not a new idea when peacebuilders stated taking it seriously in the early 2000s. The term was first used by social psychologist **Kurt Lewin** (1890–1947) in a paper he wrote in 1946. Like any social science methodology, there are now dozens of variations on the action research theme. All of them are based on the assumption that researchers cannot be and should not try to be objective when it comes to topics like conflict resolution. Instead, it makes more sense for them to be actively involved with the people they are studying in the design and implementation of all aspects of the project. Similarly, as systems theory (of which Lewin was a pioneer) also suggests, the researchers and the members of the communities they study should work together to constantly refine their goals and actions in the light of what they all learn from their work on the ground.

In time, the McConnell team honed in on three engagement areas that reflected both the diversity of the country and the issues that seemed to best lend themselves to cooperative solutions:

- expanding the use of community mediation
- focusing on conflicts over the use of natural resources
- building a rural women's empowerment network

These issue areas were not chosen randomly. The team picked them because their first few months of research and experimentation suggested that there were efforts already underway that could be expanded in a way that led to years of slow and reasonably steady improvement in the ways the Nepalese dealt with each other.

In this case, the McConnell team learned something that perhaps should have been obvious before they started. The approaches to **community mediation** that they initially drew on were couched in a language that was not familiar to rural Nepalese. As a result, the first thing the team had to do was to translate those ideas into terms and use training tools that truly drew on experiences that their clients would understand.

Once that happened, the projects accomplished a lot. The community mediation centers heard more than twenty-six thousand cases, eighty-five percent of which were resolved. More importantly, the mediators themselves—especially young women from lower castes—also empowered themselves, which drew more and more people into these efforts. As Lederach put it in his final report:

> When the mediators actually worked in and with local communities, their language shifted, otherwise few of their local listeners would have understood what they were saying. When women and low caste participants become mediators in their local communities, self-respect, social status, and power relationships shift. Developing a specific skill that permitted them to provide a role useful to and highly respected in rural communities did more for their fair treatment, inclusion, and empowerment than many awareness-raising workshops. In particular, capacity to facilitate and help transform concrete local conflict had significant impact on inclusion and status.

The action research findings reinforced the team's decision to focus on women. They already knew that many women were themselves victims of the violence. Now, they learned that many had to support their families after their husbands were killed in the fighting and do so in villages where other women had lost husbands who had fought for the other side.

More surprisingly, the team found that many poorly educated Nepalese women had trouble even telling their personal stories when asked to do so. As a result, Lederach and his team spent a lot of time empowering women so that they would feel comfortable laying their hearts out to their friends and neighbors which, of course, had little to do with their lack of formal education and everything to do with addressing gender imbalances. After just a little bit of training, hundreds of women discovered skills they didn't know they had while also realizing that they actually had a lot in common with each other.

The work with community mediators, too, surfaced trends whose importance would normally be missed in projects that only lasted for a year or two. Given the fact that they had a decade's worth of projects to plan, the team invested resources in developing the organizational capacity of the networks it funded so that they could continue their work and continue to adapt indefinitely—even after McConnell's involvement ended. In a move unheard of among all but the wealthiest global NGOs, they even talked about providing Nepalese groups with endowments that would provide them with permanent funding so that they were not constantly struggling to raise money. Last, but by no means least, they began talking about creating a nationwide infrastructure for peace that was woven around the local networks they formed, a point I will return to toward the end of this chapter in discussing peacebuilding in countries in the Global North, including the US.

Leveraging bright spots. In systems terms, there was evidence that each success could be used as **leverage** in reducing what Galtung and other theorists referred to as structural violence and chronic inequality. These are the forces that are deeply ingrained in a society's institutions and culture that cannot be wiped away with the passage of a single law or the adoption of a single peace agreement. Instead, the McConnell team realized that it had to experiment, identify initiatives that worked, and then build on them.

In short, the team sumbled onto what public health scholars call **positive deviance** or what the management scholars Chip and Dan Heath more elegantly label **bright spots**. Put simply, no matter how messy a situation is, something is bound to be "working" somewhere for someone. These are always what statisticians call **outliers** that defy the norm and was the logic behind Mary Anderson's decision to study communities that opted out of war, like Tuzla, Bosnia, as discussed in part 3.

In the Nepalese case, one of those bright spots surfaced fairly quickly. As is the case throughout much of South Asia, women were an untapped resource when it came to problem solving. In a way, the newly empowered women discussed in the previous section actually turned themselves into positive deviants. In the process of working with the McConnell team and its projects, they found ways of defying the odds and overcome past discrimination that might also have included some time being trafficked. In so doing, they surprisingly found themselves transformed into leaders who helped steer their communities in new and dramatically more constructive directions.

Similar insights emerged from the work on natural resources. Although he did not end up playing an active role in the project, Ury's work on what I called the third side in part 3 did help shape the way the Nepalese teams worked. As you also saw there, Ury himself had moved away from the notion that mediators had to be third party neutrals. However, he rarely envisioned situations in which the people he referred to as "third siders" would also be parties to the dispute on one side or the other. But as Lederach's team worked with people they initially disagreed with to find common solutions, something unexpected happened. They turned into entrepreneurs. The skills that led them to settle disputes also led them to be willing to take risks, experiment with new ideas, and learn from their mistakes in general and not just on conflicts over the use of local woodland.

They also learned the importance of patience, something that also would not have been as readily apparent in a typical project that lasted for a few months rather than a decade. The first time or even the first few times people dealt with a problem, they didn't get very far for a number of reasons, including the fact that they hadn't internalized what they had learned in their training sessions. However, once they had to explain those ideas to their colleagues—including the people they disagreed with—new possibilities emerged. In some ways, the specifics of the initial project's goals drifted away from center stage, and the members of the community began to define the social change they themselves wanted to create. Policy entrepreneurs were born—who also happened to be mediators and conflict resolvers.

Build Upward

In parts 2 and 3, it was easy to distinguish between the grassroots and public policy and deal with them in separate chapters. It is much harder to do so today for reasons that I will focus on throughout the rest of part 4. For now, it is enough to see that the McConnell team reached out to Ury as well as Lederach because it already realized that its work had major policy implications.

Many of the country's leaders knew that they would need help in finding a lasting end to the civil war. Few of them, however, were willing to take part in the kind of Track II negotiations discussed in part 3 or agree to the kind of negotiations facilitated by a third party around which Ury had built his reputation.

CONFLICT LAB 11.1

Take the two conflict maps you have been building and think of them in systems terms which is also the way Lederach's team built their strategies for Nepal:

- What are the most important patterns and feedback loops in your maps?
- What would a healthier version of the system look like? In particular, how would the map have to change to make it healthier?
- Is there any potential for change built into the system? If so, how would you unlock it?

What could you do to make the system more flexible and better able to change in the light of unexpected events?

The impetus for major policy changes would have to come from within Nepal, and that would require a grassroots-based effort, which also have been in short supply in countries like Nepal.

Therefore, the McConnell team decided to rely on what they referred to as an **inside partial** approach to building that kind of pressure from the Nepalese people themselves. In other words, it was understood from the beginning that "insiders" from Nepal would be running the project, not Lederach, the McConnell team, or any other expatriates. It was "partial" in the sense that not all of the key parties to the dispute were involved from day one. Instead, the team planned to add new participants, especially national level leaders, as the core projects produced results which led others to want to come on board.

By the end of the twelve-year project, there were tangible signs that the grassroots initiatives were beginning to have a national impact. As noted earlier, more and more of the participants in the pilot projects had assumed policy-making positions at the local level and, occasionally, in Kathmandu. About thirty of the local agreements had broad enough implications that they reached the national level and began to reshape land use policy throughout.

At that point, Lederach's decade-long commitment came to an end. So, too will our discussion of the Nepal Project, but not of the themes we have been discussing so far in this chapter.

NARRATIVES, NORMS, AND NETWORKS

The Nepal Project may have set the gold standard for locally based peacebuilding projects when it began fifteen years ago. At the same time, it could not be the model that the rest of us copied in our own work for at least two reasons. First, it is hard to imagine another funder being willing and able to either make this kind of long-term commitment or attract someone of Lederach's stature to lead it. Second, there are other projects in which practitioners have undertaken challenges that were not on the McConnell team's radar screen when they worked in Nepal.

In some ways, the less comprehensive projects that I will turn to in the rest of this chapter and the next one reflect a deeper understanding of wicked problems, a VUCA world, and system dynamics. They demonstrate, too that there has been a veritable explosion of new initiatives, some of which have expanded the field by taking on new issues or bringing in new partners. Some of them also dramatically expanded what we normally think of as the domain of peace and conflict studies, including partnerships with evangelical Christians and the military.

In fact, there are so many initiatives currently underway in global conflict zones and I cannot hope to cover them all here. Instead, what follows is a representative sample of the most promising ways in which conflict resolution and peacebuilding experts either experimented with new ideas or sought allies we had never worked with before or both. I will track them here by using the three rough categories used in AfP's Peacebuilding 3.0 framework.

Narratives

In the last twenty years, postmodernist thinking has had a huge, but also controversial, impact on academic life. Whatever you think about deconstructionism and related tools, there is no denying that these new scholarly methodologies have properly focused our attention on the very idea of dominant **narratives** or master "stories" that we use to make sense of the world.

As far as peace and conflict studies are concerned, there are probably hundreds of these storylines that vary from place to place and time to time, and it would be a waste of your time to try to delineate them all. Whatever the variation a thorough analysis might have uncovered, one theme would stand out. The dominant narratives do not revolve around cooperative problem solving or win-win outcomes when it comes to intense, divisive, and intractable conflicts.

If anything, their tone has swung back toward militaristic, vengeful, and polarized, and other memes in the first twenty years of this century. Whether you look at television news, popular video games, or award-winning dramas, our media tend to portray bellicose and violent outcomes more than they did a generation ago.

Transforming these narratives will be a key theme in the rest of this book. Let's start, however, with one example that has largely turned into a dead end before turning to more promising examples.

Countering violent extremism. In that sense, the peace and conflict studies community has fallen into a familiar trap in which we try to *counter* or dismantle the dominant narrative about terrorism or violent extremism. Media scholars tell us that once you try to take on other people's arguments on their terms, you make it harder to create an entirely new narrative that transforms the way that these stories are told. When we spend our time trying to refute an argument we disagree with, we lose the ability to propose credible alternatives that start with different premises, such as those embedded in Lederach's haiku. That, in turn, all but eliminates prospects for a paradigm shift, because you lose the ability to actually present a more attractive new paradigm which, of course, is another way of referring to a new narrative.

Nothing illustrates the need to change the dominant narrative than the ways we understand terrorism and the other forms of political violence that have preoccupied the world since 9/11.

You don't need to think in terms of narrative analysis to understand why most people around the world responded to the events of that day with anger and fear. Few objected to the Bush administration's desire to topple the Taliban regime, destroy al-Qaeda, and protect the world from future attacks. That was easy to see in public opinion polls, displays of patriotism the likes of which hadn't been seen in decades, and the speed with which NATO countries rallied to support their American ally in its moment of need.

As Lederach noted in his remarkable *Quo Vadis* article which I mentioned at the beginning of chapter 10, the desire for revenge or to at least hold the perpetrators accountable made sense. In fact, I was one of many veteran peacebuilders who could not envision a purely nonviolent response to them in the days and weeks that followed.

However, as the crisis dragged on after the fall of the Taliban regime in Afghanistan and, especially, following the defeat of Saddam Hussein's regime in Iraq, it became clear to a growing number of people in the peacebuilding community that the narrative had to go beyond military and law enforcement. From our perspective, it had become clear that what became known as the **Global War on Terror (GWOT)** could not defeat terrorism. It might be able to reduce the number of terrorists or their impact on innocent civilians. But, as we have seen time and time again, spasms of violence continue to take place. Indeed, on the morning I put the finishing touches on this paragraph, fifty-one people were killed in attacks on two mosques in Christchurch, New Zealand.

Despite the quagmire of what is sometimes and ruefully referred to as the forever war, we have not enjoyed much success in getting people to see that countering violent extremism cannot be achieved using the military and law enforcement personnel alone. It isn't that we object to strategies aimed at identifying and then "deradicalizing" individuals who might join the radicals' ranks and, if necessary, using some force to destroy organizations like ISIS or al-Qaeda.

Rather, we began to realize that we also had to provide an alternative narrative which is just now beginning to emerge. Once again, Lederach offered us a starting point in *Quo Vadis* In it, he acknowledged the need many felt at the time to seek some kind of vengeful justice that holds terrorists accountable for their actions. But, as a good peacebuilder, he also made the case that we cannot rid the world of terrorism unless and until we address its root causes, which lie in the inability to guarantee that people get to enjoy lives characterized by the values in his haiku.

In the last few years, a consensus around a different narrative has begun to emerge that shows signs of appealing to people beyond the immediate conflict resolution and peacebuilding communities. At its core are three principles:

- an acknowledgment that any effective response has to include some law enforcement, deradicalization, and the like
- a realization that violent extremism (or whatever euphemism you choose) is not a "Muslim problem." Political violence comes in dozens of forms and is committed by a wide variety of people, including the alt-right that is at the heart of so much of the turmoil in the US today and that seems to have inspired the perpetrator of the attack in Christchurch
- a viable long-term solution couched in human security terms in which radical extremism and terrorism are seen as an outgrowth of what I called imagined communities in part 3, which are themselves by-products of unmet human needs, which we have been focusing on since the birth of our field

There are two initiatives underway that are specifically aimed at changing those narratives that were just getting off the ground as I finished this book. Therefore, I will wait and consider them in part 5. For now, the projects described in the rest of this chapter and the next one should be seen as laying the foundation not only for a new narrative but also for a new kind of conflict resolution and peacebuilding movement which I will also discuss in more detail in the final two chapters

Mass media. The narrative problem also starts with the fact that we have yet to have much of an impact on the mainstream media whose coverage goes a long way toward determining the values in any individual's personal mind-set. We all know that the media landscape has changed dramatically in the last twenty years. Traditional outlets such as daily newspapers and the major television networks (and their equivalents outside the US) have seen their audiences and, therefore, their impacts shrink. More of us, instead, turn to social media and other online providers of information which has led to the creation of filter bubbles, fake news, and the like.

Despite all this turmoil, there has been one constant in the media world, which is summed up by the catchphrase "if it bleeds, it leads"—shorthand for the fact that reporters tend to concentrate on the problems we face at the expense of everything else. Below the clichéd radar screen, however, two sets of initiatives are beginning to change the problem-laden narrative with more hopeful and solutions-oriented alternatives. The first reflects what peacebuilders themselves have done. The other grows out of changes in the journalistic community itself.

First are a number of ways conflict resolution NGOs have used the mainstream media. Search for Common Ground has been the global leader in making conflict-related radio and television programming since its formation in the 1980s. At first it focused on the news. It made and distributed interviews with Soviet and American leaders using the then state-of-the-art medium—the video tape. It also created a common ground news service whose staff members both wrote stories of their own and distributed the work of others that stressed ways of building peace in the Middle East and beyond.

But Search is best known for making television soap operas whose plot lines deal with conflict-related themes. Unlike its news programs, the soap operas are aired as entertainment television. Therefore, they can can't be preachy, nor can they resemble documentaries. Instead, they are based on stories derived from with the kinds of conflicts average viewers experienced in their everyday lives.

Two examples should be enough to show what its programs are like. You can then use these examples to think of others that might help viewers deal with the conflicts you have been tracking since chapter 1.

Nashe Maalo (Our Neighborhood) ran on Macedonian television stations between 1998 and 2003. It was set in a typical, dreary apartment complex in the capital city Skopje, which would have been familiar to any Macedonian viewer. Everything else about the series was unusual. To begin with, the series starred three teenagers, one from each of the country's major ethnic groups—Macedonian, Albanian, and Roma. The thee of them deal with problems teenagers face everywhere. Dating. Parents. Bullying. Improbably, the three live in the same complex, which rarely happens in that highly segregated country. Even more improbably, once the kids reach an impasse in dealing with their problem, the apartment house (named Karman) came to life and helped them work things out.

Audience research showed that *Nashe Maalo* was the most widely watched children's television program in the country. More importantly, the young people who watched it and their family members who watched with them all became more tolerant of other groups than a sample of their peers who were not *Nashe Maalo* viewers. Once *Nashe Maalo* ran its course (in other words, its producers ran out of believable plots), it spun off bilingual kindergartens in which the children often had to interpret for their parents when they came for their teacher's meeting.

Search made soap operas in a half dozen other countries, including ones set in fictitious television news stations in Egypt and Nigeria. By far its biggest project began in Africa in the run-up to the 2010 football World Cup in South Africa and soon spread to about a dozen countries around the world that had two things in common—ethnic strife and a love for soccer. The specifics of the plot line varied from country to country. In each case, however, the fictional players dealt with social issues as well as the athletic ones they encountered in the field—or as soccer fans would prefer to call it, the pitch.

More recently, journalists have begun structuring the way they cover events in ways that stress solutions as well as problems for reasons of their own. The audience for serious journalism has been declining in recent years. That holds for print (newspapers and magazines), television and radio news, and even news-focused websites. All this is happening at a time when critics point to the role that "fake news" and social media have played in skewing recent elections and inflaming extremists on all sides.

A small group of journalists is trying to address the problems in their own industry by bringing conflict resolution themes into their reporting. Amanda Ripley of the Solutions Journalism Network has gone further than most of her colleagues by taking part in a training program run by Resetting the Table, sitting in on experiments conducted at the Difficult Conversations Laboratory, and observing projects conducted by Essential Partners.

Once Ripley finished her "basic training," she looked at her own reporting and that of her colleagues and reached six conclusions about what journalists could and should do today in ways that mirror what I have been discussing in this book since I first mentioned *Getting to YES* and win-win conflict resolution:

- **Amplify contradictions.** Journalists should ask questions that deepen our understanding of a dispute. Among other things, that means probing the men and women they interview so that their reporting can include the ambiguities involved in an intractable conflict.
- **Widen the lens.** She also discovered that good journalists tell stories in which they broaden the picture so that their readers can see multiple options in much the same way that mediators try to reframe questions. In this case, it is important for journalists to "zoom out" away from the individual story they are covering to include the larger questions it raises.
- **Get at people's motivations.** Journalists have a tendency to print or broadcast politicians' stock answers and talking points. She has found that if you dig deeper and get the people you are covering to talk about their story and how their experiences led them to the positions they hold, it becomes easier for everyone to see the nuances on all sides of an issue. She also finds that these kinds of complex stories hold people's attention for a longer period of time.

- **Listen more and listen better**. Like action researchers, Ripley finds that it helps journalists to listen deeply and empathize with the people they are covering. By engaging in what Resetting the Table calls **looping** or giving interviewees "a distillation of what you thought they meant," journalists can both make certain that they have accurately heard their interlocutors' perspective and allow them to ask deeper and more probing questions that amplify contradictions and widen the lens of everyone involved, including the source, the reporter, and the reader/viewer.
- **Expose people to the other side**. She finds that stories are the most engaging when journalists bring the people who disagree with each other together as part of their reporting. Good journalists, like good mediators, structure conversations so that people on each side understand what the other one thinks. Similarly, they can steer the conversations by asking hard-to-answer questions or emphasizing potential areas of agreement that pop up.
- **Counter confirmation bias**. The new journalism has intellectual roots in social psychological research that shows that we all tend to listen to and trust sources that confirm our predispositions. Good journalists can challenge that **confirmation bias** in at least two ways. First, they can present credible alternatives to those predispositions especially those that come from a member of a person's own "tribe." Second, they help give the readers/viewers the sense of **agency** by presenting ways that they can personally get involved.

Ripley and her colleagues are journalists, not conflict resolvers. Therefore, their main goal is to build new audiences for their own media outlets, which has led her to call on her colleagues to flip the way newsrooms work so that reporters and editors start out by covering stories that their readers or viewers want to learn about and do so in ways that will convince members of their audience to keep coming back for more.

Hearken is perhaps the leading organization actively training newsroom staff in this new approach. The subscription service was being used by more than one hundred newsrooms in the US and abroad. It helps users literally hearken or hear better in generating story ideas and, in Lederach's terms, having community members accompany journalists as they do their stories.

You rarely hear about Hearken because it works with journalists while they prepare their stories. However, if you go to its web site (www.wearehearken.com) and listen to the stories that have been done about the region you live in or on issues that you care about, you will probably have the same reaction I did. When I looked at the Hearken inspired stories carried on my local National Public Radio station, I remembered many of them as exemplars of what conflict resolution media should be like—before I had heard of Ripley or Hearken.

Norms

Changing narratives only matters if social norms change along with them. Sociologists and psychologists usually define **norms** as conventional, expected, or typical ways of thinking. Although often not part of an individual's conscious thought, norms do shape the way we behave because they help us determine which actions are appropriate and which ones are not. Anthropologists and some political scientists are more likely to use the term culture in describing the norms that shape an entire society.

In peace and conflict studies, norms can apply to an individual's core values and assumptions as well as those of an entire community, country, or the planet as a whole. In that sense, almost all of us would situate such values and beliefs near the heart of any conflict map. Not surprisingly, much of our work has focused on using new narratives to build and strengthen support for norms that are more conducive to cooperative problem solving as discussed around the exercise that ended chapter 5.

That has been particularly true for activists whose work has led them to focus less on what I have called **transactional** rather than **transformative** conflict resolution. Here, for once, complicated looking jargon terms are actually helpful.

Fisher, Ury, and many of the early pioneers in conflict resolution built their models and their professional reputations around a single or a small set of related negotiations—or transactions. A collective bargaining agreement. A baseball trade. A divorce settlement. A property dispute. Their assumption was that you could reach a single agreement that might not end the dispute once and for all, but would at least defuse tensions for a considerable period of time.

Intractable conflict and wicked problems are a different matter altogether. They defy simple solutions. Changes made in one part of a system can have spillover effects elsewhere, some of which might actually make the overall situation worse later on. What's more, the parties to the dispute usually cannot go through anything that resembles a simple divorce after which you may no longer have to deal with each other again. Intractable conflicts typically take place in communities whose differences will continue to exist and disrupt peaceful relations for the foreseeable future.

There is still a place for transactional conflict resolution, including a need to learn how to conduct those kinds of negotiations better. Most of us, however, have been drawn to the more complicated and, frankly, more interesting and challenging intractable disputes. The continued impact of race. Power in international affairs. The legacy of imperialism. Economic inequality.

On these kinds of issues, it makes more sense to transform a conflict so that the participants see it in a new light by doing the same kinds of things in an entire society that Amanda Ripley asks journalists to do in crafting their stories. Once those norms change, the conflict will still exist but it will play itself out differently and, presumably, more constructively.

Norms and cultures rarely change quickly, but, occasionally, they do. When and if that happens, the new norms can transform key relationships in ways that would have been hard to imagine just a few years before.

One recent example has been the acceptance of same sex marriage. In little more than a decade, it went from a fringe issue to the law of the land in much of the world. Once that happened, it became harder not to begin addressing other, related issues, including the status of transgendered people, what became the #MeToo movement, discrimination in the work place, the content of our mass media, and, of course, the resentments of the men and women who objected to change in some or all of these areas.

Thinking in terms of conflict transformation also brings us to a point that has been inching its way toward center stage in this book from the beginning—the importance of **relationships**. As you know from your own experience, building good working relationships in the microcosm of your daily life is never easy.

Understanding the role of norms can help you see another central point that has also lurked further below the surface so far. Lasting conflict resolution and peacebuilding has to include the adoption of new norms in people's lived experiences. These are not trivial values like (I assume) your preference for Pizza Hut over Domino's (or vice versa). Rather, these are often core beliefs some of which we all but take for granted. Challenging and changing them takes lots of hard work, and such efforts do not always succeed.

Add to that one more set of terms that conflict resolution and peacebuilding professionals use whose meaning and importance are not always obvious to outsiders. There is a growing consensus that such efforts have to shift the balance away from **top-down** toward **bottom-up** initiatives which often are referred to as **local peacebuilding**. Because they are now key parts of the peacebuilder's lexicon, the three terms emphasized in the previous sentence deserve a bit more attention.

Until recently, we emphasized initiatives that start with elites—hence top-down. That can take the form of public policies that are forged and implemented by national and other officials. They can also originate with third party neutrals serving as mediators. Perhaps most importantly for the purposes of this section, the elites can be people who rarely think of themselves as experts—the development professionals and NGO employees whose expertise is used to design peacebuilding programs.

Producing peace and the widespread use of win-win conflict resolution will require change at the elite level as well, which we will turn to in the next section. That said, more and more of us are convinced that we have to build a lot more grass roots support before we can expect the elites to change.

Because you have already seen the Nepal Project, the rest of this section will focus on four other initiatives that use local peacebuilding to begin changing norms and, in turn, provide precisely those kinds of building blocks.

Rondine and trauma healing. There is no question that conflict traumatizes people who get caught up in it, whether they are combatants who come home with physical and mental wounds or the innocent victims around the world who have seen their lives disrupted—or worse. Physicians and mental health workers have multiple definitions of what trauma is, what causes it, and how best to treat it, all of which would take us far beyond the scope of this book.

Indeed, some of that work has to be left to trained psychotherapists who normally work with individual victims. Peace and conflict resolution professionals have a role to play when it comes to helping entire communities or societies engage in one form or another of **trauma healing**. Today, much of that work revolves around yet another popular buzz word of the 2010s, **resilience**, which literally means the ability to bounce back from and adapt to wrenching events, including the trauma of war. On the other, there is so much work underway that it is impossible to highlight any one of them as reflecting the state of the art.

The most comprehensive is the one developed by **Rondine, Cittadella della Pace** (Citadel or Oasis of Peace), situated on a hillside near Arezzo in the Tuscany region of Italy as you can see on this book's cover. In 1977, the village of Rondine was abandoned and falling apart when the Bishop of Arezzo asked two families to restore the village and its castle and turn them into a refuge for needy families. In 1995 Rondine's founders shifted gears and welcomed five Chechens and Russians who had fought on opposite sides in the first war there. Two years later, the Cittadella della Pace was formed and since then, the tiny (and beautiful) hamlet has become one of the world's leading centers for reconciliation. Indeed, the site is so beautiful and its work is so important that I decided to use a photograph of it for the cover of this book after I visited Rondine for the first time in 2019.

Each fall, about twenty young men and women who have experienced violent identity-based conflict come together for a two year work/study program. Over the years, students have come to Rondine from the Caucuses, the Balkans, the Middle East, and Africa. During their time in Rondine, they go through a program of academic study that leads to a master's degree. More importantly, they work with trained professionals—including psychotherapists—who help them deal with the trauma they have suffered and build relationships with "the other" in the form of their fellow students. The students are then expected to return "home" and apply what they have learned personally and academically to promote reconciliation. From what I can tell, the two hundred or so Rondine alumni have already made a significant difference in places as different as Sierra Leone and Serbia.

Rondine stands out from other trauma healing programs, too, since it addresses the whole person and not just the causes and consequences of the traumatic experience. Because it extends over two years, and includes formal classroom education, Rondine gives participants the luxury of time like Lederach did in Nepal.

Parents Circle and Breaking the Impasse. You didn't have to read the first ten and a half chapters of this book to know that the prospects for peace in the Middle East are not very good. That does not mean that peace movements in the Middle East have disappeared. Far from it.

It is true that few organizations put on the kinds of problems solving workshops discussed in chapter 8, and no one holds out much hope for Track II dialogues like the ones that led to the Oslo Accords. Instead, groups with a narrower focus have been working to build bridges within more narrowly defined communities and take action on the basis of those common understandings, two of which should show you what they are like.

The first thing visitors to the Parents Circle/Family Forum (PCFF) web site see is this perplexing line:

> We are the only association in the world that does not wish to welcome any new members into its fold.

After spending a few more seconds on the site, you realize why. PCFF's six hundred activists have all lost family members in the violence between Israelis and Palestinians.

Since the end of the Second Intifada in 2000, its members have met to explore their common grief and find ways in which they can work together to prevent further violence—and more bereaved families. Even more importantly, teams including at least one Israeli and one Palestinian member have led seven thousand dialogues with more than two hundred thousand participants that are designed to begin reconciliation in much the same way that the TRC hearings did in South Africa.

PCFF's sessions are truly moving. I attended one in Washington in which the Paletinian had taken part in a riot in which the Israeli facilitator's son had been killed. The two of them had gone through the wrenching process of reconciling with each other at which time they decided that the best thing they could to honor the memory of that young Israeli was to work together to find peace between their two communities.

However encouraged you may be by PCFF, I should point out two problems which all peacebuilding groups in the region face today. First, voices like those of PCFF members struggle to be heard at a time when the relationship between Israelis and Palestinians is as strained as it has been at any time since the 1960s. Second, most of the people who attend those dialogue sessions come to them predisposed to accept a peaceful settlement to the overall dispute to the begin with. In other words, PCFF members spend much of their time "preaching to the choir."

These concerns are not limited to Israelis and Palestinians. They apply to initiatives of this sort around the world. They may try to reach out to communities of people who do not share their commitment to a peaceful settlement of the larger dispute, but few such initiatives have able to reach many of the people who actively or passively support the violence. This is an important enough issue that I will return to it chapter 13 when considering the next steps the field could or should take.

Another glimmer of hope that has had mixed success in Breaking the Impasse. Created in 2012 by the World Economic Forum, this movement could not have been described as bottom-up. When the group met that winter in Davos, the Arab-Israeli peace process was in one of its periodic troughs, and members of the Forum staff decided to take a new tack and bring the business communities from the two sides together to see what they could do to literally break the impasse.

In fact, a number of business leaders on both sides rose to the challenge because they saw that they could also grow their companies while creating new opportunities to build peace. Israel, for example, has a thriving technological sector that includes both global companies like Intel and local ones that have made major contributions, most notably the widely used app, Waze. There are also a lot of underemployed Palestinian engineers who could be hired by Israeli firms who currently have to outsource work to India. Why not, the Israelis argued, hire Palestinians who were literally around the corner?

Given the Davos connection, the initiative got a lot of publicity when it was launched. However, as has been the case with many new initiatives, the politics in the region posed problems that made it difficult to establish and sustain business relationships. It is, in fact, legally difficult for companies based in Israel to hire Palestinians. It is also hard to keep any kind of initiative alive at a time when travel between the Occupied Territories and Israel is difficult, if not impossible, for most Palestinians (see the Out on a Limb box on BDS and SodaStream on the next page).

If nothing else, the connections forged by Breaking the Impasse and similar initiatives could help spur the next peace process forward whenever and however it happens. Emphasis on could.

Indicators of everyday peace. The same **Mary Anderson** who brought the idea of do no harm to peacebuilding and conflict resolution coined a one-liner of her own early in the 2000s—peace writ large. She argued that NGOs could point to successes in individual communities which her team had documented in her book *Opting Out of War*, which provided me with the example of Tuzla, Bosnia. The research that led to that book helped us all see that any enduring agreement

OUT ON A LIMB

Boycotts and Divestment

There is another reason to use Breaking the Impasse here. It lets us deal with a more controversial issue that some of my colleagues would not include in a course on peace and conflict studies, the BDS movement. BDS (Boycott, Divest, and Sanction) tries to convince consumers around the world to do just that when it comes to certain Israeli products, especially those manufactured in the West Bank or Gaza.

BDS made a splash in the US when it called for a boycott of SodaStream, which grabbed my attention because my wife and I had recently bought one because it was the most environmentally efficient way to carbonize water! We did not know that SodaStream was Israeli owned, that its main production facility was in the West Bank, or that most of its employees were Palestinians. Pressure from BDS activists eventually led to the closure of that facility with production shifting to other sites in Israel proper, which also employed large numbers of Palestinian citizens of Israel whose families already lived near its headquarters in Beersheba.

There is nothing new to this kind of campaign. Earlier ones focused on companies that did business in apartheid-era South Africa, while others targeted firms that were accused of sweatshop practices. BDS campaigns are always controversial because they invariably have two trade-offs.

First, how should we weigh their costs and benefits? BDS has undoubtedly raised awareness about injustices that take place in the Occupied Territories. But, they also come with costs, including the welfare of workers who lose their jobs and the ability of companies like SodaStream to operate freely in the marketplace.

Second, how big a role should these campaigns play in peace and conflict studies? For many, these kinds of mildly coercive tactics are part and parcel of what I have been calling contentious politics throughout this book. More skeptical analysts point to the fact that these kinds of tactics tend to deepen divisions and make reconciliation more difficult.

BDS itself is controversial for another reason. It involves criticizing Israel, which many are loath to do.

For what it's worth, we decided to keep using our SodaStream. We bought it before we learned about the boycott, so we don't know if its existence would have led us to buy a different brand. We certainly would have thought about it. SodaStream may find its way back into the BDS debate now that PepsiCo announced plans to purchase the company.

at the national level has to be based on deep-seated local support. If that doesn't exist, fighting is likely to break out again.

What's more, analysts like Anderson and Lederach have made the case that each conflict is unique, and that each conflict resolution project has to be unique, too.

That led another group of scholars to question the very indicators we use to measure the degree to which people on the ground experience peace and the lack thereof. The indicators used to compute the Global and Positive Peace Indexes or Goal 16 of the United Nations' Sustained Development program (see chapter 12) are collected at the national level.

These data can be helpful for some purposes, but improving people's lived experiences is rarely one of them. Peace agreements reached by political leaders in national capitals often do not have much of an impact on the day-to-day conditions of average citizens, especially those who live far from those national capitals. They experience peace—as well as the lack thereof—when and where they encounter others, especially individuals who are not part of their in group.

Critical here is the idea of **Everyday Peace Indicators (EPI)** which were developed as part of a project coordinated by my former George Mason colleague, Pamina Firchow, and Roger Mac Ginty of the University of Durham in the UK. Their team realized that we do not have a very good idea of what peace on the ground actually looks like. They decided to find out, first, what peace means to average citizens who have direct experience in dealing with conflict and, second, why some local peacebuilding projects are more successful than others.[2]

In a blog post, Firchow described why their work is important both for students in a classroom and for practitioners in the field:

> International peace-support actors often make decisions on intervention based on data that is collected via top-down methodologies. Such interventions may fail to match the expectations of local communities who use bottom-up ways of seeing the world around them. This in turn has implications for the effectiveness and sustainability of peace interventions. By analyzing community-generated indicators of peace, Profs. Firchow and Mac Ginty conclude that by utilizing research methods oriented toward local communities, it is possible to understand the differences in the politics of the narratives, which could potentially have implications in terms of how to achieve sustainable peace in conflict areas.[3]

Like any academic theory or model, thinking about everyday peace indicators can get technical and abstract. So, before we get to the details, think about two stories Mac Ginty tells when he presents their approach to nonacademic audiences.

He was raised in a small town in Northern Ireland during the Troubles (see part 3). His father ran a clothing store. After the first IRA bomb blew out the store window, the insurance company paid to replace it. Not after the second bomb. That time, Mr. Mac Ginty put up a cheap piece of plywood. A few years later, he put in new glass. When he first got interested in peace studies, Mac Ginty asked his father why he had put in the glass window. The senior Mac Ginty said it was simple. He now felt it was safe to do so.

In rural parts of the world, people go to the bathroom outside because they don't have indoor plumbing. When fighting breaks out nearby, people are afraid to go outdoors for any reason, especially at night. So, as Mac Ginty puts it, they use chamber pots and pee inside. Like his father and his new glass window, an increase in the willingness of people to go outside and urinate is an indirect sign that a community is becoming more peaceful.

The Everyday Peace Indicators project is designed to turn anecdotes like these into systematically gathered evidence. Oddly enough, the way they go about doing it is actually more important than what they have found so far.

That's the case, first of all, because they, too, engage in action research that is designed to surface what the political scientist James Scott calls people's hidden narratives. We could explore what that means in technical terms, but Scott really had in mind getting people to talk about how conflict and related issues touch their lives, much like the windows in Mr. Mac Ginty's shop or the urination habits of people living in conflict zones.

They are usually invited in by local leaders, who may or may not be involved in implementing whatever peace agreement has been reached by national leaders. The Everyday Peace Indicators team then conducts a series of focus groups with members of the local community whose lives have been touched by the conflict. As is the case with focus groups run for political candidates in a country like the US, the researchers allow their subjects to talk with a minimum of guidance and then seek recurring themes in those conversations.

The researchers usually find that the responses fall into four clusters, few of which are included in the national settlement and all of which reflect the overlapping dimensions of human security—physical safety, economic well being, social cohesion, and human rights. The specifics, of course, vary from place to place and time to time.

Pure researchers might stop there, but peacebuilders then use the survey results in designing projects that might expand everyday peace in that community as we will see in the next section. The EPI team keeps reconvening the focus group to learn how to improve the project again and again, each time measuring the impact of their interventions. In the terms I used in discussing systems in chapter 3, local residents turn their own communities into learning organizations in which research produces action and vice versa.

The EPI team has conducted preliminary research in South Sudan, South Africa, Uganda, Zimbabwe, and Colombia. Preliminary research clearly suggests that average, everyday people can define what peace means to them and that their definition is often quite different from the solutions that national and international leaders have in mind. More worrisome and much more tentative is their finding that the kinds of peacebuilding initiatives discussed in part 3 often do not make much of a difference. Sometimes, they can even make things worse.

Children and youth. A related set of initiatives should also help you see why we now pay a lot of attention to local peacebuilding. Children and young adults are at the heart of most peacebuilding projects around the world at least in part because many of the countries experiencing intractable conflict today have large youth bubbles. A disproportionate share of their population is under thirty, which puts tremendous pressure on education, employment, and other systems that should be providing aspects of human security. When and if they fail, conflict is often the result.

World Vision International (WVI) is the world's largest NGO. Inspired by Evangelical Christianity, WVI, devotes the vast majority of its $2.6 billion budget to projects that directly meet children's needs. Over the years, it has realized that children need peace as well as food, clothing, shelter, education, and health care. As a result, it has integrated peacebuilding into everything it does:

> World Vision builds peace with and for children by weaving a fabric of resilience through their communities. From Bogotá to Beirut and from Bujumbura to Banja Luka and beyond, World Vision's peacebuilding helps communities protect and empower children affected by violence. Our tools aim to help these communities resolve their own conflicts, build capacities to heal broken relationships, and nourish more just systems and structures.[4]

As the use of capital cities beginning with the letter *B* suggests, World Vision operates just about everywhere there is conflict, including the US. It started out as a development-driven NGO, but soon discovered that if it wanted to foster capacity building, resilience, empowerment, healing, and the like, it also had to help the people it worked with cope with the conflicts that were often at the heart of their social and economic problems. That led it to become the first leading NGO to create a peacebuilding divisions whose work is now integrated into everything World Vision does.

It does not use the Everyday Peace Indicators framework despite the fact the two teams frequently work together. Instead, it has developed its own set of guidelines that are attuned to the needs of their main constituency, children and youth.

Children under the age of twenty bear a disproportionate share of the cost of conflict. Some of them get caught up in the conflict with a small, but disturbing number of them forced to serve as child soldiers. Even more important is the indirect impact violent conflict has on young people's lives, including disrupted schooling, poor health and nutrition, the grief that comes from losing family members, and more.

Over the years, World Vision has found that children as young as eight years old are mature enough to take part in defining a community's response to conflict. Therefore, much like the EPI team, they gather focus groups, in this case composed exclusively of children and youth. They ensure that all key groups are represented, including members from communities that typically find themselves in conflict with each other.

They don't ask preteens to draw a full systems map like the one you started building in chapter 1. Instead, they use the metaphor of a tree, often having the group to fill in something like the tree outlined in figure 11.1.

FIGURE 11.1
A Conflict Tree

They start a typical workshop by having the young people talk about the conflict. For the same reason that the EPI team does not have a predetermined way of looking at the conflict in mind, they let the young people tell their own stories—and their own versions of Mr. Mac Ginty's store window or the use of the outdoors rather than twenty-first century chamber pots.

The discussions invariably jumble together the conflict's immediate causes and effects. Some of the participants are under ten years old after all. After a few minutes, the facilitator helps the group focus on the specifics of the conflict, which are put on the tree trunk section of the chart.

The facilitators next lead a discussion of how the conflict has affected the young peoples' lives. Each new effect becomes a branch or a leaf depending on the nature of the problem—and on the artistic talent of the facilitators. Finally, the facilitator asks the children to discuss why they think the conflict exists in the first place, which go on the chart as the roots. The young people are almost always able to see that a conflict's roots are tangled and intertwined just like those of a mature tree—or any wicked problem.

After that, the facilitators help the children take the next step. They set goals and design projects they can do on their own and/or with their elders. The facilitators normally have to curb their enthusiasm and narrow the list down to a goal or two that they could possibly reach, focusing on the ones that have the best chance of changing either the "roots" or the "branches" which is the same idea systems thinkers get at when they use the term leverage.

The facilitators then do something one absolutely has to do with children and probably should do with any group planning to start a peacebuilding or conflict resolution project. They do a risk assessment. They help the children work through what could go wrong and what the costs would be if the worst were to happen. If the proposed initiative passes that de facto do no harm test, the World Vision team helps the young people carry it out.

Both the EPI and World Vision projects show tremendous potential. However, they are new and have only been used in a few places. In particular, because the two teams do most of their work in rural areas, we don't know how well they will work in cities where as much as two-thirds of the world's population will live by the middle of this century and which are home to very different kinds of conflict. Similarly, we don't know how effective they would be either in analyzing or responding to conflict in the Global North—a topic I will be paying more and more attention to in the rest of this book.

Still, there is every reason to believe that we will continue making progress on all aspects of local peacebuilding and community-based conflict resolution. We could say the same thing about projects that focus on almost any theme you can imagine. Gender. Race. Climate change. Sports. The arts.

You could profitably spend time on any and all of them here and we will, in fact, return to some of them in part 5 when I consider the next steps peace and conflict studies could and should take. I will not do so here, because covering them at this point would do little more than repeat the most important lesson from this chapter—how and why we have focused on bottom-up approaches to peacebuilding.

Networks

The third category in AfP's list of Peacebuilding 3.0 activities helps you see why it is harder to neatly differentiate between grassroots and public policy initiatives here than it was in parts 2 and 3. As much as we have come to emphasize local peacebuilding and bottom-up initiatives in general, we all realize that they have to go farther. Peace writ large requires more than just local peacebuilding. As the citizens of Tuzla learned, a single community that opts out of war is not enough. Somehow, entire societies have to do so, too. And, they have to have something to propose and implement instead—perhaps even a new paradigm.

I will wait until chapter 12 to consider the public policy implications of conflict resolution and peacebuilding, per se. Here, it is enough to see that by the early 2000s, many of us had seen that we had to work together. No single NGO was big enough to produce the kinds of system-level changes we were now talking about—even one as big as World Vision.

To use the language of high tech start-up companies, we have to take our work to scale. Since the turn of the century, that has led the umbrella organizations which I mentioned toward the end of chapter 7 to dramatically expand what they do.

Each defines its job differently. Nonetheless, they all have come to see the importance of networks that can amplify the impact of any single project or idea as implied in figure 2.4. All started as loose coalitions of academic programs or grassroots activists. Most have become larger and more ambitious. Most started in a single country (often the US) but have become at least multinational if not global in scope.

As has been the case throughout the case study sections of this chapter, there is no way to cover them all in a book of this length. So, you will have to be satisfied with seven of the most important and representative organizations.

Peace and Justice Studies Association. The **Peace and Justice Studies Association (PJSA)** is the oldest of the groups and is the North American affiliate of the International Peace Research Association which is even older, dating to 1964. PJSA, per se, was created in 2001 when COPRED (the Council for Peace Research Education) which focused on elementary and secondary schools merged with the Peace Studies Association at whose inaugural conference George Lopez gave his Gloom and Doom 101 speech, which featured so prominently in part 1.

Today, PJSA is a professional association of scholars who explore alternatives to the use of violence. Unlike other academic organizations like the American Political Science Association or the International Studies Association, PJSA explicitly includes activists among its members. It should, therefore, come as no surprise that it has more members with long-standing interests in contentious politics than any of the other organizations profiled here.

Perhaps because it has always had members who defined themselves as activists more than they did as scholars, PJSA has always been willing to expand the boundaries of peace and conflict studies. More than the other organizations discussed below, it has actively addressed racial inequality in the US, the unequal distribution of economic and other resources, and other traditional left wing causes. And, because most of its members teach undergraduates, it has constantly sought ways of engaging students in community peacebuilding and conflict resolution efforts.

The odds are that your instructor or someone else at your institution has ties to PJSA, so if you want to learn more about it, ask him or her.

Association for Conflict Resolution. With funding and other support from the Hewlett Foundation, three groups of dispute resolution professionals merged to form **ACR** in 2001. Hewlett also helped create learning centers at the leading universities that had graduate level conflict resolution programs at the time.

After the Hewlett Foundation stopped funding the conflict resolution field as a whole a few years later, ACR settled into its current role as an association of dispute resolution professionals that seeks to "gives voice to the choices for quality conflict resolution."

Although everyone is welcome, most of its members are Americans and work primarily on:

- internal management issues in government agencies
- peer mediation and other programs in schools
- issues that revolve around divorce mediation and family law
- environmental and other regulatory disputes
- arbitration, especially involving corporate misbehavior

Given its roots in mediation, ACR has emphasized the importance of third party neutrals, which means that some of its members have shied away from controversial and politically divisive issues. In the last few years, more and more of its members have realized that their skill set is needed in dealing with the kinds of disputes you will see in the next section and the rest of this book.

ACR is not the only group working on professional mediation. The **National Association for Community Mediation (NAFCM)** chose not to join ACR and has been more willing to take on divisive issues in the US in ways which we will see toward the end of this chapter. There are active dispute resolution programs in the American Bar Association, the American Arbitration Association, and dozens of other professional groups. Other countries have similar bodies, all of which are easy to identify on the Internet.

Alliance for Peacebuilding. The Hewlett Foundation also provided the funding to create what is now AfP in 2003. Originally, AfP was an organization of American-based peacebuilding NGOs who worked abroad. When I joined its staff and board of directors in 2005, it was little more than a club of like-minded organizations that sought ways of working together better.

All of that changed at about the same time when we brought on a new leadership team. Since then, we have actively sought new members so that we could become the voice of all peacebuilders to the point that it had more than one hundred organizational members at the beginning of 2019. Although we have never tried to attract members whose headquarters are outside of the United States, a number of those international groups are now members. Although we have not sought them either, AfP now has a few hundred individual members, including me.

More importantly, AfP's self-definition has changed in two main ways that make it different from any of the other associations considered in this section.

First, we provide intellectual leadership for our members and the peacebuilding community as a whole. We also initiate projects that our member organizations couldn't or wouldn't do on their own, including our work with the military which I will discuss in the next chapter. As Senior Fellow for Innovation, part of my job includes identifying ideas from other fields that our members should know about, some of which will also feature in this book.

That work is showcased at our annual conference in Washington. When I started in 2005, we held a retreat that attracted about forty people. Now, the annual conference is spread over three days, is held in Washington, and is attended by about five hundred people. PeaceCon (as we have been calling it of late) has keynote speakers from inside and outside of the field. In 2018, they included veteran peacebuilding and Harvard professor Donna Hicks who spoke about her book on dignity. We also had retired Marine General Anthony Zinni who commanded American forces in the Middle East between the two wars in Iraq and Abby Disney, who is Walt's grandniece and a renowned filmmaker in her own right. The real value of the conference, however, lies in the workshops and panels in which members and guests share experiences about what works—and what doesn't.

Second, we represent their interests in Washington, at the UN, and elsewhere. We removed the ban on advocacy work from our bylaws shortly after I came on board, which has led us to emphasize public policy which I will explore in more detail in the next chapter. Here, simply note that we rarely do the kind of lobbying that has gotten such a bad name in recent years. Instead, we spend time on Capitol Hill and with members of the executive branch talking about peacebuilding issues in general. We have also joined with a number of our larger members to launch a **Global Peacebuilding Campaign**, one of whose goals is to change the way the general public thinks about peace and conflict. Because that is so new, I will defer writing about it until chapter 13.

Global Partnership for the Prevention of Armed Conflict. AfP does not go out of its way to recruit international members because it doesn't have to. The **Global Partnership for the Prevention of Armed Conflict (GPPAC)** was created in 2003 and has succeeded in living up to the word global in its name from the beginning. Today, it supports fifteen networks of CSOs that together cover most of the world. These networks work on their own and are coordinated by rotating regional facilitators, a role which AfP occasionally performs in North America.

As a global organization, it does not have—because it cannot have—a single strategy. However, as its title also suggests, it has focused more on preventing armed conflicts than many other organizations that have tended to concentrate on the right end of Michael Lund's curve and emphasize postconflict reconstruction and reconciliation.

Precisely because it is based and funded outside of the US, GPPAC has experience in places where AfP's members find it hard to operate. Thus, long before President Trump began negotiations with the Democratic Republic of Korea (North Korea), GPPAC had sponsored Track II discussions that included North Koreans and Americans. Similarly, its Syria PPAC was created after the ongoing war began and therefore could not have prevented it. Still, it is by far the broadest coalition of CSOs working either in Syria itself or with the diaspora in refugee camps and beyond.

Build Peace. There are also dozens of specialized networks that are also global in scope but limit themselves to a single issue or topic. Clearing land mines. The law. Dialogue and community mediation. Human rights. Gender. Religion. You could undoubtedly add issues and topics to that list. If so, there undoubtedly is a network of CSOs working on it.

I only have room to describe one of them, **Build Peace** along with its parent company, Build Up^. It is by no means representative of these initiatives. No single organization could be. However, because it focuses on the use of information technology and was created by people who were then in their twenties, it is often used by my colleagues as a good illustration of the ways the conflict resolution and peacebuilding field could and should grow.

Build Peace and Build Up^ were created in 2014 by four remarkable men and women still in their twenties. Two of them had extensive experience in peacebuilding (to the degree that twenty-somethings can have extensive experience in anything). One was already a successful entrepreneur. The fourth was a graduate student in computer science.

I met them at their first annual conference that drew more than two hundred attendees to MIT's iconic Media Lab for what was billed as the first serious discussions of the ways IT could help peacebuilders. We watched a documentary on how Kenyans used data gathered through their flip phones to prevent electoral violence, heard talks on the ways people were already using IT in peacebuilding work, and participated in workshops on how we could do that even better.

Build Up^ has held Build Peace conferences every year since then, often choosing to hold them in conflict zones, including Cyprus, Colombia, and Northern Ireland. The 2019 conference will be held on the US-Mexican border after this book is published. At each venue, the organizers include sessions that focus on the use of IT and the arts.

Even more interesting are the initiatives that the Build Up^ team has taken on.

Every year, it funds and mentors three to five Build Peace fellows whose projects combine IT and peacebuilding. The fellowships operate more like a Silicon Valley incubator than a traditional conflict resolution training program. Mentors from the Build Up^ staff encourage their mentees to develop prototypes and minimum viable products that they can into the field quickly and learn from their mistakes. Recent fellows have included:

- a young Argentinian who built an app that allows teenagers in Myanmar to share music and then have dialogues about their troubled country's future
- the first woman to serve in the Pakistani air force, who used her fellowship to add peacebuilding to work she was already doing that incorporated technology and public participation into rural economic development
- a Bosnian psychotherapist and dancer who is creating theater groups that engage young people in creatively imagining what the future of their country could be like

The Build Peace fellows receive a year's worth of funding, training supervised by its staff, and a subsidy to attend the annual conference at which their work is featured—and critiqued.

The team also takes on peacebuilding projects of its own. They range from training programs helping London's LGBT community deal with conflict among its various stakeholders to training young people in South Sudan to make videos about their experiences.

CONFLICT LAB 11.2

For both of the conflicts you have been considering since chapter 1, outline a ten-year project that:

- addresses the key norms that are at the heart of the conflict.
- defines new narratives that might point toward peace and conflict resolution.
- takes advantage of existing networks or builds new ones if the ones you think you would need do not exist (yet).

THE HOME FRONT

The last section of this chapter deals with an important transition in peace and conflict studies that was still taking shape when I had to stop adding new material to this book. We peacebuilders are beginning to give serious attention to conflicts in our own backyards, including some that touch our own personal lives.

That put us in an awkward, but eventually creative, position. We had all used statements like "conflict is a fact of life" for decades. Now, all of a sudden, we had to take that statement seriously for the conflicts in our own lives as well as those of the clients we worked with around the world.

In my own case, I found myself wondering how I could tell people in Venezuela how to solve their conflicts when I can't solve my own here in my home state of Virginia. Similarly, how can mediators avoid the large social and political questions when the disputes they work on touch on issues raised in the #MeToo, Black Lives Matter, Climate Change, and other movements?

What Happens Over There Matters Back Here

We have always known that countries like the US have faced serious conflicts of their own. Many conflict resolution and peacebuilding professionals in the Global North have long been part of movements that address divisions over race, gender, the environment, economic and inequality. For the most part, however, we did so in our capacity as citizens rather than as peace and conflict studies professionals.

The 9/11 attacks and their aftermath demonstrated that our professional skills could help deal with the wicked problems that confront Western Europe, North America, Japan, South Korea, Australia, and New Zealand. That started as we began dealing with widespread Islamophobia. Add to that the issues of the 2010s, including climate change, everything that eddies around gender, culture wars, immigration, populism, Brexit, the election of Donald Trump, and more.

The reason for that is simple. These problems could tear our own countries apart, too.

My colleague, Col. Christopher Holshek (US Army, retired) often used to tell the civil affairs soldiers whom he trained for overseas deployments, "what happens over there matters over here." He wanted them to understand that they were being sent far from home to work with civilian populations on problems that mattered to the US.

Today, I use the same line to illustrate the fact that many of the world's problems have come home to roost. The 9/11 attacks, the subsequent conflicts in Afghanistan and Iraq, and what the **George W. Bush** administration called the Global War on Terror forced us to see that Holshek was right. Americans and Europeans had to deal with everything from Islamophobia and related fears, which continue to this day in concerns over immigration.

It wasn't just issues that eddied around 9/11. The established democracies are as prone to intractable conflicts as any country in the Global South. It is true that they have strengths that most of those other countries lack that help cushion the impact of those conflicts at least *for now*. The fact that they are democracies and have gone through the kinds of transitions that Pinker and others charted means that they already have some viable dispute resolution mechanisms in place. Most have political cultures that make it relatively easy for people to tolerate—if not embrace—people they disagree with and give their institutional arrangements a degree of bedrock support that is so lacking in much of the rest of the world. And because they are wealthier, it is easier for them to meet their citizens' social and economic needs.

I italicized the words for now in the preceding paragraph for a reason. As the dozens of books on the threat to democracy point out, those strengths could easily be eroded to the point that the democratic nature of our regimes could be put in jeopardy.

Given all that, you might assume that conflict resolution and peacebuilding professionals were quick to respond to the tensions facing the advanced democracies face. In fact, it took us even longer to find our footing here than it did to devise a response to twenty-first-century terrorism.

Many of the people we encountered had not been exposed to conflict resolution and peacebuilding solutions before. Some doubted that they would be as effective as traditional forms of activism. Also, because these were not new issues, other individuals and organizations were already working on them, but not necessarily from a peacebuilding or conflict resolution perspective.

In other words, we had to find our niche in an already crowded political space. To use the terminology introduced in part 1, we may have agreed on some core principles involving the use of nonviolence and cooperative problem solving for the good of the system as a whole. However, we did not always view the context we were working in or the goals we were trying to reach in the same way. That, in turn, led to quite a bit of flailing and quite a few false starts before we could find even a few ways to make a difference.

We also had to deal with the fact that it is not easy to work on our own turf. Mediators and others whose background is in either the law or organizational behavior prize their neutrality. Much like doctors and therapists who do not accept friends and relatives as patients, mediators and arbitrators assume that working on issues they care a lot about make it hard for them to take a step back from the specifics of a dispute and provide the dispassionate judgments that they think is needed. As we began to deal with issues that by definition hit close to home, that distance or neutrality seemed to vanish out the clichéd window.

By the same token, peacebuilders who have spent their professional lives abroad now had to adapt to working in their own cultures. In much the same way that John Paul Lederach had a lot to learn about Nepal, we discovered that we had to do the same thing when we started working at home. In particular, we had a hard time disentangling the fact that it is hard to apply core conflict resolution principles like neutrality and fairness when you are, yourself, a party to the dispute. That is particular true in the countries like the US and the UK where Donald Trump's election and the Brexit debate have made political and social life toxic.

We also had to deal with the fact that there was no single goal that all of us were working toward. That started with the fact that we were not interested in the same issues. Similarly, some of us were focused on reforms, while others wanted sweeping change. Some wanted to work through elections and/or existing institutions, while others felt the need to start from scratch. Last but by no means least, plenty of those individuals who had long track records working in those countries reacted skeptically (at best) when peacebuilders who had spend all of their time working abroad decided to get involved at home.

Building an Architecture for Peace

Let me start the discussion of the home front with the most important but least well defined concept that a handful of us have borrowed from some of the initiatives I hinted at in part 3—creating an **architecture for peace**. As suggested there, an architecture refers not to a building but to the structure or outline around which something can be built. As you will see in the next chapter, those kinds of frameworks have been built largely from the top down in the Global South. By contrast, an American or European architecture for peace will have to be built from the ground up on the basis of grassroots building blocks, some of which already exist, adding new ones, and, most importantly, combining them into a movement that truly makes a different society-wide.

I will mostly limit myself to the US in what follows. It is, of course, where I have spent most of my life. More importantly, almost all of the issues facing any of these countries are on our agenda. And, perhaps because so many of the ideas discussed in this book had their origins in the US, it should not come as a surprise that we started working on domestic issues before our European colleagues did.

In any event, keep one fact in mind. I am only describing projects that are just getting off the ground, and everything that follows will probably be out of date by the time you read these words. That said, you can keep up with breaking news along these lines through www.charleshauss.info.

The architectures that currently exist in the Global South (see the next chapter) were designed to prevent another genocide or other crime against humanity. The architecture being envisioned for the US and other industrialized democracies is both less and more ambitious than the ones that already exist.

The plans are less ambitious because no one realistically expects anything like a genocide to occur in North American or Western Europe any time soon. Instead, they are designed to warn us about looming dangers so that we can avoid the kinds of devastating conflicts we saw in part 3. At the same time, they are also more ambitious. The ones existing ones are "only" designed to prevent mass atrocities, which, of course, is no mean feat. For some of us, an architecture for peace in a country like the US should help us deal with all kinds of conflict and could lead to the kind of paradigm shift first discussed in chapter 2.

Building a fully articulated architecture for peace anywhere in North America or Western Europe will undoubtedly be harder than doing so in the Global South. These countries typically have larger and more intertwined social and economic systems. Many also have well-established political systems with roots in a deeply embedded political culture in which expectations revolve around continuing to do things as usual. In other words, it going to be harder to change peoples' norms on issues that are so ingrained in our popular culture that we take their existence for granted—if we think about them at all.

That said, some of the building blocks for such an architecture do exist. I will devote the rest of this section to describe a few of them.

Beyond Transactional Mediation

That starts with changes that are already afoot among mediators. For reasons that had little to do with the broader social turmoil at the heart of this chapter, they have been expanding their work beyond the interest-based or transactional practices that Fisher and Ury championed in the 1980s. As you saw in part 3, that had begun when mediators and began thinking in terms of intractable conflicts in the 1990s.

Until then, they spent most of their time and energy professionalizing the field amid the dramatic expansions in the use of mediation. Practitioners and academic analysts alike focused on how best to carry out negotiations in legal and other professional settings.

Since the turn of the century, many mediators and other conflict specialists have had to take on the emotionally wrenching and socially divisive issues that have been at the heart of this chapter. Some have even gone so far as to use terms like wicked problems and VUCA in their work.

Whatever terminology one uses, there has been a virtual tidal wave of new insights and programs in interpersonal and organizational conflict resolution that parallel those in peacebuilding. The newest innovations in that part of the field involve the explicit inclusion of values, norms, identities, gender, and other issues that have been in the headlines for the last twenty or thirty years.

Some of the most interesting insights come from practitioners who have had to rethink their conventional wisdom because their work takes them beyond the courtroom and workplace settings that gave rise to the first waves of alternative dispute resolution work in the 1980s and 1990s. When they had to deal with the intense emotions that emerge when you deal with the kinds of issues raised in the previous paragraph, new goals and strategies emerged that involved many of the same terms you saw in global peacebuilding, including fostering empathy, resilience, and the like.

First are community mediators. In the US, about half of the roughly four hundred community mediation centers belong to the National Association for Community Mediation. Many of those centers do the kind of transactional mediation alluded to in earlier chapters. Indeed, few of them could have survived for the last twenty years financially without the family mediation and other cases that local judges routinely sent their way.

But, because they try to use mediation techniques to address all of the issues that a given community faces, they have had to deal with the identity and other divisions that have been at the heart of the peacebuilding side of our field since the 1990s. Even though their projects reflect local conditions, all of these centers try to help people address conflicts before they reach the boiling point and develop what they call "collaborative community relationships to affect positive systemic change." Not only are the centers available to people who need them (including the courts), but they also have outreach programs so that potential clients can learn about their services.

The Piedmont Community Mediation Center in Warrenton VA is a typical NAFCM member. The center serves a five county area that stretches from the edge of the Washington DC metropolitan area to the heart of rural Virginia. The most important thing to know about the Piedmont Center is that it is small, with an annual budget of less than $500,000 a year, much of which comes from work it does for the local courts. More importantly for our purposes, it is a trusted community resource that trains local residents in alternative dispute resolution, provides assistance for resolving neighborhood disputes, and helps promote better relations between the police and the community, especially local residents of color.

The Piedmont Center is one of twenty-four NAFCM members that has received financial support from the JAMS Foundation. The Foundation is funded by the JAMS company which is world's largest alternative dispute resolution firm that handles more than fourteen thousand cases a year from twelve offices in the US and one in London. Because most of those cases involve large corporate clients, the company created the foundation to help support community mediation.

In addition to the centers like the one in Warrenton, JAMS also helps fund the **Divided Community Project**, which is housed at the Moritz College of Law at the Ohio State University. Its first major initiative deals with community violence, which is hardly surprising since two of its staff members ran the Community Relations Service under the Obama administration and led the federal response to the violence in communities like Ferguson MO and Baltimore MD. As you read their key principles, note how much their recommendations reflect the kinds of systems thinking that was at the heart of the Nepal project:

- Identify respected community leaders who are willing to take the lead and engage other stakeholders.
- Perform an assessment of the community's ability to handle divisions and their social and economic costs.
- Organize a planning group that includes government officials, other leaders, and average citizens that would allow anyone and everyone to raise issues of concern.
- Establish some sort of early warning system that could alert everyone to looming hot button issues before they reach a boiling point.
- Create institutions and practices that could actually take constructive actions to prevent violence from breaking out.
- Develop contingency plans for dealing constructively with a dispute the very moment that violence does begin as well as longer-term plans for dealing with protracted crises.

There are other new initiatives in which people are taking traditional conflict resolution tools into new communities. The major academic programs have started programs often literally in their own backyards. George Mason University, for example, is helping state and local officials and their citizens deal with the difficult issue of renaming schools and highways that were named for Confederate leaders and other prominent slave owners. The Kroc Institute at the University of San Diego has a number of ongoing projects on immigration and border security.

Cure Violence

That leads us to the next set of initiatives which address urban conflict in a way that has little to do with the approaches to peacebuilding and conflict resolution discussed so far in this book and thus break new conceptual and political ground. Among the most promising is **Cure Violence**, whose operations and underlying philosophy have little to do with anything you have seen so far. Its successes have turned it into one of the most respected NGOs in the world today.

Cure Violence was created after Dr. Gary Slutkin returned to his native Chicago after spending fifteen years working as a public health physician in Africa. Almost as soon as he settled in, he heard commentators claim that the city was suffering from an epidemic of teen violence, much of it gang related. Being an epidemiologist, Slutkin took the word epidemic seriously—and literally. He concluded that Chicago's violence was indeed spreading like an epidemic and decided it had to be treated as such.

Little in his medical training prepared him to deal with this kind of epidemic. There was, of course, no vaccine or other medical intervention that would cure urban violence. And, as a middle aged, white doctor, he had little in common with the perpetrators or victims of the shootings.

So, he combined his expertise with his ignorance and helped develop an innovative way of intervening which the Public Broadcasting Service portrayed in the 2012 documentary, *The Interrupters*, the full version of which is available for free on many video streaming services. It showed how the Cure Violence team went out of its way to recruit young men and women who knew the streets, many of whom had actually taken part in the violence at one point or another in their lives. As the title of the documentary suggests, their job was to interrupt the violence before it got started. It turns out that some of the most effective interrupters had themselves spent time in prison because of their own involvement in gang violence.

The methods Cure Violence uses are based on a standard model public health workers use to prevent the outbreak of an epidemic:

- They stop the spread of the "disease" at its source. In the most widely publicized part of its work, the interrupters stop the contagion in much the same way that public health workers stopped the spread of cholera in nineteenth-century London by providing clean drinking water in poor neighborhoods. In this case, the trained Cure Violence staff help prevent their neighbors and, in some cases, their friends from picking up their guns.

- After these crisis interventions, the broader Cure Violence team identifies the individuals who are at the highest risk of using violence and works with them to begin considering alternatives.
- They then move further out into the community to address forces that could make it more resilient and better able to resist the "disease" of violence, which is urban America's equivalent of nineteenth-century public hygiene campaigns in British cities. Eventually, this requires addressing what I earlier called the upstream, underlying, or structural causes of violence.

Because of Slutkin's background as a physician and because its funding came from donors who insisted on rigorous monitoring and evaluation of its work, Cure Violence has been studied more than any other project covered in this book. The results are amazing. The neighborhoods it first worked in experienced a forty to seventy percent reduction in armed violence within a. year. It has since started projects in New York, Baltimore, and other American cities and in a number of major conflict zones around the world including Iraq and South Africa. In every case, it has produced significant reduction in local rates of violence. The other two goals listed in the bullet points in the previous paragraph have seen less progress, but that is to be expected of any program that uses urban violence as a leverage point to address the numerous wicked problems that plague cities around the world.

Public Dialogue

The newly intensified divisions in the industrialized democracies are keeping political scientists and sociologists busy. How polarized are we? Why is that the case? How dangerous are those divisions, including for democracy itself?

The conflict resolution and peacebuilding community has not played a major role in the debates over why those divisions exist. Rather, we have focused our attention on what should be done about them.

We were not the first group of activists to enter this space. That honor goes to the **National Coalition for Dialogue and Deliberation (NCDD)** that held its first conference in 2001. Its web site describe NCDD as "a gathering place, a resource clearinghouse, a news source, and a facilitative leader" for "this extraordinary network of innovators who bring people together across divides to tackle today's toughest challenges."

Its seven hundred members live and work in thirty-four countries and incorporate dialogue and deliberation in their professional lives, not all of which centers on identity-based conflicts. Still, most NCDD members have a lot in common with the organizations described so far in this book, especially those whose roots lie in the mediation side of our field. Many of them, however, do not see themselves as part of the peace and conflict studies community. Still, its annual meetings and other activities have gone a long way toward spreading new ways of solving problems in the political arena.

More important are the dozens of new organizations that have been formed in the last decade to limit the effects of polarization in the US. Many of them belong to the aptly named **Bridge Alliance**, which is a loose coalition of about ninety organizations that are trying to revitalize American democracy. It is relevant here because about a third of those members promote and organize dialogues that are aimed at literally bridging the political divide, including NCDD.

Three of its other members are worth mentioning because they reflect the degree to which conflict resolution and peacebuilding practices are—and are not—incorporated in their work.

Living Room Conversations has deservedly garnered the most public attention. Its co-founders are as unlikely a pair as you can find. Joan Blades is a very liberal activist whose family unexpectedly made a lot of money when it sold their company that made the 2000s hit flying toasters screen saver. Mark Meckler, by contrast, is a rancher and one of the driving forces behind one wing of the Tea Party movement. They met through mutual friends and realized that they could actually talk about issues together and that doing so helped ease tensions as you can see in this excerpt from a 2018 PBS documentary, *American's Creed.*

> www.pbs.org/video/mark-meckler-and-joan-blades-political-enemies-dbuthb

Living Room Conversations has been successful for many reasons, including its founders' charisma. It has attracted support, too, because it does not ask much of its participants and facilitators. Conversations typically last no more than two or three hours. There is no expectation that they will lead to further action, although it is the founders' hope that they will do so. After all, they have both built national political movements themselves. Similarly, the conversations are designed to be very easy to run and don't require the skill set of a trained facilitator.

Another Bridge Alliance member does take the discussions further. Like Steven Pinker, these activists drew their name **Better Angels** from a line in Abraham Lincoln's first inaugural address. Like Living Room Conversations, Better Angels intentionally brings Americans from both sides of the political divide together. However, it is more focused on fostering dialogues that extend beyond a single session. Its discussions are designed to dig deeper so that the participants have a better chance of understanding and empathizing with the other side. It wants participates to consider searching for possible areas of agreement and, in some cases, even working together. Its facilitators, too, receive some basic training in hosting what the Better Angels team calls "constructive, nonpolarizing conversations between people who disagree politically."

You may actually have encountered the third Bridge Alliance member, **Sustained Dialogue**, because much of its work takes place on college campuses. The organization was created by Harold Sanders who had helped negotiate the first agreements between Israel and Egypt when he was an American foreign service officer. Sanders and his successors have tried to apply the lessons they learned from his high level work to campuses. As such, its work is based on the need for long-lasting and intense dialogues among the participants to a dispute.

They have created Sustained Dialogue groups on dozens of campuses in the US and abroad. The campus itself determines what the Sustained Dialogue project is like, including the topics it covers and the people who are involved. Sometimes, it takes on an issue that divides the campus itself, such as the role of fraternities and sororities. Sometimes, it tackles broader social issues, such as how racism affects campus life. Sometimes, it is organized by students. Sometimes, the faculty and administration take the lead—and pay the bills. Sometimes, Sustained Dialogue programs are extensive and rigorous enough that they are offered for academic credit.

However a specific program is organized, the Sustained Dialogue team has to spend a lot of time training its student leaders because the organization gives equal emphasis to the two words in its title. It wants to run dialogues that are so intense that they leave no party to the discussion unchanged. And they have to be sustained, because they are designed to last for an entire semester and have an impact on the participants for the rest of their lives.

Two other organizations that are not part of the Bridge Alliance reflect the value of including conflict resolution and peacebuilding principles even more explicitly in a program's design.

Hands Across the Hills was created in the aftermath of the 2016 presidential election by Paula Green. Green had had a long and distinguished career as an international peacebuilder and peace educator and was heading toward retirement when the divisive election convinced her that she should use her forty years of experience to help resolve America's own conflicts. Serendipitously, she discovered a comparable group in Letcher County, Kentucky. At first, Green thought that Letcher County and her home town, Leverett, Massachusetts, only had their hilly location in common. But, she soon discovered that strong social networks existed in both communities and that residents of both of them were yearning for contact with people who came from the "other side" socially and political.

She started by contacting and getting to know her counterpart in Kentucky. Gradually, the two of them identified friends and neighbors who were interested in getting to know the "other." After months of preparation, a delegation from Kentucky came for a weekend visit. They stayed in the homes of their Massachusetts counterparts and spent the weekend having political discussions, but also sharing the day-to-day experience of a Berkshire mountains weekend. Later, the Bay State residents paid a return visit to the hills of eastern Kentucky.

One of their blog posts sums up the entire program: "They came with curiosity, they left in love." The initiative has gotten significant media exposure, and plans are underway to continue this exchange and build others like it around the country.

Even more grounded in conflict resolution theory is **Resetting the Table (RTT)**. It was created by the husband and wife team, Melissa Weintraub and Eyal Rabinovich. She is a rabbi; he is an experienced mediator and former college professor.

Given their backgrounds, it is not surprising that they started doing work on the divisions with the Jewish community, including on the stance American Jews should take toward Israel. If that were all it did, Resetting the Table would not even be mentioned in this book. I included it because it is pioneering two other features both of which revolve around what it calls deep conflict transformation.

First, it puts its facilitators through extensive training which it normally spreads out over a series of weekends. In other words, its facilitators themselves develop the in-depth skills required to guide others through the personal paradigm shifts that lead to new mind-sets that the term transformation conveys.

Second, it has begun to reach beyond the Jewish community by launching its own initiative to heal America's divisions. Like many in the conflict resolution and/or Jewish worlds, RTT staff were surprised and confused by Trump's election. So, it decided to send a team of thirty-six trained facilitators and student interns to spend a few weeks listening to and learning from residents of eight counties in rural Wisconsin and Iowa that swung to support Trump after giving President Obama a majority four years earlier. The teams sought out local leaders, especially conservatives and members of the working class. They also brought larger groups of residents together to talk about everything from health care to immigration to various interpretations of Christianity, the last of which intrigued the RTT team, most of whom, of course, were practicing Jews. Then, in 2018, it piloted a project that no one else in the peace and conflict community had considered. It reached out to journalists and trained them in mediation skills. As discussed above, that produced real interest among reporters who were already trying to find an alternative to both the if-it-bleeds-it-leads style of journalism.

All of these projects have tremendous potential. All of them have problems, two of which will be at the heart of part 5, but should at least be mentioned here.

First is the difficulty we have had taking them to scale, which I will return to at the end of this section. Having small groups of people from Kentucky and Massachusetts visit each other is terrific. So are the intense discussions facilitated by Resetting the Table or Sustained Dialogue. However, if we are going to change the way millions of people in the US or Great Britain or Japan or New Zealand think, we need to reach more people and do so as quickly as possible.

Second, we are not yet reaching everyone, despite the best efforts of Living Room Conversations or Resetting the Table. So far, these efforts have appealed primarily to liberal, well-educated voters. In other words, people of color, Evangelical Christians, and other key social groups have not found these initiatives all that welcoming perhaps because of the ways that implicit biases get in the way of even the best intentioned bridge builder.

Although we realize that we have to reach out across these and other divides, we have not done a great job of doing so. To cite but one example. I attended the first NCDD conference in 2001. One of the speakers was demonstrating the then revolutionary technology that lets you do instant polling. She asked the group how they had voted in the 2000 presidential election. Only two of the two hundred attendees admitted to have voted for President George W. Bush. Four or five times that many had cast their ballot for the Green Party candidate, Ralph Nader, who only won about two percent of the vote nationwide.

We have made some progress since then. Still, when I attended the 2018 ACR and AfP conferences, there were very few Republicans in sight.

Lessons from the Corporate World

A small number of business leaders were active in the 1960s movements against the war in Vietnam. Echoes of their involvement can be seen today in the twenty-first century version of business executives who promote peace and the far larger movement for corporate social responsibility.

For the purposes of this book, however, the corporate world's importance lies in some of its own professional innovations that have lessons that conflict resolution and peacebuilding practitioners are just beginning to learn. Few of these ideas and practices were developed with conflict resolution or peacebuilding in mind, despite the fact that mediators have found steady work as coaches and advisors because of their understanding of organizational dynamics.

Despite what I said a few paragraphs ago, don't ignore the growing interest in **corporate social responsibility** through which companies commit themselves to causes that go beyond the bottom line. Thirty years ago, that meant refusing to doing business in places like South Africa. These kinds of boycotts are still used today, most notably in the BDS movement aimed at Israel. More often now, companies are choosing to use some of their profits to meet broader social goals involving the environment, social and racial equality, and, in some cases, peace. Most visible here are the 204 billionaires (as of 2019) who have signed the **Giving Pledge**, and have committed themselves to giving away at least half of their wealth.

But that is just the beginning. The corporate thinkers you are about to encounter reached conflict resolution related conclusions because practices much like the ones discussed so far in this book contributed to their businesses' success. This is not the place to go into the management literature in any detail. It's enough to cite some key themes that are beginning to find echoes among peacebuilding and conflict resolution professionals because these new management ideas, too, have origins in systems theory.

Many of today's most dynamic corporations are run by managers who stress teamwork. Companies that continue to use traditional forms of top-down leadership tend to find themselves in trouble, even those in the high-tech world as you can see in recent press coverage of companies like Uber and Facebook. By contrast, more of the highly successful new companies stress management strategies in which workers are empowered as much as possible both in terms of taking responsibility for doing their jobs and in helping shape the decisions about their team's or even the entire company's future.

The corporate world and business education have changed so much that one of the career options I will discuss in part 5 is getting an MBA. When I graduated from college in the late 1960s, none of the activists I knew even gave a moment's thought to business school. Now, the best MBA programs incorporate issues at the heart of their curricula that parallel the main themes raised in this book.

At times, that has led management experts to explicitly use some of the ideas developed in this book. No one did so more than the late Stephen Covey, who may have also been the most influential management guru of his generation. Consider these words drawn from a collection of his best writings that his family assembled after his untimely death in a bicycle accident in 2012:

> Most of life is not a competition. We don't have to live each day competing with our spouse, our children, our workers, our neighbors, and our friends. "Who's winning in your marriage" is a ridiculous question. If both people aren't winning, both are losing.
>
> The win-win mentality is fundamental not just to business but to all of life's relationships. It's the ticket to entry into any human being's heart.
>
> We assume that the whole point of an argument is to win—to beat the other side. Just try that on your friends and family and see how far you get toward a loving and creative relationship.
>
> Win-win is not a personality technique. Win-win is a frame of mind and heart that constantly seeks mutual benefit in all human interactions. It is a total philosophy.[5]

That has led to literally hundreds of exciting new ideas about cooperative problem solving. Without taking you too far away from the main topic of this book, consider six of these themes all of which have implications for conflict resolution and peacebuilding.

Disruptive innovation. I did not put innovation at the top of this list because it is in my job title. Rather, it is in my job title because we live in a world of disruptive change, whether it was the invention of the cell phone or social media in the tech world or the rise of modern terrorism for peace and conflict studies. As you will also see in part 5, it would be foolish of us not to be ready for the disruptive innovations that would be our equivalents of the iPhone or Facebook.

Design thinking. Design thinking has become the rage in the most creative parts of the corporate world in ways that go far beyond the use of scenario planning discussed in part 3. Now, companies like IDEO use multidisciplinary teams that include consumers of the product they are designing. Together, they go back to the clichéd drawing board, harness their collective creativity, and often end up building innovative products wholly or largely from scratch. And, they do so by quickly creating prototypes, trying them out until they reach a minimum viable product, and learning from their mistakes before they think about taking that product to scale. There are more risks involved in trying out prototypes with real-world conflicts than you get with early mockups of the next cell phone. However, there have to be ways in which the benefits of failing fast and learning from your mistakes can be brought into our work, too.

Lessons from improv. Second City is known for its comedy routines. However, it also has a thriving practice that helps workers and managers use improv in their work. The same tactic of never saying "yes, but" and always saying "yes, and" to people you work—and disagree—with that leads to great humor can lead to the kinds of breakthroughs you reach using the most advanced versions of transformative mediation.

Empowering the workforce. As we move into what is often called a knowledge economy, not only are assembly line jobs disappearing but so is the mentality of just showing up and doing your job. In today's high-tech world, in which you will likely build your career, the emphasis is on knowledge, creativity, initiative, and other traits that are easier to reach if your employees feel as if they can make a difference not just in their own jobs but in the company as a whole.

The benefits of diversity. Almost all successful executives now understand that the more diverse their workforce is, the more successful their company will be. They also know that diversity can also lead to more conflict. But there is little doubt that the more diverse your staff is—however you choose to measure diversity—the more creative ideas you will have to choose from.

Embracing change. Today's businesses cannot afford to ignore the fact that we live in a world in which change is the only constant. Indeed, management analysts are even more likely to use terms like VUCA or wicked problems than we peacebuilders are. An executive has no choice but to prepare for life in an increasingly globalized and interconnected economy in which what worked today almost certainly won't work tomorrow. Far more than my colleagues in peace and conflict studies, they know they have to be ahead of the clichéd curve, which has led them to use terms like agile and to seek the bright spots or outlying cases that can be taken to scale.

Personal Growth

This growing convergence between the mediation and peacebuilding strands of the field did not occur in a vacuum. During these same years, but for other reasons, the Western world has seen a sharp upsurge of interest in ideas and practices that promote personal growth, emotional intelligence, and self-awareness. This can be seen in the numbers of people doing everything from studying meditation or practicing yoga or attending twelve step programs.

Few people start meditating or attending AA meetings primarily out of a desire to build peace or resolve conflicts. Nonetheless, there is an overlap between the two worlds that actually goes in both directions. Many activists I have worked with over the years have discovered that personal self-awareness and even some kind of spiritual practice enhances conflict resolution work. That is especially true among the colleagues who have committed themselves to projects that require a long-term commitment and/or are transformational in nature. Some—but probably fewer—people who become adept at some spiritual practices or emotional intelligence techniques discover that the empathy that they develop slides into sympathy, compassion, and a desire to build a more peaceful world.

A number of organizations have explicitly tried to draw connections between personal growth of a spiritual nature and building peace. To see how and why that takes place, consider the Shift Network, which has little in common with the other organizations considered in this book. To begin with, it is a for-profit company that offers courses and trainings online that deal with spirituality, holistic health, wellness, shamanism, relationships, enlightened business, and peacebuilding. As unlikely as it may seem, 1.3 million people from 170 countries have participated in the courses and events it sponsors.

While there are other and larger spiritual organizations, none does more explicitly to have a social and political impact through its peace programs, which are run by Philip Hellmich, who has a long history of working in the secular peacebuilding world, during which time he has maintained an active meditative practice. The Shift Network's peace programs revolve primarily around a Summer of Peace, in which it hosts online sessions (and occasionally face-to-face ones) that the Alliance for Peacebuilding has helped organize for the last few years.

It also attracts some surprising participants to these events. You would not be surprised to find the head of Search for Common Ground, AfP's staff, or some of the leading lights in spirituality on its roster. You might, however, be shocked to find names like Marla Maples (the actress who was also Donald Trump's second wife) or Pete Carroll, the longtime coach of the NFL's Seattle Seahawks.

The Return of Contentious Politics

The individuals and organizations described so far in this chapter are not the only ones working for a more peaceful world. As has always been the case, the kinds of activism I have emphasized here have had an uneasy relationship with others which focus on what's wrong with the world and place more demands on our leaders.

Arthur Brooks and the Dalai Lama

The Dalai Lama and Arthur Brooks

Much of the rest of this book will revolve around two themes—the importance of self-awareness and the need to build broader coalitions. No two people epitomize both points better than Arthur Brooks and the Dalai Lama.

His Holiness needs no introduction. Arthur Brooks probably does. By the time this book comes out, he will have stepped down after a decade as CEO of the American Enterprise Institute, which is one of Washington's most prominent conservative-leaning think tanks. In other words, he does not come from a part of the world where conflict resolution or peacebuilding have gotten a lot of traction.

Brooks, however, has a long-standing relationship with the Dalai Lama. As I was finishing this chapter, they wrote an op-ed article in the *Washington Post*, "All of Us Can Break the Cycle of Hatred." On the same day, his book *Love Your Enemies* was published. I read it immediately and realized that I would have to squeeze at least a box in this chapter though I had already submitted the final manuscript to my editor. Brooks and the Dalai Lama have been talking about the link between inner peace and political peace for decades.

The two of them focus on the role that contempt plays in our lives and how it contributes to wicked problems. The best introduction to their thinking and its implications for this book comes in a talk Brooks gave at a symposium on the transition in power in Washington during the week before President Trump's inauguration—www.usip.org/passing-the-baton-2017-the-day-in-video.

In it, he puts his own spin on your line that conflict is a fact of life. As he put it in that video, "don't take disagreement out of it, but learn to disagree better." The Dalai Lama showed him how to do it. When Brooks asked for advice on how to deal with the contempt he felt for people whose views he disagreed with, His Holiness said, "Show warm-heartedness. I defeat my enemies when I make them my friends."

The Dalai Lama indeed does it himself. Every morning he prays for the Chinese leadership, who are the very same people who forced him into exile in 1959.

The people I work with the most often have a tendency to avoid organizations that—as we often put it—stress "naming and shaming" the people they disagree with. Doing so, we worry, leads to the kind of contempt and unbridgeable divisions that Arthur Brooks worries about, which I thought was important enough to put into a box of its own on this page.

At the same time, it is important to understand that contentious politics not only has a place in peace and conflict resolution, but that place may well be growing in importance given the events of the last twenty years.

That began with the antiglobalization protests of the early 2000s in Seattle, Geneva, and other cities. They drew attention primarily because some of their participants used tactics that bordered on violence in ways that would have led some of my colleagues to leave them out of a book like this one.

The 2010s, of course, have seen a tremendous deepening of ideological tensions and the polarization of most democratic electorates. Protest movements like the ones that toppled communist and other dictatorial regimes continued, most notably in Iran during its Green Movement following the 2009 presidential election and in the various Arab spring protests of the 2010s that started so promisingly but ended up in new dictatorships and, in some cases, bloody civil wars in Syria, Yemen, and Libya.

In Europe and North America, the protest movements have not tried to topple regimes—at least not yet. Still, social and political life has been tumultuous. Protests against the wars on terrorism. France's yellow vests. Britain's movements for and against Brexit. Demonstrations for and against the wave of migrants that have moved to Europe since 2015. The rise of populist candidates. Black Lives Matter. #MeToo.

Not all of these movements belong in a book like this one, especially the ones that have endorsed the use of violence. Still, the world of peace and conflict studies which had largely focused on bridge building during the 1990s has had to come to grips with the world of protest politics, which, of course, was an important part of its origins.

The dramatic reappearance of contentious politics has had two significant implications for peace and conflict studies.

The first is the tension that has always existed within our community between those who primarily say "no" to perceived injustice and those who are convinced that building bridges across ideological divides is the best way forward. I know that this is a tough question because I have personally supported both sides of it at one point or another in my professional and political career.

The second raises a tension that I will return to frequently in the rest of this book. Most people I have worked with over the years have been very good at working with all sides, especially when they were mediating or playing bridge building roles. Most of them, like me, have their roots on the left side of the political spectrum.

Yet, there is no obvious reason why peace and conflict resolution have to be equated with progressive politics. In fact, there are some people in these fields who are self-identified conservatives on at least some issues. There are, for instance, plenty of peacebuilding Evangelicals for Peace, some of whom explicitly combine their commitment to peace to their commitment to spreading the teachings of Jesus.

In the end, we have found it relatively easy to work with people from more conservative faith traditions who share our basic commitments to ethical principles like the Golden Rule. It is also increasingly clear that we have to build new political partnerships if we are to succeed in producing something approaching a paradigm shift in the way we deal with conflict.

It is by no means clear who—if anyone—should not be welcomed into our efforts. On one level, if we take our values seriously, we should be as inclusive as possible and not exclude anyone. However, most of our colleagues feel the need to draw the line somewhere. Most of us are at least reluctant to work with anyone who accepts the use of violence as a viable tactic under all but the most unusual circumstances. Most, too reject the idea of working with anyone who denies the fundamental equality of all human beings or works openly against efforts to reduce barriers that stand in the way of true equality because the roots of structural racism (or any other disliked "ism") and those of structural violence are largely the same.

KEY TERMS

Concepts

accompaniment, 233
action research, 236
agency, 244
architecture for peace, 260
bottom-up, 246
bright spot, 238
community mediation, 236
confirmation bias, 244
corporate social responsibility, 268
emerge, 234
Everyday Peace Indicators (EPI), 249
inside partial, 239
intrapersonal, 270
leverage, 237
local peacebuilding, 246
looping, 244
narratives, 240
norms, 244
outliers, 238
positive deviance, 237
relationships, 245
resilience, 246
top-down, 246
transactional, 245
transformational, 245
trauma healing, 246
wicked problem, 233

Individuals

Anderson, Mary, 248
Bush, George W., 259
Lederach, John Paul, 233
Lewin, Kurt, 236

Organizations, Places, and Events

9/11 Attacks, 258
Alliance for Peacebuilding, 270
Association for Conflict Resolution (ACR), 255
Better Angels, 265
Bridge Alliance, 265
Build Peace, 257
Cure Violence, 263
Divided Community Project, 262
Giving Pledge, 268
Global Partnership for the Prevention of Armed Conflict (GPPAC), 256
Global Peacebuilding Campaign, 256
Global War on Terror (GWOT), 241
Hands Across the Hills, 266
Living Room Conversations, 265
McConnell Foundation, 233
National Association for Community Mediation (NAFCM), 255
National Coalition for Dialogue and Deliberation (NCDD), 264
Nepal Project, 233
Peace and Justice Studies Association (PJSA), 254
Resetting the Table, 266
Rondine Cittadella dela Pace, 246
Sustained Dialogue, 265
World Vision International (WVI), 251

DIG DEEPER

Brooks, Arthur. *Love Your Enemies: How Decent People Can Save America from the Culture of Contempt.* New York: Broadside, 2019. By the then CEO of the American Enterprise Institute, this book explores how we could and should disagree better.

Firchow, Pamina. *Reclaiming Everyday Peace: Local Voices in Measuring and Evaluation after War.* New York: Oxford University Press, 2018. A bit technical in places, this thoughtful book describes the everyday peace indicators methodology and the first attempts to use it.

Heath, Chip, and Dan Heath. *Made to Stick: Why Some Ideas Survive and Others Die.* New York: Random House, 2007. An intriguing look at how innovations take hold.

Johnson, Steven. *Where Good Ideas Come From: The Natural History of Innovation.* New York: Riverhead, 2011. Like the Heaths, Johnson is not part of our field. His ideas are worth exploring.

Lederach, John Paul. *Memoirs of Nepal: Reflections across a Decade*. Redding, CA: McConnell Foundation, 2015. An evocative, first-person account of the one truly holistic, long-term peacebuilding project.

Ripley, Amanda. "Complicating the Narratives." https://thewholestory.solutionsjournalism.org/complicating-the-narratives-b91ea06ddf63. Not a book but the most thoughtful article I've ever read on how journalists could and should change.

Senge, Peter. *The Fifth Discipline: The Art and Practice of the Learning Organization*. New York: Doubleday, 1990. Still the classic on how systems work within organizations.

United Nations/World Bank. *Pathways to Peace: Inclusive Approaches to Preventing Violent Conflict*. www.worldbank.org/en/topic/fragilityconflictviolence/publication/pathways-for-peace-inclusive-approaches-to-preventing-violent-conflict. A book-length report filled with state-of-the-art data.

NOTES

[1] John Paul Lederach, *Memoirs of Nepal: Reflections across a Decade* (Redding, CA: McConnell Foundation, 2015), 37.

[2] Pamina Firchow, *Reclaiming Everyday Peace: Local Voices in Measuring and Evaluation after War* (New York: Oxford University Press, 2018).

[3] https://everydaypeaceindicators.org/2017/07/09/measuring-peace-the-epi-way/.

[4] www.wvi.org/peacebuilding.

[5] Stephen Covey, *The Wisdom and Teachings of Stephen Covey* (New York: Simon and Schuster, 2012), 154–155.

CHAPTER 12

Toward the Grown-ups' Table

THINK ABOUT IT

I will be making a fairly conventional "glass half full/glass half empty" case in this chapter. We have made some progress in getting to the grown-ups' table but have fallen far short of our ultimate goal of having peacebuilding and conflict resolution values routinely shape public policy making. So, in figuring out just how close we are to "half full" or "half empty," ask yourself the following questions:

- How have the events of the last twenty years changed the broader policy-making dynamics at the national and global levels?
- In what ways have peacebuilding and conflict resolution groups tried to influence public policy?
- Given the material in this chapter, how effective have those efforts been? Why did you reach that conclusion?
- Given what you have learned about systems theory and other themes raised in the first eleven chapters of this book, what other realistic options should we be considering?

CORE CONCEPTS

international community—an informal term referring to the UN, the International Institutions, and, sometimes, the leading industrialized democracies

Overton Window—reflects the range of policy options that are generally considered viable at a moment in time

peace writ large—the understanding that peace has to be built at more than just the local level

populism—a political strategy that allegedly speaks for "the people" but usually has nationalistic overtones

Sustainable Development Goals—the UN's guiding document for the years 2015–2030

Peace Writ Large is a term [used] to describe changes at the macro level of society, comprising two basic goals—stopping violence and building just and sustainable peace by addressing the political, economic, and social grievances driving conflict.

—CDA Collaborative

THE POLITICAL SCIENTIST JOSEPH LAPALOMBARA used to make his graduate students quake in their boots when he asked three simple questions after they made a seminar presentation: Oh yeah? How come? So what?

Ever since my own days as a political science graduate student (when we were told about LaPalombara's questions on the first day of class), the "so what" question has always given me the most trouble. I got a lot of training in research methods for use in gathering data (oh yeah) and then analyzing the results (how come). I've always found it is much harder to figure out how to answer his "so what" question. Yet, that is the one that brought me both to political science and then to peace and conflict studies.

The one time I heard Professor LaPalombara discuss his idiosyncratic teaching method he said that "so what" was really two questions rolled into one, both of which will be at the heart of this chapter because they let us bring Julia Roig's concerns about the grown-ups' table up to date. The first is relatively simple. How much change could you observe in the public policies or whatever else that you were interested in? The second is far harder to measure. In the simplest possible terms, how big of an impact did a particular set of activities have on that outcome?

At first glance, the answer to both questions could well be "not much." If anything, the public policies pursued by governments around the world seem to have become less and less cooperative and peaceable over the last twenty years. And, as Roig's initial comment suggested, most of us are convinced that if we did have a regular seat at the grown-ups' table, things would be different.

On the other hand, if we put LaPalombara's questions and Roig's lament in historical perspective, things do not seem quite so bad. Don't get me wrong. As you are about to see, the national and global policy-making challenges we face dwarf those of either the 1980s or the 1990s. But first impressions aside, we can point to a series of policy changes, some of which could be the kinds of **bright spots** I talked about in the two previous chapters. I won't be able to show you how much of an impact our community has had in shifting what pundits often call the policy needle in a more peaceful direction. Nor will I try to make the case that we have come anywhere near close to reaching our goals.

Nonetheless, by the time you finish this chapter, I suspect you will be surprised by how many partially successful initiatives we can point to. I also suspect that you will be frustrated by how little progress we have made, which should prepare you for part 5 in which I will discuss where this field is likely to head next and how you could be a part of it.

NATIONAL GOVERNMENTS I: THE GLOBAL SOUTH

The rest of this chapter is devoted to a representative sample of these initiatives which I have divided into three sections. This first one focuses on four types of initiatives in the Global South, two of which build on what you saw in part 3, which means I can deal with them briefly here. The other two are newer and will be carried over into the discussions of governments in the Global North and international institutions that follow.

Outliers. That starts with the first time you met **Mary Anderson** in this book as the author of *Opting Out of War*. Currently, peacebuilders are trying to figure out why places like Idlib in Syria had largely been able to avoid the fighting until 2019 and how those findings could be used as first steps in "adding up to peace" when and if the fighting actually ends.

Truth and reconciliation commissions. As of late 2018, almost fifty countries had created some kind of truth and/or reconciliation commission. None of them went as far or were as successful as South Africa's (see chapter 9). More importantly, we are also beginning to understand why some enjoy more success than others. In her study of one of perhaps the least well publicized TRC in the Solomon Islands, Karen Brounéus has uncovered circumstances in which such a body is most likely to have an impact.

That starts with something that might seem obvious at first glance. People who are part of the identity group that was responsible for most of the atrocities have to take what the victims say seriously and be prepared to apologize. In addition, Brounéus relies on the concept of **perspective taking**, which is a version of empathy, but one in which all sides have to be willing to "take" the other side's perspective seriously, something that has not happened enough in many TRCs other than South Africa's.

It helps if it is clear which side was morally in the wrong and key members of that community are willing to accept responsibility for their actions. Otherwise, these commissions can turn into exercises in which each primarily criticizes the other in what peacebuilders often call **naming and shaming** exercises.

In the Solomon Islands where these conditions were not fully met, the TRC's truth telling process may actually made things worse. More generally, that is likely to be the case when overall trust in "the other side" is low and little effort is made to forge more respectful relationships.

Special attention has to be paid to the reintegration of former combatants on all sides, but especially those who fought for the state. If they aren't willing to show genuine remorse, the TRC as a whole is not likely to get very far.

Many TRCs also have a limited impact because they do not serve as springboards for addressing the structural causes of conflict. This criticism, of course, could be levied against South Africa under Presidents Thabo Mbeki and Jacob Zuma.

The implications of Brounéus's research can perhaps be seen most easily in three places in the Global North where something akin to a TRC has been tried. In 2009, Canada organized a TRC to investigate the forced placement of indigenous children in residential school programs that were little more than what we in the US call reform schools. Six years later, the commission issued a report that laid out the evidence and made a series of plausible recommendations. Unfortunately, few of them were converted into official public policies. To begin with, the commission did not have the legal authority to take perpetrators to court. Similarly, Prime Minister Steven Harper largely ignored the recommendations, which languished until his government was defeated at the polls and replaced by one headed by Justin Trudeau who had made indigenous rights a central issue in his election campaign. A similar effort by the Wabenaki tribe and the state of Maine in the US led to similar and underwhelming results. Finally, a self-appointed group in Greensboro, North Carolina, convened a TRC twenty-five years after a group of civil rights protesters were killed by a Ku Klux Klan member who supposedly had the tacit support of the local police department. In this case, the TRC had next to no impact because it was unofficial and was only convened because the statute of limitations had run out, making any legal prosecutions of the perpetrators impossible. In other words, like many TRCs that have fallen short of their goals, the one in Greensboro was widely seen as a way for one side to get a bit of revenge against the other.

Architectures for prevention. In chapter 11, I briefly mentioned creating an **architecture for prevention** of conflict in the US. As I said there, those networks will have to be built upward from grassroots organizations. The existing ones in Africa and South America were created by political elites and all have some sort of official standing.

As you will see in more detail when we consider the UN later in this chapter, three overlapping categories of crimes are currently prohibited by international law—war crimes, crimes against humanity, and genocide. Many countries in the Global South have either experienced mass atrocities in the past thirty years and/or worry that they might do so at some point in the future. As a result, a few of them have created architectures or integrated collections of institutions that bring together government officials and civil society organizations. None have yet been fully authorized in law. However, they typically work through a single national office such as the Ombuds, while leading civil society networks focus on potential hot spots around the country where violence could well break out. Most are also affiliated with the Global Network of R2P Focal Groups, which was created by the governments of Denmark and Ghana and now has sixty member states.

Their work varies from country to country. Perhaps the closest there is to a typical example is the Kenya National Committee for the Prevention of Genocide, War Crimes, Crimes against Humanity, and All Forms of Discrimination, whose title is truly a mouthful. The KNC (for short) was created in the aftermath of the electoral violence that killed more than one thousand and displaced another six hundred thousand Kenyans in 2007. Before the 2017 election, the KNC enlisted the support of thirty stakeholder groups and held training sessions and community forums around the country, while concentrating on regions thought to be at greatest risk, like Isiolo County and the national capital, Nairobi. That year, only sixty-seven people were killed in electoral violence. We obviously cannot attribute that sharp a reduction in violence to the KNC alone. However, it had to have had something to do with the peaceful nature of an otherwise extremely heated election campaign that was filled with allegations of fraud and abuse.

Ethiopia's Ministry of Peace. The final example is the most recent and the most promising. In October 2018, the new Ethiopian prime minister Abiy Ahmed named **Muferiat Kamil** to be the country's minister of peace. The then forty-two-year-old Muferiat had already been leader of an insurgent movement, a cabinet minister, and speaker of the parliament before she became the world's first minister of peace.

The term does not always have positive connotations, since George Orwell had created one in his epic dystopian novel *1984*, in which the ministry's efforts yielded anything but peace. In the Ethiopian case, however, it will probably be an important force in the transition toward democratic rule since it has responsibility for the police and the national intelligence service and is led by one of the country's most dynamic young leaders.

The Ministry of Peace may be just the beginning of a broader shift toward state-driven peacebuilding in that troubled country. Although it was never formally colonized, Ethiopia was unable to escape the identity-based conflict that swept Africa, especially following the assassination of long-time emperor Haile Selassie in 1975.

The young Abiy (also forty-two at the time) committed his government to an inclusive policy that would extend representation to the country's underserved minority groups from which both he and Muferiat came. He also has made it clear that his would be a different government in symbolically important ways. Within weeks of taking office, a group of disgruntled and armed soldiers showed up at his office demanding a pay raise. A former soldier himself, the prime minister invited the soldiers into his office and, before negotiating with them, got down on the floor and did a series of pushups with them. At least this time, the crisis was defused.

At the same time, I do not want to leave you with the impression that policy makers in the Global South have made a significant turn toward peacebuilding. Even a brief look at the Global Peace Index will quickly disabuse you of that notion. If anything, conditions have deteriorated in far too many parts of the world. To make matters worse, as we come to grips with wicked problems and the VUCAed nature of today's world, we have learned that that the challenges we face are all the more daunting precisely because they are so multifaceted.

That said, one reason for introducing **Clayton Christensen** and his notion of a job to do in chapter 10 is that we are beginning to see some convergence in the way economists like him and peacebuilders see the path(s) forward in countries like Ethiopia, Kenya, or the Solomon Islands. Like my peacebuilding colleagues, Christensen was frustrated by how little we had to show for our efforts after decades of spending hundreds of billions of dollars on economic development and a smaller but still considerable amount on peacebuilding. Again, like my peacebuilding colleagues but unlike many mainstream economists, Christensen has long emphasized the importance of grassroots-based economic development in which entrepreneurs create markets where none had existed before which in turn lead to jobs, stability, prosperity, and, in due course, peace. Like Lederach, Christensen argues that such grassroots efforts have to be combined with better governance, but there seems to be a growing consensus that lasting prosperity and lasting peace best starts with grassroots initiatives that put pressure on political leaders to follow suit.

Muferiat Kamil, Ethiopia's (and the World's) First Minister of Peace

I could pursue this line of speculation farther here. However, it makes more sense to return to these notions of integrated development and peacebuilding in part 5.

NATIONAL GOVERNMENTS II: THE GLOBAL NORTH

The Global North presents us with a different picture in two main ways. First, because we had not been engaged in the policy process there to any great extent before 2000, we had to find our political footing. Second, while we discovered that the Global North needs peacebuilding every bit as much as the rest of the world, we learned that we could not simply import tool kits we had used in the Global South.

That second point is important enough to explore before turning to concrete examples. These words were written early in the third year of Donald Trump's presidency. Polarization was at an all-time high in the US and other industrialized democracies, which was reflected in outbursts of racism and intolerance of all sorts. All of a sudden, we were no longer only worrying about political disputes taking place in far-away countries.

They were on our own doorsteps.

The problems antedate Trump's election and extend far beyond the problems posed by his leadership. To see why, consider three obvious examples. Islamophobia has been a problem at least since the 9/11 attacks, if not before. Similarly, Donald Trump had nothing to do with causing the waves of immigrants who have flocked to the US and Western Europe over recent decades. And, the political right does not get all the blame for our problems. Political conservatives properly point to the chilling impact of so-called politically correct limitations on freedom of expression on university campuses throughout the developed world.

My goal is not to take a stand on these or other issues. Rather, I want to spend the rest of this section outlining the belated ways that the conflict resolution and peacebuilding communities have responded to the crises they now face at home. We will do so in three steps by considering some:

- general dilemmas that apply everywhere in the North
- specific challenges we face in the US and how we are beginning to respond to them
- ways in which some other governments have gone farther than the US

Why Adding Advocacy Matters

As noted several times earlier in this book, many conflict resolution and peacebuilding NGOs in the Global North only started doing advocacy work in the last fifteen years. The decision to do so was not taken lightly.

That was especially true in the US where the initial concerns about losing our third party neutral status were compounded by a peculiarity in American tax laws. Almost all of the US-based NGOs covered in this book have been granted tax-exempt or 501(c)3 status as nonprofits. According to the laws governing the Internal Revenue Service, donations to all certified nonprofits are tax deductible.

There is one important catch here for our purposes. Tax-exempt organizations cannot engage in lobbying, which many colleagues interpreted as meaning that they could not do any advocacy work at all.

In practice, the law is far less draconian than many of my colleagues thought a decade ago. Trying to shape public opinion or even "educate" members of Congress on issues is not considered lobbying and is therefore perfectly legal. Most experts also agree that nonprofits can spend as much as twenty percent of their annual budget working to promote particular pieces of legislation without jeopardizing their tax-exempt status. The only thing that is explicitly prohibited is giving direct support to a particular candidate or political party in an election campaign, which next to no peacebuilding organization would do under any circumstances.

Other countries' legal systems are far less restrictive, and many make little or no distinction between for profit and not for profit entities. Still, since most of the leading peacebuilding and conflict resolution NGOs are based in the US and many of the other receive a good bit of their funding from American foundations, the unusual American tax law did limit our willingness to engage in political activity of any kind before the beginning of this century.

Things began to change after 9/11. As you have already seen, the issues conflict resolution and peacebuilding professionals dealt with were now increasingly controversial and increasingly involved their home governments. Although there was some resistance to doing so, organizations that emphasized peacebuilding gradually began explicitly doing advocacy work. AfP changed its bylaws in 2007. Twelve years later, AfP actually does a small amount of lobbying as we have done in support of the Global Fragility Act (see the box on page 286). Other peacebuilding organizations made the transition more easily for the simple reason that their bylaws never prohibited advocacy work or they were based in countries where taking a stand on issues was not legally problematic.

By the start of the 2010s, there still were plenty of conflict resolution organizations that maintained strict political neutrality. However, more and more of them had joined the peacebuilding groups in taking a stand on some specific causes.

I should add one caveat here which has appeared in other contexts throughout this book. In most of the Global North, the conflict resolution and peacebuilding communities are perceived to be on the left end of the political spectrum. There are some exceptions, including Evangelical and Mormon peacebuilders in the United States. Nonetheless, we do have to confront the popular perception—and often the reality—that we draw our support primarily from political progressives.

That is to some degree an inescapable problem. It is hard to see, for example, how someone who holds explicitly racist or nationalistic views could also support the bridge building or egalitarian sides of our work. Still, as you will see in part 5, one of the next challenges facing conflict resolution and, especially, peacebuilding is to find a way to change that popular equation that supporting peace also means supporting the left.

None of these issues have much bearing on what happens in the Global South, where, of course, most peacebuilding work has been concentrated since the end of the Cold War. There, the left–right division is not as important as it is in Europe or North America. And, we find people from almost all political and faith traditions taking part in peace processes though, as in the North, it is rare that rabid nationalists or overt racists join those efforts until circumstances all but require them to do so, as we saw in South Africa.

Theories of Change and Beyond

In at least one key respect, we have not taken our own advice. As far as I know, no one has developed a theory of change that is any more specific than the one Chigas and Woodrow laid out in *Adding Up to Peace* (see chapter 10). That comment is not meant to be a criticism of their work, because they had no intention of devising anything that resembled a concrete strategy. That said, we are just beginning to develop ideas that could eventually be turned into sophisticated theories of change and provide the intellectual grounding for a policy-related project that is as holistic and ambitious as the one in Nepal.

Insider partial. Recall from chapter 11 that the McConnell Foundation team adopted what they called an **insider partial** strategy in working with Nepal's government. They assumed that they could not expect to gain access to all critical policy-making networks on day one. Rather, they decided to pick specific policy areas and institutions to work on first and gradually add others as circumstances warranted.

Most American and European NGOs have gradually moved in that kind of direction usually without explicitly saying so. We focused on aspects of foreign policy making in which we had the most expertise and the best contacts inside of government. In the US, that started with civil servants at the State Department and USAID. Gradually, we have extended our outreach to Congress, the military, and beyond.

To be honest, this kind of limited access to policy makers can be frustrating. Indeed, it is what prompted Julia Roig to make her comment about the grown-ups' table in the first place. Still, as you will see in the section on the Overton Window and the box on the Global Fragility Act, there are signs that our version of the insider partial strategy is beginning to show results.

Cumulative strategy and OODA loops. Over the course of this book, I have been arguing that we should be open to the possibility of a paradigm shift in the way we deal with conflict at all levels. In doing so, I've also been making the case that paradigm shifts almost never occur all at once but tend to build gradually. Add to that the logic of systems theory as presented in chapter 3 with its notion that one constantly has to adapt one's strategy and tactics in the light of experience. Taken together, that suggests that one cannot normally define a pathway that inevitably leads to a paradigm shift or any other dramatic change.

That also doesn't mean that we could or should act in a chaotic of willy-nilly manner. Here, consider two helpful ideas come from the American military, which has rarely been a source of ideas for the peacebuilding community! However, both have gained widespread support in the corporate world where the ability of a system to "learn" from its experience is highly prized. We are beginning to do the same in peacebuilding and conflict resolution circles.

Admiral Joseph Caldwell Wylie championed the idea of **cumulative strategy** in which a military planner does not set out to win a campaign in a single battle. Rather, he or she sets something akin to the Omidyar Group's guide star and steers an ever changing course toward it in which small, seeming disconnected actions end up having a significant impact, which, in this case, amounts to adding up to peace.

Similarly, US Air Force colonel James Boyd introduced cadets training to be pilots to what he called **OODA loops**. A pilot or anyone else seeking a complicated goal should keep repeating (hence the notion of loops) a pattern of **O**bserving, **O**rienting, **D**eciding, and **A**cting. Presumably, like cumulative strategists, the OODA planners keep getting closer to the target by learning from their mistakes. In our case, of course, the target is world peace rather than a bombing site!

Do no harm and public policy. Mary Anderson introduced the idea of not doing harm as a guideline that NGOs should follow in their grassroots projects. It actually has implications for policy advocacy as well in ways that lead to the Out on a Limb box in this chapter.

When we worked in places and on conflicts that were far from home, we rarely had a stake in the outcome. Even if we preferred one side or the other as in South Africa, we could usually leave after our project was finished, knowing that our work would not have a huge impact on our lives back home.

That is not the case when we work on conflicts that can literally take place in our own back yard. In that case, you do have a stake in what happens. You often care passionately about the outcome. As my entrepreneurial friends put it, you have skin in the game.

The invocation to do no harm gets more complicated here because of two overlapping questions, neither of which is easy to answer.

First, how do we take stands on policy issues and not deepen existing ideological and other divisions? The logic of systems analysis suggests that we can normally seek policy solutions that work for everyone because they benefit the entire system in the long run. It is not always obvious that we can avoid policies that do no harm to anyone in the short term. There are, of course, policy-related decisions that invariably lead to less than win-win outcomes, most notably elections. Consensus policy making, as discussed in chapter 9, is a step in that direction, but it should have been obvious at that point that we are still a long way from having answered that question.

Second, how should we treat the people we disagree with? In earlier chapters, I wrote extensively about the very human habit of demonizing our opponents by relying on the image of the enemy and other traits that social psychologists have been studying since they first tried to understand the Holocaust. When you are dealing with conflicts in which you have skin in the game, that ceases being an academic discussion.

These questions are also hard for me to answer personally. I have spent my whole adult life on the left and today find myself aghast at what President Trump and his administration have done. How do I show my anger toward the administration, but do so in a way that does no harm?

If you happen to like President Trump, you should ask the same question about your attitude toward former President Obama. If you are not an American, find an equivalent politician, other leader, or issue that makes sense to you. Brexit. President Putin. Chancellor Merkel. President Duterte. Kim Jong-un. Ayatollah Khamenei.

Whichever camps you fall into, you face some version of the quandary that I do with the Trump administration in which some of my friends and neighbors work. It is hard to resist venting that anger and engaging in the kind of naming and shaming behavior I mentioned earlier.

Yet, if you do, you can deepen the ideological and emotional wedges and run the risk of doing personal and political harm. Even when you are convinced that you are on the right side of the issues from an ethical perspective.

The best answer I've been able to come up with—which I know is less than satisfying—comes from the world of improv as discussed in chapter 11. There, I talked about the value of always saying "yes, and" even when you disagree with someone, because doing so tends to expand the available options to you. However, when a conflict hits close to home, sometimes you morally have to say no.

Here I extrapolated from improv and came up with a different way of doing so. When I respond to opponents with a line that begins with something like "no, but," I typically go on and point out why their point of view is even worse than they thought.

What would it take to say "no, and?" Following Amanda Ripley's advice to journalists, that means expressing disagreement but also at least showing curiosity about why someone has what seem like outrageous beliefs, at least from your perspective. It could also mean disagreeing and then suggesting an alternative point of view that you might both agree with. In other words, in Ripley's terms, we can complicate the narrative. Or, as we saw in chapter 7, it is possible to play one of William Ury's third sider roles while also taking a strong stand on an issue.

But do read the Out on a Limb box before you agree with me.

And remember that there is a place for the anger you feel toward the people you disagree with.

Between the Grass Roots and National Government

The chapters on policy making in parts 2 and 3 focused all but exclusively on the national and global levels. That made sense given the issues that both scholars and practitioners focused on at the time.

The interest in local peacebuilding led us to pay more attention to policy initiatives that unfold closer to home. The definition of "closer to home" varies from country to country because of their different constitutional arrangements. Everywhere, however, we have seen a proliferation of local initiatives, some of which have spread upward to whatever other subnational units have substantial decision-making power in that country, sometimes referred to as the **grass tops**.

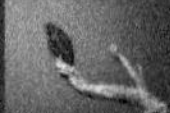

OUT ON A LIMB

The Role of Contentious Politics

It should be clear from the text that I have cast my lot with strategies that stress bridging political divides, finding common ground, and adopting other cooperative approaches to conflict resolution. It is not the only plausible strategy for people in the peace and conflict studies community to follow.

I know that's the case because I spent the first third of my career studying and practicing contentious politics. Therefore, www.charleshauss.info has discussion forms that allow visitors to debate these issues that will still be up for grabs when you read these lines.

The Global Fragility Act

A single example should show you how far we have come and how far we still have to go as far as advocacy is concerned.

In early 2019, a bipartisan group of members of the US House and Senate introduced the Global Fragility Act, which was pending in both houses of Congress when I wrote these lines. The act grew out of the work Mercy Corps' public policy team had done over the previous few years and had attracted the support of nearly sixty leading NGOs, including AfP.

When and if it is passed, the bill would commit the US government to a ten-year-long strategy that would:

- help stabilize the countries that are most at risk of civil war and other kinds of mass violence
- create pilot projects for conflict prevention in the countries deemed most at risk
- define and use state-of-the-art measures for evaluating the impact of those efforts
- regularly report on progress made under the act both to Congress and to the American people

At this point, it is hard to tell if the bill will become law. A previous version did pass the House of Representatives by an overwhelming 376 to 16 vote in the final days of the previous Congress but was never take up by the Senate. The new version will probably gain House approval, face an uncertain future in the Senate, and might or might not be vetoed by President Trump. It should also be noted that the leadership of both parties in both houses have yet to show any significant interest in the act.

Those pessimistic realities notwithstanding, this marks the first time that the conflict resolution and peacebuilding communities have supported a single piece of legislation or that it can seriously anticipate securing a major public policy victory.

You can learn more about the initiative and why it is so important by watching this short video made by Mercy Corps.

www.youtube.com/watch?v=aZYgP53z0y8&feature=youtu.be

Two rather different examples should suggest the variety of opportunities peacebuilders and their allies have been exploring.

Community policing. Ever since modern police forces were created in the nineteenth century, the relationship between law enforcement and community members has been problematic. Today, the resulting tensions tend to play themselves out in difficult relations between police officers and members of minority communities, American readers will recognize this in movements like **Black Lives Matter** and broader concerns about how people of color are treated by law enforcement personnel. Europeans and Canadians view similar problems through a lens that focuses on the relationship between recent immigrants with law enforcement and city government in general.

If you only paid attention to the mass media and its coverage of events, like police shootings of young people of color, you might conclude that little progress has been made on this front. In practice, many police departments and other law enforcement professionals around the world have gone out of their way to improve relationships with members of minority communities and the rest of the population. For reasons of their own, more and more law enforcement officers have adopted **community policing** and other similar approaches to their work. As the name suggests, these programs were designed to help police officers work in partnership with members of their community in addressing two key issues, the importance of which, of course, varies from city to city:

- improving law and order, especially when it touches on deep social and political divisions over race, religion, and other identity-based issues
- preventing and countering the recruitment of young people to violent extremist networks at home or abroad

You already encountered one organization in chapter 11 that focuses on the first of these bullet points, **Cure Violence**. Its work routinely puts its staff in contact with local police forces. In addition, because many Cure Violence staff members are themselves ex-offenders, their interactions are the first instance of something I will focus on a lot in the rest of our book—a desire to forge unusually broad coalitions as suggested in the box on the next page.

Cure Violence is by no means the only organization bringing strange political bedfellows together. In the US, the **Divided Communities Project** at the Ohio State University has built coalitions of activists, local officials, and others in five conflict-ridden cities as part of a program it is gradually taking nationwide.

The project works with community mediation centers and other grassroots leaders to develop dialogues that help:

- initiate and design a project that could bridge some of those divides
- convene meetings of key stakeholders both in the community and in local government
- enhance constructive social interactions

The project does not necessarily advocate passage of new legislation because it realizes that the rules and regulations themselves are rarely the problem. Rather, difficulties arise because of the ways existing policies are implemented when officials and citizens come together which led them to the awkward sounding phrase—enhancing constructive patterns—which is another way of referring to norms or a community's political culture.

You can see that in one of its intriguing early projects which I also alluded to in chapter 11. **Orlando Speaks** was spearheaded by Rachel Allen, who is a humanities professor at Valencia College and a member of an ongoing network of community college peace studies faculty members. In the aftermath of the disturbances in Ferguson, Missouri, and a year before the PULSE nightclub shootings, she realized that police–community relations in Orlando had to be

Strange Political Bedfellows

One often unspoken assumption underlying the policy side of Peacebuilding 3.0 is that it will not succeed unless our community can build coalitions that bring together individuals and organizations who are not used to working with each other and may actually have been hostile toward each other at some point in the not so distant past. Not everyone in the field is always happy with the prospect of creating these coalitions. Thus, many Black Lives Matters are reluctant to work with the police—for good reason. Similarly, those of us who come out of the peace movement often have trouble envisioning partnerships with the military, a topic I will cover later in this chapter. Nonetheless, working with people one disagrees with is part of what defines much of our field and makes us different from traditional peace and social change activists.

improved given the number of young black men who had been arrested and even killed by law enforcement officers.

So, she began promoting the idea of holding open dialogues between community members and police officers and quickly gained the support of the college's academic dean who happened to be a seventeen-year veteran of the local police force. Between them, they were able to convince Mayor Buddy Dyer and leading police department officials to participate despite their initial concerns that Orlando Speaks would devolve into a session at which angry citizens complained about the police and little was accomplished.

Plenty of forethought went into planning and organizing six meetings, each of which was held in one of the city's tensest neighborhoods. Average citizens, activists, and police officers began by sharing a light dinner before settling in for an evening of discussion. Police officers were encouraged, but not required, to attend. Those who did were asked not to sit at a table with other officers, and everyone was encouraged to eat dinner with people they did not know beforehand.

The meetings did have their dramatic and tension-filled moments. A group of local activists picketed outside the first one, protesting long-standing biases in the way the police treated community members, especially people of color. Allen went outside and explicitly asked the picketers to join the discussions. Participants scrambled to make more room at the tables for their new dinner partners. Allen makes the case that these turned out to be the best set of discussions Orlando Speaks has held so far.

The discussions were designed to build awareness, create new and more constructive relationships, build trust, and enhance citizen engagement in community policing. Sessions used a technique known as serial testimony in which each participant at a table was given time to present his or her perspective before a general discussion began.

The discussions have not led to many formal changes in police department policies. However, participants and average citizens alike acknowledge that important steps have been taken that "enhanced constructive patterns" not only in police–community relations but in the way city officials deal with average citizens in general.

Divided communities are not a purely American phenomenon. Cities around the world have conflicts of their own and have also become key recruiting grounds for terrorist networks like ISIS or the insurgents fighting against the government of Ukraine. As a result, organizations like the **Strong Cities Network** are creating forums through which urban officials and their constituents can share best practices and lessons learned—another theme I will return to in the rest of this book.

The network was formed at the UN General Assembly meeting in 2015 and had grown to 120 member cities by the end of 2018. Its members include some of the biggest cities in the world (London, Los Angeles, Paris) and others that have been the site of terrorist or other forms of urban violence in recent years (Sarcelles, France, Kano State, Nigeria, and Medellin, Colombia).

I will focus on its work in the Western Balkans, because of the conflicts that erupted there after Yugoslavia collapsed, as featured in part 3. The region is important for SCN for twenty-first-century reasons, too. As many as fifteen hundred fighters from the region have joined ISIS, and several hundred more are part of the Russian-backed insurgency in eastern Ukraine. Although there have been relatively few outbreaks of violence within the region in the last twenty years, many of the same causes that led to the fighting in the 1990s helped convince those young men to join struggles in the world's other hot spots.

By the end of 2018, the SCN's projects had created:

- cooperative mechanisms through which police officers and community leaders work together
- services that could identify and counsel the young men and women who were susceptible to recruitment into extremist networks
- media and other campaigns that address the rise of right-wing nationalist as well as Muslim extremism
- networks that would reduce the duplication in existing efforts
- exchanges through which officials in one community could learn from colleagues in the rest of the Balkans region and beyond

Urban design. It's not just physical security. Conflict resolution and peacebuilding professionals have been involved in ingenious efforts to reimagine what cities should be like. Here, consider a very different example that took me halfway around the world.

In 2003, I got an email from Janette Hartz-Karp inviting me to help facilitate what the government of Western Australia was calling a **Dialogue with the City** to help chart the long-term growth of Perth. Western Australia occupies about one-third of the country's territory but only has 2.6 million residents, eighty percent of whom live in the Perth metropolitan area.

When we met in Washington, Hartz-Karp described the city as being a lot like San Diego, but without the congestion. She also said that its population was expected to grow by more than half in the next thirty years. Most of the new residents would be immigrants from Asia who would change the demographic makeup of a country that had only recently begun allowing nonwhites to move there.

State and local officials had decided that they wanted the newer, bigger, and more diverse Perth to resemble the existing city as much as possible. That, in turn meant, that it had to plan its future. The state's minister of development decided to host a session with twelve hundred local residents and civil leaders at which the participants would agree on a basic growth strategy that the professional planners would then implement.

Hartz-Karp asked America Speaks to facilitate the larger discussion because it had had tremendous success holding similar events regarding recovery from Hurricane Katrina in New Orleans and rebuilding Ground Zero after 9/11. Because of my involvement in the US Consensus Council (see chapter 9), I was asked to help work with the professional planners, because Hartz-Karp worried that they would be reluctant to accept whatever this group of amateurs came up with.

The discussion went so well that I wasn't needed.

Equal numbers of participants were drawn from a list of local leaders, individuals who explicitly volunteered to participate in the session, and randomly selected voters. Aboriginal and immigrant attendees came to an earlier session that addressed their particular concerns. Then, everyone turned up early one morning in a converted warehouse on the city's docks. There, they were assigned to sit at round tables, each of which had three citizens from each group, a facilitator, and a scribe who sat in front of a personal computer.

The morning was split into forty-five-minute sessions in which each table discussed transportation, environmental, and development policies. After each of them, a speaker took the stage while a team in the back room compiled the tables' results, distilled them down into the three top options for each topic. By the end of the morning, the tables had agreed on a key priority item for each of the three policy areas.

After a box lunch, people reassembled at their tables that now had a table-sized map of the Perth region and a pile of board game tokens representing the number of people, vehicles, buildings, and so on that planners expected would be added to the region by 2030. Each table then had to distribute the tokens on the map in keeping with the goals that the group had reached in the morning. It was frankly amazing to watch these groups of nine people who had never met each other before that morning dig into moving their tokens around the map spread out on their table. During the afternoon, the scribes again sent in each table's progress, and the data base experts in the backroom summarized the results, and the tables then fine tuned their plans.

By the end of the day, there was a clear consensus on what a congestion free Perth would look like in 2030. The once reluctant planning staff agreed. The expected tension-filled meeting I was asked to facilitate lasted about twenty minutes. A few weeks later, the state legislature passed the enabling legislation.

As a result, when you visit Perth in 2030, it will still feel a lot like San Diego without the congestion.

Adding Up to Peace I: The United States

Orlando and Perth are one thing.

Local peacebuilding is terrific, but it only take us so too many decisions in too many countries have to get made at higher levels of governmnent.

Therefore, the acid test will come when we begin to have a significant impact at the national level and beyond. And, it is safe to say that we rarely have that kind of an impact when it comes to formal legislation. More importantly, prominent national level politicians still tend to emphasize nationalism and treat their opponents with something less than a spirit of what the Dalai Lama would call warm heartedness whether at home or abroad.

However, as you are about to see, a significant number of senior civil servants, serving and retired military officer, and some sub-cabinet-level elected officials have moved toward the peacebuilding and conflict resolution communities. Most of the examples that follow will probably be unfamiliar ones, even if you follow world news closely. For good or ill, the world's media have yet to practice the kind of journalism Amanda Ripley recommended (see chapter 10) and the old truism still holds about news coverage: "if it bleeds, it leads."

Growing areas of agreement exist in dozens of policy areas. In order to to keep the length of this section manageable, I will limit myself to the kinds of foreign policy and national security issues where the progress has been the most extensive and perhaps the most surprising. I will start with the US because it is the most powerful county in the world by orders of magnitude, and members of the peace and conflict studies community have properly been highly critical of its behavior, starting long before Donald Trump won the presidency.

Diplomacy. You have already seen hints of the changes that are taking place in the American diplomatic community with the discussion of the **States Institute of Peace (USIP)** in chapter 9 and the **US Agency for International Development (USAID)**'s Conflict Assessment Framework in chapter 3. Both saw their role grow dramatically after 9/11.

USIP has not grown dramatically in size, although it has gotten a spectacular permanent home, a photograph of which is on page 117. Its congressionally funded budget of about $40 million a year is but a tiny fraction of the State Department's, let alone the Pentagon's. Republican legislators have periodically targeted it for elimination. Yet, USIP survives as one of the few places in Washington where liberals and conservatives work together on foreign policy.

In fact, that may be its most important function. It makes the news when it hosts foreign dignitaries or publishes insightful books and articles, including the first versions of the diagram that begins chapter 3. But its real impact lies primarily with its ongoing working groups and the projects they have sponsored.

Over the years, it has created teams that focus on gender, economics and peace, the role of the military, technology, and more. It isn't just the working groups themselves. In addition, people meet each other and forge relationships that carry over into activities that USIP has no role in whatsoever, including some of the work with the military which I will describe in a few paragraphs. It has even spun off a new nonprofit, the **PeaceTech Lab**, which resembles a high-tech start-up more than a peacebuilding NGO.

USAID exists to promote economic development in the Global South. Much like Steve Killelea's reasoning in creating the Global Peace Index, USAID planners realized that its funding was being lost because the schools, hospitals, and other facilities it built were destroyed in the fighting. As a result, it started hiring consultants and staff members who gradually integrated conflict resolution into its efforts, as you saw in the second version of its Conflict Assessment Framework (figure 3.4). Beginning with the Clinton administration, USAID has dramatically increased its funding of and organizational capacity for preventing conflict and intervening if prevention fails. Even under the Trump administration, much of that work has continued.

Conflict resolution and peacebuilding have also gained a toehold in the State Department. In this case, the impetus came during the George W. Bush administration at the height of the debate about the war in Iraq. On December 7, 2005, the White House issued **National Security Presidential Directive 44 (NSPD 44)**, which began:

> The purpose of this Directive is to promote the security of the United States through improved coordination, planning, and implementation for reconstruction and stabilization assistance for foreign states and regions at risk of, in, or in transition from conflict or civil strife.[1]

The Directive created a unit that is now known as the Conflict and Stabilization Office, which ostensibly coordinates all US government efforts along these lines. I used the term *ostensibly* in the previous sentence because CSO lacks the staff, funding, or power to actually "improve coordination, planning, and implementation for reconstruction and stabilization assistance." But, as with Directive 3000.05, which I will be discussing next, it is a significant—if largely symbolic—step in our direction.

It is impossible to make the case that American foreign policy has changed all that much. But we do have a seat at the grown-ups' table whenever USAID or CSO is involved.

The military. Because so many of us became peacebuilders because of our opposition to war, we rarely thought of the military as a potential partner before 9/11. Now, we routinely work with current and retired military officers and enlisted personnel in ways that continue to amaze me and suggest just how fast the scope of peacebuilding and conflict resolution is changing.

To some degree, we have become more sanguine about the military. As noted frequently in part 3, it is hard for peacebuilding NGOs to operate in the middle of a conflict zone while the fighting is going on. To be effective, we need a modicum of physical security, which is typically provided by the military and law enforcement personnel.

Far more importantly, many members of the military have changed their own positions. I first sensed that one day fifteen years ago when I was walking from one meeting to another with an army colonel who had just finished a tour of duty identifying the remains of soldiers killed in Vietnam nearly forty years earlier. Before that, he had been deployed in Iraq during the early stages of the invasion. So I was surprised when he put his arm around my shoulders and said words that came as such a surprise that I remember them verbatim:

> Chip. You will find your strongest supporters among soldiers and their families. We've been there. We've done it. We don't want to do it again.

We were heading to a meeting with assistant secretary of defense Linton Wells, who was writing **Department of Defense Directive 3000.05**, although I did not know that he was working on something that momentous at the time. When it was issued a week before NSPD 44, it declared that:

> stability operations are a core U.S. military mission that the Department of Defense shall be prepared to conduct and support. They shall be given priority comparable to combat operations and be explicitly addressed and integrated across all DoD activities including doctrine, organizations, training, education, exercises, materiel, leadership, personnel, facilities, and planning.[2]

I happened to be in the Pentagon the day it was issued for an appointment with Wells. He had warned me that something was afoot, although I did not know that he was actually working on something this dramatic. Until that moment, I never expected that the Bush administration would issue an official document declaring that the kinds of activities covered in this directive and NSPD 44 should "be given priority comparable to combat operations and be explicitly addressed and integrated across all DoD activities." If anything, subsequent versions of the Directive have gone further, in particular noting that the Department of State must take the lead in all prevention and reconstruction efforts.

No one who pays even the slightest attention to the news would argue that the American military has turned into a group of pacifists! Even my closest military friends—like the colonel quoted above—are prepared to fight, kill, and die if necessary. However, thinking within the military has clearly begun to shift.

AfP staff members are now routinely invited to trainings and to make presentations at military "schoolhouses" where troops get the equivalent of a civilian's continuing education. A team we led wrote a handbook on human security training which is being used both by faculty at those schoolhouses and at NGO training sessions. I have personally been to West Point, the Air Force Academy, the Army and Navy War Colleges, Marine Corps headquarters, and Fort Polk, where all deploying soldiers go through simulated wartime exercises. Every time I make a presentation, I'm treated with respect, and my words are taken seriously.

This is one of many places in this book's narrative at which I don't want to overstate my case. A mere glance at today's news will show you that the world's militaries still spend most of their time either fighting or preparing to fight. Still, the fact that professional peacebuilders and professional soldiers can find any common ground is a testament to the fact that we can build unusual coalitions and find strange political bedfellows.

The Overton Window and Violent Extremism

The last point about the US is the hardest one to make with any degree of precision. Nonetheless, it may be the most important.

When discussing their successes since the days of leaders like Ronald Reagan and Margaret Thatcher, conservative analysts focus on the ways that they have shifted what they call the **Overton Window** in their direction. Joseph Overton was a policy analyst at the libertarian leaning Mackinac Center for Public Policy in Michigan before he died in an ultralight aircraft accident at the age of forty-three in 2003. His legacy lives on in the "window" that bears his name in which he suggested that the libertarians had succeeded in shifting elite and public opinion to such an extent that free-market related policies that had once been outside of the mainstream were now squarely on the public policy agenda.

The conflict resolution and peacebuilding committees have moved their version of the Overton Window, too. As you are about to see, policy proposals that would have seemed absurdly idealistic in the days of Peacebuilding 1.0 or 2.0 are now plausible.

In other words, we may not be able to point to many concrete policy victories on specific issues. It is clear, however, that the men and women who sit at the grown-ups' table take the kinds of ideas we promote in Peacebuilding 3.0 far more seriously than they ever did before 9/11. We may not have a place at that table when formal policy is made. But we are often consulted beforehand. Perhaps more importantly, some of the people with "permanent" seats at the table have begun to share at least some of our perspectives on some key issues.

The easiest way to see the Overton Window in practice is to consider American policy toward violent extremism. If you could transport yourself back in time to the early 2000s, policy-making discussions would have assumed that Muslims were the only community we had to worry about and that we had to meet force with force that was applied by both our military abroad and law enforcement at home. The best way to treat extremists we captured was harsh punishment. The most lenient approaches involved trying to "deradicalize" them.

Now, as the 2010s draw to a close, just about everyone understands that violent extremism is not a Muslim problem. In fact, most terrorist acts in the US are now carried out by white supremacists and other members of the alt-right. Similarly, the peacebuilding community has led successful efforts to convince at least a few conservative policy makers that we cannot eliminate the terrorist threat until we address its "drivers," which lie in the causes of structural violence that have played such an important role in this book so far.

I am not trying to make the case that there has been a sea change in American public policy in these respects. Many decision makers still see these issues in essentially the same way they did in 2001. Nonetheless, the Overton Window has moved in directions most conflict resolution and peacebuilders would appreciate. Public policy itself is beginning to follow in its wake.

Adding Up to Peace II: The Other Democracies

While only time will tell if the initiatives discussed in the previous section will last or reach the potential I see in them, we can at least take solace in the fact that similar changes are taking place in the other industrialized democracies, some of which have gone a lot further than the US. The clearest example lies in funding as reflected in table 12.1, which provides data for official peacebuilding spending in 2016, the last year for which all the data were available.

Overall, the world's governments spent $3.4 billion on peacebuilding that year, a point we will return to in the next section. Of that total, the US contributed about $300 million, a figure that has probably declined a bit since then. That was slightly more than the EU's expenditure but was dwarfed by the funds provided by its member states, including the UK and Germany, which each outspent the US.

Canada and the UK both have offices akin to the State Department's CSO. Germany's foreign ministry officially supports Track I and Track II diplomacy. Other militaries have obviously found it easier to take on tasks that that do not involve combat operations, especially Canada and the Scandinavian countries whose militaries have done little but peacekeeping for the last fifty years.

There is one key area in which a handful of other democracies have moved in directions that have not come close to entering the Overton Window in the US. Attentive readers may have noticed the relative absence of gender-related

TABLE 12.1 | State Spending on Peacebuilding, 2016

Country	Expenditure in millions USD
United States	299
Germany	483
United Kingdom	338
European Union	251
Worldwide total	3,400

Source: Adapted from ECDPM, "Supporting Peacebuilding in Times of Change," https://ecdpm.org/publications/supporting-peacebuilding-change-europe/.

themes in this book so far. That is particularly surprising in a field whose professional ranks have always had more women than men. Nonetheless, it has only been in the last few years that mainstream conflict resolution and peacebuilding professionals have been addressing the field's issues through a gendered lens.

That began with the UN Security Council's adoption of **Resolution 1325** in 2000. It committed the UN to including a focus on women in all of its conflict resolution and development projects. The UN's offices were also expected to include more women on their staffs and to include what it called a gender perspective in all of its reports and in the trainings it did for NGOs and others in the field.

As is the case with most of the official policy initiatives discussed in this chapter, Resolution 1325 has been honored in the breach. Still, Seventy-nine countries have adopted some gendered foreign policy provisions since Resolution 1325 was signed, including the United States.

Of them, Sweden has led the way in defining and implementing what it calls a **feminist foreign policy** which it first adopted in 2014. It commits the government to enhancing the representation and role of women everywhere from the parliament to the country's development initiatives, the bureaucracy, and even the corporate board room, which means that the policy extends far beyond peacebuilding.

Since the election of Prime Minister Justin Trudeau in 2015, Canada has followed closely in Sweden's footsteps by adopting a feminist international aid policy. Australia, the UK, and the US all have appointed enjoys at the ambassadorial level who focus on women's issues involving peacebuilding and more.

The most progress has been made in the use of ADR-like practices in governments' internal workings. Japan, Australia, New Zealand, the Western European countries, Canada, and the US all have created mediation and arbitration offices for handling disputes both in their legal systems and in the internal workings of their government agencies.

In the US, state courts began adopting alternative dispute resolution systems as early as the late 1970s because they cost less and often left fewer lasting scars than litigation on family and other matters. Early in President William Clinton's administration, legislation was passed establishing dispute resolution services in every federal agency and instructed them to use ADR procedures to settle internal disputes.

It is hard to tell if the US is ahead of or behind the other industrialized democracies as far as adopting these procedures is concerned because its political system is so fragmented both within Washington and between the national, state, and federal levels. As a result, it is easier to see some of these principles in other countries that have more centralized states and therefore more uniform practices and procedures.

John Major's conservative government asked Harry Woolf, then the Lord Chief Justice of England and Wales, to chair a commission on ADR during the mid-1990s. Its report triggered the widespread adoption of ADR techniques in many areas of the British legal system. All small claims court cases that involve a sum of less than £10,000 (about $13,000) must go to mediation before they can be scheduled for trial. The government has also created a national mediation hotline to help parties to a dispute locate ADR service providers. In the 2010s, while British governments have faced ever tightening budgets, political leaders have promoted the financial benefits of ADR, estimating that its use saves the taxpayer about £400 million ($500 million) a year.

The use of ADR procedures was given a boost when the EU issued a directive in 2008 that forced all of its member states to adopt and/or strengthen existing ADR offices. In this case, Germany took the lead by completely rewriting its national mediation laws, extending the use of ADR into some criminal proceedings.

There have, of course, been laggards. France, in particular, has been slow to adopt mediation, in part given the structure of its highly centralized legal system, in which the roles of judge and prosecutor are frequently mixed. That said, France is also the global hub of international arbitration in which an official chooses between proposals made by the two sides to a dispute. Because arbitration does not involve third-party neutrals in the way that mediation does, it often is left out of courses on conflict resolution. However, others include it in ADR because it limits the adversarial nature of a dispute.

In concluding this section, note that these offices and procedures emphasize transactional rather than transformational conflict resolution and thus may not seem all that interesting if you were drawn to this field out of a desire to change the world. Still, it is hard to deny the fact that these kinds of legal and other bureaucratic procedures have helped give ADR and ideas like win-win unprecedented visibility and credibility.

THE GLOBAL DIMENSION

Last—but increasingly not least—is the **international community**. As you saw in chapter 9 the international agencies had already began to play a major role in peacebuilding during the 1990s. While the new political pressures of the twenty-first century have hamstrung all of them, it is safe to say that they have had a growing and constructive impact that extends to real policy as well as to moving its version of the Overton Window.

Limited Resources

Before turning to that growing involvement, I should temper your enthusiasm with some sobering statistics that reinforce the point I made with table 12.1. As you saw there, global spending on peacebuilding reached about $3.4 billion in 2016. Private foundations spend about $400 million more. In all likelihood, other sources contributed about another billion dollars bringing total global spending on peacebuilding to about $5 billion a year.

Five billion dollars is also the annual budget for United Nations' regular expenditures, although it is able to raise money from members states for special purposes, including some of its peace operations. The UN's peacekeeping efforts did have a budget of almost $7 billion for the fiscal year that began in July 2018. However, that only goes for the kinds of stabilization efforts discussed in part 3, and, as you will soon see, that does not include state-of-the-art peacebuilding activities.

Five billion dollars may seem like a lot of money. Before you reach that conclusion, contrast that figure along with a few others. The best estimate is that the total annual expenditure on the military and defense amounts to $1.7 trillion or more than three hundred times what is spent each year on peacebuilding projects. Even development assistance is better funded, with about $150 billion a year coming from governmental sources alone. Shifting away from statistics on spending, two hundred million people were in need of humanitarian assistance, while sixty million people have either been forced into exile or live in internally displaced persons camps as de facto refugees within the borders of their home countries.

To put this in perspective, Wyoming is the least populated American state with under six hundred thousand residents. Its annual budget routinely tops $10 billion which is far more than the most liberal definition yields for the UN's commitment to peacebuilding.

The United Nations Family

Add to that the fact that international institutions are not always held in high regard. The realists among international relations scholars have long argued that the UN, the EU, and the other intergovernmental organizations (IGOs) remain all but powerless because they lack a military and other coercive tools that would allow them to implement their policies. At the other end of the spectrum, many conservatives argue that these international governmental institutions have too much power that should properly reside with nation-states, something we have seen plenty of in recent years with the renewed interest in nationalism and **populism** in Europe and North America.

In fact, both of these criticisms are overstated. As you are about to see, these institutions have gained some ability to deal with the world's conflicts and overcome at least some of the realists' doubts. At the same time, there are few signs that they will become powerful enough that they can compel most governments to act against what they perceive to be their national interests.

Peacekeeping. At the end of 2018, the UN operated fourteen peacekeeping missions. Some of them antedate the time period covered in part 4, like the one located in the Green Zone separating the Turkish northern half of Cyprus from the overwhelmingly Greek southern half of the island. It is hard to argue that these decades old missions are no longer needed, but it is also hard to make the case that they are doing a lot to keep the peace either.

About half of the current peacekeeping missions were begun after the 9/11 attacks, and all have been deployed to active combat zones. A single example should illustrate the ways in which they are—and are not—effective.

On July 9, 2011, South Sudan became the newest UN member state when it was granted its independence from Sudan after a long and bloody civil war. On the day before, the Security Council authorized the creation of UNMISS (United Nations Mission in South Sudan) because everyone knew that the new country was not going to get off to a smooth start. Not only did it face hostile neighbors, but its own leaders were deeply divided and those disagreement turned violent within a matter of months. Once those hostilities turned into an full-blown civil war in December 2013, the Council expanded UNMISS's mandate to include the protection of civilians and of humanitarian workers who tried to deliver aid to the region.

In late 2018, UNMISS had about sixteen thousand soldiers and police officers, about half of whom came from Rwanda, India, Ethiopia, and Nepal. At best, its track record has been mixed, but we do not know what the situation would have been like had the force not been there. In all likelihood, things would have been far worse.

The UN forces were hindered by their terms of engagement. In other words, they are only allowed to use their weapons if they are fired on first. Even then, there were limits placed on how much force they could use. As a result, UNMISS has not been able to stop the fighting between rival South Sudanese factions that has continued in an on and off fashion literally since independence day. The UN has undoubtedly saved quite a few civilian lives by creating camps for internally displaced Sudanese who might have been killed otherwise. Nonetheless, even those camps have been subject to attacks, and violence and accidents have claimed the lives of several dozen UN personnel.

Peacebuilding. The UN created a **Peace Building Commission** in 2005 which could become a major player in the not so distant future, although it represents little more than a shift in the UN's Overton Window for now.

Unlike many of the world's political leaders, the UN's permanent staff has taken much of what this book has covered to heart. In its core document, the UN's Peacebuilding Office lays out an agenda that is so similar to what we've seen so far in part 4 that we can deal with it in a single paragraph. Its staff members understand peacebuilding, conflict prevention, and postconflict reconciliation in the same basic ways that Michael Lund or the architects of USAID's CAF do. It also understands that peacebuilding efforts have to be locally run, while the UN staff and other outsiders have to practice the kind of cultural sensitivity that Lederach was committed to in Nepal. The office has been able to intervene in a number of the world's hot spots, including South Sudan, the Central African Republic, Guatemala, Bosnia, and Timor-Leste. Its staff has also convincingly made the case that peacebuilding efforts aimed at prevention cost a lot less than sending in the blue helmets.

There is, however, a huge problem here. The Peacebuilding Office does not have the funds it needs. Unlike traditional peacekeeping operations, its operations cannot be funded out of the UN's regular budget. Instead, the Secretary General and Security Council have to ask for supplemental appropriations from the individual member states. More often than not, their governments have refused to grant the PBO the money it asks for. In short, there have been times when relatively inexpensive prevention programs in countries like the Central African Republic were not funded only to find that the UN later had to send in far more expensive peacekeeping troops who had to cope with a more complicated and dangerous situation. What's more, UN spending on peacebuilding is likely to go down in the near future if the US continues to reduce its UN contribution, which amounts to more than one-fourth of what the international body spends in these areas.

Terrorism and other new threats. The same internal disagreements have limited the UN's ability to adopt programs that could address the terrorist threat. Given its charter, it is hard for the UN to act if it is perceived to be violating the national sovereignty of a member state unless that state has invited it in. Those restrictions have been reduced to some degree with the adoption of the R2P provisions discussed in chapter 9, but the fact of the matter is that the UN is not likely to act decisively if even one reasonably powerful member state is involved and objects to its intervention.

In addition, the US and other countries have largely ignored the UN in their plans to combat terrorist groups. Because they assumed that a strong show of military force would be needed to defeat terrorism, there was little place for the UN in their planning for the very reasons that the realists properly raise.

More generally, decisive action by the UN remains elusive because the Security Council normally requires the unanimous agreement of the five permanent members before it can do anything. And, whenever Israel, Syria, Iran, or any of the world's other major hot spots in recent years, the threat or the reality of a veto by one or more of them has normally kept the UN on the sidelines.

The SDGs and *Pathways to Peace*. Far more important was the UN's 2015 adoption of the **Sustainable Development Goals (SDGs)** and of the Millennium Challenge Goals (MCGs) fifteen years earlier. They marked the first two times that the international community laid out a reasonably integrated set of plans that would guide development strategy for an extended period of time.

Many of my colleagues were disappointed by the omission of peacebuilding from the MDGs. Still, the UN and international community as a whole did go a long way toward reaching those goals, which included a sharp reduction in the number of people in absolute poverty who suffered from the ill-health and other problems that go along with it.

Although progress on the Millennium Development Goals was mixed, the UN community decided to take on an even more ambitious set of targets for the fifteen years after the period dedicated to reaching the MCGs came to an end. Because the SDGs marked such a major step forward for the UN, we will concentrate on them here.

That starts with the fact that the SDGs broke with UN tradition by including peace in its list of seventeen overarching goals and came up with a number of specific targets to measure progress toward meeting each of them.

Their authors also understood that development had to be understood as an integrated process. To be sure, both its definition of human security in the 1990s and the MDGs later in the decade worked on the assumption that you could not separate any one aspect of development policy from the rest. To cite but one example, one could not improve overall standards of living in a community that was characterized by gender discrimination, environmental decay, or, of course, ongoing violence.

Last but by no means least, the SDGs made it clear that development and its correlates were everybody's problems. All countries fell short on more than one of the SDGs. And in an acknowledgment of the interconnectedness of life, they minced no words. Rich countries as well as poor ones had a vested interest in seeing the entire world develop. Although it got less attention than the rest of the SDGs, its authors made it clear that the rich countries also had plenty of problems of their own, which also have to be addressed before they can talk about sustainable development at home.

Finally, the SDGs opened the door to a new partnership with the **World Bank**, which culminated in the unprecedented publication of a joint report, *Pathways to Peace*, which I discussed earlier. Although the World Bank agreed to become part of the UN "family" in 1947, each organization worked largely on its own until the SDGs were signed. At that point, the leaders of the Peacebuilding Support Office and other UN agencies along with the Bank's Fragility, Conflict, and Violence unit, realized that they had to work together since they both had to deal with the consequences of the upsurge in political violence during the second decade of this century.

Over the course of the next two years, their researchers worked with thought leaders from the world's leading political and economic think tanks to address a problem they saw growing out of the SDGs. They could not be reached without paying even more attention to the effects of conflict. The end result was their joint report, the importance of which can perhaps best be seen in its subtitle—inclusive approaches to preventing armed conflict.

The report is important here both because peacebuilding researchers played a major role in drafting it and because it points the two organizations and many others in new and promising directions. Most of its themes had already been raised by some of the more intellectually sophisticated NGOs. What matters here, however, is the fact that the report was issued by two staid institutions that have never been known as risk takers. Yet, that is exactly what the report commits them—and the governments and NGOs they fund—to doing.

That starts with the fact that the report is anchored in the kind of systems and complexity theories that have been at the heart of part 4. That alone gave credibility to some of the concepts that only the most intellectually precocious peacebuilders had used beforehand, including:

- Solutions emerge from the experience of local peacebuilders who lead their own projects with advice coming from outsiders, as we saw with John Paul Lederach's involvement in Nepal in chapter 11.
- Whoever runs a project has to do so in ways that address the root causes of conflict as they play themselves out in the complex series of feedback loops they are a part of.
- Those projects also have to find leverage points that can turn dysfunctional vicious cycles into virtuous circles in which feedback helps systems grow rather than deteriorate.

Even more importantly, the report's authors set out to shift what they believed is an important imbalance in the way that the international community envisions peacebuilding. Prior to its publication, most government officials and NGO leaders had only paid lip service to the idea that we would all be better off if we prevented conflict from turning violent in the first place.

In practice, however, most of our efforts were focused on postconflict reconstruction because that was what funders were willing to pay for. Our rhetoric may have given equal importance to the two ends of the conflict mapping curve at the beginning of chapter 3. Most of our experience—and therefore most of our expertise—resulted from work done after the fighting stopped.

Michael Lund, who first created that curve twenty years ago advised *Pathways to Peace*'s research team. In particular, he helped them see that preventive conflict resolution could have the same effect as preventive medicine. It might stop the conflict (or disease) from breaking out in the first place. Even if it failed, preventive efforts could keep the conflict from escalating out of control, leading the report's authors to envision future conflicts having a less disruptive—and dangerous—impact.

Even though we did not have as much experience in preventing conflict, the report also suggests that the very tools laid out in the list of SDGs and the indicators the UN would be using to measure progress also lent themselves to practical work in conflict prevention. That is where the "inclusive approaches" of their subtitle comes into play. Although the evidence on this front is limited, the UN and the World Bank's researchers did marshal what data they could find and developed simulations that showed that inclusive approaches to problem solving were likely to reduce the severity of conflict that takes place in transitional societies.

Other International Bodies

As you also saw in part 3, other international intergovernmental organizations played a role in Peacebuilding 2.0. Most of them have stepped up their role in the last twenty years as well.

International Financial Institutions. At the end of World War II, the estern allies also created three economic organizations, the World Bank, the **International Monetary Fund (IMF)**, and the Global Agreement on Tariffs and Trade (now the **World Trade Organization**). All have played a role in most areas of global economic life and been the recipient of plenty of criticism over the years. The IMF, in particular, is often blamed for much of today's growing inequality and for the solidification of what is often referred to as the neoliberal or neo-imperialistic world order. Similarly, the WTO focuses on trade disputes and reducing barriers to the global exchange of goods and services. Oddly enough, its decisions and even the issues it deals with have rarely made it into the most recent wave of engagements by the peacebuilding community.

For the purposes of this book, the key is the World Bank. One should never lose sight of the fact that it is a bank whose primary concern is economic development in poor countries in the Global South and the former communist world. As such, it is firmly part of the capitalist power structure.

However, as you have just seen, it recently became a strong supporter of conflict resolution and peacebuilding. Its professional staff members have seen the way that violence and conflict in general have stood in the way of rapid economic development in country after country where the Bank has made investments over the years. As a result, its economists and other professional staff members have spent much of this century exploring the relationship between economic development and peace, which culminated in the 2011 publication of its annual *World Development Report* and the recent joint report with the UN.

Regional organizations. The world has also seen the creation of a number of regional governments and security alliances since 1945. None of these come close to having the power of a conventional national government. However, some like NATO, the EU, the Organization of American States, and the African Union have begun to have an impact on peace issues.

The EU and NATO have even been willing to exert their influence beyond their collective borders. Together, they are in the process of developing a rapid deployment force that could intervene to stop fighting and begin peacekeeping and peacemaking operations anywhere in the world. Elsewhere, these institutions have taken important steps to address conflict that occurs throughout their region with the African Union having the widest-ranging impact.

For instance, its troops have been deployed in Somalia since 2007 in an attempt to both maintain the fragile ceasefire among its warlords and use more traditional military means in its so far failed attempt to destroy al-Shabab.

NGOs. We cannot leave NGOs themselves out of this discussion for two reasons. First, they have tried to influence policy making at the international as well as the national level. Second, in the eyes of some, however, they have become part of the problem, especially as bulwarks of the liberal peace.

The NGOs' policy-making role is new on both fronts. In the late twentieth century, the global NGOs largely stayed out of policy debates about world peace. The large ones like World Vision or CARE argued that they only dealt with development and humanitarian issues—not war and peace. Many of the smaller but growing peacebuilding organizations valued their position as third party neutrals, in particular because they were working in countries and on issues that were quite different from the ones they worried about back home, wherever home happened to be.

That began to change after 9/11. More and more NGO leaders came to realize that they could not separate peacebuilding from economics, gender, public health, and the other issues they had considered separately before.

There was no single incident that marked that change. However, if you had to focus on one that had a disproportionate and visible effect it would have been the tsunami that hit much of South and Southeast Asia on December 26, 2004.

To be sure, its size and devastation were both unprecedented. More central for our purposes, it struck in a number of conflict zones in poor parts of the region, none of which was more important here than the Indonesian province of Aceh. Like many other regions that were hit by the tsunami, much of coastal Aceh was destroyed. The region was also home to the GAM Muslim guerilla force that had been fighting against the Indonesian government since the 1970s. Despite a number of conflict resolution initiatives that had been undertaken over the years, little progress had been made until the earthquake and tsunami hit.

At that point, a number of unusual things happened. Despite its preoccupation with the wars in Afghanistan and Iraq, the US sent an aircraft carrier flotilla on an aid mission during which military and NGO personnel realized that they had a common purpose at least on humanitarian issues. More importantly, the shock provided by all the destruction led both the rebels and the leaders in Jakarta to reconsider their position. Within a year, a peace agreement had been reached which has largely held ever since.

More generally, NGOs increasingly realized that they had little choice but to become advocates for more congenial public policies (at least in their eyes) in all the venues they worked in, including their home countries, the international organizations.

The same held true for some multinational corporations. They, too, now understand that they cannot do business without considering the direct and indirect impacts of their actions on conflicts in the countries or regions in which they operate. Many, too came to see that it was also in their economic interests to be seen as playing a constructive role in developmental, humanitarian, and environmental affairs, which ultimately led a smaller subset of them to realize that their **corporate social responsibility** efforts had to be extended to conflict resolution as well.

MEASURING IMPACT

I have shied away from discussing research methodology in this book, but this is one point at which it is important to see why peace and conflict studies researchers do what they do. In this case, it will help you see both why we have been making progress and that we have done so by not pursuing what Thomas Kuhn calls normal science as defined in chapter 2.

Recall that normal science is the norm when a field has a clear paradigm that everyone accepts. At that point, it makes sense to test hypotheses using tools like randomized control trials whose origins lie in the modern natural sciences that often do have such a paradigm.

Peace and conflict studies is a new field and has not yet reached that kind of maturity. In scientific terms, we are still in the theory-building stage. Under these circumstances, the kind of inductive tools I introduced in part 1 make more sense. That's the case because our goal is to create new hypotheses or paradigms that could then be subjected to traditional scientific research.

Things have begun to change on this front.

Conflict resolution and peacebuilding professionals now have to pay more attention to the impact of their work—or the lack thereof. Like anyone else, we have always wanted it to be as effective as possible. In practice, it took pressure from two groups of outsiders to get us to pay serious attention to whether our projects and programs worked or not.

The first outside pressure came from our funders who, not surprisingly, wanted to make certain that the several billion dollars a year that go toward conflict resolution was money well spent. A few major donors, including the Hewlett Foundation, indeed, did decide that their money could be better spent elsewhere. Others continued to fund conflict resolution and peacebuilding but began insisting that we measure just how effective our efforts were.

Even more important were the critics who were not about to change their minds and support conflict resolution and peacebuilding policies unless and until they were presented with incontrovertible evidence that "it" works. To some degree, we will never be able to satisfy their concerns, especially when the demand for evidence is really a smokescreen for ideological opposition to our work. Enough of those critics, however, were open to being convinced that many of us decided to focus on **monitoring and evaluation** or measuring how much of a difference we were making.

This work is often very technical and filled with debates over which research methodologies are most appropriate. Little of that adds value to an introductory course. However, it is important for you to see how we have responded to the critics, if for no other reason than this is one of the areas in which the most entry level jobs are to be found.

In 2010, AfP, the United States Institute of Peace, and others began systematically assessing what we have accomplished. In the last ten years, other government agencies and foundations who fund projects in the field have built monitoring and evaluation consortiums around the world on our work in general and on projects with an explicitly faith-based perspective.

By the time I wrote these lines, all of the major peacebuilding and conflict resolution organizations had accepted the fact that they have to evaluate their work and learn from what went wrong as well as what went well. Most now include funds for conducting that kind of research in their budgets, and both AfP and GPPAC regularly advise their members on best practices in learning and evaluation.

The GHR Foundation asked a consortium led by AfP to specifically examine the impact of religiously based peacebuilding which is one of its top funding priorities. The mostly small NGOs it supports had rarely thought about measuring their impact, and we have used GHR's funds to develop tools for that faith-based community and to provide seed funding to some of those NGOs who want to develop evaluation programs.

In the process, we have learned that measuring the impact of any peacebuilding program is easier said than done. Few projects start with clear baseline measures about conditions before the project began making it impossible to determine how big (or small) an impact it had. It is rarely possible, let alone ethically acceptable, to do the kind of randomized control trials that have become the gold standard for measuring success. We also discovered one key way in which not having a paradigm slows progress in all areas of the field. Because we do not have a common point of departure, let alone an agreed on set of tools for conducting and evaluating our work, it is very hard to compare projects undertaken by two different organizations, let alone the dozens of initiatives that are being conducted in a single country at a given moment in time. Among other things, that means that it is all but impossible to do the kinds of meta-analyses that combine the data from dozens of studies that have paved the way to progress in dozens of other disciplines.

Nonetheless, progress has been made on at least two fronts.

First, there is all but universal agreement that individual projects have to be rigorously evaluated from start to finish. That starts with the way they are designed. That leads us to choose projects so that they meet an existing need *and* add to what we already know which is a pair of criteria any scientist asks when designing a research experiment. Data has to be collected in such a way that results from your project can be compared with those from mine so that we actually learn from each other.

Second, those results have to be combined into an **evidence-based** statement about what works—and what doesn't. It probably is true that neither our funders nor our critics will be completely persuaded by data that shows that we have had an impact. On thing is clear, however. They are not going to do so in the absence of that kind of evidence.

PEACEBUILDING 4.0? TOWARD A MOVEMENT

This chapter started on a pessimistic note for good reason.

When it comes to having a noticeable and regular impact on public policy making regarding peace and conflict–related issues, we undoubtedly fall far short of our own expectations. However, my goal in this chapter and in part 4 in general has been to document just how much progress we *have* made.

That said, the trajectory we are currently on is not likely to get us where we want to go, which might require moving to Peacebuilding 4.0. As you have seen, we moved from Peacebuilding 1.0 to 2.0 to 3.0 in the wake of a dramatic and unexpected event that set us back to the clichéd drawing board.

This time, we can make the transition without experiencing any such cataclysmic event because many of us understand that something new and bigger has to come next. Until now, we have largely built peace and conflict studies and the real-world initiatives discussed in the first nine chapters of this book largely by working within our own **silo**.

When business or public policy executives use the term silo, they obviously are not referring to those large, cylindrically shaped towers that are used to store grain, let alone those underground pits where intercontinental range missiles are stored in the hope that they never get used. In this case, silo is a (usually) pejorative terms that describes the reluctance to work outside of our normal professional or commercial community and the comfort zone that comes with it.

To be fair, we have expanded our silo quite a bit, as you have seen several times already. Still, we have largely talked to individuals and organizations that were already heavily and professionally engaged with the kinds of conflicts we were dealing with. Now, it is time to spread our networks far more broadly and build the kinds of popular movements that will not only get us to the grown-ups' table but that will also produce profound changes in the ways that we all deal with conflict.

That's how I will end *From Conflict Resolution to Peacebuilding*.

KEY TERMS

Concepts

bright spot, 276
community policing, 285
corporate social responsibility, 301
cumulative strategy, 282
evidence-based, 303
feminist foreign policy, 294
grass tops, 284
insider partial, 282
international community, 295
monitoring and evaluation, 302
naming and shaming, 277
OODA loop, 283
Overton Window, 292
perspective taking, 277
populism, 296
silo, 303
Sustainable Development Goals (SDGs), 298

People

Anderson, Mary, 277
Christensen, Clayton, 279
Kamil, Muferiat, 278

Organizations, Places, and Events

Black Lives Matter, 285
Cure Violence, 286
Department of Defense Directive 3000.05, 291
Dialogue with the City, 288
Divided Communities Project, 286
International Monetary Fund (IMF), 300
National Security Presidential Directive 44 (NSPD 44), 290
Orlando Speaks, 286
Peace Building Commission, 297
PeaceTech Lab, 290
Resolution 1325, 294
Strong Cities Network, 287
United States Institute of Peace (USIP), 290
US Agency for International Development (USAID), 290
World Bank, 298
World Trade Organization, 300

DIG DEEPER

Brounéus, Karen. *Truth and Reconciliation Processes: Learning from the Solomon Islands*. Lanham, MD: Rowman and Littlefield, 2019. This short book (the Solomon Islands are a small country, after all) explores the potentials and pitfalls of truth and reconciliation commissions.

Chigas, Diana, and Peter Woodrow. *Adding Up to Peace: The Cumulative Impacts of Peace Processes*. Boston: CDA, 2019. The best systematic analysis of taking peacebuilding to scale.

Cortright, David, Conor Selye, and Kristin Wall. *Governance for Peace: How Inclusive, Participatory, and Accountable Institutions Promote Peace and Prosperity*. New York: Cambridge University Press, 2018. The only book to review the literature on everything its title suggests.

Richmond, Oliver. *Peace: A Very Short Introduction*. New York: Oxford University Press, 2014. Puts the liberal peace in a policy-making context.

UN/World Bank. *Pathways to Peace*. www.worldbank.org/en/topic/fragilityconflictviolence/publication/pathways-for-peace-inclusive-approaches-to-preventing-violent-conflict. The best book-length analysis of the state of peacebuilding policy today.

NOTES

[1] https://fas.org/irp/offdocs/nspd/nspd-44.html.

[2] http://faculty.nps.edu/dl/hfn/documents/DoD_Directive_d300005p.pdf.

PEACEBUILDING 4.0?

(With Bethany Gen and Nora Malatinszky)

Next Gen Peacebuilding

THINK ABOUT IT

There are three overarching issues to think about while reading these final two chapters.

- When Nik Gowing and Chris Langdon use the phrase *thinking the unthinkable*, they urge us to think about a future that many us find so unpalatable that we prefer to shy away from thinking about it altogether. Here, I want you to think about a far more pleasant future and how we might get there.
- Donald Rumsfeld's categories do lend themselves to bewilderment and bemusement. You should also take them seriously, especially the unknowns in our future. How do you prepare yourself, your community, and the planet as a whole for them?
- The Conflict Lab at the end of this chapter will ask you to design social movements to build support for solutions to the two conflicts you have been working on since chapter 1. It's a good idea to begin thinking in these terms now.

CORE CONCEPTS

black swan—following Naseem Nicholas Taleb, an unlikely even that forces us to rethink some previously unspoken assumptions

known unknowns—Donald Rumsfeld's notion that there are future trends that we can predict, although we may not be able to predict specific events

mind-set—a social psychological term used to describe one's personal paradigm

movement—a formal or informal group that promotes one or more social causes

paradigm—a scientific theory or other all-encompassing mind-set that covers an entire field

unknown unknowns—Donald Rumsfeld's notion that there are some utterly unpredictable events in the future that will shake us up

Most of the things worth doing in the world had been declared impossible before they were started.

—Louis D. Brandeis

People are very open-minded about new things—as long as they're exactly like the old ones.

—Charles Kettering

IN THE FIRST SENTENCE OF THIS BOOK, I told you that I wanted to make it unusual, interesting, challenging, and empowering.

So far, I have tried to emphasize its intellectual challenges in ways that I hope were interesting and unusual.

Now, I want to focus on aspects of that statement that I have largely kept on the back burner since that first paragraph—the practical challenges, which I hope can be as empowering for you as they have been for me. I emphasized the words intellectual and practical because I will be shifting gears once again. This time, I will turn your attention away from an emphasis on intellectual explanations of how and why the field of peace and conflict studies has evolved toward discussions of where it could and should be heading.

In so doing, I will also have to be more speculative than I have been so far. However, I intend to be speculative in a practical way by focusing on concrete steps that we could take in this chapter and then the ones that you could take to find your place in the next generation of conflict resolution and peacebuilding in the final one.

That starts with a dilemma non-fiction authors face. Most of us have a harder time ending our books than novelists do. To see why, think about the last novel you read or movie you saw. Typically, they end when the author ties together all the loose ends and resolves whatever conflict he or she was dealing with.

Some mystery novels I read do have a concluding chapter in which the characters talk about what happened. Some movies and novels lay the groundwork for the sequels to come. But, basically, a work of fiction has what screenwriters call a story arc that runs from the beginning to the (hopefully) climactic conclusion.

Think now about nonfiction books you've read recently. The climax usually comes a bit before the end. Authors then use the conclusion to recap the case they have been making throughout the book. Academics also typically go on to suggest areas for future research.

None of those typical endings were going to work if I wanted to deliver on my promise of an unusual, interesting, challenging, and empowering book. So, I kept the filmmaker's idea of a story arc in mind. In addition to learning once again that I don't have the creative spark it takes to be a successful creative writer, I also realized that this book's story arc could not end with its chronological conclusion in part 4. It has to look into the future, too.

Before you accuse me of becoming a science fiction writer, let me explain.

Peacebuilding 3.0 is a good shorthand term to use in describing the state of peace and conflict studies today. It *does not*, however, tell us where it is heading in two key ways that I need to cover if I want *From Conflict Resolution to Peacebuilding* to be truly challenging and empowering. That starts with two ways in which I am impatient with our progress, which I hear echoed frequently from members of your generation—albeit in different form.

First, despite everything we have accomplished in the last thirty years, we have not changed the way most people deal with conflict. We have not succeeded in convincing the vast majority of the world's people that chapter 1's title is correct. Some people have come to see that conflict is a permanent fact of life. As a species, however, we have not yet learned that responding to conflict with violence involves a choice and that there are almost always alternatives to lashing out in fury.

Second, we have yet to secure our "permanent invitation" to Julia Roig's grown-ups' table. For all the progress we've made, it is rare to find senior policy makers who approach their jobs using the kinds of values Fisher and Ury wrote about in *Getting to YES*, let alone the ones that lead to conflict transformation along the lines that I discussed in parts 3 and 4.

I often express my version of Clayton Christensen's job to be done with my hands as reflected in the three photographs on the next page. The first reflects where we were when the Cold War ended. We had made some progress as a result of the work of the European Greens, the American disarmament movement, and organizations like Beyond War. The second depicts where we are today. We've made plenty of progress. Words like win-win are part of our everyday vocabulary. My colleagues often are invited to the grown-ups' tables in Washington and elsewhere around the world. The third one shows the progress we still have to make. It is because we have so much work to do at both the grassroots and elite levels that I am convinced that we need something like a paradigm shift as I suggested with figures 2.5 and 2.6.

That leads me to two conclusions, each of which will get a chapter in part 5. And if I've done my job, you will finish this book more challenged and more empowered.

The challenging conclusion lies in the need to build movements that can mobilize entire populations in ways that will eventually compel our leaders to follow our lead. We have always tried to build more support for the professional work we do. Now, the challenge is to create broader movements in which people from all walks of life see the need to change the ways in which we all deal with conflict. My colleagues and I are beginning to start them as I write, but the emphasis truly is on beginning.

The empowering conclusion comes in the next chapter. which will focus on ways that you can find a career in this field. More importantly, I will make the case that you have a role to play in its evolution whether you want to or not, precisely because you are one of the "people from all walks of life" I referred to in the previous paragraph.

In short, I want to end this book on an upbeat and challenging note, which is where the question mark in part 5's title comes in. While I am excited about what we can accomplish in the next few years, I also have to make it clear that there is tremendous uncertainty about what those next steps could lead to.

EPIGRAPHS, FOURTH GRADERS, AND UNDERGRADUATES

That leads me to the two epigraphs, the opening photograph, and the unusual way I went about writing part 5.

The first statement is by US Supreme Court justice Louis Brandeis. He was right. History is filled with accomplishments that everyone had once assumed were impossible. People can't fly. Or talk live to friends anywhere in the world in real time. Or stay cool in hot weather and warm when it is freezing outside.

At first glance, peace might seem like one of those unreachable goals. But, as Brandeis implied, why assume that it can't be reached? After all, we have already seen important signs that we are heading in that direction.

The second is from Charles Kettering, who was a contemporary of Brandeis's and a talented inventor who gave the world electric engine starters, colored automobile paint, duco glue and other adhesives, along with some things we don't remember quite so fondly, including leaded gasoline and Freon. His statement urges us not to fall into a trap that often snares people who think that the best we can do is to tinker with the status quo. From his point of view, the most important thing change agents can do is to keep an open mind especially when it comes to ideas that would take you out of your comfort zone, as we would say today.

Both are terrific pieces of advice as you head into the world of conflict resolution and peacebuilding after this course is over. Reach for the unreachable while questioning yourself.

Just as useful in setting the agenda for part 5 is **John Hunter's** awe-inspiring experience working with fourth graders. Hunter is an award-winning elementary school teacher and author of *World Peace and Other Fourth Grade Achievements* who now also runs the **World Peace Game Foundation.**[1] He presents them with a four foot by four foot by four foot structure that has three Plexiglass levels which you can see in the photograph on page 308. When playing the game, the students have to deal with fifty overlapping global problems (including peacebuilding) over the course of eight weekly sessions by rearranging pieces that represent those issues around the levels, which represent the earth's surface, atmosphere, subsurface regions, and outer space (home to the all-important weather god, who helps students out when they get stuck). Almost every time children play the game, they figure it out. It usually only happens at the last possible moment, but they do figure it out.

www.youtube.com/watch?v=klJcBj1v7mc

In Brandeis's terms, they accomplish the impossible. In Kettering's, they do so by thinking the unthinkable and turning it into reality, fourth-grade style.

Now, we will explore how that could happen for adults as well.

Thus, the rest of this chapter lays out some exciting uncertainties about where peace and conflict studies is heading. I could build that around the research my academic colleagues are doing. However, if my own years in the classroom are any indication, you are more interested in the practical or applied sides of the field, so that is what I will be concentrating on here.

The unusual content of part 5 also led me to make some unusual decisions about how to write it. I was seventy years old when I started writing this book. The future is not going to belong to my generation. In other words, someone my age should not be the only person developing a vision of Peacebuilding 4.0 or whatever we end up calling the next phase.

So, I did two things as I was finishing the first draft. First, I asked two undergraduate students—Bethany Gen (Oberlin College) and Nora Malatinszky (George Mason University) to work with me on part 5. While the two chapters are written in my voice to make things flow, you will have no trouble seeing their influence (you can also meet them in the box on this page and talk with them through my web site, www.charleshauss.info).

When this book went to press, Bethany Gen was finishing her second year at Oberlin. We met early in her first year, when she asked me for career help, something I often offer to students at my alma mater as part of a long-term mentoring project organized by its Career Services office. We discovered lots of interests in common, ranging from peacebuilding to soccer. I asked Bethany to help out on part 5 largely because she keeps me up to date on gender and campus issues from her perspective as a mediator at Oberlin's Yeworkhwa Belachew Center for Dialogue and as a trainer for the college's Preventing and Responding to Sexual Misconduct (PRISM) program.

At the same time, Nora Malatinszky was finishing her junior year at GMU. We met at the end of her second year at S-CAR's library, where she had a student job. I quickly learned that, like Bethany, she was as smart as any student I'd ever worked with. Unlike Bethany, our partnership has been almost exclusively academic. That began with our joint interest in postcommunist Hungary, where she was born, and soon expanded to include her own ambitious research project on that country and the career to which she hopes it will lead.

Second, because I was auditing my friend Doug Irvin-Erickson's introductory course at George Mason University, he agreed to give his students an unusual final assignment. On the first day of class, he told them that they would write two papers instead of a traditional exam. The first would explore what they thought peace and conflict studies had to deal with next. The other would discuss how they might fit into the field after the course was over. Of course, he told them that they would be graded on how well they defended the positions they took and that it was perfectly all right to say either that the field had no future or that they did not expect to be a part of it after the course ended. He also told them that I would base the final two chapters in part on what they wrote.

Bethany Gen and Nora Malatinszky

DONALD RUMSFELD'S LEGACY

When I talked with Nora and Bethany and read the students' finals, I realized that something was missing in the first four parts of this book. I didn't go outside of the clichéd box enough. If we were going to get beyond the limits implicit in my second photograph, we had to think differently.

That led me to take a detour and consider words from a strange source for a book about peace and conflict studies. Former US secretary of defense **Donald Rumsfeld** (1932–) was the primary architect of the George W. Bush administration's response to the 9/11 attacks, which means he bears a lot of responsibility for the wars in Afghanistan and Iraq. Needless to say, he does not get much respect from my colleagues. And deservedly so.

Nonetheless, Rumsfeld is responsible for the bizarre phrasing of a useful insight about the world in which we peacebuilders work. At his February 12, 2002, news briefing, he uttered these words, which continue to confuse everyone who encounters them for the first time until they dig a bit deeper into their meaning:

> Reports that say that something hasn't happened are always interesting to me, because as we know, there are known knowns; there are things we know we know. We also know there are known unknowns; that is to say we know there are some things we do not know. But there are also unknown unknowns—the ones we don't know we don't know. And if one looks throughout the history of our country and other free countries, it is the latter category that tend to be the difficult ones.[2]

His terms baffled many of the reporters who covered the press conference. But, once we got through the humor associated with yet another Rumsfeldism—he also called email suggestions he sent to his subordinates "snowflakes"—we realized that he was actually on to something.

That "something" may not have helped us avoid the Global War on Terror, but it does help us begin pulling the themes of *From Conflict Resolution to Peacebuilding* together. It also takes us back to the logic behind scenario planning that I raised in chapter 7 and have mostly ignored since then. In his own peculiar way, Rumsfeld was asking us to think about the various ways the future could unfold and to prepare for them.

I know that I said that I do not like books that spend a lot of time summing up what the author has already said in the conclusion, and I do not plan to do so here. Still, taking some of the key (and I hope somewhat catchy) phrases that I've used throughout this book and seeing them in Rumsfeld's terms should help you see where peace and conflict studies has to go if we want to reach the goals implied by the three pictures taken of me at Rondine on page 309.

Known Knowns

In fact, there are a few things that anyone reading this book—including those of you who don't think this field has a future—would agree about. Barring changes that we cannot begin to anticipate, they are our equivalents of the commonly accepted scientific facts that water is made up of hydrogen and oxygen atoms or that the force of the earth's gravity makes most objects fall at the rate of thirty-two feet per second squared. We may not know everything about them, but we have a reasonably clear sense of where our work on them should be heading, both academically and practically.

Conflict will still be a fact of life. Even if we were somehow able to end war, we will not end conflict. If you think back to the definition of conflict in chapter 1 and add to it everything you have learned since then, you will have no trouble understanding how and why conflict is a by-product of being human. The question is what we do about it.

Violence is costly. Whatever you think about the research on the decline in our use of violence and war, there is no question that our continued reliance on force as a tool for problem solving costs us a lot. Just count the number of casualties in wars and crime or the economic cost of our militaries and police forces. You may decide that we need to bear some or all of those human and financial expenses. However, next to no one relishes the fact that violence and its costs are such a common theme in our lives—including my friends who serve in the military or law enforcement, who have volunteered for jobs in which the use of armed force may be necessary.

Violence is a choice. The evidence gathered by peacebuilding scholars as well as neuroscientists and evolutionary psychologists all suggests that the definition of human nature I learned as an undergraduate was off target. We are not simply aggressive, selfish creatures. Every one of us has instincts that can lead us toward violence. But that's not the only thing you need to know about our human nature. We also have "wiring" that leads us to be cooperative, sympathetic, and empathetic.

The evidence suggests, too, that each of our brains is wired differently. Some of us are more prone to being cooperative. Others are more likely to engage in violence or use force. The challenge facing conflict resolution and peacebuilding professionals is to create environments in which the cooperative—and not the violent—side of our human nature rises to the fore.

We can envision alternatives to war, if not to violence and coercion. By that same token, it is not hard to envision a more peaceful world. There are lots of ways of demonstrating that. Among the best is the conflict lab John Hunter created in his fourth-grade classroom.

Even in his classroom experiment some force was required. In this case, it is exercised by a character he calls the weather god who adds a bit of coercion as she helps the children deal with climate change, world peace, economic inequality, and more.

Speaking in real-world terms, it seems highly unlikely that we will be able to totally shed Robert Dahl's definition of power as something I exert over you (see chapter 1). But, in the logic of systems analysis as developed in chapters 3 and 5, we have made enough progress that we can think of peace and cooperative problem solving as a guide star or long-term goal as well as a near star, by which we define concrete steps for reaching that future goal.

Mind-sets matter. Given the way my academic and activist career has evolved, I emphasize personal **paradigms** and **mind-sets** more than many of my colleagues. Even my skeptical friends, however, acknowledge that they matter—if less than I am inclined to argue. The same holds for my argument that we can change what Albert Einstein called our **modes of thinking**, which I first discussed in chapter 2. In this case, I may make changing our core values and assumptions seem easier than it will prove to be. Still, it is hard to argue that we cannot make significant progress in that direction—because we already have.

Big pictures need new eyes. Thinking in terms of paradigms and mind-sets also makes it easier to take a step back from the specifics of a conflict, put it in perspective, and analyze it by what Marcel Proust called seeing with new eyes. There is no question that we can make marginal improvements in the way we deal with a given conflict. However, any time you begin thinking about wholesale change, it is hard to do so without questioning some core assumptions we currently tend to take for granted. Luckily, that is much easier to do—and a lot more important to do—in peace and conflict studies than it is in comparative politics, in which I spent the first half of my professional career.

Gender. Three issues that need more of our attention stood out in what Irvin-Erickson's students wrote. I alluded to the first in part 4—gender. It might seem surprising that gender has not gotten all that much attention from conflict resolution and peacebuilding professionals. After all, we live in a world in which #MeToo and more have raised everyone's gender sensitivity. However, perhaps because men were at the heart of so many wars and other forms of conflict, gender issues received relatively little attention even as our field comes to be led by women both in our academic and applied work.

That has begun to change, and not just because of movements like #MeToo. We have also learned a lot about the impact gendered issues play in our work. In particular, we know that when women are involved in negotiating a peace agreement, it is more likely to last than if only men are involved. Similarly, if you believe that the way we are raised (nurture) is more important than our genetic predispositions (nature), there is reason to believe that the way women are socialized leads many of them to act more cooperatively than men.

Youth. We have also increasingly become aware of two things. First, like women, young people tend to be the victims of conflict. Second, evidence from around the world suggests that your generation—like mine did half a century ago—will demand radical change from its elders (who now, of course, include me). At AfP and elsewhere, we have begun aiming more and more of our programming toward attracting and actively engaging young people—and not just students in peace and conflict studies courses, a theme I will revisit in the next chapter.

Climate change. Climate change is the challenge of this generation. We know that climate change already contributes to the outbreak and/or worsening of some conflicts around the world, and we have to assume that it will continue to do so. Even more importantly, we know that the debate over what to do about climate change itself is likely to be a make-or-break issue with implications not just for the rest of your lifetime but for those of the next generation(s) that have yet to be born.

Unknown Unknowns

Rumsfeld's most perplexing—and perhaps most important—expectation about the future revolves around the **unknown unknowns**. On one level, worrying about them might feel like a fool's errand since we cannot predict what they are going to be like.

However, we can anticipate that they will occur and that we should be prepared to deal with them. Unfortunately, we are ill equipped to do so. You know that because you have already encountered two unknown unknowns in this book. Next to no one anticipated the end of the Cold War until a few months before the Berlin Wall came down. Very few of us had any inkling that terrorists were about to fly airplanes into the World Trade Center and the Pentagon when we woke up on September 11, 2001.

In both cases, unknown unknowns of that magnitude threw us for a loop. We had to go back to the clichéd drawing board and redesign much of this entire field twice in the course of my professional lifetime.

We also know that the number of unknown unknowns is likely to grow exponentially in the future. In popular culture, their discovery is often referred to as the **black swan** effect after the book of the same name by Nassim Nicholas Taleb.[3] Taleb starts with the "discovery" of black swans. Until the Europeans "discovered" Australia, "everyone" "knew" that all swans were white. Then, in 1697, a group of Dutch explorers led by Willem de Vlamingh saw the "first" black swan while visiting what is now Western Australia.

Discovering the existence of black swans itself actually had an impact on modern science and is now integrated into the part of evolutionary theory which covers members of the same species that get separated and evolve on their own.

That is not why black swans are relevant here, however. As Taleb developed the idea, he made the case that black swan–like events:

- would occur more frequently because the world is becoming more interconnected (see Metcalfe's law in chapter 2) and is increasingly defined by accelerating rates of change (see Moore's law, also in chapter 2)
- could have extreme and devastating effects
- are only surprising because our mind-sets keep us from anticipating them

Again, we have no way of knowing what those unknown unknowns will be. We can grasp at straws and try to do so by thinking about how the long-term consequences of trends like climate change could shape the future of conflict. When we do so, of course, we are beginning to touch on Rumsfeld's most important category for our purposes—the known knowns.

Known Unknowns

Although Rumsfeld himself may not have realized it, the distinction between unknown unknowns and known unknowns is actually quite blurry. Some people did anticipate the collapse of the Soviet Union. As I pointed out in chapter 10, I was part of a focus group that predicted that terrorists might fly hijacked airplanes into big buildings, though we had no inkling that such an attack would happen or that the World Trade Center and the Pentagon would be targets.

In fact, Taleb wrote *The Black Swan* in part because some unknowns were, well, somewhat knowable. As he sees it, we would be well advised to shed mind-sets that keep us from seeing that certain trends could emerge and that certain events could occur. We might not be able to predict the specifics of black swan event, but we can explore the trends that could well produce one.

That is the premise on which **scenario planning** is based. You start with, in Rumsfeld's terms, the known knowns about the future. Then, you consider the most plausibly **known unknowns** and project the likely futures to which they could lead. Once you've done that, you can plan accordingly.

One does all that knowing that unknown unknowns or black swan events are going to occur. If the complexity scientists (including Taleb) are right, we will see more such events with more serious consequences in the future.

Some companies try to plan for known unknowns, starting with Royal Dutch/Shell, where the idea of scenario planning was invented. That is less true of governments, whose policies are often driven by short-term forces, most notably election cycles. Many NGOs, too, focus excessively on the short run because, as we saw with John Paul Lederach's project in Nepal, their funders insist that peacebuilders show results at the end of one- or two-year grants.

In fact, as far as I know, only the government of Singapore has taken these metaphorical black swans and their implications seriously. It has had to. Singapore is a tiny, wealthy, heterogeneous country in Southeast Asia that has pulled itself out of extreme poverty because it has been able to adapt to social and economic trends that swirl largely out of its control. For the last decade or so, it has conducted an annual **Remote Areas Horizon Scan (RAHS)**, in which its civil servants and outside experts try to identify those long-term trends and help policy makers adapt to them, as you can see in this video by RAHS creator Peter Ho:

www.youtube.com/watch?v=KOHpXvUgpcs

It is in this sense that known unknowns become a useful tool in concluding this book. In decreasing order of importance and uncertainty, we can think of the following known unknowns that we "know" are going to be important for the future of conflict resolution and peacebuilding.

Reaching a fork in the road. If we are at such a fork, we have to make a choice. If we were satisfied with what we have achieved so far, we could just continue along on our current path. I, for one, am not satisfied with our accomplishments.

Getting a seat at the grown-ups' table. If we want to produce a paradigm shift, we are going to have to engage with people who are currently in power. We may have to convince them to go along with what we want. We may have to replace them. In either event, we are not likely to get that seat unless we take a fork at the road that sets us off in a very different direction from the one(s) we have been following for the last thirty years.

Seeing with new eyes. We can't make the kind of progress we want to make unless we see the world of conflict and our role in it through new mental lenses. This, of course, is why I have spent so much time on the idea of a paradigm shift.

Bright spots. The various components of the conflict resolution and peacebuilding communities have traditionally focused on the problems we face. In recent years, we have identified unusual cases (hence the term outliers), where "things" seemed to "work," however you chose to define things and work. We have not, however, spent much time focusing on how we can build off of those successes to produce a movement for change.

THINKING ABOUT TWENTY-FIRST-CENTURY MOVEMENTS

The final five words in the previous section are important enough to repeat here—produce a movement for change. If I'm right, they point us in some clear directions—but do see this chapter's Out on a Limb box.

That, in turn, leads me to one theme in Peacebuilding 3.0 that did not feature prominently in part 4, but will have to be at the heart of dealing with all of these knowns and unknowns. We assumed that people would be drawn to the conflict resolution and peacebuilding community more or less as we ourselves had defined it. You saw that in a number of guises, almost all of which involved asking how we could add to our impact by expanding our grassroots networks or getting ourselves a permanent seat at the grown-ups' table.

OUT ON A LIMB

I'm taking myself farther out on a limb here than I did anywhere else in this book. That's the case because the argument being made here is largely incompatible with the kinds of contentious politics I have discussed at various points throughout this book.

I am well aware that there are times when we may have to nonviolently coerce people we disagree with into change. But I am also well aware that the logic of this argument sharply limits when and how it makes sense to build the kinds of movements I was a part of in the 1960s and 1970s.

If you disagree with me, I'd love to hear why and how you do.

There is nothing wrong with that. In fact, I plan to continue doing just that for the rest of my life.

That said, we are increasingly aware that there has to be a broader cultural shift in the ways everyone—from everyday citizens to the world's most prominent leaders—deals with conflict. That is, after all, why forks in the road, bright spots, mind-sets, and grown-ups' tables all matter.

That, in turn, suggests building movements that take us beyond the conflict resolution and peacebuilding communities and toward the next stage of our growth that involves the entire population—not just our fellow professionals or the people who are at the heart of the world's most intractable conflicts.

Note, too, that the kinds of movements that I will be describing will not resemble those of the 1960s. Times have changed. So, too has our understanding of how social change occurs. We now, for instance, think in terms of theories of change or the long-term impacts of our actions, which we rarely did when we opposed racial segregation or the Vietnam war.

I also spoke of movements in the plural two paragraphs ago because I am convinced that given what we know about social movements and about the world we live in, no single movement will do. Therefore, I conclude this chapter by outlining the logic behind two ways that movements grow and briefly discuss four of them that were just getting underway as I was finishing this book.

In other words, we may not be talking in terms of Peacebuilding 4.0, or even use that meme by the time you read this book. Still, the field is going to change because it has to change if it is going to both continue the dramatic growth of the last thirty years and if it is going to overcome the problems that have kept us both from changing popular culture or getting a seat at the policy makers' metaphorical grown-ups' table.

Everett Rogers's Legacy

Once you rule out violent revolution, building a successful social movement has two key components. First, you have to build support for the new idea or ideas. Second, you have to turn that change in public opinion into a strong movement that can either convince or compel the powers that be to change public policy. Although the two are clearly interconnected, two separate strands in social movement theory help us understand two somewhat different, but complementary, ways to proceed.

The key thinker behind the first one was **Everett Rogers** (1931–2004). Rogers himself had little or nothing to do with social movements. Rather, he was among the first scholars to systematically study the way innovations spread. Even here he was an anomaly. Today, we tend to think of innovations as coming from places like Silicon Valley. Not Rogers. He was born and raised on a farm in Iowa, trained as an agronomist, and began developing his ideas about innovation by studying how and why farmers adopted new corn seeds.

As his career progressed, Rogers built on what he knew about seed corn and created a model of how any innovative idea took hold in any population. I first came into contact with Rogers when he taught at the University of Michigan while I was in graduate school, but his work only began to have a major impact on my work a decade later, after he had moved to Stanford and attracted the attention of Beyond War's founders (see chapter 5). We were among many aspiring social movement leaders who adopted his ideas about a successful movement's trajectory which I have reproduced here as figure 13.1.

Focus first on the bell-shaped portion of the chart, which resembles what statisticians call a normal curve. It reflects one general way a lot of human characteristics are arrayed, including height, weight, intelligence, and even positions on the pollster's left–right scale.[4] Rogers's research showed that new ideas gained acceptance along a trajectory that normally mirrors that curve. In this case, do not focus too much on the percentages, since they represent the share of the population that lies one, two, and three standard deviations away from the mean (if you are statistically inclined) and may not apply to every innovation.

In the early days of a movement, only a handful of creative thinkers have adopted an idea. To be honest, I doubt that even one-tenth of Rogers's 2.5 percent of the American population has even begun to grasp what win-win conflict resolution and peacebuilding are all about. So, there are clearly more

FIGURE 13.1
The Movement of an Idea through a Population

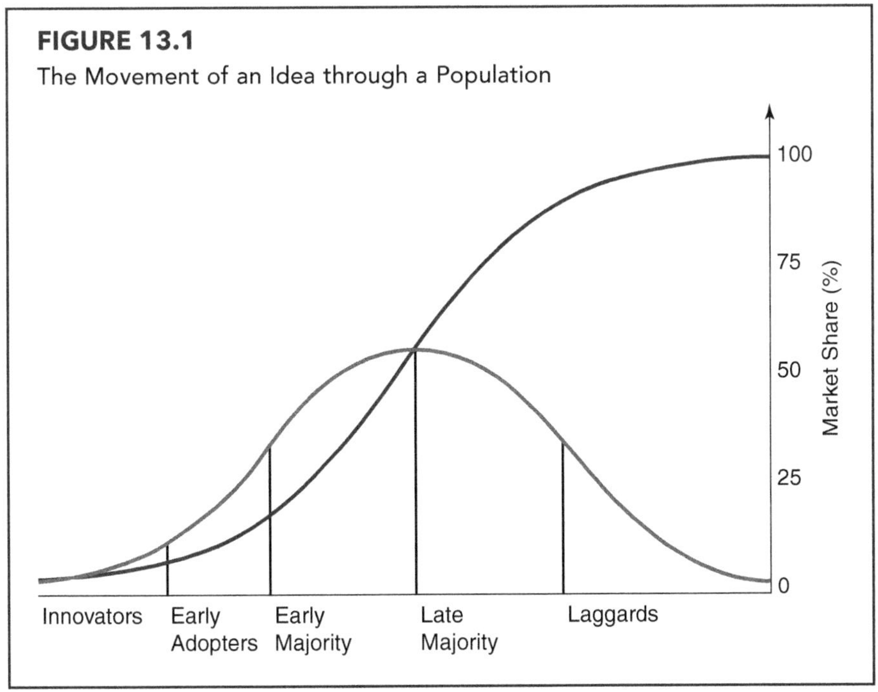

potential innovators to be found using the same kinds of techniques we have been using over the years.

Rogers's real contribution lies in the fact that he drew our attention to the rest of the population. To succeed, a movement has to reach at least a critical mass of its target audience. As you are about to see, it does not have to win everybody over. But to the degree that a movement wants to win democratically and, therefore, largely through winning over public opinion, it has to build broad and deep support.

The people whom he calls innovators can actually be broken down into two subgroups. First are the people who come up with new ideas in the first place, which includes men and women like Johan Galtung, John Marks, Roger Fisher, Kenneth and Elise Boulding, Mary Anderson, and John Paul Lederach. Next come people like me, who do not develop the ideas per se but are good at synthesizing them, which is why we get asked to write textbooks.

It turns out that neither of those groups are particulary good at reaching out to the population as a whole. Here, another set of individuals–the early adopters–play a critical role in determining if and how a society adopts a new idea.

When illustrating this point, Rogers's protégés often cite the case of the young Dr. Martin Luther King Jr., when he was a pastor in Montgomery, Alabama at the time of the famous boycott that many believe launched the modern civil rights movement. King was then in his late twenties and leading his first church. He was far from being the beloved icon he would become over the course of the next decade. However, he was a respected member of the clergy whose words were taken seriously by members of his own congregation and others in Montgomery's African American population.

Opinion leaders like the young Dr. King exist in all communities, not just in Black churches. When Rogers started writing in ways that applied to social movements in the 1960s and 1970s, he was thinking largely in terms of local, geographically based communities. Today, we also have to think about online and other communities that can be built through the use of technologies that were not even on the drawing board in his day.

As you move along his curve, the pace of change can speed up. By the time you have reached about five percent of the population, Rogers argued that the idea was embedded. By that time, enough community leaders around the country (or conceivably around the world) have adopted and spread the innovative idea that it becomes part of everyday conversation.

Then comes the heavy lifting. When and if you have convinced all of the early adopters, you have reached about twenty percent of the population. At this point, thought leaders of all stripes have begun to come on board. Once that happens, a once novel idea is beginning to become conventional wisdom.

By then, Rogers claimed that an innovation had become unstoppable. It might not become the norm quickly, but it is now so deeply rooted in popular culture that it is likely to gain the support of more and more of the population. Analysts today would have chosen other terms to describe his remaining categories. The key point, however, is still the same. On most questions, most people tend to follow suit once key opinion leaders are on board.

Shift your attention here to the second curve that looks a bit like an S, which presents the numbers in the first one on a cumulative basis. It shows you the percentage of the total population that has adopted a new idea at each stage in the process. Here note that after a slow start through the various forms of early adopters and opinion leaders, support for the new idea can begin to take off, and quickly.

That's the case because other members of the population tend to follow the lead of people whose opinions they trust. Not everyone ever comes on board, as we Americans can see in the continued open support for white supremacy. However, the people Rogers called laggards end up playing a rearguard role because their once dominant position in public opinion has disappeared.

Charles Tilly's Legacy

Ideas like these do help us understand how support for new ideas can spread and go viral. In other words, they can help us figure out how to convince the public to buy the latest new cell phone or some other new product. Marketing is, in fact, one of the areas where Rogers's insights have had the most influence.

You didn't need to read first twelve and a half chapters of this book to understand that changing public opinion and/or mind-sets alone is not enough to produce lasting change at any level, from the interpersonal to the global. That is where the research about contentious politics returns to center stage, albeit with a slightly different slant from the one I've used in previous chapters.

Here research done and inspired by **Charles Tilly** (1929–2008) is all but indispensable. Unlike Rogers, I knew Tilly well. He was one of my mentors at Michigan, and we spent the next forty years pleasantly disagreeing with each other about the use of force and violence in social movements.

Tilly was a historical sociologist who did most of his own research on eighteenth- and nineteenth-century social movements in Europe. During those years, most of the working class and other progressive movements he researched lost, however much public support they might have amassed. The history of the Vendée counterrevolution or the Paris Commune need not concern us here, other than to note Tilly's four key lessons, which are summarized in figure 4.1.

First, shifts in public opinion have to be converted into organized demands for social change. Tilly and his colleagues referred to these as contending groups, which come in a wide variety of forms. Few of the organizations profiled in parts 2 through 4 of this book even thought of themselves as contending groups even when making claims (let alone issuing demands) on the state.

Second, as the two headed arrows in figure 4.1 suggest, power flows in both directions. Often, states resist these claims and do their best to keep us from Julia Roig's grown-ups' table. More often than Tilly or his students (of whom, of course, I was one) wanted to admit, the state and other powerholders are able to keep contending groups out through the use of force or other forms of power as I defined it in chapter 1. Sometimes, contending groups have to force the powers that be to give way either by compelling them to adopt new policies or by forcing them out of office altogether.

Third, neither the state nor the contending groups are fully masters of their own destiny. There are other domestic (in Tilly's research, French capitalists) or international ones (again, in his research, the German government) who limit what either contending groups or the state can hope to accomplish.

Finally, the one area in which Tilly and I disagreed is a highly important one for anyone interested in peace and conflict studies. How much force does it take to get the state to go along? Is it ever ethically appropriate to use force because it compels the other side to go along with the contending group's wishes? Is physical violence ever appropriate? How coercive can our tactics be?

TWENTY-FIRST CENTURY MOVEMENTS IN EMBRYO

Everything covered so far in this chapter points toward a single conclusion. The biggest known unknown for peace and conflict studies in the third decade of the twenty-first century is how we should go about building a movement or, more likely, movements. The "known" is the need for a movement or movements, if we want to take the fork in the road that dramatically increases our impact. The "unknown" is how to do it.

As I write in early 2019, there are dozens of such embryonic movements underway, four of which are worth considering here. The first deals with a reasonably narrow but vitally important topic and is being coordinated by **Cure Violence**, which you met in part 4. The second is one of the more innovative efforts to address climate change. AfP has a leading role in the other two, both of which are attempting to transform cultural norms about conflict and violence in ways that could ultimately lead to new public policy initiatives, if not a full-blown paradigm shift.

I have called them all embryonic movements, because they were in their initial stages when I had to stop writing *From Conflict Resolution to Peacebuilding*. You can follow their progress on their own websites and through www.charleshauss.info.

End the Violence Epidemic

After years of dramatic growth, Dr. Gary Slutkin realized that Cure Violence could not end urban violence on its own. Without abandoning his organization's own efforts, he teamed with former surgeon general Dr. David Satcher and former dean of the Johns Hopkins School of Public Health Dr. Al Sommer to form the **End the Violence Epidemic** movement.

The movement is limited. It does not have every issue peacebuilders care about on its radar screen. It is only focused on the kinds of violence that Slutkin and his colleagues think can be treated using the epidemiologist's tool kit. And, although it is open to anyone, the three founders have decided to mobilize health care professionals first.

Still, it is a movement that will help define a common framework for treating violence as a disease, identify new forms of medical and other intervention, and promote policies that promote racial, economic, and what it calls health equality in the US. Although the movement is still in its early stages, it plans to mobilize support in every sector of the ecosystem in which violence-as-epidemic occurs as depicted in its framework map as you can see on the bottom of the next page.

At the heart of that system are the panels depicted in the middle of the map—the city's residents, the **civil society organizations** they form, and local social service providers. Just as important are networks that serve the community, including everyone from law enforcement to faith-based institutions to whatever mental and behavioral health institutions are located there.

It is, as far as I know, the first movement anywhere in the peacebuilding and conflict resolution world to be explicitly built on systems principles. Thus, although Slutkin rarely uses the term explicitly, they treat urban violence as a wicked problem that has to be diagnosed and treated as an integrated syndrome or pattern of interconnected symptoms and ailments.

If you are considering a career that involves aspects of urban affairs or public health, End the Violence Epidemic is well worth following. If your interests lie elsewhere, you will probably be able to find a silo-stretching movement in your field, because I know they exist for everyone from environmentalists to engineers.

Fridays for Future

When I was in college and graduate school, I was part of a youth movement that changed everything from political to sexual mores. We did not reach the political goal we wanted most—ending the war in Vietnam right away. But, we did help usher in the modern women's and environmental movements and helped spark some basic changes in cultural norms that resonate today, wherever you stand on the strategies and tactics we used at the time.

Today's young people are beginning to launch their own movements. They do not resemble ours, nor should they. The 2020s and the 1960s are more than half a century apart, and a lot has changed in between.

One new movement emerged while I was writing this book. And, although **Fridays for Future** focuses on climate change rather than conflict resolution and peacebuilding, it attracts plenty of young people who are interested in both.

It was started by a young Swede, **Greta Thunberg** (2003–). Her protest career began in 2018, when she started quietly sitting on the steps of the Swedish parliament to protest her government's failure to take climate change seriously. Her story was picked up by the Swedish media and soon went viral.

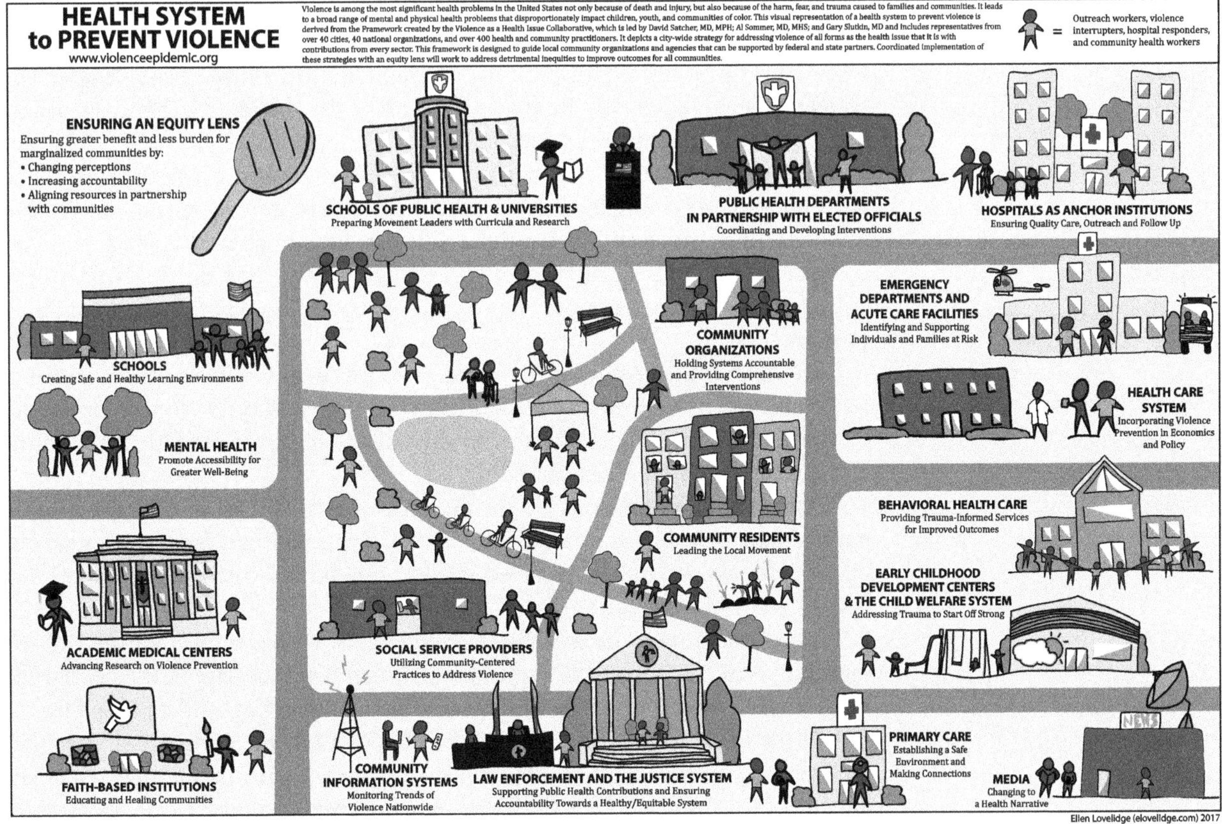

Mapping the Violence Epidemic

Her personal strike morphed into the organization Fridays for Future. After she appeared at the COP24 global conference in Katowice, Poland, she began getting global attention. On March 19, 2019, roughly 1.4 million high school students boycotted classes in 125 countries to demand swift and decisive action on climate change. Meanwhile, three members of the Norwegian parliament nominated her for the Nobel Peace Prize.

All by the time she turned sixteen.

https://youtu.be/rzNDO5Umut4

+Peace

In early 2019, AfP and fifteen other global peacebuilding NGOs began what is known as a soft launch of **+Peace**, as the previously mentioned Global Peacebuilding Coalition is now known. A soft launch essentially means that the organization has a website, ambitious goals, and very few clearly defined initiatives. Because it includes most of the largest peacebuilding organizations that have the greatest access to what I've referred to as the grown-ups' table and to the mass media, it has decided to focus on changing the narrative of how the world understands and deals with conflict.

+Peace will be the first peacebuilding movement that Tilly would have recognized. It is explicitly aimed at changing the state and its policies. It expects to do so by building a coalition of existing groups and adding new ones that will focus on building support for peacebuilding as defined in part 4.

The movement began with a seemingly simple, innocuous, and not very earth-shattering campaign—to get the word peacebuilding into the dictionary. As you saw in part 3, the word is relatively new. No one is quite sure where and when it was first used. However, my colleagues and I started using it after UN secretary general Boutros Boutros-Ghali drew the distinction between peacekeeping, peacemaking, and peacebuilding.

We soon discovered that our word processors balked every time we typed peacebuilding as a single word. In the days before autocomplete and instant spell checking, you would type those thirteen letters without a space and end up with red squiggly lines on your screen. The reason was simple. None of the online dictionaries recognized the word. Peace building was fine. Peacebuilding was not.

We all, of course, know how to add new words to our software package's list of acceptable words. Getting to the dictionary developers was far more complicated. By the time I sent this manuscript to my editor, the three most popular online dictionaries had added peacebuilding.

Fixing the dictionary is by no means the same thing as achieving world peace. Nonetheless, it is a start. +Peace's steering team had far more audacious plans in the works when I finished writing this book, which will be rolled out later in 2019 and thereafter.

We expect this to be a global movement. However, more than half of the founding NGOs are based in the US, and American issues are at the heart of so many of the world's problems that much of its initial efforts will be based there.

At the time I wrote this chapter, the idea of a **Green New Deal** was a hot topic among progressive activists. The leadership team is in the process of creating an equivalent Peace New Deal that could become a central issue discussed in the 2020 presidential election campaign and beyond.

That will require a wide variety of efforts. Some will look like conventional political activism, ranging from offering position papers to all of the major candidates to organizing grassroots activist campaigns at key moments in the calendar, including on the UN International Day of Peace which occurs every September. The steering committee is also working on an advocacy tool kit that would bring together everything its members have learned about getting access to the policy-making grown-ups' table, including the lessons we can learn from other successful movements.

Most importantly of all, +Peace will be seeking new allies. As the discussion of strange political bedfellows in chapter 12 suggested, most of the larger peacebuilding and conflict resolution NGOs now understand that we cannot change the world unless we draw interest in and support for our work from social and political groups that have never identified themselves with either peace or conflict resolution.

The +Peace team is reaching out to media celebrities and other well-known figures who could serve as champions for the cause in much the same way that Bono did for global poverty. Another is working on what we have tentatively called a PeaceMark or a set of guidelines corporations should follow to be seen as both profitable and peaceful that would function much the same way that the various LEED categories are used to certify the degree to which a new building was constructed along sound environmental lines.

In short, however +Peace evolves, it will build out from what its member organizations have already accomplished. What's new is the realization that we have to act like the kind of nonviolent contending groups that Tilly focused on. Few of these organizations are likely to be taking to the streets and leading the kinds of angry protests that brought down leaders in the former communist world and the Middle East in the so-called colored revolutions of a generation ago. Our roots are still too closely tied to the polite protesters of the 1980s.

We know that others will be in the streets. We may join them at times, but the desire to find a place at the grown-ups' table will mean that our priorities will lie elsewhere.

Where People Take Their Conflict

The other movement had not really gotten off the ground when I wrote these words, but I feel confident including it here because I will be one of its leaders. At the same time that the +Peace team realized we had to try new approaches if we ever wanted to get the grown-ups' table, another group, which included my editor at Rowman and Littlefield, some ACR members, and my colleagues at AfP and George Mason, came to a slightly different but overlapping conclusion.

We had spent the last generation trying to build support for conflict resolution and peacebuilding on the assumption that people should join us in our efforts. Then, we realized that we work with a lot of teachers, social service workers, coaches, law enforcement officers, and members of the clergy who deal with conflict all the time, and do so in ways that parallel what I have been talking about throughout this book, but don't think of themselves as part of our tribe. My editor, who has published peace and conflict–related books in as many as a dozen different academic disciplines, was frustrated by how scattered the overall field seemed to be.

So, we held a series of focus groups at national conferences and ended up with three broad goals for another movement in which we would:

- reach out to what I began calling our "first cousins" in those other fields
- train as many as two million people in basic conflict resolution skills
- focus on reaching the next generation, a point on which I will focus in the next chapter

In so doing, we expect to create the kind of movement Everett Rogers would have recognized, because we have to build support in ways that will mirror the trajectories he sketched forty years ago. That means reaching out to the target communities I just mentioned (and perhaps others) and building partnerships with them without expecting them to join us *as* peacebuilders. One will definitely include building on and coordinating work that is already being done by American high school and college students.

Most of the members of this team have been deeply impressed by the ideas behind local peacebuilding; the logic that Diana Chigas and Peter Woodrow (who is part of the planning team) used in *Adding Up to Peace*, discussed in part 4, and the whole idea of taking things to scale that we have borrowed from the corporate world. Central to any such approach is John Paul Lederach's notion of **accompanying** local peacebuilders. Rather than coming in as an outside expert who has the answers, our goal is to work with people in those communities on the ways they deal with conflict, learn from what they have done, and serve as a network that amplifies and aggregates their efforts so that they can be taken to scale.

We are less interested in attracting celebrities or accessing corporate C Suites, though we will not turn down support from either of them. Rather, we expect to publish handbooks and other short documents that end up in public libraries, prepare curricula that my grandchildren's teachers can use in the normal course of elementary school education, and help the members of your generation build your own movement, which, of course, is the subject of the next chapter.

CONFLICT LAB 13

Return to the two conflicts you have been working on since chapter 1, keeping in mind that the national- and global-level issue you picked might not lend itself to this exercise.

For one or both of your conflicts:

- Design a movement that would address one or more of its underlying causes as determined in previous conflict labs.
- Design a Rogers-like shift in public opinion that could be taken to scale.
- Chart how it could be used to build a Tilly-like movement that could add up to peace in ways that are consistent with the principles of nonviolence I began developing in chapter 3.

If you don't find any of these approaches compelling, design your own, but be sure you can justify doing things your way.

KEY TERMS

Concepts

People

Organizations, Places, and Events

DIG DEEPER

Bahcall, Safi. *Loonshots: How to Nurture the Crazy Ideas That Win Wars, Cure Diseases, and Transform Industries.* New York: St. Martin's, 2019. A must-read if you think peacebuilding is an impossible dream, even though Bahcall never mentions peacebuilding in the entire book.

Heimans, Jeremy, and Henry Timms. *New Power: How Power Works in Our Hyperconnected World—and How to Make It Work for You.* New York: Doubleday, 2018. A readable and thought-provoking book on how power could and should be in a VUCA world.

Hunter, John. *World Peace and Other 4th Grade Achievements.* New York: Houghton Mifflin, 2014. The most enjoyable book you will ever read on peacebuilding by far. And credible, too.

Taleb, Nassim Nicholas. *The Black Swan: The Impact of the Highly Improbable.* New York: Random House, 2007. A tough read, but a remarkable book on how unlikely events will have a huge impact on our lives in the future.

NOTES

[1] John Hunter, *World Peace and Other 4th Grade Achievements* (New York: Houghton Mifflin, 2014).

[2] http://archive.defense.gov/Transcripts/Transcript.aspx?TranscriptID=2636.

[3] Nassim Nicholas Taleb, *The Black Swan: The Impact of the Highly Improbable* (New York: Random House, 2007).

[4] The fact that it resembles Michael Lund's curve in figure 3.3 is also no coincidence, but the overlap is not of any importance here.

CHAPTER 14

And That Leaves You

THINK ABOUT IT

You will not be asked to master any new concepts or facts in this chapter. Instead, I want you to think about if and/or how everything you have learned since you started this book changed the way you think about conflict resolution and peacebuilding.

Even more importantly, I am asking you to think about how you will deal with the conflicts you encounter in the future, a future that will begin the moment you put this book down for the last time.

CONCEPTS

decision—when truly made, an irrevocable choice; from the Latin for "cut away from"

Golden Rule—in Judeo-Christian and other faiths, the notion that you should do unto others as you would have them do unto you

growth mind-set—values that stress the positive lessons one can draw from experience

PACE—problem solving, adaptability, creativity, empathy

If you could overcome just one conflict this year, what would it be?
—*Sarah Federman*

SARAH FEDERMAN TEACHES CONFLICT resolution at the University of Baltimore. As I was getting ready to write this chapter, I noticed that she had begun using the above epigraph in her email signature. All at once, two of the threads I had been thinking about using in ending this book came together.

First, she didn't say *resolve* but used the term *overcome* instead. If you think about the conflicts covered in the first thirteen chapters of this book, few of them will ever be fully resolved. Most, however, can be overcome in the sense that they will no longer take us to the brink of a literal or metaphoric war. You only have to turn on the news to see that we are a long way from ending racism or sexism in the United States or anywhere else for that matter. However, Sarah draws our attention to the fact that we have overcome some of them. No serious political leader is ever likely to propose, for example, that slavery be made legal or that women be barred from voting ever again.

Second, and even more importantly, Sarah understands that we are all human. None of us—and that definitely includes me—can overcome all of the world's problems. So, she asks us to redefine our priorities and think about the single conflict we can realistically hope to overcome this year.

I'll be asking you to set your sights a bit higher than that. But, echoing Sarah's words, I assume that you will not be doing this kind of work 24/7. After all, I don't. So, it is incumbent on me to suggest ways you could be involved in the course of your everyday lives.

PROFESSIONAL PATHWAYS

I spent most of my academic career teaching courses in comparative politics as well as peace and conflict studies. My comparative politics students rarely came to my office seeking advice on building a career in that field.

Peace and conflict studies students do so every day. Even now, when I'm no longer standing in front of a class for fourteen weeks at a time, students routinely ask me for career advice.

That is no coincidence. Unlike comparative politics, many—maybe most—students take courses in peace and conflict studies because they already already have an abiding interest in the subject. Many already have had experience in some aspects of it. Others are thinking about pursuing a major or even a career in it.

When I have discussions along those lines these days, I routinely start with Federman's question. For the purposes of this book, however, it makes more sense to start with professional careers and end with her challenge.

That said, if you are certain you do not want to take more courses or find a career in the field, you can probably skip ahead to the section titled "Sarah Federman's Question," since I doubt your instructor will include anything in this chapter on the final.

Further Study

As an academic, it would be remiss of me not to start out by urging you to take more courses in conflict resolution and peacebuilding. After all, as I have suggested several times, all this book and presumably the course you are taking can do is scratch the surface of this fascinating, new, and constantly changing field.

At the same time, I am at a disadvantage, because I don't know what other courses you can take at your college or university. That said, I *can* point you in three main directions, two of which you can follow whether your school offers more courses in the field or not.

More courses in the field. More and more colleges and universities do offer specialized courses in conflict and peace studies. Many now even have minors and majors in aspects of conflict resolution and peacebuilding.

My own alma mater, Oberlin College, is a case in point. When I was a student there in the late 1960s, there were no such courses in the curriculum. If there had been, I probably would have majored in peace and conflict studies rather than political science, which is where I ended up after abandoning my initial hopes of becoming either an engineer or a physicist. After all, I jokingly refer to myself as having majored in ending the war in Vietnam, and a peace studies minor or major would have been an obvious fit.

Today, few schools only have a single course like the one you are about to finish. Therefore, you probably have others you could take. I think you should do so. Obviously, the place to start is with your instructor, because he or she will have a lot better idea of what those options are than I possibly could.

If your school does have a minor or major in either conflict resolution or peacebuilding, it probably includes some kind of requirement for an internship or a practicum. If so, that is something I can probably help you with.

Broaden your horizons. Since I have intentionally drawn on plenty of research from other academic disciplines, it should be obvious by now that I don't think you can master conflict resolution and peacebuilding by taking courses in those fields on their own. Even if you major in the field, you could and should benefit from courses in related fields. And, of course, if you have read this book at a school that doesn't have additional courses in conflict and peace studies and are still interested in the field, you have no choice but to pursue offerings in those other disciplines.

Professional training and career building. If your instructor and I have done our jobs well, some of you reading this book will at least be entertaining the possibility of working in this field at some point in the future. It is possible to get some jobs with only an undergraduate degree in peace and conflict studies or some related discipline, but it is getting harder and harder to do so.

As a result, most people wanting to build a career in it will have to get a graduate degree. It does not have to be in a formal peace and conflict studies program like the one at George Mason University. In fact, most people I've worked with over the years on the AfP staff have graduate degrees in other fields, including law, international relations, Middle East studies, public policy, history, economics, engineering, and even an MBA.

It also makes sense to get some practical experience along the way before or during your graduate career whatever field you choose to pursue. That, too, can take dozens of forms, ranging from the Peace Corps and AmeriCorps (as well as its foreign and nongovernmental equivalents) to time working in the corporate sector. It is no longer surprising to have backgrounds in yoga, banking, or the military.

Careers

Once you've finished your formal education, you will probably want to find a job and start a career in the field. What follows is by no means an exhaustive list. Instead, I simply want to highlight options that you can easily pursue with professional advisors, starting with your own school's career services office.

Once again, you will have multiple options—though be certain to read the next section on the need to have a Plan B. That's the case because while there are jobs in which expertise in peace and conflict studies is needed, there aren't enough of them to go around.

It's easiest to start with jobs that are directly in the field and located in the sectors where I've spent the most time in recent years—the conflict resolution/peacebuilding NGO community, teaching, and public service.

NGOs come in all shapes and sizes. Many are located in big, capital cities like Washington, where I live. Most do the bulk of their work in the field, which means you could end up living and working just about anywhere in the world.

Luckily, there is one source that lists many of the available jobs, the **Peace and Conflict Development Network (PCDN)**, managed by former Georgetown professor Craig Zelizer. He doesn't list everything, but Zelizer does as good a job as anyone possibly could of finding the positions that are available, including ones in academia.

Do not assume that you will only find relevant jobs at peacebuilding NGOs. In fact, many of the larger ones, like CARE or Save the Children, do not have offices that deal explicitly with peacebuilding. However, you may well find interesting positions there. The same holds true for think tanks. Neither the American Enterprise Institute nor the Brookings Institution (which I can see from the window of my office at AfP) have peacebuilding divisions. Both have peacebuilders on their staffs.

Teaching jobs require academic credentials. The few available professorships require a PhD or its equivalent. There are surprisingly few opportunities for teaching younger students, although more and more schools are hiring conflict resolution professionals as support personnel. These jobs also require specialized training, which varies from place to place and subject to subject.

Finally, there are jobs with national governments and international organizations, such as the UN or the World Bank. These include a country's diplomatic service and a wide variety of positions in the international bodies. As noted in chapter 13, most governments in Europe and North America now have ADR services in most of their agencies. The international agencies typically have research and administrative jobs in their headquarters and field offices that actually do peacebuilding work.

You Need a Plan B

When he lived in Washington, Craig Zelizer ran a workshop on careers for young peacebuilders at AfP's annual conference. People in the room gasped when he stated that "half of the people in this room will not get jobs in the field." After the groans and shrieks subsided, Craig would add that they would find more interesting and more lucrative jobs elsewhere.[1]

Unfortunately, Zelizer is right. We cannot and will not be able to offer enough jobs unless and until we take the kinds of steps outlined at the end of chapter 13. Even more importantly, I'm also convinced that the conflict and peacebuilding fields are not providing the right kinds of jobs. When I put on my political scientist or futurist hat, I look out at a world that is experiencing experiential rates of change in almost all aspects of life. Or, as Heraclitus of Ephesus allegedly said twenty-five hundred years ago, "change is the only constant." That may or may not have been true in ancient Greece. It certainly is the case today.

No one has thought more about the implications of accelerating change for the workforce in general and for the kinds of young people I work with in particular than Gary Bolles, who is chair for the Future of Work at the Singularity University. Singularity is a peculiar university. It doesn't have a football team. It doesn't even give degrees. Instead, it helps prepare people to live in a world of constant and often mind-numbing change.

As Bolles sees it, to survive in such a world, people will have to develop a new set of skills, which he sums up with the acronym **PACE**, which stands for a commitment to a lifetime of:

- problem solving
- adaptation
- creativity
- empathy

We do some of that in the training programs we use with young people, both inside and outside of conventional universities. However, I am not convinced that our Plan A jobs rarely call for PACE-equipped people. Even worse, I'm convinced that many PACE-oriented young people will get frustrated by working for peacebuilding and conflict resolution groups that don't have accelerating rates of change at the heart of their organizational DNA.

Some Plan B Options

So, now that I've depressed you about the state of our professional world, what should an effective Plan B look like? What are the alternatives that young professionals could explore that Craig and the others of us who have run those workshops never find time to get to?

Here are four possibilities. They aren't the only ones.

Get an MBA (at least from the best schools). If I were thirty-one or forty-one instead of seventy-one, I would get an MBA from one of the top business schools—assuming I could get in. Not because I want to get rich or love capitalism. Rather, some of the most creative new ideas for social change and interpersonal relations are coming from business schools, especially the ones that emphasize design.

Over the last few years, I've learned more about peacebuilding and conflict resolution from the likes of Adam Grant, Amy Edmondson, Sam Arbesman, Dolly Chugh, John Kotter, Clayton Christensen, Peter Senge, Jessica Wattman, Ravi Venkatessan, Chip and Dan Heath, and Bruce Nussbaum than I have from people who have peacebuilding or conflict resolution in their job descriptions.

This is actually something I initially stumbled onto in the 1980s. I first became a peacebuilding professional through the Beyond War movement, which was led by men (and a few women) who were in the first generation of Silicon Valley entrepreneurs. One of my contemporaries, who was then a vice president at a leading tech start-up, once summed up the difference in mind-sets between leftist activists like me and his fellow business executives. After listening to me, he realized that I became involved politically and assumed that I would lose. He responded by saying that if he had that kind of a mind-set, his company would go bankrupt.

The bottom line is simple. Manyof today's MBAs are being prepared for a world of constant change, including the conflicts that come with it.

Think like a start-up. I still find myself drawing on what I learned from my mentors in Beyond War about the companies they had founded in two ways that reflect what start-up culture has to teach us—despite the bad reputations some of the greedier entrepreneurs have justifiably earned.

First, start-ups have to be built around what Stanford psychologist Carol Dweck calls a **growth mind-set**. If you don't want to create a cool product *and* take it to scale, it isn't worth thinking about joining the start-up world. We peacebuilders often talk about scaling our initiatives. However, we rarely act that way. There are a few exceptions to that rule, such as **Build Up^** (see chapter 11), but it is no coincidence that several of its founders began their careers in corporate start-ups.

Second, I increasingly find myself suggesting to young people who have adopted some aspects of start-up culture that they create their own conflict resolution or peacebuilding organization. This is not for everyone. In addition to Gary Bolles's "e for empathy," start-ups require an "e for entrepreneurship," which is not something all the young people I work with are good at.

Build Up^ is a great example of what peacebuilding start-ups could look like. When its founders first came together in 2013, next to no one else was thinking about the interconnection between peacebuilding, technology, and the arts. Its small team of four twenty-somethings did. They have held five annual conferences around the world, each of which has attracted a *minimum* of 250 people. They have raised money for an annual fellows program through which Build Up^ staffers mentor even younger peacebuilders who live in conflict zones and have cool, scalable projects of their own. They also have an ongoing project that identifies potential extremists in the US online and invites them into facilitated, long-term dialogues with people from the "other side."

There is no reason why today's young people can't emulate Build Up^ in other parts of the field. If nothing else, if they have gone to a school like Oberlin, they will have been exposed to start-up culture through campus incubators that exist at every major undergraduate institution I'm aware of.

Bring conflict resolution into the economic mainstream. There are also ways for young people to work in corporate America, make a difference, have fun, and earn a decent income. Until recently, I would steer students toward the human relations departments that are explicitly charged with dealing with conflict at the workplace.

Now, I see signs that the space open to conflict-sensitive professionals inside the corporate world is beginning to broaden. Again, there is no systematically gathered evidence here, but a few examples should illustrate the point.

Most of us (especially those of us with children and grandchildren) have watched dozens of Pixar movies. Few of us know, however, how much its writers and producers draw on themes one finds in our work, something Ed Catmull, Pixar's CEO, documents in his book on the company, *Creativity, Inc.* Similarly, IDEO and other design companies incorporate a whole array of social science insights about people's lived experiences into their projects. Even Second City has a successful business consulting practice in which it helps clients learn how to use improv tools in improving everything from workplace culture to their company's bottom line.

It's easy to take a list like this one and say that it only applies to a handful of particularly cool and trendy companies that are very much the exception to the rule. However, as we have discussions about building a sector that is able to make a profit while building peace as a direct or indirect product of their business, we are noticing something intriguing in the corporate world, even in the extractive industries. Corporate executives are figuring out that their companies cannot survive, let alone thrive, unless they, too, adapt to a world of exponential change.

Not so long ago, this was the realm of a company's corporate social responsibility arm, which often was not taken to be anything more than a dispenser of charity by C-Suite executives who, of course, focused on making money. However, as Nik Gowing and Chris Langdon discovered in interviewing more than one hundred of those titans of industry and government for their book *Thinking the Unthinkable*, there is a growing realization that a company's very survival depends on its being able to navigate conflict-filled metaphoric waters.

In short, we can help.

Go work with *THEM*. Last, but by no means least, there are plenty of jobs in the government, including in the military and the intelligence community. I would actually go so far as to say *especially* with the military and the intelligence community.

As a product of the 1960s, it took me a while to recognize that "they" had also changed in the years after the end of the Cold War and then again after 9/11. I should have seen it earlier. In the early 2000s, I worked at Search for Common Ground, while my wife was a senior analyst at what is now the Open Source Center at the CIA. Each year, the two organizations held their holiday parties on consecutive nights. The political discussions at the two events (yes, we were all policy wonks) were the same. The only difference between the parties was that Searchers didn't sing Christmas carols at John and Susan Marks's house.

Seriously, in the years since 9/11, many professionals in the American and European militaries and intelligence communities have changed dramatically. The experiences in Iraq and Afghanistan convinced a surprising number of senior officers that there is no purely military way out of what we used to call the war on terror and now euphemistically refer to as combatting violent extremism.

To cite but one example, two days before my birthday in 2005, the US Department of Defense gave me an unexpected birthday present. Donald Rumsfeld's Pentagon issued Directive 3000.05, which gave conflict prevention and postconflict reconstruction the same priority as war fighting. In the fifteen years since then, the directive lives primarily on paper, but it has given rise to a bevy of new offices (and jobs) in the military–industrial complex where young peacebuilders could easily work.

As a conscientious objector who has never fired a gun and still cannot support the use of violence, I find it hard to suggest that someone consider enlisting, even though the world's militaries now have civil affairs officers and other specialists for whom conflict resolution training is a real asset. Even if you don't want to join the military, there are civilian jobs for people with training in peacebuilding and conflict sensitivity. Most North American and European governments also have an equivalent of the State Department's Office of Conflict Stabilization and Recovery, USAID's Office of Conflict Management and Mitigation, or the quasi-independent United States Institute of Peace.

More generally, plenty of the young people I work with do not want to work directly for "them." However, military installations as different at the Army War College's Peacekeeping and Stabilization Operations Institute and Fort Polk's massive training base in Louisiana are increasingly reaching out to the NGO world for advice. In fact, the day after I finished this chapter, I headed to Quantico to take part in a training exercise so that young marines can encounter NGO employees here and don't do so for the first time in the middle of a conflict zone.

SARAH FEDERMAN'S QUESTION

No one knows how many students who take an introductory course in peace and conflict studies go on to careers in the field of either the Plan A or Plan B variety. I would guess that at least half of the students who took Doug Irvin-Erickson's course and took the final exam I mentioned in chapter 13 will build their careers elsewhere, even though most of them were majoring in conflict analysis and resolution. When I work with Oberlin students, the proportion of them who go on in any variation on the theme of peace and conflict studies is far lower.

But that doesn't let them—or you—off the hook.

And that's why Sarah Federman's statement in her email signature matters.

Conflict Is a Fact of Life

Whatever you end up doing for a living, your life is going to be filled with conflict.

Even if we succeed and pull off the paradigm shift I have been talking about since chapter 1, there will still be plenty of conflict, and it will come in forms that neither you nor I can predict. In the statement from Donald Rumsfeld quoted in chapter 13, he was referring to global unknown unknowns. You will encounter plenty of them that appear much closer to home in the years to come—whatever you choose to do personally, professionally, or politically.

In other words, you *will* have to deal with conflict everywhere from your own home to your planet as a whole.

There is only one thing you can control—how you deal with it.

Violence Is a Choice

That involves making choices.

Evolutionary psychologists have spent a lot of time in recent years exploring the ways our brains are "wired" and how our basic predispositions reflect our genetic past. There is still a lot of uncertainty about what our human nature is. However, those same scientists are convinced that we do all have a violent side that is part of our evolutionary inheritance. We all carry traces of a past when our ancestors would have been killed if they did not lash back at their predators, whether they were members of other species or other groups of humans.

It is also clear that we have inherited the capacity to cooperate. Again, the historical causal chains are murky. Still, we know that we survive—whether as individuals or societies—because we can solve most of our problems without resorting to violence.

One other thing about our evolutionary past is clear. When members of a community or ethnic group or country or any other body of people resorts to violence, they choose to do so. There are always alternatives. Those alternatives may not have worked in every instance. There are times—perhaps including the days after 9/11—when we don't have a lot of realistic nonviolent options available to us.

But we *do* always have options.

My own involvement with the Beyond War movement in the 1980s began an exploration of those choices and my personal mind-set that continues to this day and led to the final Out on a Limb box of this book. It also helps explain why I have drifted away from contentious politics as is also reflected in that final box.

Beyond War's origins lay in the thinking of Henry Burton Sharman (1865–1953), a Canadian theologian who tried to strip the world's religions of their ritual and take them down to the ethical imperatives they held in common. The founders of Beyond War expanded on those ideas to stress interdependence (which we would now call globalization) ethical principles, like the **Golden Rule**, that are found in all of the world's major spiritual traditions, and taking personal responsibility for solving problems.

That brings me to the picture of the earth from space that begins this chapter. No one had ever seen the photograph before December 7, 1972. It may be commonplace today, but it was riveting for members of my generation. Later in that decade, the leaders of what became Beyond War met Russell Schweikart, who had commanded the first mission that orbited the moon. Schweikart also spent some time outside the space capsule and recorded his reactions, which we later turned into a video that combined the beauty of the view of the earth with the Golden Rule and calls for peace.

www.youtube.com/watch?v=7y7O_9WB3ZU

Thirty years later, it is still eight minutes of captivating video. Even more importantly for the purposes of this book, we used it to help the people we worked with see that systems theory demonstrates the empirical as well as the ethical power of the Golden Rule and its equivalents.

In an interdependent world, systems theory tells us that everything one does affects everything and everyone else directly or indirectly. In other words, if I don't do unto others as I would like them to do unto me, it is likely to come back to haunt me. On the other hand, if I help them reach their own goals and help us define and then reach goals we hold in common, the whole system benefits, as I argued at more length in chapter 3.

At the end of that series of workshops, we asked the people we worked with to make a decision to live their lives according to five commitments. Doing so changed the way I approach conflict at all levels—from the way I deal with members of my family, my students, my coworkers, and even the many people I disagree with politically.

It starts with the word **decision**. It seems like a simple enough concept. But, in fact, it is hard to make and stick to a decision. I've decided to do lots of things in my life and not carried through on them. From this perspective, those weren't real decisions.

As is often the case, the etymology or history of the word tells us a lot. In this case, the root is based on the Latin word for "cut." Thus, a surgeon makes an incision into your body so that she or he can repair a torn ligament. By that same logic, a *de-cision* is a cut away from something.

I used to smoke. In fact, I was still smoking some when I encountered this definition of decision. I had thought I'd made the decision to quit smoking dozens of times. Literally speaking, I had never made the decision, because I eventually picked up my pipe again.

When truly made, a decision is irrevocable. You choose to live your life differently. You decide not to smoke or drink anymore. Or, you decide to get regular exercise or meditate every day.

Living up to these kinds of decisions is hard. It takes practice. You will probably have relapses, as anyone who struggles with addiction will tell you.

Still, a decision is a conscious choice to do things differently.

In this case, we asked people to make a decision and commit themselves to these five principles when they deal with conflict which I first presented at the end of chapter 5 but which might make more sense to you now:

I will resolve conflict.
I will not use violence.
I will maintain a spirit of goodwill.
I will not preoccupy myself with an enemy.
I will work together with others to build a world beyond war.

We knew full well that no one could live up to those principles all of the time. We knew it because we couldn't do so ourselves.

However, we also knew two things. Our own experience showed that the conflicts in our own lives turned out better to the degree that we lived up to these principles. And, we discovered that people around us noticed and started asking us how and why we acted differently. To use the terminology of part 4, we could see some signs that following these principles could begin adding up to peace.

We also knew at the time that following these principles alone would not lead us to world peace and that we would have to build a social movement to go

OUT ON A LIMB

Is the Personal Political?

This final Out on a Limb box is hard for me to write. After all, I'm a political scientist by training, which means that I have studied national decision-making for most of my career.

Yet, I'm making a very different argument here. I'm suggesting that building peace writ large starts with how I deal with the conflicts in the microcosm of my daily life. In Everett Rogers's terms, more and more of us have to change the ways we resolve our own conflicts before the political and other leaders can be expected to follow suit.

As a result, I have wrestled with the two questions that eddy out of the term *decision* and the five principles since I first encountered them in 1983.

- How do I maintain a spirit of goodwill (or the Dalai Lama's warmheartedness) and stick with those other principles with someone whose views I truly despise?
- In Diana Chigas and Peter Woodrow's terms, how do we make personal change "add up to peace"?

You should think about them, too.

along with these profound and hard-to-live-with personal changes. We failed to do so then, and, as I suggested in the previous chapter, we are just beginning to do so now.

But rather than returning to these points, let me make an assumption or two. You decide not to go into any part of peace and conflict studies for your career. But, you are still going to get into conflict with your parents, your children, your coworkers, your neighbors, the people you disagree with politically, and ... That list goes on and on.

Ask yourself how your life would be different if you were to use those principles in your everyday life. Then do the final Conflict Lab.

There is now quite a bit of evidence from neuroscience, management studies, and social psychology that suggests that the attitude we bring to a conflict affects not only the outcome of the dispute but our personal health as well. The Dalai Lama has inspired a lot of high-end biological research about the impact of mindfulness and of what he and Arthur Brooks call warmheartedness. What's remarkable about those data is the impact of what Beyond War called a spirit of goodwill on the person who exercises it as well as on the resolution of the conflict itself. In other words, if I treat you with dignity and respect, I tend to feel better even if you don't reciprocate.

No one argues that it's easy to break old habits, whether the habits involve an addiction to a substance or an addiction to naming and shaming. Journalists like Charles Duhigg have helped us see how we can break old habits, social psychologist Adam Grant has shown the conditions under which those of us who are "givers" fare better than those of us who are "takers." Social worker Brenée Brown has outlined how to lead when all seems to be lost.

In the peacebuilding field, no one has done a better job of underscoring the personal side of conflict than the leaders of the **Arbinger Institute**. Their books often have the term *peace* in their titles, but the institute works mostly with corporations, police forces, and addicts rather than governments and their opponents. As you can see from this short video, Arbinger's trainers stress the importance of our individual mind-sets or, as I have called them more often, our personal paradigms.

www.youtube.com/watch?v=qnwzDfOQJFM

But unlike the positive mind-sets I have concentrated on, they focus on the need to get beyond a personal paradigm that revolves around what they call self-deception. If Arbinger's consultants are right, we all engage in self-deception when we deal with conflict because we are products of our own societies. Unless we make a conscious decision not to. Unless we decide to adopt something like the Beyond War principles.

Even if you don't go as far as I do in the final Out on a Limb box, successful peacebuilding and conflict resolution involves a hefty dose not just of self-awareness but of our equivalent of preventive medicine as well. Recall from the diagram that begins chapter 3 that Michael Lund stressed the importance of conflict prevention. Recall, too, that I argued on numerous occasions that we have honored his point in the breech.

What the Arbinger consultants—along with my doctor and therapist—are advising is to prepare ourselves for the next conflict. If we're lucky, we can prevent it in much the same way that healthy people can prevent many crippling diseases by eating well, staying in shape, or not drinking too much alcohol.

CONFLICT LAB 14

Take the grassroots conflict you have been working on since chapter 1. Then add one more—a hard-to-resolve conflict in your personal life. What could you personally do to answer Sarah Federman's question for those conflicts?

Preventive conflict resolution may not keep the next conflict from happening, but it can leave us better prepared for handling it when it does arise.

Fragile. Handle with care.

MY COFFEE MUG

At the beginning of chapter 13, I confessed that it is harder for textbook writers to end books than it is for good novelists who end their books by pulling all the strings of the plot together into a neat climax or, dare I use the word, resolution. I made that point to get you ready for a textbook whose "plot" would still be unfolding until the end—and beyond.

Even so, I had trouble figuring out what to say in the last few paragraphs until I remembered how I ended the first edition of my comparative politics textbook in 1993. I finished it during the first Christmas vacation I spent with my then fifteen-year-old stepdaughter (who is now a lot older and a clinical psychologist).

First holidays with stepparents and stepchildren are always awkward, but Evonne handled it with grace, dignity, and good cheer. The thing I will never forget, still use, and always talk about is the coffee mug she gave me that showed a picture of a tabby cat holding up the globe and had the caption:

> Fragile. Handle with care.

KEY TERMS

Concepts

decision, 334
Golden Rule, 334
growth mind-set, 331
PACE, 330

Organizations, Places, and Events

Arbinger Institute, 336
Build Up^, 331
Peace and Conflict Development Network (PCDN), 329

DIG DEEPER

There aren't a lot of book on careers in peacebuilding. In fact, I'm only aware of one.

Smith, David J. *Peace Jobs: A Student's Guide to Starting a Career Working for Peace*. Charlotte, NC: Information Age, 2016. A wonderful introduction by someone who has focused on community colleges.

There are other books worth reading on the way to align your personal life trajectory with peace and conflict studies.

Arbinger Institute. *The Anatomy of* Peace. San Francisco: Berrett-Koehler, 2015. As is the case with most of their books, the Arbinger Institute tells the story of self-deception and its impact on peace and conflict resolution through allegories'.

Brooks, David. *The Second Mountain: The Quest for a Moral Life*. New York: Random. House, 2019. Brooks is one of the most prominent conservative commentators in the mainstream American media. I was reading this while writing this chapter. It reinforces what I called Sarah Federman's question here.

Duhigg, Charles. *The Power of Habit: Why We Do What We Do in Life and Business*. New York: Random House, 2012. I've never read a better book on why we get into habits—good and bad—and why it is so hard to break out of them.

Grant, Adam. *Give and Take: Why Helping Others Drives Our Success*. New York: Penguin, 2013. This young, hip business professor explores how helping other helps you, too.

Stone, Douglass, Bruce Patton, and Sheila Heen. *Difficult Conversations: How to Discuss What Matters Most*. New York: Penguin, 2010. By three current and former staff members at Harvard's Project on Negotiations. This book discusses how to have those tough discussions.

NOTES

[1] An earlier version of this section appeared in http://mobileservices.texterity.com/acresolutionmag/december_2018?pg=1#pg1.

GLOSSARY

A

accelerating rates of change—when change in a phenomenon occurs at an ever greater rate; often referred to as an exponential rate of change or a power function.

accompaniment—in local peacebuilding, the notion that outside conflict resolution experts follow the lead of people on the ground.

action research—a methodology that combines dispassionate analysis with engaged activism.

Adams, Gerry—leader of Sinn Fein and, many claim, the IRA during the Troubles in Northern Ireland.

adaptive leadership—an approach to management that stresses adjustment in the face of experience.

adjacent possible—in evolutionary theory, the notion that species adapt by making incremental changes on the basis of available opportunities.

advocacy—public or private support for specific public policy proposals.

African National Congress (ANC)—the leading organization opposing apartheid in South Africa.

agape—a conception of love as concern for others as championed by Martin Luther King, Jr. and others.

agency—An individual's sense that he or she can control his or her own life.

Alliance for Peacebuilding—a US-based network of peacebuilding organizations.

alternative dispute resolution (ADR)—approaches to problem solving that stress alternatives to adversarial processes and outcomes, including mediation.

anarchy—in international relations, the absence of a viable international state capable of maintaining order or reaching other core policy goals.

Anderson, Benedict—academic responsible for the term *imagined communities*.

Anderson, Mary—founder of CDA collaborative, first applied the idea of do no harm to peacebuilding.

apartheid—the South African policies of strict racial segregation in place until the 1990s.

appreciative inquiry—an approach to conflict resolution and management that stresses what has worked in the past and builds off of it.

Arafat, Yasir—founder and first head of the PLO.

Arbinger Institute—American consulting firm that focuses on how personal blind spots keep us from living up to our responsibilities.

Arbitration—a form of ADR in which a third-party neutral chooses between two options proposed by the parties to the dispute.

architecture for peace—a term used to refer to the basic framework of a peace agreement.

asymmetrical wars—like many of today's conflicts, one side has far more power than the other, although the stronger side often doesn't win.

B

basic needs—in John Burton's terms, the core necessities which, if unmet, lead to conflict.

BATNA—from *Getting to YES*, the best alternative to a negotiated agreement.

Beslagic, Selim—Mayor of Tusla during the Bosnian war.

Better Angels—American organization that brings left and right together.

Black Consciousness—movement in South Africa during the 1980s against apartheid.

Black Lives Matter—contemporary American movement that focuses on alleged police brutality.

black swan—following Naseem Nicholas Taleb, an unlikely even that forces us to rethink some previously unspoken assumptions.

Bloody Sunday—in Northern Ireland, shootings by British troops that catalyzed the Troubles.

Bosnia-Herzegovina—former Yugoslav republic that had a bloody civil war and genocide in the 1990s.

both/and—an alternative to either/or thinking in which the parties seek a solution that add value for everyone.

bottom-up—in local peacebuilding, the notion that successful peace processes start at the grass roots and build upward from there.

Boulding, Kenneth and Elise—peacebuilding pioneers.

Boutros-Ghali, Boutros—former Secretary General of the UN.

Bridge Alliance—network of transpartisan organizations in the US.

Bridging social capital—social networks that involve people of opposing viewpoints.

bright spot—unusual example that "worked," often referred to as outlier or positive deviant.

broker—someone who helps forge deals.

Build Up^—a network of international peacebuilding entrepreneurs that focuses on technology and arts.

Bull, Hedley—British Australian academic who coined the term *international society*.

Burton, John—Australian academic and diplomat, founder of George Mason University's School of Conflict Analysis and Resolution.

Bush, George H. W.—forty-first president of the US.

Bush, George W.—forty-third president of the US.

C

CAF—USAID's Conflict Assessment Framework.

Caldicott, Helen—head of Physicians for Social Responsibility in the 1980s.

capacities—generic term for the resources and abilities of an individual or organization.

CDA Collaborative—NGO founded by Mary Anderson.

Christensen, Clayton—professor at Harvard Business School who studies disruptive innovation.

Citizen diplomacy—efforts by average citizens working with each other across national lines to reach common goals.

civil society—generic term for voluntary organizations.

civil society organizations (CSO)—formal or informal bodies created by average citizens to work for social goals.

community mediation—a form of mediation that revolves around community level disputes rather than those between individuals or organizations.

community of practice—a network of professionals who share research and practical tools.

community policing—an approach to law enforcement that has police officers cooperating as much as possible with the people in the areas they are responsible for.

complex adaptive systems—a term used to define complicated systems, often beset by wicked problems.

complexity—a version of systems theory that stresses the complicated interconnections among its component parts.

compromise—a conflict resolution technique that involves both sides giving up part of what it wants.

confirmation bias—the tendency to interpret all new information as conforming to one's preconceived beliefs.

conflict—a disagreement (usually intense) between two or more parties.

Conflict Analysis Framework (CAF)—the United States Agency for International Development's Conflict Assessment Framework.

conflict habit—the normal style or approach one uses in dealing with conflict.

conflict management style—the same basic thing as conflict habit.

conflict map—in systems approaches, a way of visually presenting the contours of a dispute.

conflict prevention—stopping conflict from breaking out.

conflict trap—the tendency to fall into bad conflict habits.

consensus—a form of decision-making in which unanimity or something close to it is required.

constructivists—international relations school that focuses on domestic politics.

contact theory—early but still popular approach that suggests that bringing people together helps defuse tensions.

contentious politics—involves the use of disruptive tactics to change state policy.

Convergence Center for Public Policy—a leading consensus-based network in the US.

Cooperrider, David—creator of appreciative inquiry.

corporate social responsibility—philosophy that businesses should help solve social problems.

corporatism—academic term to describe representation through professions rather than population.

crisis—a turning point.

culture—in anthropology and other social sciences, basic values and assumptions.

cultural sensitivity—the requirement that conflict resolution be in line with a community's cultural norms.

cumulative strategy—a military notion that we should learn from our successes.

Cure Violence—an American-based NGO that works on urban violence and treats it as an epidemic.

Cyprus—divided island in the Mediterranean.

D

Dallaire, Roméo—commander of UN forces in Rwanda during the genocide.

Dayton Accords—agreement that ended the Bosnian war.

De Klerk, F. W.—last apartheid-era leader of South Africa.

decision—When truly made, an irrevocable choice; from the Latin for "cut away from".

deep ecology—in green politics, the notion that all aspects of a system are interconnected.

deep structure—in systems theory, the most important "loops" that define the outlines of the entire system.

democratic peace—the theory that democracies do not go to war with other democracies.

Department of Defense Directive 3000.05—statement that gave conflict prevention and post conflict reconstruction the same status as warfighting.

design thinking—in systems theory, the notion that one should plan and iterate one's activities.

dialogue—intense discussions that leave neither party unchanged.

Dialogue with the City—urban renewal project in Perth, Australia.

diplomacy—formal negotiations and other interactions between national governments and/or other decision makers.

disruption—innovations and other actions that profoundly alter the status quo.

do no harm—for peacebuilders, our version of physicians' commitment in the Hippocratic Oath.

downstream—in systems theory, the long-term consequences of an action.

dysfunctional—in systems theory, events that worsen its condition.

E

Elias, Norbert—leading theorist of modernization.

emerge—in complexity theory, the notion that structures grow out of realities.

empathy—the ability to put oneself in the "shoes" or mind-set of someone else, especially one's adversary.

End of history—Francis Fukuyama's theory about the end of the Cold War.

End the Violence Epidemic—a project of Cure Violence.

engagement—a generic term that focuses on simply being involved in solving problems.

English school—an academic theory that stresses international society and other cooperative forms of international relations.

Enlightenment—a term used to describe the rebirth of Western thought, especially in the seventeenth and eighteenth centuries.

environment—in systems theory, key forces that lie outside the formal system itself.

ethnic cleansing—originally used to describe the genocide in Bosnia, now used more generically.

eufunctional—a system whose performance improves over time.

European Union (EU)—the world's largest regional intergovernmental organization.

Everyday Peace Indicators (EPI)—a set of technical tools used to measure the degree to which people actually live under peaceful conditions in the microcosm of their daily lives.

evidence-based—the belief that our actions should be assessed on the basis of hard evidence.

evolution—the science of how species and individuals change in profound ways over time.

exponential—rapid, accelerating growth.

F

facilitators—individuals who manage conflict resolution and similar initiatives.

feedback—in systems theory, the notion that events at one time loop back and affect the entire system later.

feminist foreign policy—in Canada, Sweden, and elsewhere, foreign policies that prioritize gender related issues.

Fridays for Future—a movement to address climate change run by high school students.

Fukuyama, Francis—scholar best known for the end of history theory.

future shock—an idea developed by Alvin and Heidi Toffler that we are having trouble dealing with accelerating rates of change.

G

Galtung, Johan—creator of the idea of positive peace.

Gandhi, Mohandas—leader of India's nonviolent independence movement.

General Assembly—the UN body representing all countries.

genocide—the systematic killing of all or most of a population on identity grounds.

Getting to YES—title of a book that came to symbolize win-win conflict resolution.

Giving Pledge—a group of mostly American billionaires who have agreed to give away at least half of their wealth.

globalization—the interconnection of world wide systems of interaction.

Global Partnership for the Prevention of Armed Conflict (GPPAC)—a global network of peacebuilding NGOs.

Global Peacebuilding Campaign—*see* +Peace.

Global Peace Index (GPI)—the leading, national-level statistical indicator of how peaceful a country is —or isn't.

Global South—a generic term used to describe countries in what used to be known as the Third World.

Global War on Terror (GWOT)—one of many terms used to describe the American-led response to 9/11.

Golden Rule—in Judeo Christian and other faiths, the notion that you should do unto others as you would have them do unto you.

Good Friday Agreement (GFA)—ended the Troubles in Northern Ireland.

good offices—a generic germ to describe initiatives by leaders who informally help deal with conflict.

Gorbachev, Mikhail—last head of the Soviet Union.

grass tops —a term used to describe local leaders in peace processes and beyond.

Green—political movements that are based on deep ecology and, initially, opposition to nuclear power.

green line—a term used to describe unofficial borders in countries like Cyprus and Israel/Palestine.

Green New Deal—initiative to address climate change by American members of Congress first elected in 2018.

Green Party—political parties that promote environmental and related views.

grievances—in the CAF, a generic term for the issues people are concerned about.

grown-ups' table—a metaphor for our access or lack thereof to major public policy making circles.

growth mind-set—values that stress the positive lessons one can draw from experience.

guide star—the Omidyar Group's term for a long-term or overarching goal.

Gutteres, António—Secretary General of the UN.

H

Hands Across the Hills—a project bringing together residents of rural Massachusetts and Kentucky.

hierarchy of needs—Abraham Maslow's term for the values we tend to stress as societies become more affluent.

Hobbes Thomas—seventeenth-century philosopher known for his pessimism.

holistic—the belief that everything is interconnected.

horizontal—the relationship among actors at more or less the same level of a hierarchy.

human needs—the notion that we all have many "needs" that are part and parcel of our existence as people.

human security—the new belief that security cannot simply be defined in geopolitical terms.

Huntington, Samuel—a leading American political science known for his ideas about the clash of civilizations.

I

identity—the often emotional ways we define ourselves along racial, religious, gender, ethnic, linguistic, and other lines.

IFOR—the International Force for the Former Yugoslavia.

image of the enemy—a psychological term for the ways we tend to stereotype or demonize our adversaries.

imagined communities—Benedict Anderson's notion that things like national identity and race are human creations and not inherent.

implicit biases—the belief that many of our prejudices are deeply rooted and often unconscious.

incremental changes—reforms that do not change the basic structure of a system.

ingroups—in social psychology, our tendency to identify with people who are most like ourselves.

inside partial—John Paul Lederach's notion that one has to start with incremental changes and build on them by working within the system.

intentionality—the conscious decision to seek a particular goal in response to a particular set of circumstances.

international community—an informal term referring to the UN, the international institutions, and, sometimes, the leading industrialized democracies.

International Criminal Court (ICC)—the new UN body that has responsibility for crimes against humanity.

International Financial Institutions (IFIs)—the generic term for the World Bank, International Monetary Fund, and World Trade Commission.

International Fund for Ireland—a quasi-official capital fund that has helped build infrastructure to help the Northern Ireland peace process.

international governmental organizations (IGOs)—formal international bodies representing governments.

International Monetary Fund (IMF)—the IFI that focuses on monetary matters.

International Physicians for the Prevention of Nuclear War (IPPNW)—a network of doctors that played a major role in the peace movements of the 1980s.

international society—the belief that national governments can and do cooperate through shared norms, informal organizations, and international regimes.

Intifada—a series of Palestinian uprisings against Israeli rule and occupation.

intractable conflict—a conflict that has multiple causes and consequences that cannot be settled quickly or easily.

intrapersonal—addressing conflict within an individual.

Irish Republican Army (IRA)—the leading Catholic fighting unit in Northern Ireland during the Troubles.

J

job to do—Clayton Christensen's notion that we need to prioritize goals.

K

Kamil, Muferiat—Ethiopia's (and the world's) first Minister of Peace.

Kelman, Herbert—peacebuilding pioneer known for problem-solving workshops.

Killelea, Steve—Australian philanthropist and founder of the Institute for Economics and Peace.

King, Martin Luther, Jr.—iconic American civil rights leader.

known unknowns—Donald Rumsfeld's notion that there are future trends that we can predict, although we may not be able to predict specific evens.

L

Lederach, John Paul—peacebuilding pioneer now known best for his work on reconciliation and in Nepal.

leverage—in systems theory, exerting influence where it makes the most difference.

leviathan—Hobbes's theory of the (all) powerful state.

Lewin, Kurt—social psychologist and systems pioneer.

liberal Peace—a definition of peace that also includes a commitment to liberal democracy and market capitalism.

linkages—connections between two or more elements in a system.

Lived experience—term used to describe the way people experience phenomena in their daily lives.

Living Room Conversations—an American initiative to bring left and right together.

Local peacebuilding—the (as yet unproven) belief that lasting conflict resolution and peacebuilding have to be built from the bottom up.

looping—Resetting the Table's approach to rephrasing what someone else says to deepen a dialogue.

low-intensity conflict—military term to describe small-scale wars.

Lund curve—visual way of understanding conflict developed by Michael Lund.

M

Mandela, Nelson—South African leader of the ANC and the first post-apartheid president.

Marks, John—founder of Search for Common Ground.

Maslow, Abraham—social psychologist known for his theory about the hierarchy of needs.

mass atrocity—another term for genocide.

McConnell Foundation—American philanthropy that funded a decade-long project in Nepal.

mediators—a term to describe conflict resolution professionals who help disputants reach agreements.

Metcalfe's law—measures the density of networks.

Millennium Development Goals (MDGs)—UN priorities for the first fifteen years of this century.

mind-set—a social psychological terms used to describe one's personal paradigm.

Mitchell, George—former American senator who led the negotiations that culminated in the Good Friday Agreement.

models—depiction of social and other phenomena that fall short theories.

modernity—a term used to define the generic state of affairs over the last two or three centuries.

mode of thinking—another term for a personal paradigm or mind-set.

monitoring and evaluation—the part of any academic or public policy field in which practitioner's work and its impact are assessed.

Moore's law—a term used to describe the accelerating rates of of change, especially in technology.

movement—a formal or informal group that promotes one or more social causes.

multitrack diplomacy—informal negotiations carried out by people without diplomatic status.

mutually hurting stalemate—the belief that two sides can continue fighting but that neither can win, at least at an acceptable cost.

N

9/11—terrorist attacks in New York and Washington in 2001.

naming and shaming—the notion that one side should call out the worst in another.

narratives—the stories individuals or organizations tell about reality.

National Association for Community Mediation (NAFCM)—a leading American organization of locally based conflict resolution centers.

National Coalition for Dialogue and Deliberation (NCDD)—a mostly American network of dialogue professionals.

National Peace Accord—South Africa's framework agreement during the transition away from apartheid.

National Security Presidential Directive 44 (NSPD 44)—signed by George W. Bush; created conflict resolution offices within the State Department and elsewhere.

negative peace—peace as the absence of war.

negotiation—a generic term for conflict resolution and related discussions that do not lead to war.

neoliberal—a term used to describe economic policies that stress classical, free market capitalism.

Nepal Project—a decade-long peacebuilding project.

network—collection of interdependent components of an integrated system.

Neutrality—the belief that one should not take sides in a dispute.

new left—a term used to describe wide-ranging protest movements in the 1960s and 1970s.

new world order—a generic term used to describe hoped for peace following the end of the Cold War.

nongovernmental organization (NGO)—term used to describe private, voluntary organizations that work for social change, public health, peace, and more.

nonviolence—philosophies and related political strategies that reject the use of physical violence.

norms—core values and beliefs in a country's or community's culture.

North Atlantic Treaty Organization (NATO)—western alliance created by the United States during the Cold War.

Nuclear Freeze—a campaign in the US that primarily wanted to "freeze" the size of the American and Soviet nuclear arsenals during the 1980s.

O

Omidyar Group—a leading group funding peacebuilding and other systems-related initiatives.

OODA loop—observe, orient, decide, act.

opportunity structures—the leeway in a given situation that allows actors to move forward.

Orlando Speaks—a movement in that city to improve police/community relations.

orphaned agreement—an agreement that fails because it does not lead to further and deeper agreements.

Oslo Accords—the failed agreement between Israel and the Palestinian authority from the 1990s.

other—social psychological term used to describe members of outgroups.

outgroups—social psychological term used to (disparagingly) refer to people not like oneself.

outliers—unusual cases in a regression equation that can be thought of as exceptions to the rule.

Overton Window—reflects the range of policy options that are generally considered viable at a moment in time.

P

PACE—problem solving, adaptability, creativity, empathy.

pacifism—commitment to nonviolence in all aspects of life.

Palestine Liberation Organization (PLO)—leading opponent of Israel, now ruling the West Bank.

paradigm—a scientific theory or other all encompassing mind-set that covers an entire field.

paramilitaries—unofficial and often illegal militaries.

paying forward—rather than paying back, investing the future.

+Peace—a campaign to change public opinion and public policy on conflict related issues.

peace—the absence of violent conflict.

Peace and Conflict Development Network (PCDN)—a professional networking organization.

Peace and Justice Studies Association (PJSA)—one of several academic peacebuilding groups.

peacebuilding—processes that lead to stable or positive peace.

Peace Building Commission—the official UN body that supposedly coordinates all of its activities in these regards.

peace churches—denominations that renounce war.

peace enforcement—the imposition of peace by military or other means.

peacekeeping—processes that prevent former adversaries from returning to war.

peacemaking—the continued enforcement of a cease-fire or other tentative agreement.

PeaceTech Lab—a spin-off from USIP that is building a peace/technology sector.

peace writ large—the understanding that peace has to be built at more than just the local level.

perestroika—Soviet-era economic restructuring policies.

permanent members—the five countries that have permanent seats on the UN Security Council: the US, the UK, Russia, China, and France.

perspective taking—the belief that we can make conflict resolution easier ty understanding the other side's point of view.

Physicians for Social Responsibility—the American branch of IPPNW.

Pinker, Steven—leading American psychologist who writes about violence and peace.

plasticity—the neuroscientific notion that our minds are flexible and can even be "rewired".

polite protesters—used to describe 1980s peace movement activists and others who were reluctant to exert pressure on the US and other governments.

populism—a political strategy that allegedly speaks for "the people" but usually has nationalistic overtones.

positive deviance—outliers who move a system in a constructive direction.

positive peace—occurs when people settle their differences constructively and their basic human needs are met.

Positive Peace Index (PPI)—the Institute for Economics and Peace's measure of how peaceful a country is.

positive-sum—an outcome that benefits all parties.

power—normally, the ability to get others to do what you want.

power law—another term for some exponential rates of change.

prevent—to stop something from happening.

proactive—to act before something (bad) happens; the opposite of reactive.

problem-solving workshops—one of many tools for conflict resolution.

Project on Negotiations (PON)—a leading mediation program, based at Harvard Law School.

public judgment—Daniel Yankelovich's notion that mass publics occasionally do reach new agreements on new principles.

public policy—the process by which governments at all levels determine what they will do.

Q

Quakers—the Society of Friends.

R

Rabin, Yitzhak—former Israeli prime minister.

reactive—the notion that one is not proactive and acts in response to events that have already occurred.

realism—academic theory that sees international relations in Hobbesian terms.

Reagan, Ronald—American president as the Cold War ended.

reconciliation—the process whereby parties to a dispute restore their relationship after it has ended.

Reformation—the period in which Protestants broke away from the Catholic Church.

regimes—a term used to describe the basic institutional arrangements followed by a country.

relationships—ongoing interactions among two or more individuals, organizations, or governments.

Remote Areas Horizon Scan (RAHS)—Singapore's long-term-planning office.

Renaissance—the period of intellectual reawakening in Europe, especially in the fifteenth and sixteenth centuries.

Resetting the Table (RTT)—an American peacebuilding NGO.

resilience—literally, the ability to bounce back or respond constructively to adversity.

resolution—a settlement that ends or eases a conflict.

Resolution 1325—UN Security Council resolution that mandates including gender related issues in foreign policy.

Responsibility to Protect (R2P)—UN notion that the international community has to prevent crimes against humanity.

restorative justice—legal proceeding that seeks to improve long-term relationships rather than seeking punishment.

right relationships—conflict resolution principle that stresses finding the right balance in the relationship among two or more actors.

ripeness—the point at which a conflict is "ready" to be resolved, usually after a mutually hurting stalemate has been reached.

Rogers, Everett—a leading American scholar on how innovations become adopted.

rondine—Italian community that works with victims of traumatic conflict.

Rosling, Hans—public health doctor who researched social and economic progress.

rules of engagement—term used to describe the conditions under which soldiers are (supposedly) allowed to use deadly force.

Rumsfeld, Donald—American secretary of defense during and after 9/11.

Rwanda—site of the 1994 genocide.

S

Sant'Egidio, Community of—a leading Catholic peacebuilding and social justice NGO.

scale—the notion that we should make businesses and other institutions grow.

scenario planning—a technique developed by Shell Oil to help planners choose among several alternative futures.

School for Conflict Analysis and Resolution—the world's first conflict resolution graduate program, housed at George Mason University.

Search for Common Ground—one of the first peacebuilding NGOs.

Security Council (United Nations)—the UN agency with responsibility for peacekeeping and peacebuilding initiatives.

self-limiting revolution—the notion developed by Adam Michnik of Solidarity that protesters would end or limit their revolution if and when they felt the need to run violent.

Serbia—the former Yugoslav republic normally held responsible for the civil wars of the 1990s.

Sharp, Gene—influential theorist of nonviolence.

silo—a disparaging term used to describe the way people tend to work in isolation.

Solidarity—the Polish civil society organization that helped bring down the communist regime in that country.

sovereignty—the critical principle at the heart of realist international relations.

spoiler—individual or institution who can and wants to jeopardize a fragile agreement.

stable peace—the notion that countries can remain at peace with each other indefinitely.

state—as used by political scientists, the institution that at least in theory has a monopoly of the legitimate use of force in a given territory.

stereotypes—our tendency to demonize another group.

stickiness—in information technology, the notion that what starts as a fad can become a permanent phenomenon.

Strong Cities Network—a coalition of urban governments that deal with violent extremism.

structural violence—causes of conflict that reflect inequalities of power.

superordinate goal—a goal that can be only be reached through the cooperation of all or most of the parties involved.

Sustainable Development Goals (SDGs)—the UN's guiding document for the years 2015–2030.

Sustained Dialogue—an American-based NGO that works on US-Russian relations and has a significant presence on college campuses.

systems—an approach to studying conflict (or anything else) that views it as a wholly interdependent phenomenon.

T

terrorism—violence by nonstate actors designed primarily to instill fear.

Thatcher, Margaret—prime minister of the UK during the 1980s.

theory—an attempt to explain or predict behavior.

theory of change—a series of "if/then" statements about what might happen if peacebuilders do a certain thing.

third side—term developed by William Ury to describe neutral facilitators and others who help conflict resolution processes succeed.

third world—increasingly obsolete term used to describe the newly independent countries of the postcolonial world.

third-party neutral—mediators, facilitators, and others who manage conflict resolution processes.

Thunberg, Greta—Swedish teenager who began Fridays for Future.

Tilly, Charles—American sociologist of social movements and protest.

tipping point—Malcolm Gladwell's argument that focuses on the moment when a movement or an accelerating rate of change seems to take off.

top-down—elite-driven social change.

Track II diplomacy—negotiations conducted by private citizens, many of whom have close ties to governmental officials.

transactional—agreements that simply reach a short-term outcome and normally do not address the root causes of a dispute.

transformational—forms of conflict resolution in which the underlying causes of a dispute are addressed and the relationships involved are literally transformed.

trauma healing—a term used to describe a variety of techniques used to help people overcome the emotional impact of genocide and other crimes against humanity.

Troubles—a generic term used to describe the conflict in Northern Ireland from the 1960s through the 1990s.

Trump, Donald—forty-fifth president of the US.

trust—the ability to count on and/or predict the behavior of another.

Truth and Reconciliation Commission (TRC)—official bodies in South Africa and elsewhere that promote reconciliation by exploring what happened during a violent conflict.

Tutsis—the minority ethnic group, victimized by the genocide in Rwanda.

Tutu, Desmond—former Anglican Archbishop of South Africa who led the Truth and Reconciliation Commission.

Tuzla—a city that "opted out" of the Bosnian war.

two state solution—the generic term used to describe the policy that might someday produce separate and independent Israeli and Palestinian states.

U

ubuntu—an African phrase best translated as "a person is a person through another person".

UNAMIR—the UN's mission in Rwanda.

UNFICYP—the UN's mission in Cyprus.

United Nations (UN)—the world's largest IGO.

United Nations Office of the High Commissioner for Refugees (UNHCR)—has responsibility for most of the UN's work on such issues.

United States Institute of Peace (USIP)—congressionally chartered and funded think tank in the US.

unknown unknowns—Donald Rumsfeld's notion that there are some utterly unpredictable events in the future that will shake us up.

UNPROFOR—UN mission in the former Yugoslavia.

US Agency for International Development (USAID)—the development agency of the US government.

V

vertical—a generic term used to describe relationships that run up and down a social hierarchy.

veto power—a power held by the five permanent members of the UN Security Council.

vicious cycles—in systems theory, continuously deteriorating situations.

violent extremism—a euphemism used to describe terrorism since 9/11.

virtuous circles—in systems theory, continuingly improving situations.

VUCA—volatile, uncertain, complicated, and ambiguous.

W

Walesa, Lech—leader of Solidarity in Poland.

War crimes—a generic term used to describe genocide and other crimes against society.

Weber, Max—the leading social theorist of modern and bureaucratic organizations.

wicked problem—problems whose causes and consequences are so inextricably intertwined that you cannot solve them quickly, easily, or separately, if you can solve them at all.

win-lose—outcomes in which only one side can win; zero sum.

win-win—outcomes from which everyone benefits; positive sums.

World Bank—the IFI that focuses on development.

World Peace Game Foundation—promotes the game of the same name developed by John Hunter.

World Trade Organization (WTO)—the IFI that focuses on trade.

World Vision International (WVI)—an Evangelical Christian NGO that focuses on the intersection of children and peace, among other things.

Z

zero-sum—outcomes in which only one side can win; win-lose.

INDEX

CREDITS

2 "March for Our Lives Boston 2018" by AnubisAbyss is licensed under CC BY-SA 2.0
30 Clip Art by Vector Toons
58 Niccolò Caranti / Courtesy John Paul Lederach / Kenneth E. Boulding / Steve Larson/Denver Post/Getty Images
74 Designed by Gerald Holtom, 1958
79 National Archives
88 © Community of the Ark of Lanza del Vasto
105 Interfoto/Alamy Stock Photo
113 White House Photo
117 U.S. Institute of Peace
120 "Genocide Memorial" by schacon is licensed under CC BY 2.0
149 Louis-F. Stahl/CC BY-SA 3.0 DE
153 Paul Weinberg/Wikicommons, CC BY-SA
159 Wikimedia, Creative Commons
166 Motimeiri/iStock
170 Vince Musi/The White House
195 Ross Setford/AP Images
206 John Spencer/Philadelphia Business Journal
219 Courtesy of Steve Killelea
232 DanielPrudek/iStock
235 Courtesy of John Paul Lederach, with permission from MSBKN
271 © 2019 by Patrick G. Ryan
275 Sustainable Development Goals © World Health Organization
279 Anadolu Agency/Getty Images
306 Nikki Boertman, The Commercial Appeal/AP Images
321 © Ellen Lovelidege
326 NASA/NOAA/GOES Project